Springer Series in Information Sciences 23

Editor: Thomas S. Huang

Springer Series in Information Sciences

1 **Content-Addressable Memories**
By T. Kohonen 2nd Edition

2 **Fast Fourier Transform and Convolution Algorithms**
By H. J. Nussbaumer 2nd Edition

3 **Pitch Determination of Speech Signals**
Algorithms and Devices By W. Hess

4 **Pattern Analysis and Understanding**
By H. Niemann 2nd Edition

5 **Image Sequence Analysis**
Editor: T.S. Huang

6 **Picture Engineering**
Editors: King-sun Fu and T.L. Kunii

7 **Number Theory in Science and Communication** With Applications in Cryptography, Physics, Digital Information, Computing, and Self-Similarity By M.R. Schroeder
2nd Edition

8 **Self-Organization and Associative Memory** By T. Kohonen
3rd Edition

9 **Digital Picture Processing**
An Introduction By L.P. Yaroslavsky

10 **Probability, Statistical Optics, and Data Testing** A Problem Solving Approach By B.R. Frieden
2nd Edition

11 **Physical and Biological Processing of Images** Editors: O.J. Braddick and A.C. Sleigh

12 **Multiresolution Image Processing and Analysis** Editor: A. Rosenfeld

13 **VLSI for Pattern Recognition and Image Processing** Editor: King-sun Fu

14 **Mathematics of Kalman-Bucy Filtering**
By P.A. Ruymgaart and T.T. Soong
2nd Edition

15 **Fundamentals of Electronic Imaging Systems** Some Aspects of Image Processing By W.F. Schreiber
2nd Edition

16 **Radon and Projection Transform-Based Computer Vision**
Algorithms, A Pipeline Architecture, and Industrial Applications By J.L.C. Sanz, E.B. Hinkle, and A.K. Jain

17 **Kalman Filtering** with Real-Time Applications By C.K. Chui and G. Chen
2nd Edition

18 **Linear Systems and Optimal Control**
By C.K. Chui and G. Chen

19 **Harmony: A Psychoacoustical Approach** By R. Parncutt

20 **Group Theoretical Methods in Image Understanding**
By Ken-ichi Kanatani

21 **Linear Prediction Theory**
A Mathematical Basis for Adaptive Systems By P. Strobach

22 **Psychoacoustics** Facts and Models
By E. Zwicker and H. Fastl

23 **Digital Image Restoration**
Editor: A. K. Katsaggelos

24 **Parallel Algorithms in Computational Science**
By D. W. Heermann and A. N. Burkitt

25 **Radar Array Processing**
Editors: S. Haykin, J. Litva, and T. J. Shepherd

26 **Signals and Systems**
Hankel-Operator and Hardy-Space Approach
By C. K. Chui and G. Chen

Aggelos K. Katsaggelos (Ed.)

Digital Image Restoration

With 86 Figures

Springer-Verlag
Berlin Heidelberg New York
London Paris Tokyo
Hong Kong Barcelona
Budapest

Professor Aggelos K. Katsaggelos, Ph. D.
Northwestern University,
Department of Electrical Engineering and Computer Science
R. R. McCormick School of Engineering and Applied Science
Evanston, IL 60208, USA

Series Editors:
Professor Thomas S. Huang
Department of Electrical Engineering and Coordinated Science Laboratory,
University of Illinois, Urbana, IL 61801, USA

Professor Teuvo Kohonen
Laboratory of Computer and Information Sciences,
Helsinki University of Technology,
SF-02150 Espoo 15, Finland

Professor Dr. Manfred R. Schroeder
Drittes Physikalisches Institut, Universität Göttingen, Bürgerstrasse 42–44,
W-3400 Göttingen, Fed. Rep. of Germany

Managing Editor: Helmut K. V. Lotsch
Springer-Verlag, Tiergartenstrasse 17,
W-6900 Heidelberg, Fed. Rep. of Germany

ISBN 3-540-53292-7 Springer-Verlag Berlin Heidelberg New York
ISBN 0-387-53292-7 Springer-Verlag New York Berlin Heidelberg

Printed in the United States of America

Typesetting: Data conversion by Springer-Verlag
54/3140 – 5 4 3 2 1 0 – Printed on acid-free paper

Preface

The field of image restoration is concerned with the estimation of uncorrupted images from noisy, blurred ones. These blurs might be caused by optical distortions, object motion during imaging, or atmospheric turbulence. In many scientific and engineering applications, such as aerial imaging, remote sensing, electron microscopy, and medical imaging, there is active or potential work in image restoration.

The purpose of this book is to provide in-depth treatment of some recent advances in the field of image restoration. A survey of the field is provided in the introduction. Recent research results are presented, regarding the formulation of the restoration problem as a convex programming problem, the implementation of restoration algorithms using artificial neural networks, the derivation of nonstationary image models (compound random fields) and their application to image estimation and restoration, the development of algorithms for the simultaneous image and blur parameter identification and restoration, and the development of algorithms for restoring scanned photographic images. Special attention is directed to issues of numerical implementation. A large number of pictures demonstrate the performance of the restoration approaches.

This book provides a clear understanding of the past achievements, a detailed description of the very important recent developments and the limitations of existing approaches, in the rapidly growing field of image restoration. It will be useful both as a reference book for working scientists and engineers and as a supplementary textbook in courses on image processing.

I would like to thank Professor Thomas S. Huang, University of Illinois, Urbana, for suggesting that I edit this volume. I would also like to acknowledge him along with Professors Henry Stark, Illinois Institute of Technology, John W. Woods, Rensselaer Polytechnic Institute, and Abraham H. Haddad, Northwestern University, for sharing their expertise in editing with me.

Chicago, Illinois
December 1989

Aggelos K. Katsaggelos

Contents

Contributors

Angwin, D.L.
Advanced NMR Systems
46 Jonspin Road
Wilmington, MA 01887, USA

Auyeung, Ch.
Digital Technology Laboratory
Chicago Corporate Research and Development Center
Motorola Inc., Schaumburg, IL 60196, USA

Chellappa, R.
Department of EE-Systems, University of Southern California
Los Angeles, CA 90089-0272, USA

Jeng, F.-Ch.
Bell Communications Research
MRE2A261, 445 South Street
Morristown, NJ 07960, USA

Katsaggelos, A.K.
Department of Electrical Engineering and Computer Science
R. R. McCormick School of Engineering and Applied Science
Northwestern University, Evanston, IL 60208-3118, USA

Kaufman, H.
Department of Electrical, Computer and Systems Engineering
Rensselaer Polytechnic Institute, Troy, NY 12180-3590, USA

Lay, K.-T.
Department of Electrical Engineering and Computer Science
R. R. McCormick School of Engineering and Applied Science
Northwestern University, Evanston, IL 60208-3118, USA

Lichtenstein, Z.
Department of EE-Systems, University of Southern California
Los Angeles, CA 90089-0272, USA

Mersereau, R.M.
School of Electrical Engineering, Georgia Institute of Technology
Atlanta, GA 30332-0250, USA

Pavlović, G.
Department of Electrical Engineering, University of Rochester
Rochester, NY 14627, USA

Sezan, M.I.
Imaging Science Laboratory, Research Laboratories
Eastman Kodak Company, Rochester, NY 14650-1816, USA

Simchony, T.
Department of EE-Systems, University of Southern California
Los Angeles, CA 90089-0272, USA

Stark, H.
Electrical and Computer Engineering Department
Illinois Institute of Technology, Chicago, IL 60616, USA

Tekalp, A.M.
Department of Electrical Engineering, University of Rochester
Rochester, NY 14627, USA

Woods, J.W.
Department of Electrical, Computer and Systems Engineering
Rensselaer Polytechnic Institute, Troy, NY 12180-3500, USA

Yeh, S.-J.
Department of Electrical, Computer and Systems Engineering
Rensselaer Polytechnic Institute, Troy, NY 12180-3590, USA

1. Introduction

A. K. Katsaggelos

With 1 Figure

1.1 The Digital Image Restoration Problem

Digital image processing is concerned with the manipulation and analysis of images, or two-dimensional (2D) data in a broader context, by computer. The three subareas of digital image processing are *enhancement, restoration and reconstruction*; *digitization and compression* and *matching, description and recognition* [1.1]. The computer graphics area may also be considered to be a subarea of image processing [1.2], although the general objective, that of synthesizing an image, as well as the mathematical tools used, are very different.

The goal of image restoration is to recover the original scene from the degraded observations. Image restoration techniques are oriented towards modeling the degradations, blur and noise, and applying an inverse procedure to obtain an approximation of the original scene. This is distinct from image enhancement techniques, which are designed to manipulate an image in order to produce results more pleasing to an observer, without usually making use of particular degradation models. Reconstruction techniques are also treated separately from restoration techniques, since they operate on a set of image projections and not on a full image, although the two groups of techniques share the same objective, that of recovering the original image, and end up solving the same mathematical problem, that of finding a solution to a set of linear or nonlinear equations.

The problem of image restoration has been extensively studied for its practical importance as well as its theoretical interest [1.3]. Literature on the subject is abundant and varied since the problem arises in almost every branch of engineering and applied physics, as is evident from the lists of references at the end of the chapters in the book. Perhaps the most prominent example of successful image restoration is the work done at the Jet Propulsion Laboratory with images of the Moon, Mars, and other planets taken by TV cameras on board artificial satellites [1.2]. They have succeeded in compensating for various image degradations, including random noise, interference, geometrical distortion, field nonuniformity, contrast loss, and blurring. Another problem which has spurred much of the research in image restoration is imaging through the atmosphere [1.4]. The problem is to obtain good images of planets, stars, and artificial satellites by imaging systems based on earth. The dominating degradation in this case is the blurring due to atmospheric turbulence. Atmospheric turbulence is also a severe limitation in remote sensing and aerial imaging, as used for geographic purposes, weather prediction and conserva-

Springer Series in Information Sciences, Vol. 23
A. K. Katsaggelos (ed.): Digital Image Restoration

tion studies. Even if stellar images are acquired not through the atmosphere, there are applications where these images need to be restored. A prime example are the images obtained by the Hubble Space Telescope, which are seriously degraded due to the spherical aberration of its primary mirror. Finally, the study of motion blur becomes important when longer exposures are necessary to record relatively dark scenes or when, for example, the image motion-compensation system on a satellite fails.

The various restoration approaches that have appeared in the literature depend on the particular degradation and image model assumed. For example, the degradation model can be linear or nonlinear with additive or signal-dependent noise. The image can be modeled to represent a sample of a stochastic random field or respresent a deterministic quantity. Furthermore, various models for stochastic random fields can be used and various constraints can be placed on a deterministic quantity.

The aim of this chapter is to classify the existing restoration techniques and introduce the new approaches presented in the remaining chapters of the book. In the following, degradation and image models are reviewed first. Ill-posed problems are defined and regularization techniques are discussed, since the image restoration problem is an ill-posed problem and most restoration algorithms have a common structure expressed by regularization theory. Finally, the existing restoration algorithms are categorized and briefly reviewed.

1.2 Degradation Models

Let us denote by $x(i,j)$ and $y(i,j)$ the original undistorted image and the observed noisy-blurred image, respectively. The discrete images result from the sampling of the corresponding continuous light quantities. A general degradation model is

$$y(i,j) = S\left\{\sum_m \sum_n d(i,j,m,n)x(m,n)\right\} \odot v(i,j) , \tag{1.1}$$

where $S\{\cdot\}$ represents a nonlinear function, $d(i,j,m,n)$ is the response of the blurring system to a two-dimensional (2D) impulse at the (i,j) spatial location, $v(i,j)$ denotes the corruptive noise process, and $\odot$ represents a pointwise operation. The function $S\{\cdot\}$ usually defines a pointwise (memoryless) operation, and it is used to model the response of the image sensor [1.3]. If, for example, photographic film is used as the recording medium then the function $S\{\cdot\}$ is described by the *Hurter-Driffield* (H-D) curve. *Andrews* and *Hunt* [1.3], *Cannon* [1.5], and *Trussell* and *Hunt* [1.6], among others (see also the list of references at the end of Chap. 8), have proposed restoration techniques with the nonlinearity taken into account, when the blurring system is linear space-invariant (LSI) and the noise additive. A general conclusion reached by all of them is that there is no significant improvement in the restoration results by taking the nonlinearity into account. Using the same degradation model *Tekalp* and *Pavlović* in Chap. 8 also derive a deconvolution filter in the "exposure domain". In contrast to the previous researchers, they conclude, based on their experimental evidence, that without taking the nonlinearity into account, certain scanned photographic images result in unacceptable restorations. However, in most of the work in the image restoration area, the function $S\{\cdot\}$ in (1.1) is ignored.

The noise process $v(i,j)$ in (1.1) may originate in the image formation process, the transmission medium, the recording process or any combination of these. When photographic film is used as the detection-recording mechanism, the noise, called *film-grain noise*, is due to the randomness in size, shape and separation of the silver grains. Film-grain noise is signal dependent and has a Poisson distribution [1.3]. A simple approximation is to consider the noise as signal independent, in which case the film grain noise is approximated by an additive white Gaussian (AWG) process in the density domain or a multiplicative process that obeys log-normal statistics in the intensity domain. *Chellappa, Simchony* and *Lichtenstein* in Chap. 5, model the image as a Gauss-Markov Random Field (GMRF) which is corrupted by film-grain noise and obtain its maximum a posteriori (MAP) estimate, using either a stochastic or a deterministic relaxation technique.

When photoelectronic systems are used for image detection and recording, the noise is due to the random fluctuations in the number of photons and photoelectrons on the photoactive surface of the detector and the random thermal noise sources in the circuits that sense, acquire, and process the signal from the detector's photoactive surface. Although the first process generates signal-dependent noise, both photoelectronic and thermal noise are usually modeled by a zero-mean, AWG process. Some representative restoration algorithms with signal dependent and multiplicative noise can be found in [1.7–10]. However, in most of the work in the image restoration area the process $v(i,j)$ in (1.1) is zero-mean AWG, uncorrelated with $x(i,j)$. Therefore, due to two basic simplifications the degradation model of (1.1) takes the form

$$y(i,j) = \sum_{m}\sum_{n} d(i,j,m,n)x(m,n) + v(i,j)\ . \tag{1.2}$$

The degradation model of (1.2) has found limited use, due primarily to the difficulty in estimating $d(i,j,m,n)$ in most applications but also due to the high computational requirements of the resulting restoration techniques. *Sawchuk* [1.11], for example, developed transformation-based algorithms, while *Schafer* et al. [1.12] used constrained iterative algorithms for the removal of space-variant blurs. In most practical situations, however, the blur can be modeled as being, at least regionally, space-invariant [1.13]. That is, the following degradation model applies:

$$y(i,j) = \sum_{m}\sum_{n} d(i-m,j-n)x(m,n) + v(i,j)\ . \tag{1.3}$$

We assume, without loss of generality, that both images are square of size $N \times N$, that is, $0 \le i \le (N-1)$ and $0 \le j \le (N-1)$. By stacking or lexicographically ordering the $N \times N$ arrays $y(i,j), x(i,j)$ and $v(i,j)$, Eqs. (1.2) and (1.3) become

$$\boldsymbol{y} = D\boldsymbol{x} + \boldsymbol{v}, \tag{1.4}$$

where $\boldsymbol{y}$, $\boldsymbol{x}$ and $\boldsymbol{v}$ are $N^2 \times 1$ vectors and D is an $N^2 \times N^2$ matrix. For the space-invariant blur case D is a block Toeplitz matrix. Such matrices can be approximated by block circulant matrices. Block circulant matrices are easily diagonalized since their eigenvalues are the 2D discrete Fourier transform (DFT) values of the defining 2D sequences, and their eigenvectors are defined in terms of Fourier kernels [1.3, 14]. Then, (1.4) is written in the discrete frequency domain as

$$Y(k,l) = D(k,l)X(k,l) + V(k,l)\,, \tag{1.5}$$

where $Y(k,l), D(k,l), X(k,l)$ and $V(k,l)$ represent respectively the 2D DFTs of $y(i,j), d(i,j)$, $x(i,j)$ and $v(i,j)$, for $0 \le k \le (N-1)$ and $0 \le l \le (N-1)$. The $D(k,l)$ are the "unstacked" eigenvalues of the matrix D, as was already mentioned. Clearly we can arrive at (1.5) by taking the 2D DFT of both sides of (1.3), under the assumption that it represents circular convolution. The 2D arrays can always be appropriately padded with zeros, for example, so that the result of circular convolution equals that of linear convolution.

The model of (1.3) or, equivalently, the model of (1.4) or (1.5), has been primarily used in the field of image restoration. Most of the image restoration algorithms in the literature were derived under the assumption that the point spread function (PSF) of the blur, as well as the required information on the noise field, is exactly known. The types of these algorithms will be reviewed and classified in Sect. 1.5. It is noted here that although the degradation model is linear space-invariant (LSI), the restoration filter may be nonlinear or space-variant or both. Finally we mention that there are applications where the PSF of the blurring system is random. *Ward* and *Saleh* [1.15] and *Combettes* and *Trussell* [1.16] have proposed algorithms for the restoration of stochastically blurred images.

1.3 Image Models

The use of an image model expresses our prior knowledge about the undistorted image. The resulting restoration filter clearly depends on the specific image model. The incorporation of a priori information into the restoration process is essential in obtaining acceptable solutions or regularizing the ill-posed image restoration problem, as will be explained in the next section.

The basic distinction between image models is that of *deterministic* and *statistical* or *stochastic*. According to *Andrews* and *Hunt* [1.3], deterministic image models can be divided into parametric (an image is represented in terms of primitives) or nonparametric. With a stochastic model an image is considered to be a sample function of an array of random variables called a *random field*. This characterization of an ensemble of images is useful in developing image restoration techniques that are valid for an entire class and not just for an individual image, as is the case with deterministic image models.

A possible division of stochastic models is into *parametric* and *nonparametric*. An example of a parametric stochastic image model is to assume that the image field is described by a 2D Gaussian probability density function (pdf). Such a pdf is specified in terms of two parameters, the covariance matrix and the mean vector. Such an image model is commonly used in maximum likelihood estimation problems, as is the case in Chap. 6. If the mean and covariance are still used in modeling the image but not as parameters of a pdf (the pdf is unknown), then a *nonparametric stochastic model* results. Both models.can be defined as *covariance models* [1.17], regardless of whether the covariance is a parameter of a pdf or not. Covariance models can be divided into *stationary* or *homogeneous* and *nonstationary* or *inhomogeneous*. A stationary model is defined as one having a constant or stationary mean and a stationary covariance, which results in the covariance matrix being block Toeplitz. Stationary models have been extensively used in image restoration [1.3]. However, in general, an image is an inhomogeneous random field, and hence, it cannot be fit very well by a homogeneous model. Three types of nonstationary covariance models result by assuming that the mean and/or the covariance is nonstationary. For example, *Hunt* and *Cannon* [1.18] proposed a Gaussian image model with nonstationary or space-variant mean and stationary covariance. The local mean and the local variance were used, for example, by *Wallis* [1.19], *Lee* [1.20] and *Kuan* et al. [1.7] for image estimation and restoration. This model was generalized by *Jeng* and *Woods* [1.21], who proposed two inhomogeneous image models.

An alternative to representing random fields by mean and covariance functions is to characterize them as the outputs of linear systems whose inputs are random fields with known or desired statistical properties (for example, white noise inputs) [1.17]. Such linear systems are represented by difference equations and are often useful in developing computationally efficient image processing algorithms, as shown by *Jain* [1.22]. A linear stochastic difference equation model that realizes the covariances of an ensemble is determined by spectral factorization.

The most commonly used linear system model for representing the image random field is the autoregressive (AR) model. According to this, the value at the "present" pixel is expressed in terms of the intensity values of pixels belonging to the "past". That is, $x(i,j)$ is equal to

$$x(i,j) = \sum_{(m,n)\in S_a}\sum a(i-m, j-n)x(m,n) + u(i,j)\,, \tag{1.6}$$

where $a(i,j)$ are called the prediction coefficients. Depending on the support of the prediction region S_a, three types of AR models result: causal, semicausal and noncausal, which are related, respectively, to the hyperbolic, parabolic and elliptic classes of partial differential equations [1.17]. The characteristics of the driving process $u(i, j)$ depend on the shape of S_a, as described by *Jain* [1.22]. In all cases, (1.6) represents a homogeneous random field. Of the three types of AR models, causal (nonsymmetric half-plane: NSHP) models have been primarily used for restoration, since they are recursively computable and thus result in recursively computable restoration filters (for iterative restoration algorithms, however, no causality requirement need be imposed on the AR model, [1.23]). Furthermore, a finite recursive Markov representation of the image field is desired. As shown by *Woods* [1.24], one cannot find a finite-order NSHP model corresponding to every 2D Markov field. However, since the inverse is true, that is, a finite order NSHP model driven by spatially white noise generates a Markov field, instead of fitting the spectral density to given spectral data, one can take a factored form and fit this to the data. This then converts the modeling problem to one of filter design.

A space-variant or nonstationary image model is obtained from (1.6) by allowing the prediction coefficients to be a function of the spatial position [1.25]. As a more tractable alternative, instead of allowing the coefficients to change at each pixel, a finite number of image structures can be assumed (different edge orientations and an isotropic region) and thus the prediction coefficients become a function of the particular image structure. This way, a multi-model recursive estimation/restoration algorithm results, which switches (based on a MAP decision logic, for example) between a finite number of available filters [1.26–29]. Recently, stochastic image models have been developed that govern this switching among the available restoration filters [1.30, 31]. Such models represent *compound random fields*. Two compound random fields are introduced and used for estimation and restoration in Chap. 4 by *Jeng* and *Woods* and Chap. 5 by *Chellappa, Simchony* and *Lichtenstein*.

Autoregressive moving average (ARMA) image models have had limited use in image restoration [1.32, 33]. This is due to the fact that modeling a given 2D random field by an AR model for estimation purposes yields results comparable to those achievable using an ARMA model, as reported by *Woods* and *Dravida* [1.32]. Furthermore, the identification of ARMA models is more complicated than that of AR models.

1.4 Ill-Posed Problems and Regularization Approaches

1.4.1 Ill-Posed Problems

The concept of a well-posed problem was introduced by *Hadamard* in the early 1900s, in an attempt to clarify what types of boundary conditions are most natural for various types of differential equations. As a result of his investigation, a problem characterized by the equation $Ax = y$, where $x \in H_1$, $y \in H_2$ (both H_1 and H_2 denote Hilbert spaces) and A is a bounded linear operator, is defined to be well-posed provided the following conditions are satisfied:

(i) for every element $\boldsymbol{y} \in H_2$ there exists a solution in the space H_1;
(ii) the solution is unique;
(iii) the problem is stable on the spaces (H_1, H_2), which means that the solution depends continuously on the data.

Otherwise the problem is ill-posed. *Nashed* [1.34] introduced the concept of well-posedness in the least-squares sense, according to which $A\boldsymbol{x} = \boldsymbol{y}$ is well-posed if for each $\boldsymbol{y} \in H_2$ there exists a unique least-squares solution (of minimal norm), which depends continuously on the data. For years, ill-posed problems had been considered as mere mathematical anomalies. Indeed, it was believed that physical situations only lead to well-posed problems. However, this attitude was erroneous and many ill-posed problems arise in practical situations. A detailed list of the ill-posed problems arising in mathematical physics is provided in the monograph by *Lavrentiev* [1.35].

If the image formation process is modeled in a continuous infinite dimensional space, the distortion operator $\boldsymbol{D}$ becomes an integral operator and (1.4) becomes a Fredholm integral equation of the first kind. Then the solution of (1.4) is almost always an ill-posed problem [1.34, 36–39]. This means that the unique least-squares solution of minimal norm of (1.4) does not depend continuously on the data or that a bounded perturbation (noise) in the data, results in an unbounded perturbation in the solution, or that the generalized inverse of $\boldsymbol{D}$ is unbounded [1.34]. The integral operator $\boldsymbol{D}$ has a countably infinite number of singular values that can be ordered with their limit approaching zero. Since the finite dimensional discrete problem of image restoration results from the discretization of an ill-posed continuous problem, the matrix D has (in addition to possibly a number of zero singular values) a cluster of very small singular values. Clearly, the finer the discretization (the larger the size of D) the closer the limit of the singular values is approximated. Therefore, although the finite dimensional inverse problem is well-posed in the least-squares sense, the ill-posedness of the continuous problem translates into an ill-conditioned matrix D.

In quantifying the conditioning of a matrix the condition number $P(D)$ can be used, defined according to the inequality [1.40]

$$\frac{\|\boldsymbol{e}\|}{\|\boldsymbol{x}\|} \leq \|D\| \, \|D^{+}\| \frac{\|\boldsymbol{v}\|}{\|D\boldsymbol{x}\|} = P(D) \frac{\|\boldsymbol{v}\|}{\|D\boldsymbol{x}\|} , \tag{1.7}$$

where D^{+} denotes the generalized inverse of D, $\boldsymbol{x}$ is the solution when the noiseless data are available, and $\boldsymbol{e}$ denotes the error in the solution when the noisy data $\boldsymbol{y}$ are available. If the value of $P(D)$ is small, a small relative change in $\boldsymbol{y}$ cannot produce a very large relative change in $\boldsymbol{x}$. If $P(D)$ has a large value, a small perturbation in the data may result in large (although bounded) perturbation in the solution, and the system is said to be ill-conditioned. By using the l_2 norm for vectors and matrices, $P(D)$ takes the simplified form

$$P(D) = \|D\|_2 \cdot \|D^{+}\|_2 = \frac{\mu_1}{\mu_r} , \tag{1.8}$$

where $\mu_1, \ldots, \mu_n$ are the singular values of D, r is the rank of D, and it was assumed that $\mu_1 \geq \mu_2 \geq \ldots \geq \mu_r > \mu_{r+1} = \ldots = \mu_n = 0$. Since the largest singular value of D is different from zero due to the assumption of lossless imaging, $P(D)$ is an increasing function of the image dimensions.

The problem of noise amplification can be further explained by using a spectral approach. That is, the minimum norm least-squares solution of (1.4) can be written as [1.41]

$$\bar{\boldsymbol{x}} = \sum_{i=1}^{r} \frac{(\boldsymbol{w}_i, D\boldsymbol{x})}{\mu_i} \boldsymbol{z}_i + \sum_{i=1}^{r} \frac{(\boldsymbol{w}_i, \boldsymbol{v})}{\mu_i} \boldsymbol{z}_i \,, \tag{1.9}$$

where $\boldsymbol{w}_i$ and $\boldsymbol{z}_i$ are respectively the eigenvectors of DD^{T} and $D^{\mathrm{T}}D$ and $(\boldsymbol{z}, \boldsymbol{w})$ denotes the inner product of the vectors $\boldsymbol{z}$ and $\boldsymbol{w}$. Clearly, since D is an ill-conditioned matrix some of its singular values will be very close to zero, so that some of the weights μ_i^{-1} are very large numbers. If the ith inner product $(\boldsymbol{w}_i, \boldsymbol{v})$ is not zero (as is true when the noise is broadband), the noise [second term of (1.9)] is amplified. Similar observations can be made by using the spectral decomposition of an orepator in infinite dimensional spaces [1.42]. If matrix D is block circulant then the singular values μ_i are equal to $|D(k,l)|$ in (1.5), where $|\cdot|$ denotes complex magnitude.

1.4.2 Regularization Approaches

"Regularization of ill-posed problems" is a phrase used for various approaches to circumvent lack of continuous dependence (as well as to impart existence and uniqueness if necessary). Roughly speaking, a regularization method entails an analysis of an ill-posed problem via an analysis of an associated well-posed problem, whose solution yields meaningful answers and approximations to the given ill-posed problem. According to *Tikhonov* [1.43], the regularization method consists of finding regularizing operators that operate on the data, and determining the regularization parameter from supplementary information pertaining to the problem. The regularization operator depends continuously on the data and results in the true solution when the regularization parameter goes to zero, or equivalently when the noise goes to zero.

Numerous methods have been proposed for treating and regularizing various types of ill-posed problems. The various approaches to regularization involve essentially one or more of the following intuitive ideas [1.42,44]:

(a) change of the concept of a solution;
(b) restriction of the data;
(c) change of the space and/or topologies;
(d) modification of the operator itself;
(e) the concept of regularization operators; and
(f) well-posed stochastic extensions of ill-posed problems [1.45]. The various approaches to regularization overlap in many aspects. Usually several of the above ideas manifest themselves in any particular approach to regularization.

Most existing image restoration methods have a common estimation structure, in spite of their apparent variety. This common structure is expressed by regularization theory. Such a statement can be also made for most early vision problems [1.46]. *Titterington* [1.47] and *Demoment* [1.48] in a recent review paper, provide a Bayesian interpretation of regularization problems. No details are provided here regarding the interpretation of restoration techniques as regularization approaches, due to lack of space. A qualitative interpretation should be kept in mind, however, according to which the use of prior information on the solution or the parameters to be estimated expresses the underlying idea in many regularization approaches. This prior information is combined with the data information and defines a solution by trying to achieve smoothness and yet remain "faithful" to the data. In other words, a regularized solution is a solution between the "ultra-rough" least-squares solution and an "ultra-smooth" solution based on a priori knowledge [1.47].

1.5 Overview of Image Restoration Approaches

The main image restoration approaches that have appeared in the literature are overviewed in this section. A classification of these approaches is shown in Fig. 1.1. This classification is based primarily on the image model assumed, that is, deterministic or stochastic, stationary or nonstationary, dynamic or static, but also on the algorithmic procedure used for obtaining the solution. The restoration approaches considered assume a linear degradation model with additive (white Gaussian) noise, as expressed by (1.2) or (1.3). A number of restoration algorithms can be implemented in the discrete frequency domain. If a matrix-vector representation of an algorithm is shown, a discrete frequency domain representation can be obtained if the matrices involved are block-circulant (the sum, product and inverse of block-circulant matrices is also a block-circulant matrix). Block-circulant matrices can be obtained as approximations to block-Toeplitz matrices [1.3].

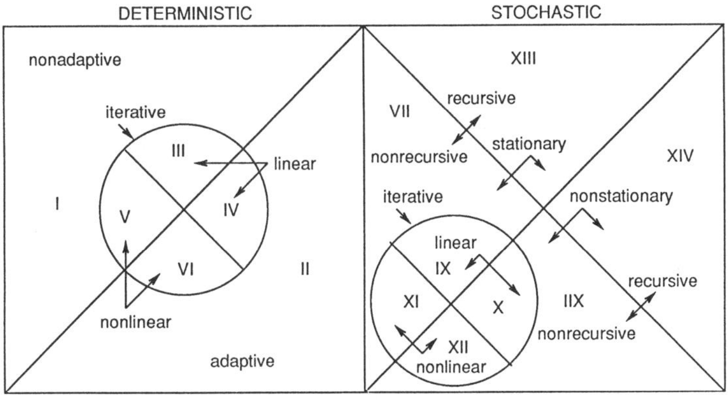

Fig. 1.1. Classification of image restoration algorithms

1.5.1 Deterministic Restoration Algorithms

For this class of restoration algorithms the original image is a deterministic signal completely unknown or with a known bound.

a) Group I. Consider the case of a completely unknown $\boldsymbol{x}$ first. If no information is assumed about the noise (or equivalently, if the noise is ignored) then according to the least-squares approach, the error norm $\|\boldsymbol{v}\| = \|\boldsymbol{y} - D\boldsymbol{x}\|$ is minimized with respect to $\boldsymbol{x}$, resulting in the normal equations

$$D^{\mathrm{T}}D\boldsymbol{x} = D^{\mathrm{T}}\boldsymbol{y} , \tag{1.10}$$

where ^{T} denotes the transpose of a matrix or a vector. An $\boldsymbol{x}$ satisfying (1.10) represents a least-squares solution. If D is square invertible, then $\boldsymbol{x} = D^{-1}\boldsymbol{y}$ represents the inverse filter. If $D^{\mathrm{T}}D$ is not invertible, then the solution of (1.10) of minimum-norm, denoted by $\bar{\boldsymbol{x}}$, is chosen. This solution is used in defining the generalized inverse of D, denoted by D^{+}, according to the relation $D^{+}\boldsymbol{y} = \bar{\boldsymbol{x}}$. The truncated singular value decomposition [1.3], represented by (1.9) with r replaced by a smaller number, is another related method in group I. According to this method, regularization is performed through control of the dimensionality of the solution space.

Consider next the case when the noise is modeled as zero mean with known covariance Φ_v. In this case, a linear unbiased estimator which yields the minimum error covariance matrix is equal to [1.49]

$$D^{\mathrm{T}}\Phi_v^{-1}D\boldsymbol{x} = D^{\mathrm{T}}\Phi_v^{-1}\boldsymbol{y} . \tag{1.11}$$

It is interesting to observe that if the noise is white, that is, $\Phi_v = \sigma^2 I$, where I is the identity matrix, (1.11) reduces to the normal equations, meaning that the white noise can be ignored.

Both (1.10) and (1.11) represent an "ultra-rough" solution. A regularized solution can be obtained by assuming that additional a priori knowledge is available. That is, let us assume that

$$\boldsymbol{x} \in Q_x , \tag{1.12}$$

where Q_x is a set in an N^2-dimensional space. Similarly, assume that the noise $\boldsymbol{v}$ belongs to a set Q_v. Since $\boldsymbol{v}$ must lie in a set, it follows that a given observation $\boldsymbol{y}$ combines with the set Q_v to define a new set which must contain $\boldsymbol{x}$. Thus the observation $\boldsymbol{y}$ specifies a set $Q_{x/y}$ which must contain $\boldsymbol{x}$;

$$\boldsymbol{x} \in Q_{x/y} = \{\boldsymbol{x} : (\boldsymbol{y} - D\boldsymbol{x}) \in Q_v\} . \tag{1.13}$$

Consider now the sets Q_x and $Q_{x/y}$. Each set contains $\boldsymbol{x}$ and therefore $\boldsymbol{x}$ must lie in their intersection [1.50]. Let $Q_{\hat{x}}$ denote this intersection. Then

$$Q_{\hat{x}} = Q_x \cap Q_{x/y} , \tag{1.14}$$

where ∩ denotes set intersection. According to (1.14) the restored image is defined not as a single vector but as a set. This set is the smallest set that must contain $\boldsymbol{x}$ and that can be calculated from the available information. We note here that the formulation of this set theoretic approach to restoration is quite straightforward and holds true for any kind of set. However, the difficulty of the approach arises when the intersection of these sets, as defined by (1.14), is to be calculated. To make the problem more tractable, ellipsoids are used for the sets $Q_{\boldsymbol{x}}$ and $Q_{\boldsymbol{v}}$. A usual form of these ellipsoids is [1.47]

$$\|C\boldsymbol{x}\|_F^2 \leq E^2 \tag{1.15}$$

and

$$\|\boldsymbol{v}\|_W^2 \leq \varepsilon^2 , \tag{1.16}$$

where $\|\cdot\|_F$ represents a weighted norm. However, since the intersection of ellipsoids is not an ellipsoid, an ellipsoid bounding this intersection is used, whose center respresents the restored image. For the ellipsoids of (1.15) and (1.16) it is shown [1.51] that the center of a bounding ellipsoid satisfies the equation

$$(D^{\mathrm{T}}W^{\mathrm{T}}WD + \alpha C^{\mathrm{T}}F^{\mathrm{T}}FC)\boldsymbol{x} = D^{\mathrm{T}}W^{\mathrm{T}}W\boldsymbol{y} , \tag{1.17}$$

where α, the regularization parameter, is equal to $(\varepsilon/E)^2$. Equation (1.17) can also be derived by considering *Miller*'s regularization approach [1.52, 53]. A number of filters result from (1.17) depending on the way the regularization parameter is specified and on the type of the a priori knowledge assumed, as expressed by the matrices C, F and W. Matrices F and W introduce the spatial adaptivity of the filter, and are discussed later (set $F = W = I$, for the time being). Clearly for $\alpha = 0$ the least-squares filter results. If one of the bounds ε or E is not known, the restoration problem is formulated as a constrained minimization problem. The parameter α, which now represents a Lagrange multiplier, is chosen in an iterative fashion, so that (1.15) and (1.16) are satisfied with equality, if ε and E are known, respectively. Pictorially, in this case, the restored image is on the surface of one of the ellipsoids at the point of minimum distance from the center of the other ellipsoid. This filter represents the constrained-least-squares (CLS) filter initially proposed by *Hunt* [1.54], with ε known (see also *Dines* and *Kak* [1.55]). Usually ε is the known parameter, which is estimated from the noisy-blurred image $\boldsymbol{y}$ [1.3], or is chosen to be equal to a parameter, such as the mode or the expected value, of the probability distribution describing the fit of the least-squares solution to the true image [1.47]. The determination of α can also be based on the minimization of a risk function. An example of this approach is the cross-validation approach [1.56]. According to (1.17) only the ratio of the parameters ε and E is required in obtaining the solution. However, the individual values of ε and E are needed in verifying the existence of a feasible set of solutions or the nonemptiness of $Q_{\hat{\boldsymbol{x}}}$.

The role of the constraint C is to impose a smoothness requirement on the solution. That is, C should represent a high-pass filter so that the energy of the restored signal at high frequencies, due primarily to noise amplification, is bounded, according to (1.15). In agreement with this, C has been chosen to be a pth order differential operator [1.36–38, 43, 54]. *Hunt* [1.3] suggests the use of a block circulant C whose properties in the frequency domain match the spatial frequency reponse of the psychophysics of the human visual system. In crossing the line between deterministic and stochastic approaches, C can be chosen to be equal to $(\Phi_x)^{-1/2}(\Phi_v)^{1/2}$, where Φ_x and Φ_v are respectively the image and noise covariance matrices. Then (1.17) represents a *parametric Wiener filter.*

In Chap. 2 by *Auyeung* and *Mersereau,* constrained image restoration is treated as a convex programming problem solved using a dual approach. More specifically, least-squares, minimum cross entropy and maximum entropy cost criteria are used under a variety of constraints on the signal to be restored and the observation noise. Iterative approaches are followed in obtaining the solution.

b) Group II. The development of spatially adaptive restoration algorithms is motivated by the fact that most of the nonadaptive filters are low-pass and give rise to unacceptable blurring of lines and edges in the restored image. The adaptivity in the deterministic restoration algorithms is introduced by considering properties of the human visual system. Psychophysical experiments confirm that noise in flat regions of the image will cause the observer to perceive spurious features or textures, and that at sharp transitions in image intensity the contrast sensitivity of the human visual system decreases with the sharpness of the transition and increases approximately exponentially as a function of spatial distance from the transition [1.57]. This masking effect in the visual system results in lower noise visibility in the vicinity of edges.

Based on this information, *Anderson* and *Netravali* [1.57] first defined the noise *masking function* as a measure of spatial detail and then based on subjective tests they obtained the *visibility function.* According to these functions for areas with high spatial activity (large value of the masking function), the visibility function goes to 0 (noise is not visible), while for flat areas the visibility function goes to 1 (noise is visible). The information provided by the visibility function was used by *Anderson* and *Netravali* [1.57] and *Knutsson* et al. [1.58] in designing noise smoothing filters. *Katsaggelos* et al. [1.59, 60] used the values of the visibility function as entries of the matrix F in (1.17). Then W is set to be equal to $I - W$ [1.61]. This way at the areas of high spatial activity the noise is allowed to go through the restoration filter, due to the action of F, while these areas are more deblurred than the areas of low spatial activity, due to the action of W. In other words, the restoration filter in (1.17) varies continuously between the two extreme forms of an inverse filter for $F = 0$ and of a noise smoothing filter for $F = I$. *Ichioka* and *Nakajima* [1.62] have also used a matrix W, determined by a feature-extracted image with the use of a nonlinear variance filter.

c) Groups III–VI: Iterative Deterministic Restoration Algorithms. Many problems in signal processing take the form of solving the equation

$$Gx = z\,, \qquad (1.18)$$

for $\boldsymbol{x}$, or equivalently solving for the roots of $G\boldsymbol{x} = 0$, by absorbing the vector $\boldsymbol{z}$ into G. If G is a nonlinear operator then, in contrast to the case of linear systems of equations, direct methods for the solution of nonlinear equations are usually feasible only for small systems of a very special form [1.63]. That is, iterative methods represent the only alternative for obtaining a solution of (1.18), provided it does indeed have solutions. However, iterative methods represent a possible alternative for solving a set of linear equations if, for example, direct matrix inversion is computationally unfeasible. More importantly, with direct restoration approaches the inverse of D is determined without considering the properties of the original undistorted image. With iterative methods it is possible to incorporate known properties of the original image into the restoration process (regularization principle). This is achieved with the use of constraints.

A number of iterative techniques from the numerical analysis literature have been used for image restoration [1.64–66]. One such iteration which has been widely used to remove the effects of many different types of distortions [1.12] is the successive approximations based iteration. It has the form

$$\begin{aligned} \boldsymbol{x}_0 &= \beta \boldsymbol{z} \\ \boldsymbol{x}_{k+1} &= \tilde{\boldsymbol{x}}_k + \beta\left(\boldsymbol{z} - G\tilde{\boldsymbol{x}}_k\right) \\ \tilde{\boldsymbol{x}}_k &= C_{\mathrm{H}}\boldsymbol{x}_k \, . \end{aligned} \tag{1.19}$$

The parameter β $(0 < \beta < 2\|G\|^{-1})$ is chosen to insure convergence and maximize the rate of convergence. With the use of the *hard constraint* C_{H} additional prior knowledge about the properties of the desired solution is incorporated into the solution process [1.12]. Examples of such constraints are the positivity, the time-limitation and the band-limitation constraints. Signals which satisfy these and other properties may define convex sets, and the application of a hard constraint is equivalent to projecting onto a convex set [1.67]. The operator C_{H} represents one hard constraint operator or the concatenation of several. Clearly, (1.18) may result from a deterministic restoration approach, like the ones described in the previous section, or from a stochastic approach. Perhaps the earliest reference to an iteration of the type of (1.19) was by *Van Cittert* [1.68] in the 1930s. In this case $G = D$, $\boldsymbol{z} = \boldsymbol{y}$, the distortion was spatially invariant, the gain β was equal to 1 and $C_{\mathrm{H}} = I$. *Jansson* et al. [1.69] modified the Van Cittert algorithm by replacing β with a relaxation parameter that depends on the signal. The successive approximations iteration applied to the normal equations (1.10) constitutes *Landweber*'s iteration [1.70]. Also, *Kawata* and *Ichioka* [1.71, 72] used iteration (1.19) for image restoration with a fixed or a varying parameter β. *Katsaggelos* et al. [1.53, 59–60] used iteration (1.19) to find a solution to (1.17), with fixed or iteration dependent F and W. The resulting iteration was used by *Lagendijk* et al. [1.61] to describe the ringing effect. Algorithms of the type (1.19) are reviewed by *Katsaggelos* [1.51] and *Meinel* [1.73]. Iterations with higher rates of convergence have been recently applied to signal restoration [1.74–76]. The multistep version of algorithm (1.19) is discussed by *Katsaggelos* and *Kumar* [1.77].

The method of projecting onto convex sets (POCS) describes an alternative iterative approach to incorporating prior knowledge about the solution into the restoration process. It first appears in the engineering literature in the early 1980s [1.67, 78], and since then it has been successfully applied to the solution of various restoration problems [1.79]. According to the method of POCS, incorporating a priori knowledge into the solution can be interpreted as restricting the solution to be a member of a closed convex set that is defined as a set of vectors which satisfy a particular property. If the constraint sets have a nonempty intersection, then a solution that belongs to the intersection set, which is also a convex set, can be found by alternating projections onto these convex sets. Indeed, any solution in the intersection set is consistent with the a priori constraints and therefore it is a feasible solution.

The method of POCS can be applied, for example, to find a vector which belongs in the intersection $Q_{\hat{x}}$ in (1.14). The projections $P_{Q_x}x$ and $P_{Q_{x/y}}x$ onto the sets Q_x and $Q_{x/y}$, respectively, are defined by ($F = W = I$) [1.51, 80]

$$P_{Q_x}x = \left[I - \lambda_2(I + \lambda_2 C^T C)^{-1} C^T C\right] x , \tag{1.20}$$

$$P_{Q_{x/y}}x = x + \lambda_1 \left(I + \lambda_1 D^T D\right)^{-1} D^T(y - Dx) , \tag{1.21}$$

where λ_1 and λ_2 need to be chosen so that conditions (1.15) and (1.16) are satisfied, respectively. The solution of (1.17) differs from the solution obtained by the POCS method; the two solutions are the same only when the starting point of the POCS iteration satisfies (1.17). *Trussell* and *Civanlar* [1.80] and *Sezan* and *Tekalp* [1.81] have applied the POCS method to image restoration.

Clearly, if the constraint C_H in (1.19) or the projection operator are nonlinear, the resulting iterative restoration algorithm is nonlinear. A representative example is an operator which projects onto the convex sets of signals whose amplitude is within specified bounds (the widely used positivity constraint represents a special case of this operator).

In dealing with iterative algorithms, the analysis of the convergence as well as the rate of convergence is very important. The contraction mapping theorem usually serves as a basis for establishing convergence of iterative algorithms [1.63, 82]. When G in (1.18) is a symmetric, semipositive definite matrix, *Bialy*'s theorem [1.83] provides a sufficient condition for convergence of iteration (1.19) with $C_H = I$. Convergence criteria for iterative restoration algorithms have been proposed by *Trussell* [1.84] and *Sullivan* and *Katsaggelos* [1.85].

1.5.2 Stochastic Algorithms

For this class of restoration algorithms a stochastic description of the image is assumed.

a) Groups VII–XII. Nonrecursive restoration algorithms are included in these groups, which are based on the use of a static stochastic image model. One of the most widely used restoration filters is the Wiener filter, described by

$$x = \Phi_x D^{\mathrm{T}} \left(D\Phi_x D^{\mathrm{T}} + \Phi_v \right)^{-1} y = \left(D^{\mathrm{T}}\Phi_v^{-1} D + \Phi_x^{-1} \right)^{-1} D^{\mathrm{T}}\Phi_v^{-1} y \, , \tag{1.22}$$

where Φ_x and Φ_v are the respective correlation matrices of the image and the noise field [1.49]. The form of the Wiener filter for an image of nonzero mean is given in [1.17]. If the matrices D, Φ_x and Φ_v are block circulant, (1.22) can be written in the discrete frequency domain. If at least one of these matrices is not block circulant, then most probably an iterative technique is necessary, due to the required inversion of a matrix of large size in (1.22). Matrix D is not block circulant if the distortion is space-variant, while Φ_x is not block circulant if, for example, the mean of the image is not constant, although the covariance matrix is block circulant. Nonlinear iterative algorithms are obtained in this case if a nonlinear constraint operator C_{H} (positivity constraint, for example) is used, according to iteration (1.19). Algorithms in groups XI and XII are obtained, in this case, depending on whether Φ_x is block circulant or not. Another member of group XI is the maximum entropy restoration algorithm [1.86, 87].

Other members of group VII are the geometric mean filter [1.3], the homomorphic type filter of *Cannon* [1.5, 88], and the MAP and maximum likelihood (ML) restoration filters. MAP restoration filters were derived by *Trussell* and *Hunt* [1.6] and *Hunt* [1.89] using the degradation model of (1.1) with additive noise. For the model of (1.4) under consideration, the ML and MAP restorations reduce respectively, to the least-squares solution of (1.10), under the assumption of AWG noise, and the Wiener filter [1.17].

b) Group XIII: Stationary Recursive Restoration Algorithms. Recursive structures are usually characterized by reduced computational complexity over that of nonrecursive filter forms and thus appear more compatible with small-scale hardware implementations, and are more suitable for real time applications. A general approach to 2D recursive restoration must incorporate the following features:

(i) derivation of a dynamic image model, yielding an exact representation of the statistics of the image,
(ii) identification of the parameters of the model, and
(iii) design of an optimal or suboptimal filter based on this model. The overview of this area can be complemented by the excellent chapter by *Woods* [1.28] and the detailed overview and references in Chap. 7 of this volume.

The first approach to recursive processing of images was the derivation of scalar signals from scanned images and application of well known 1D (Kalman) filtering techniques [1.90, 91]. Most early image estimation or restoration recursive algorithms did not take into account the correlation of a pixel to pixels from previous lines in the image. A first attempt at a true 2D recursive estimation scheme was suggested by *Habibi* [1.93]. As was pointed out by *Strintzis* [1.94] no such filter could be optimal in the mean squared error sense. An algorithm similar to Habibi's was proposed by *Panda* and *Kak* [1.95]. *Katayama* and *Kosaka* [1.96] also derived a restoration scheme based on Habibi's model, which was shown by *Murphy* [1.97] not to be optimal. The initial attempts to extend the 1D Kalman filter to two dimensions encountered both computational and storage problems. To overcome these problems *Murphy* and *Silverman* [1.98] considered line-by-line restoration, *Katayama* [1.99] used a discrete sine transform for fast restoration and *Suresh* and *Shenoi* [1.100] derived a Kalman strip filter using 2D *Roesser* models [1.101]. *Biemond* et al. [1.102] introduced a hybrid Kalman filter which is recursive in the vertical direction and transform based in the horizontal direction.

Woods and *Radewan* [1.103] and *Woods* and *Ingle* [1.104] derived an optimum 2D scalar Kalman filter for estimation and restoration. However, the support of the state was very large and therefore suboptimal approaches were derived. Suboptimal Kalman techniques have been sought by many researchers, since although they provide two to three orders of magnitude reduction in computation, the reduction in optimality is slight. The reason for this result is that the cause of the excessive computations is "purely mathematical", that is, the very uncommon but possible occurrence of high correlation at great distances from the estimated point [1.103]. For example, the Reduced Update Kalman Filter (RUKF) and a Kalman strip processors were proposed by *Woods* [1.28], and the Reduced Order Model Kalman Filter (ROMKF) was proposed by *Angwin* and *Kaufman* [1.105] and is analyzed in detail in Chap. 7. Other recent Kalman restoration filter structures have been proposed by *Wu* [1.106] and *Mahalanabis* and *Xue* [1.107].

c) Group XIV: Nonstationary Recursive Restoration Algorithms. The basic common assumption of all algorithms in the previous section is that the image is considered to be a realization of a 2D stationary process. The resulting restoration filter is therefore a stationary filter. Such filters result in smearing of edges in the image, since at the edge location the image model changes, contrary to the stationary assumption. Regarding this issue, more recent work has concentrated on the derivation of nonstationary filters.

Nonstationary image models and nonstationary restoration filters based on these models have already been discussed in Sect. 1.3. Nonstationary restoration techniques can in general be divided into continuously adaptive and region adaptive. In the first class belong filters that use the local mean and variance [1.7, 19, 20] and the filter by *Tekalp* et al. [1.25], while in the second class belong the multiple image model based filters. *Nahi* and *Habibi* [1.26] first dealt with the case of two models. *Ingle* and *Woods* [1.27] considered the case of more models (usually five models describing edges of different orientations and isotropic situations), and then derived a multiple-model recursive estimator using the RUKF. *Woods* et al. [1.31] addressed the optimal space-variant estimation of images in the presence of noise with a given number of a priori selected image models in a switching environment, where at each pixel one of the steady-state linear space-invariant filters designed for these models is chosen. An extension of this decision-directed method to deconvolution type problems is presented by *Tekalp* et al. [1.29]. Compound random fields are used and analyzed in detail in Chaps. 4 and 5. Other nonstationary filters are the 1D Kalman filter of *Biemond* and *Gerbrands* [1.110], in which edge information is used to improve the step response; the self-tuning algorithms of *Wellstead* and *Pinto* [1.111], in which a recursive identifier is used in conjunction with an ARMA filter, and the nonlinear adaptive Kalman filter of *Rajala* and *de Figueiredo* [1.108], which represents a modification of the filter by *Aboutalib* et al. [1.109] based on the masking function.

Most of the recursive restoration techniques that have appeared in the literature deal with a space-invariant distortion. More recent work deals with spatially variant blur PSF models [1.112]. In Chap. 7 by *Angwin* and *Kaufman*, both the image and blur PSF are assumed to be nonstationary. Region adaptive and continuously adaptive techniques are derived based on ML estimation.

1.6 Discussion

Algorithms developed for the restoration of a single frame or monochrome image, under the assumption that the blur is exactly known, have been discussed. In many practical situations however, the PSF of the blur needs to be identified from the noisy-blurred data. This problem is addressed in Chap. 6 by *Katsaggelos* and *Lay*, see also [1.113], where an iterative approach is derived based on the Expectation-Maximization (EM) algorithm, and in Chap. 7 by *Angwin* and *Kaufman*, where a recursive approach is followed based on the ROMKF. References on blur identification and image restoration algorithms can be found at the end of these two chapters. In certain applications image data from multiple frequency bands, multiple time frames, multiple colors, or multiple sensors need to be restored. Restoration algorithms for multichannel images has been presented by *Hunt* and *Kübler* [1.114] and *Galatsanos* et al. [1.115, 116]. Related to multichannel image restoration are the restoration of an image when multiple distorted versions of the image are available [1.117, 118] and the estimation and restoration of (video) sequences of images, which is expected to be an active future research area.

Most image restoration algorithms that have appeared in the literature were implemented on a general purpose computer. However, when fast or real-time implementations are required, special purpose computers and hardware needs to be considered. Along these lines Hopfield's artificial neural network has been used to perform constrained least squares image restoration by *Zhou* et al. [1.119] and *Paik* and *Katsaggelos* [1.120]. In Chap. 3 by *Yeh, Stark* and *Sezan*, a learning algorithm is proposed that enables the network to learn the Lagrange multipliers [regularization parameter α in (1.17)] associated with the constraints. In the same chapter Hopfield-type networks are used to implement associative content addressable memories, based on a set-theoretic approach.

Let us close this chapter with the following critical questions: Has the area of image restoration reached its saturation point? Or, can we really do much better that the existing restoration algorithms? Although the newer algorithms are more sophisticated and complicated than the inverse filter or the constrained least squares filter, for example, is the improvement they introduce very dramatic? Furthermore, how is this improvement measured? It is widely known that the mean squared error criterion does not agree with the properties of the visual system. However, it is the most widely used criterion. Should performance indices more representative of the visual system's response be obtained? Finally, how far in the future is the day when it will be "impossible to take a bad picture"?

Acknowledgement. This material is based upon work supported in part by the NSF under grant no. MIP-8614217.

References

1.1 A. Rosenfeld, A. C. Kak : *Digital Picture Processing*, Vol. 1 (Academic, New York 1982)
1.2 T. S. Huang (ed.): *Picture Processing and Digital Filtering*, 2nd ed., Topics Appl. Phys., Vol. 6 (Springer, Berlin, Heidelberg 1979)
1.3 H. C. Andrews, B. R. Hunt : *Digital Image Restoration* (Prentice Hall, Englewood Cliffs, NJ 1977)
1.4 B. L. McGlamery: J. Opt. Soc. Am. **57**, 293–297 (1967)
1.5 T. M. Cannon: "Digital Image Deblurring by Nonlinear Homomorphic Filtering"; Ph.D. dissertation, University of Utah (1974)
1.6 H. J. Trussell, B. R. Hunt: IEEE Trans. C-**27**, 57–62 (1979)
1.7 D. T. Kuan, A. A. Sawchuk, T. C. Strand, P. Chavel: IEEE Trans. PAMI-**7**, 653–665 (1985)
1.8 C. R. Moloney, M. E. Jernigan: Opt. Eng. **28**, 478–487 (1989)
1.9 J. F. Walkup, R. C. Choens: Opt. Eng. **13**, 258–266 (1974)
1.10 W. A. Pearlman, W. J. Song: "A Robust Method for Restoration of Photon-Limited Images", in Proc. SPIE, Vol. 504 (Aug. 1984) pp. 270–276
1.11 A. A. Sawchuk: Proc. IEEE **60**, 854–861 (1972)
1.12 R. W. Schafer, R. M. Mersereau, M. A. Richards: Proc. IEEE **69**, 432–450 (1981)
1.13 M. M. Sondhi: Proc. IEEE **60**, 842–853 (1972)
1.14 R. C. Gonzalez, P. Wintz : *Digital Image Processing*, 2nd ed. (Addison-Wesley, Reading, MA 1987)
1.15 R. K. Ward, B. E. A. Saleh: IEEE Trans. ASSP-**35**, 1494–1498 (1987)
1.16 P. L. Combettes, H. J. Trussell: IEEE Trans. ASSP-**37**, 393–401 (1989)
1.17 A. K. Jain: *Fundamentals of Digital Image Processing* (Prentice Hall, Englewood Cliffs, NJ 1989)
1.18 B. R. Hunt, T. M. Cannon: IEEE Trans. SMC-**6**, 876–881 (1976)
1.19 R. Wallis: "An Approach to the Space Variant Restoration and Enhancement of Images", in Proc. Symp. Current Math. Problems in Image Sci. (Nov. 1976) pp. 107–111
1.20 J. S. Lee: IEEE Trans. PAMI-**2**, 165–177 (1980)
1.21 F. C. Jeng, J. W. Woods: IEEE Trans. ASSP-**36**, 1305–1312 (1988)
1.22 A. K. Jain: Proc. IEEE **69**, 502–528 (1981)
1.23 A. K. Katsaggelos, J. Biemond, R. M. Mersereau, R. W. Schafer: Trans. Circ. Syst. Signal Proc. **3**, 139–160 (1984)
1.24 J. W. Woods: IEEE Trans. IT-**18**, 232–240 (1972)
1.25 A. M. Tekalp, H. Kaufman, J. W. Woods: IEEE Trans. ASSP-**33**, 469–472 (1985)
1.26 N. E. Nahi, A. Habibi: IEEE Trans. CAS-**22**, 286–293 (1979)
1.27 V. K. Ingle, J. W. Woods: "Multiple Model Recursive Estimation of Images", in Proc. ICASSP (1979) pp. 642–645
1.28 J. W. Woods: "Two-Dimensional Kalman Filtering", in *Two-Dimensional Digital Signal Processing I*, ed. by T. S. Huang, Topics Appl. Phys., Vol. 42 (Springer, Berlin, Heidelberg 1981)
1.29 A. M. Tekalp, H. Kaufman, J. W. Woods: IEEE Trans. ASSP-**37**, 892–899 (1989)
1.30 S. Geman, D. Geman: Trans. IEEE PAMI-**6**, 721–741 (1984)
1.31 J. W. Woods, S. Dravida, R. Mediavilla: IEEE Trans. PAMI-**9**, 245–253 (1987)
1.32 J. W. Woods, S. Dravida: "Two-Dimensional Recursive Estimation for ARMA Signal Models", in Proc. ICASSP (1982) pp. 1150–1153
1.33 M. G. Strintzis: IEEE Trans. AC-**23**, 801–809 (1978)
1.34 M. Z. Nashed: IEEE Trans. AP-**29**, 220–231 (1981)

1.35 M. M. Lavrentiev: *Some Improperly Posed Problems of Mathematical Physics* (Springer, Berlin, Heidelberg 1967)
1.36 D. L. Phillips: Assoc. Comp. Mach. **9**, 84–97 (1962)
1.37 S. Twomey: Assoc. Comp. Mach. **10**, 97–101 (1963)
1.38 S. Twomey: J. Franklin Inst. **279**, 95–109 (1965)
1.39 A. K. Katsaggelos: "Constrained Iterative Image Restoration Algorithms", Ph.D. dissertation, School of Electrical Engineering, Georgia Institute of Technology (1985)
1.40 J. R. Westlake: *A Handbook of Numerical Matrix Inversion and Solution of Linear Equations* (Wiley, New York 1968)
1.41 G. Strang: *Linear Algebra and Its Applications*, 2nd ed. (Academic, New York 1980)
1.42 M. Z. Nashed: "Aspects of Generalized Inverses in Analysis and Regularization", in *Generalized Inverses and Applications*, ed. by M. Z. Nashed (Academic, New York 1976)
1.43 A. N. Tikhonov, V. Y. Arsenin: *Solution of Ill-Posed Problems* (Winston, Wiley, New York 1977)
1.44 T. K. Sarkar, D. D. Weiner, V. K. Jain: IEEE Trans. AP-**29**, 373–379 (1981)
1.45 J. N. Franklin: J. Math. Anal. **31**, 682–716 (1970)
1.46 M. Bertero, T. Poggio, V. Torre: "Ill-Posed Problems in Early Vision", Art. Intell. Lab. Memo 924, M.I.T. (1986)
1.47 D. M. Titterington: Astron. Astrophys. **144**, 381–387 (1985)
1.48 G. Demoment: IEEE Trans. ASSP-**37**, 2024–2036 (1989)
1.49 E. L. Hall: *Computer Image Processing and Recognition* (Academic, New York 1979)
1.50 F. C. Schweppe: *Uncertain Dynamic Systems* (Prentice-Hall, Englewood Cliffs, NJ 1973)
1.51 A. K. Katsaggelos: Opt. Eng. **28**, 735–748 (1989)
1.52 K. Miller: SIAM J. Math. Anal. **1**, 52–74 (1970)
1.53 A. K. Katsaggelos, J. Biemond, R. M. Mersereau, R. W. Schafer: "A General Formulation of Constrained Iterative Restoration Algorithms", in Proc. ICASSP (1985) pp. 700–703
1.54 B. R. Hunt: IEEE Trans. C-**22**, 805–812 (1973)
1.55 K. A. Dines, A. C. Kak: IEEE Trans. ASSP-**25**, 346–350 (1977)
1.56 G. H. Golub, M. Health, G. Wahba: Technometrics **21**, 215-223 (1979)
1.57 G. L. Anderson, A. N. Netravali: IEEE Trans. SMC-**6**, 845–853 (1976)
1.58 H. E. Knutsson, R. Wilson, G. H. Granland: IEEE Trans. COM-**31**, 388–397 (1983)
1.59 A. K. Katsaggelos, J. Biemond, R. M. Mersereau, R. W. Schafer: "Nonstationary Iterative Image Restoration", in Proc. ICASSP (1985) pp. 696–699
1.60 A. K. Katsaggelos: "A General Formulation of Adaptive Iterative Image Restoration Algorithms", in Proc. Inf. Sciences and Systems (1986) pp. 42–47
1.61 R. L. Lagendijk, J. Biemond, D. E. Boekee: IEEE Trans. ASSP-**36**, 1874–1888 (1988)
1.62 Y. Ichioka, N. Nakajima: J. Opt. Soc. Am. **71**, 983–988 (1981)
1.63 J. M. Ortega, W. C. Rheinboldt: *Iterative Solution of Nonlinear Equations in Several Variables* (Academic, New York 1970)
1.64 E. S. Angel, A. K. Jain: Appl. Opt. **17**, 2186–2190 (1978)
1.65 T. S. Huang, D. A. Barker, S. P. Berger: Appl. Opt. **14**, 1165–1168 (1975)
1.66 R. Marucci, R. M. Mersereau, R. W. Schafer: "Constrained Iterative Deconvolution Using a Conjugate Gradient Algorithm", in Proc. ICASSP (1982) pp. 1845–1848
1.67 D. C. Youla, H. Webb: IEEE Trans. MI-**1**, 81–94 (1982)
1.68 P. H. Van Cittert: Z. Phys. **69**, 298–308 (1931)
1.69 P. A. Jansson, R. H. Hunt, E. K. Pyler: J. Opt. Soc. Amer. **60**, 596–599 (1970)
1.70 L. Landweber: Am. J. Math. **73**, 615–624 (1951)
1.71 S. Kawata, Y. Ichioka: J. Opt. Soc. Am. **70**, 762–768 (1980)
1.72 S. Kawata, Y. Ichioka: J. Opt. Soc. Am. **70**, 768–772 (1980)
1.73 E. S. Meinel: J. Opt. Soc. Am. A **3**, 787–799 (1986)
1.74 S. Singh, S. N. Tandon, H. M. Gupta: Signal Process. **11**, 1–11 (1986)
1.75 C. E. Morris, M. A. Richards, M. H. Hayes: IEEE Trans. ASSP-**36**, 1017–1025 (1988)
1.76 A. K. Katsaggelos, S. N. Efstratiadis: IEEE Trans. ASSP-**38**, 778–786 (1990)
1.77 A. K. Katsaggelos, S. P. R. Kumar: Signal Process. **16**, 29–40 (1989)
1.78 M. I. Sezan, H. Stark: IEEE Trans. MI-**1**, 95–101 (1982)
1.79 H. Stark (ed.): *Image Recovery: Theory and Application* (Academic, New York 1987)
1.80 H. J. Trussell, M. R. Civanlar: IEEE Trans. ASSP-**32**, 201–212 (1984)
1.81 M. I. Sezan, A. M. Tekalp: IEEE Trans. ASSP-**38**, 181–185 (1990)
1.82 V. T. Tom, T. F. Quatieri, M. H. Hayes, J. M. McClellan: IEEE Trans. ASSP-**29**, 1052–1058 (1981)
1.83 H. Bialy: Arch. Ration. Mech. Anal. **4**, 166–176 (1959)

1.84 H. J. Trussell: IEEE Trans. ASSP-**31**, 129–136 (1983)
1.85 B. J. Sullivan, A. K. Katsaggelos: Opt. Eng. **29**, 471–477 (1990)
1.86 B. R. Frieden: "Image Enhancement and Restoration", in *Picture Processing and Digital Filtering*, ed. by T. S. Huang, Topics Appl. Phys., Vol. 6 (Springer, Berlin, Heidelberg 1975)
1.87 S. F. Gull, J. Skilling: Proc. IEE **131-F**, 646–659 (1984)
1.88 M. Cannon: IEEE Trans. ASSP-**24**, 58–63 (1976)
1.89 B. R. Hunt: IEEE Trans. C-**26**, 219–229 (1977)
1.90 N. E. Nahi: Proc. IEEE **60**, 872–877 (1972)
1.91 A. O. Aboutalib, L. M. Silverman: IEEE Trans. CAS-**22**, 278–286 (1975)
1.92 M. S. Murphy, L. M. Silverman: IEEE Trans. AC-**23**, 809–816 (1978)
1.93 A. Habibi: Proc. IEEE **60**, 878–883 (1972)
1.94 M. G. Strintzis: Proc. IEEE **64**, 1255–1257 (1976)
1.95 D. P. Panda, A. C. Kak: IEEE Trans. ASSP-**25**, 520–524 (1977)
1.96 T. Katayama, M. Kosaka: IEEE Trans. AC-**24**, 130–132 (1979)
1.97 M. S. Murphy: IEEE Trans. AC-**25**, 336–338 (1980)
1.98 M. S. Murphy, L. M. Silverman: IEEE Trans. AC-**23**, 809–816 (1978)
1.99 T. Katayama: IEEE Trans. AC-**27**, 1024–1032 (1982)
1.100 B. R. Suresh, B. A. Shenoi: IEEE Trans. CAS-**28**, 307–319 (1981)
1.101 R. P. Roesser: IEEE Trans. AC-**20**, 1–10 (1975)
1.102 J. Biemond, J. Rieske, J. Gerbrands: IEEE Trans. ASSP-**31**, 1246–1256 (1983)
1.103 J. W. Woods, C. W. Radewan: IEEE Trans. IT-**23**, 473–482 (1977)
1.104 J. W. Woods, V. K. Ingle: IEEE Trans. ASSP-**29**, 188–197 (1981)
1.105 D. L. Angwin, H. Kaufman: Signal Process. **16**, 21–28 (1989)
1.106 Z. Wu: IEEE Trans. ASSP-**33**, 1576–1592 (1985)
1.107 A. K. Mahalanabis, K. Xue: IEEE Trans. ASSP-**35**, 1603–1610 (1987)
1.108 S. S. Rajala, R. J. P. de Figueiredo: IEEE Trans. ASSP-**29**, 1033–1042 (1981)
1.109 A. O. Aboutalib, M. S. Murphy, L. M. Silverman: IEEE Trans. AC-**22**, 294–302 (1977)
1.110 J. Biemond, J. Gerbrands: IEEE Trans. SMC-**9**, 622–627 (1979)
1.111 P. E. Wellstead, J. R. C. Pinto: Int. J. Control **42**, 457–478 (1985)
1.112 A. M. Tekalp, H. Kaufman, J. W. Woods: Signal Process. **15**, 259–269 (1988)
1.113 K. T. Lay, A. K. Katsaggelos: Opt. Eng. **29**, 436–445 (1990)
1.114 B. R. Hunt, O. Kübler: IEEE Trans. ASSP-**32**, 592–599 (1984)
1.115 N. P. Galatsanos, R. T. Chin: IEEE Trans. ASSP-**37**, 415–421 (1989)
1.116 N. P. Galatsanos, A. K. Katsaggelos, R. T. Chin, A. Hillary: IEEE Trans. SP, to be published
1.117 D. C. Ghiglia: J. Opt. Soc. Am. A **1**, 398–402 (1984)
1.118 A. K. Katsaggelos: J. Vis. Comm. Im. Repr. **1**, 93–103 (1990)
1.119 Y. T. Zhou, R. Chellappa, A. Vaid, B. K. Jenkins: IEEE Trans. ASSP-**36**, 1141–1151 (1988)
1.120 J. K. Paik, A. K. Katsaggelos: IEEE Trans. SP, to be published

2. A Dual Approach to Signal Restoration

Ch. Auyeung and R.M. Mersereau

With 17 Figures

This chapter looks at constrained image restoration as a convex programming program, which it solves using a dual approach. Particular attention is directed to the solution of the optimal restoration problem using least-squares, minimum cross entropy, and maximum entropy cost criteria under a variety of constraints on the signal to be restored and the observation noise. Special attention is directed to issues of numerical implementation and sequential restoration. Results from different optimization criteria are compared on some one-dimensional examples.

2.1 Background

The field of image restoration is concerned with the reconstruction or estimation of uncorrupted images from noisy, blurred ones. These blurs might be caused by optical distortions, object motion during imaging, or atmospheric turbulence. Restoration or noise removal is important when resolution and recording limitations are severe, as is the case in astronomy, and when the images are historically important.

The topic of restoring blurred imagery has been actively studied since the late 1960s. The maturity of the field can be seen by the publication of this volume and others [2.1] dedicated to this topic. This research has led to the development of many algorithms for image restoration. It has also shown that the image restoration problem is badly ill-conditioned; many feasible restorations may be consistent with a given noisy, blurred observation. The goal of this chapter is to explore this space of feasible solutions. It does this by looking at the problem in a formal mathematical setting. In this setting the problem is similar to the problems of power spectrum estimation and the reconstruction of multidimensional signals from their projections. Estimation criteria from these different problem domains can be adapted to the deblurring problem. Different constraints on the image and noise along with different optimization criteria are shown to lead to distinct feasible restorations and distinct image models.

Figure 2.1 illustrates the components of the image restoration problem. The image $y(\boldsymbol{r})$ is the noisy, blurred image that is the input to the restoration algorithm. It produces the restoration or estimate, $\hat{x}(\boldsymbol{r})$, of the unobservable, undistorted image, $x(\boldsymbol{r})$. The restoration is assumed to come from some space, $\mathcal{X}$, of functions, called the space of *feasible solutions*. The independent variables are contained in the vector

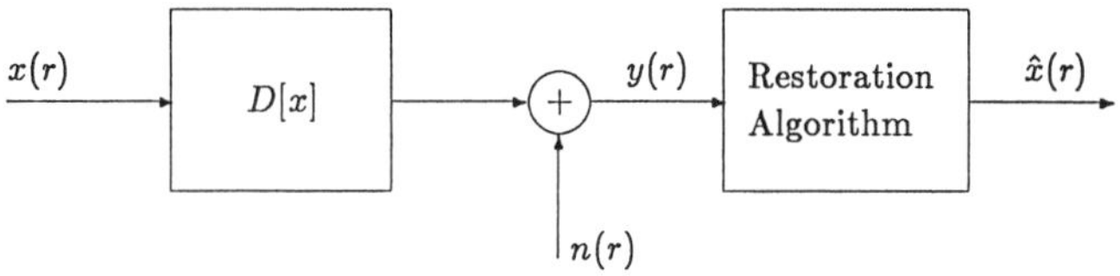

Fig. 2.1. A model which connects the signals of the image restoration problem

r which belongs to a compact set K in a Euclidean space. For image restoration K is normally a rectangular section of $\mathbb{R}^2$ and r is a 2-vector. It will also be assumed in this chapter that the distortion operator $D[x]$ is both linear and known. This is clearly a restriction, but it is the most frequently studied case. The last two chapters in this volume discuss restoration from unknown linear distortions, and Biemond et al. [2.2] allow a pointwise nonlinearity in addition to a linear blur. The only noise considered is additive.

In general $y(\boldsymbol{r})$ is not completely known either; instead only a finite number of samples are available. Mathematically, the observations can be expressed as

$$y_k = \int_K x(\boldsymbol{r}) d_k(\boldsymbol{r})\, d\boldsymbol{r} + n_k \,, \qquad k = 1, 2, \ldots, N \,, \tag{2.1}$$

where n_k is a sample of the additive measurement noise, and $d_k(\boldsymbol{r})$ is the kernel of the linear transformation that is determined by the physics of the problem. For the image deblurring problem, $d_k(\boldsymbol{r})$ represents the point spread function (PSF) of the blur at the kth sample. It is important to recall, however, that other problems can also be cast in this same framework. For the power spectrum estimation problem, x represents the unknown power spectrum, y_k corresponds to samples of the autocorrelation function, and $d_k(\boldsymbol{r})$ is the Fourier kernel associated with the kth lag. If $d_k(\boldsymbol{r})$ is a line impulse, this framework describes the reconstruction (estimation) of multidimensional signals from projections. Indeed, one of the strong motivations for considering this problem in an abstract setting is so that the results and methodologies from these other domains can be applied to the deblurring problem.

The earliest work on image restoration simply exploited properties of the blurring operator and the additive noise. This research, which led to inverse filtering, Wiener filtering, and generalized Wiener filtering [2.2], produced techniques which are still commonly used. Later work also incorporated constraints on the signal to be restored. Kalman filtering [2.3] did this by exploiting an image model. Early iterative procedures [2.4] restricted the feasible signals to come from convex sets and utilized the projection operators that were associated with those sets.

The remainder of this chapter is organized into four sections. The next one recasts the image restoration problem as a convex programming problem. A convex cost functional is associated with each possible feasible restoration and the optimal restoration is chosen to be the one that has the lowest cost. Several candidate cost functionals are discussed and various types of constraints on the restoration and the measurement noise are defined. The actual optimization, however, can be difficult to perform. Section 2.3 reformulates the optimization problem in a dual framework. If the dual problem has a solution, then the optimal restoration must be of a certain functional form with unspecified parameters. These parameters can be chosen to match the observations. The following section discusses the numerical implementations of several of these algorithms and compares the resulting restorations on a one-dimensional example. A one-dimensional example is used because the procedures are computationally efficient only for certain optimization criteria and only for certain forms of prior knowledge. The final section discusses the problem of sequential restoration. If restorations are to be made and updated as measurements are sequentially received, additional constraints are placed on the optimization criterion. These are discussed in this section.

2.2 Application of Convex Programming to Image Restoration

Some signal restoration problems can be formulated as convex programming problems. When there are many feasible solutions that are consistent with both known prior information and the measured blurred image, a restored signal can be found by defining a continuous, strictly convex functional that assigns a cost to each feasible solution and then selects the one which minimizes the cost. Two factors affect the complexity of the resulting algorithms. One is the cost functional itself and the other is the set of constraints that are placed on the restored image. Different choices for these result in quite different restorations. For convex programming to be applicable the set of feasible solutions must be a *convex* set. This means that if x_1 and x_2 are feasible solutions, their linear combinations

$$\lambda x_1 + (1-\lambda)x_2, \qquad \forall \lambda \in [0,1] \, ,$$

must be feasible solutions. In addition, the prior information about the signal and the noise must be expressed in the form of equality or inequality constraints.

In addition, for convex programming to be applicable the cost must be a strictly convex *functional* over the convex set of feasible solutions. A functional $H : X \to [-\infty, \infty]$ is *strictly convex* if, for any two feasible solutions x_1 and x_2 such that $H(x_1) < \infty$ and $H(x_2) < \infty$, the inequality

$$H\big([1-\lambda]x_1 + \lambda x_2\big) < [1-\lambda]H\big(x_1\big) + \lambda H\big(x_2\big) \, , \qquad \forall \lambda \in (0,1) \, , \tag{2.2}$$

always holds. This definition of a convex functional is different from the classical one, because it only requires that (2.2) be valid over the set of feasible solutions.

Earlier research has considered various forms of signal restoration using convex programming. This includes the least squares method of *Hunt* [2.5], the minimum cross entropy method of *Frieden* [2.6], and the maximum entropy method of *Lang* and *McClellan* [2.7, 8]. More recently, *Leahy* and *Goutis* [2.9] have suggested a unified approach to signal restoration using convex programming which includes the other three restoration methods as special cases. The approach in this chapter is similar in several respects, but differs in others. *Leahy* and *Goutis* formulated the restoration problem as an abstract optimization problem with a convex cost functional, but because their functional was very general they could not provide a parametric representation for the restored image. The approach presented here does yield such a representation.

2.2.1 The Unified Cost Functional

We need to be careful in specifying the form of the convex cost functional. The specification must be general enough to include many different feasible restorations, but it must not be so general that the resulting algorithms cannot be implemented. One useful candidate is of the form [2.10]

$$\int_K h(x(\boldsymbol{r}))\, d\boldsymbol{r} \ , \tag{2.3}$$

where $h(t)$ is a strictly convex, continuous function of a real variable t and K is the compact support of the image x. The function $h(t)$ is allowed to be infinitely positive at some points, but it is not allowed to be infinitely negative at any point on the real axis. A convex function that satisfies this condition will be called a *proper convex function.*

This objective function is an abstraction of the cost functionals used in least squares restoration, minimum cross entropy restoration, and maximum entropy restoration. When $h(t) = \frac{1}{2}t^2$, the problem reduces to a least squares restoration. Similarly, when $h(t) = t\ \ln(t/u)$ for some positive quantity u, we have the objective function corresponding to minimum cross entropy restoration. The special case $h(t) = -\ln(t)$ results in maximum entropy restoration. This is not the most general cost functional, however. A more general one would be

$$\int_K x(\boldsymbol{r}) \int_K k(\boldsymbol{r}, \boldsymbol{r}')x(\boldsymbol{r}')\, d\boldsymbol{r}'\, d\boldsymbol{r} \ . \tag{2.4}$$

However, (2.3) is adequate for the goals of this chapter.

2.2.2 Signal Constraints

The more information that is known about the unblurred image in advance the better, because this reduces the number of feasible solutions and presumably the variation among them. When this is the case it becomes less important which restoration criterion is used and we can choose the one that is the most computationally efficient. Therefore, we will accept as a premise that a good restoration algorithm should incorporate as much prior information as possible about the image being restored. Two types of prior information were considered in this study. The first of these placed bounds on the allowable pixel amplitude values. The restored image was required to belong to the set

$$R_b = \{x \in L^\infty[K] : \quad l(\boldsymbol{r}) \leq x(\boldsymbol{r}) \leq u(\boldsymbol{r}) \ , \quad \forall \boldsymbol{r} \in K\} \ , \tag{2.5}$$

where the functions $l(\boldsymbol{r})$ and $u(\boldsymbol{r})$ which are defined over the compact support K are the given upper and lower bounds on the signal $x(\boldsymbol{r})$. Special cases of these bounds are also of interest. By setting $l(\boldsymbol{r}) = -\infty$ or $u(\boldsymbol{r}) = \infty$ one or the other of these bounds can be effectively removed. Also, by setting $l(\boldsymbol{r}) = 0$ the restoration is restricted to be positive everywhere.

The second type of signal constraint is a bound on the value of its integral. This requires that $x(\boldsymbol{r})$ belongs to the set

$$R_{\mathrm{i}} = \{x \in L^{\infty}[K] : \quad I(x) \leq I_0\} \ , \tag{2.6 a}$$

where

$$I(x) \triangleq \int_K x(\boldsymbol{r})\, d\boldsymbol{r} \ . \tag{2.6 b}$$

The integral constraint together with the nonnegativity constraint can be used to constrain the total intensity of a nonnegative signal.

2.2.3 Noise Constraints

Prior knowledge about the image to be restored is not the only form of prior knowledge that can improve the performance of a restoration algorithm. Knowledge of the distortion and of the statistics of the additive noise is also important. In this chapter it will be assumed that the distortion or blurring operator is known exactly. Three types of constraints on the additive noise $\boldsymbol{v}$ will be incorporated into our restorations.

The first type of noise constraint will be known as the *variance matching constraint*. The restored signal, $\hat{x}$ will be said to satisfy this constraint if the difference $D(\hat{x}) - \boldsymbol{y}$ lies within a 95 % confidence region of the noise, $\boldsymbol{v}$. If the noise is Gaussian, this is equivalent to requiring that the difference $D(\hat{x}) - \boldsymbol{y}$ lie within the solid ellipsoid

$$S_{\mathrm{v}} = \left\{v \in \mathrm{R}^N : \quad \boldsymbol{v}^{\mathrm{T}} C^{-1} \boldsymbol{v} \leq \delta\right\} \ , \tag{2.7}$$

where C denotes the $N \times N$ covariance matrix of the additive Gaussian noise vector, $\boldsymbol{v}$, and δ is chosen from a table of a χ^2 distribution with N degrees of freedom and a 95 % confidence region.

The second type of noise constraint is the *spectrum matching constraint* [2.9]. This constrains the restoration $\hat{x}$ so that the magnitude squared of the discrete Fourier transform of the difference $D(\hat{x}) - \boldsymbol{y}$ is an approximation to the noise spectrum. One tractable way of doing this is to use 95 % confidence intervals again. This constrains the modeling error to lie within the solid hypercube

$$S_{\mathrm{s}} = \left\{\boldsymbol{v} \in \mathrm{R}^N : \quad \boldsymbol{v}^{\mathrm{T}} P_k \boldsymbol{v} \leq \delta_k \ , \quad k = 0, 1, \ldots, N-1\right\} \ , \tag{2.8}$$

where δ_k denotes the 95 % confidence region for the periodogram of the noise n at the kth frequency sample and the matrix P_k is given by

$$P_k(a, b) = \exp\left\{2\pi \mathrm{i}\left[\frac{(a-b)k}{N}\right]\right\} \ , \qquad a, b = 1, 2, \ldots, N \ . \tag{2.9}$$

The quantity $v^{\mathrm{T}} P_k v$ is the square of the magnitude of the discrete Fourier transform of the difference $D(\hat{x}) - y$ at the kth frequency bin.

The third type of noise constraint is known as the *exact measurement matching constraint*. It assumes that the measurement is error free, and hence that the difference $D(\hat{x}) - y$ is zero. Mathematically this requires that this difference belongs to the set

$$S_e = \{v \in \mathrm{R}^N : v = \mathbf{0}\} . \tag{2.10}$$

Because the image restoration problem is usually highly ill-conditioned, this noise constraint may be a poor one to use, even when the actual noise level is fairly low. It is included, however, for comparison purposes because it is implied by many classical procedures such as inverse filtering. It usually results in the simplest restoration algorithm, and in the presence of tight signal constraints may yield satisfactory results.

2.2.4 Restatement of the Image Restoration Problem

The goal of the convex programming formulation of the restoration problem is to find a signal which minimizes

$$\int_K h(x(\boldsymbol{r}))\, d\boldsymbol{r} \tag{2.11 a}$$

subject to the conditions that

$$x \in R \qquad \text{and} \qquad D(x) - y \in S . \tag{2.11 b}$$

The set R contains the prior knowledge about the signal. The set S incorporates both the measurements (observations) and the prior knowledge about the noise statistics. R will be restricted to bounds on the restoration and possibly to bounds on its integral. S is restricted to one of the three types of noise constraints discussed in the previous section. In later discussions this will be called the *constrained primal formulation* of the problem.

These restrictions do not severely limit our understanding of the problem since our goal is to understand the applicability of the method and to see how the restorations change when the cost functional and the signal and noise constraints are varied. Other types of constraints on the signal and noise can also be applied.

The constrained problem can be recast as an equivalent *unconstrained* optimization problem known as the *unconstrained primal problem*. This calls for finding a signal which minimizes the functional

$$P(x) = A(x) + B[D(x)] + C[I(x)] \tag{2.12}$$

called the *primal functional*, where $I(x)$ is the integral operator defined earlier and

$$A(x) = \begin{cases} \int_D h[x(\boldsymbol{r})]\, d\boldsymbol{r} & \text{if } x \in R_\mathrm{b} ; \\ \infty , & \text{otherwise} ; \end{cases} \tag{2.13 a}$$

$$B[D(x)] = \begin{cases} 0, & \text{if } D(x) - y \in S\,; \\ \infty, & \text{otherwise}\,; \end{cases} \tag{2.13 b}$$

$$C[I(x)] = \begin{cases} 0, & \text{if } I(x) \leq I_0\,; \\ \infty, & \text{otherwise}\,. \end{cases} \tag{2.13 c}$$

The first functional, $A(x)$, forces the restored signal to satisfy the upper and lower bound constraints and minimize the selected objective functional. The second one, $B[D(x)]$, forces compliance with the noise constraint, and the third forces the signal to satisfy the integral constraint. This representation may seem artificial at first, but it is more convenient for analysis. Another reformulation of the problem, known as the *dual formulation*, is the subject of the next section.

2.3 The Dual Approach to Signal Restoration

With the primal approach the optimization problem in (2.13) is solved directly and the free parameters are the samples of the restored signal itself. With the dual approach, on the other hand, the problem is solved indirectly after transformation into a different problem called the *dual problem*. The variables in this case are not samples of the image but instead are a set of Lagrange multipliers. Under certain conditions, the optimal restoration can be obtained from this set of Lagrange multipliers. Since the number of Lagrange multipliers is equal to the number of measurements, N, when this number is less than the number of samples in the image, dual methods are more efficient than primal ones.

The application of duality transforms to image restoration is not new. *Frieden* [2.6], *Hunt* [2.5], *Lang* and *McClellan* [2.7, 8], and *Leahy* and *Goutis* [2.9] have all used this approach. The latter research also considered its validity and limitations. All of these studies, however, were based on a form of duality known as *Fenchel duality*, which cannot be used to generate an explicit representation of the dual functionals for the restoration problem in (2.13). Fenchel duality also cannot be used to test for the existance of an optimal solution. To overcome these limitations the work described here is based on *conjugate duality*. Although the application of conjugate duality is more direct, the study of the applicability of the dual approach is more difficult, because there is no Fenchel duality theorem [2.11] and the results must be derived from more basic results in optimization theory.

2.3.1 The Primal and Dual Approaches

With the primal approach the constrained signal restoration problem is solved directly. For some signal and noise constraints this can be done using an iterative search. With the dual approach the problem is solved indirectly by transforming the objective functional and its constraints into a different functional, called the *dual functional*, and a new set of constraints using the Fenchel transform. This functional is then *maximized* subject to the constraints. The advantages of the method are that the number of free variables may be greatly reduced and the maximization may be unconstrained. More importantly, under certain circumstances the solution to the dual problem is related to the optimal solution of the original problem through a parametric model where the parameters of the model are the Lagrange multipliers. Then, the dual approach becomes a model-based image restoration method.

As an example consider the least squares image restoration problem with an exact measurement matching constraint. The constrained primal problem finds the x which minimizes

$$\frac{1}{2}\int_K x^2(\boldsymbol{r})\,d\boldsymbol{r}\ , \tag{2.14}$$

subject to

$$\boldsymbol{y} = D(x)\ . \tag{2.15}$$

The corresponding unconstrained dual problem finds the vector

$$\boldsymbol{\lambda} = \left[\lambda_1, \ldots, \lambda_N\right]^{\mathrm{T}} \tag{2.16}$$

which maximizes

$$\boldsymbol{\lambda}^{\mathrm{T}}\boldsymbol{y} - \frac{1}{2}\int_K [\boldsymbol{\lambda}^{\mathrm{T}} h(\boldsymbol{r})]^2\ , \tag{2.17}$$

where $h(r)$ was defined in Sect. 2.2.1. The optimal solution of the primal problem is related to the optimal solution $\hat{\boldsymbol{\lambda}} \in \mathrm{R}^N$ of the dual problem through the signal model

$$\hat{x}(\boldsymbol{r}, \hat{\boldsymbol{\lambda}}) = \boldsymbol{\lambda}^{\mathrm{T}}\boldsymbol{d}(\boldsymbol{r}) = \sum_{k=1}^{N} \hat{\lambda}_k d_k(\boldsymbol{r})\ , \tag{2.18}$$

where $\boldsymbol{d}(\boldsymbol{r}) = [d_1(\boldsymbol{r}), \ldots, d_N(\boldsymbol{r})]^{\mathrm{T}}$. The relationship between the primal and dual formulations is illustrated in Fig. 2.2.

The dual approach is not always better than the primal one. In determining which approach to use, one should consider the following questions:

- Is it possible to get an explicit representation of the dual functional? If not, the dual approach is not applicable. The next subsection presents a procedure for finding the dual functional for the restoration problem in (2.13).
- Will the dual approach lead to the same solution as the primal one? If not, again the dual approach is not applicable. This issue is also addressed in a later subsection.
- How many variables does the problem have? If the number of samples of the restored signal is much larger than the number of measurements, the dual approach is more efficient.
- Is the dual functional differentiable? If the dual functional is not differentiable, it cannot be minimized using the well-known gradient-based optimization methods

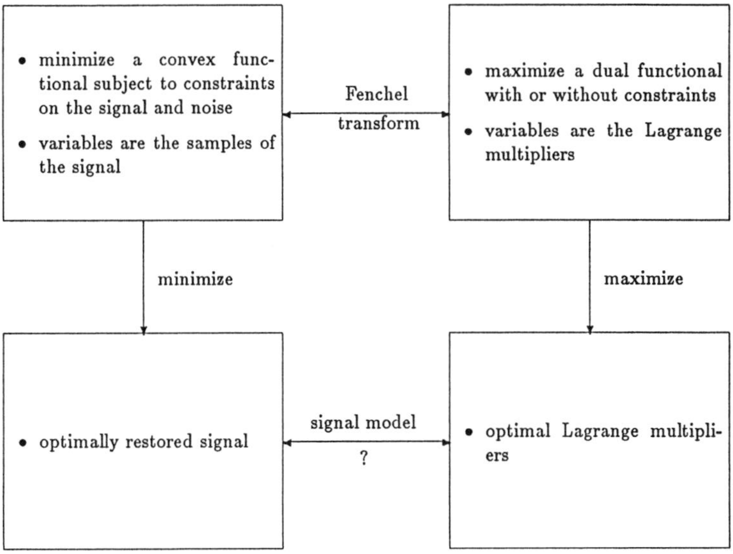

Fig. 2.2. Relationship between the primal and dual approaches to constrained optimization

such as the conjugate gradient or Newton methods. Instead, other, less well-known techniques must be used, such as those based on subgradients [2.12]. Slower techniques such as the downhill simplex method [2.13] can also be used in this case.

- Is a constrained optimization procedure available? With the primal approach, the procedure used must be able to incorporate constraints, otherwise it is useless for the restoration. In certain situations, however, it may be possible to modify the constrained problem into an unconstrained one using penalty functions. With the dual approach, the dual problem may be an unconstrained optimization problem. The relative efficiency of the primal and dual approaches may depend upon how well the optimization procedures can handle constraints.

2.3.2 Generating Dual Functionals and Signal Models

The optimally restored image is found indirectly with the dual approach. A parametric representation of the image is found first, and then the values of its parameters are found by solving the associated dual problem. There are many ways by which this can be done. The approach that has been most widely used is based on *Fenchel duality*. A more general, but less well known approach uses *conjugate duality*.

The indirect approach may seem to be strange and mysterious. This section will explain how and why this indirect approach works using conjugate duality. The explanation is simplified and not rigorous. It is based on the book by *Rockafellar* [2.14]. Only an outline of the method will be presented here to convince the reader that the dual approach can lead to the optimally restored image. For further details and a rigorous explanation, the reader is directed to the books [2.14–16].

The unconstrained version of the primal problem looks for the image x that minimizes the quantity

$$P(x) = A(x) + B[D(x)] + C[I(x)] \; . \tag{2.19}$$

The transformation to the dual problem can be broken down into three steps. First the original restoration problem is perturbed by $\boldsymbol{u}$, chosen from some vector space U, to generate a new function $\phi(x, \boldsymbol{u})$, called the *bifunction* [2.14] so that

$$\phi(x, \mathbf{0}) = P(x) \; . \tag{2.20}$$

Although there are many ways of effecting this perturbation, the one that we will use perturbs the measurement vector $\boldsymbol{y}$ by $\gamma \in \mathsf{R}^N$ and the total intensity I_0 by $\delta \in \mathsf{R}$, resulting in $\boldsymbol{u} = (\gamma, \delta)$, $U = \mathsf{R}^N \times \mathsf{R}$ and

$$\phi(x, \gamma, \delta) = A(x) + B[D(x) + \gamma] + C[I(x) + \delta] \; . \tag{2.21}$$

An alternative method perturbs the image by $\boldsymbol{u} \in L^{\infty}[K]$. Then $U = L^{\infty}[K]$ and

$$\phi(x, \boldsymbol{u}) = A(x) + E(x - \boldsymbol{u}) \; , \tag{2.22}$$

where

$$E(x) = B[D(x)] + C[I(x)] \; . \tag{2.23}$$

This latter approach results in the same dual problem as that obtained using Fenchel duality.

Once the bifunction has been found, the second step transforms $\phi(x, \boldsymbol{u})$ into a Lagrangian function:

$$L(x, \boldsymbol{\lambda}) \stackrel{\triangle}{=} \inf_{\boldsymbol{u} \in U} \{\langle \boldsymbol{u}, \boldsymbol{\lambda} \rangle + \phi(x, \boldsymbol{u})\} \; . \tag{2.24}$$

$\boldsymbol{\lambda}$ is an element in the dual space[1] Λ of U. These parameters are the Lagrange multipliers.

In the final step, the dual functional and the image model are found from the Lagrangian function. The dual functional is

$$D(\lambda) \stackrel{\triangle}{=} \inf_{x \in L^{\infty}[K]} L(x, \boldsymbol{\lambda}) \; . \tag{2.25}$$

If, for every $\boldsymbol{\lambda}$ the minimum is attained by a unique image $\hat{x}$, then the image $\hat{x}$ is dependent upon the Lagrange multipliers $\boldsymbol{\lambda}$. In other words $\hat{x}$ is a function of the position $\boldsymbol{r}$ and $\boldsymbol{\lambda}$. This function, $\hat{x}(\boldsymbol{\lambda}, \boldsymbol{r})$, is the signal model. The dual problem seeks the $\boldsymbol{\lambda}$ which minimizes $D(\boldsymbol{\lambda})$.

[1] The dual space Λ is a set which contains all the continuous linear functionals defined on U.

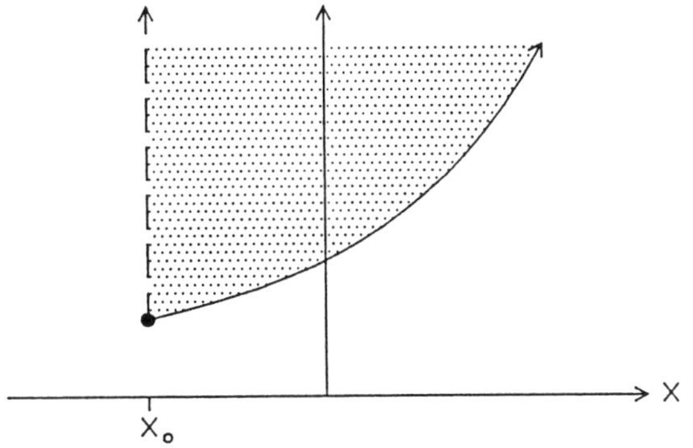

Fig. 2.3. A lower semi-continuous, proper convex function

When the solution of the dual problem leads to the optimal restored image, it is given by $\hat{x}(\hat{\boldsymbol{\lambda}}, \boldsymbol{r})$. To understand when this is the case we need to examine some of the basic properties of the Lagrangian function $L(x, \boldsymbol{\lambda})$ and the perturbed problem $\phi(x, \boldsymbol{u})$.

To simplify the explanation assume that the bifunction $\phi(x, \boldsymbol{u})$ is a *lower semi-continuous, proper convex* function in $L^\infty[K] \times U$. Figure 2.3 shows a lower semi-continuous, proper convex function H defined on a Banach space X. The function H is lower semi-continuous because, at any point x_0 where H is discontinuous, x_0 is connected to its neighbor on the graph. In general, a lower semi-continuous, proper convex function H has the property that all of the points $(x, \boldsymbol{y})$ above and including the graph $(x, H(x))$, as indicated in the shaded area in Fig. 2.3, form a nonempty, closed, convex set, and also has the property that $H(x) > -\infty$ everywhere.

The Lagrangian function $L(x, \boldsymbol{\lambda})$, obtained from the bifunction $\phi(x, \boldsymbol{u})$, is a convex function of x and a concave function of $\boldsymbol{u}$. When the bifunction is lower semi-continuous proper convex, both the primal and dual functionals can be obtained from the Lagrangian. The primal function is given by

$$P(x) = \phi(x, \mathbf{0}) = \sup_{\boldsymbol{\lambda} \in \Lambda} L(x, \boldsymbol{\lambda}) \tag{2.26}$$

and the dual by

$$D(\boldsymbol{\lambda}) = \inf_{x \in L^\infty[K]} L(x, \boldsymbol{\lambda}) \, . \tag{2.27}$$

From these we see that

$$P(x) \geq L(x, \boldsymbol{\lambda}) \geq D(\boldsymbol{\lambda}) \qquad \text{for all} \quad x \in L^\infty[K] \, , \qquad \boldsymbol{\lambda} \in \boldsymbol{\Lambda} \, , \tag{2.28}$$

and consequently

$$\begin{aligned} \inf_{x \in L^\infty[K]} \sup_{\boldsymbol{\lambda} \in \Lambda} L(x, \boldsymbol{\lambda}) &= \inf_{x \in L^\infty[K]} P(x) \geq \sup_{\boldsymbol{\lambda} \in \Lambda} D(\boldsymbol{\lambda}) \\ &= \sup_{\boldsymbol{\lambda} \in \Lambda} \inf_{x \in L^\infty[K]} L(x, \boldsymbol{\lambda}) \, . \end{aligned} \tag{2.29}$$

If the equality holds in (2.29), the common value is called the *saddle value* of L.

The saddle value exists if L has a saddle point, i.e., a pair $\hat{x}, \hat{\boldsymbol{\lambda}}$ such that

$$L(x, \hat{\boldsymbol{\lambda}}) \geq L(\hat{x}, \hat{\boldsymbol{\lambda}}) \geq L(\hat{x}, \boldsymbol{\lambda}) \qquad \text{for all} \quad x \in L^\infty[K], \quad \boldsymbol{\lambda} \in \Lambda . \tag{2.30}$$

When the saddle point exists, $\hat{x}$ is the optimal restored image and $\hat{\boldsymbol{\lambda}}$ is the optimal solution of the dual problem.

The success of the dual approach hinges on whether or not a saddle point can be found. If so and if there is a signal model $\hat{x}(\boldsymbol{\lambda}, \boldsymbol{r})$ such that

$$D(\boldsymbol{\lambda}) = \inf_{x \in L^\infty[K]} L(x, \boldsymbol{\lambda}) = L(\hat{x}, \boldsymbol{\lambda}) \tag{2.31}$$

and we can find $\hat{\boldsymbol{\lambda}}$ such that

$$D(\hat{\boldsymbol{\lambda}}) = \sup_{\boldsymbol{\lambda} \in \Lambda} D(\boldsymbol{\lambda}) , \tag{2.32}$$

then $\hat{x}(\hat{\boldsymbol{\lambda}}, \boldsymbol{r})$ is the optimally restored signal.

2.3.3 Signal Models for Common Optimization Criteria

The previous section illustrated how conjugate duality could be used to construct a dual problem and a signal model. This discussion was abstract and it might seem that the results would be difficult to apply in practice. This section presents several new and simple formulas for constructing the dual of the restoration problem in (2.13) and the signal model which defines the optimally restored signal. The mathematical details can be found in [2.10].

If we define

$$B_\mathrm{e}^*(-\boldsymbol{\lambda}) = -\boldsymbol{\lambda}^\mathrm{T} \boldsymbol{y} , \tag{2.33 a}$$

$$B_\mathrm{v}^*(-\boldsymbol{\lambda}) = -\boldsymbol{\lambda}^\mathrm{T} \boldsymbol{y} + \sqrt{\delta \boldsymbol{\lambda}^\mathrm{T} C \boldsymbol{\lambda}} , \tag{2.33 b}$$

$$B_\mathrm{s}^*(-\boldsymbol{\lambda}) = -\boldsymbol{\lambda}^\mathrm{T} \boldsymbol{y} + \frac{1}{N} \sum_{k=0}^{N-1} \sqrt{\delta_k \boldsymbol{\lambda}^\mathrm{T} P_k \boldsymbol{\lambda}} , \tag{2.33 c}$$

and

$$B^*(-\boldsymbol{\lambda}) = \begin{cases} B_\mathrm{e}^*(-\boldsymbol{\lambda}) , & \text{for exact data matching} , \\ B_\mathrm{v}^*(-\boldsymbol{\lambda}), & \text{for covariance matching} , \\ B_\mathrm{s}^*(-\boldsymbol{\lambda}), & \text{for spectrum matching} , \end{cases} \tag{2.34}$$

then the dual problem is to find the set of Lagrange multipliers $(\boldsymbol{\lambda}, \mu) \in \mathrm{R}^N \times \mathrm{R}$ that maximizes

$$D(\boldsymbol{\lambda}, \mu) = \begin{cases} \int_K \left[h(\hat{x}(\boldsymbol{\lambda}, \mu, \boldsymbol{r})) - (\boldsymbol{\lambda}^\mathrm{T} \boldsymbol{d}(\boldsymbol{r}) + \mu) \hat{x}(\boldsymbol{\lambda}, \mu, \boldsymbol{r}) \right] d\boldsymbol{r} & \text{if } \mu \leq 0 \\ \quad + \mu I_0 - B^*(-\boldsymbol{\lambda}) , & \\ \infty , & \text{if } \mu > 0 , \end{cases} \tag{2.35}$$

where the signal model is

$$\hat{x}(\boldsymbol{\lambda}, \mu, \boldsymbol{r}) = \max\left[\min\left[(h')^{-1}(\boldsymbol{\lambda}^{\mathrm{T}}\boldsymbol{d}(\boldsymbol{r}) + \mu), u(\boldsymbol{r})\right], l(\boldsymbol{r})\right] . \tag{2.36}$$

The function max(·,·) returns the larger of its arguments and the function min(·,·) does the opposite. This signal model is a generalization of the signal models in [2.9]. The function $(h')^{-1}(\boldsymbol{\lambda}^{\mathrm{T}}\boldsymbol{r}(\boldsymbol{r}) + \mu)$ is the inverse function of

$$\frac{d\,h(x)}{dx} \tag{2.37}$$

evaluated at $\boldsymbol{\lambda}^{\mathrm{T}}\boldsymbol{d}(\boldsymbol{r}) + \mu$. For the restoration without signal bounds this model reduces to

$$\hat{x}(\boldsymbol{\lambda}, \mu, \boldsymbol{r}) = (h')^{-1}\left(\boldsymbol{\lambda}^{\mathrm{T}}\boldsymbol{d}(\boldsymbol{r}) + \mu\right) . \tag{2.38}$$

In the special case where the total intensity is not constrained, the Lagrange multiplier μ is zero, the dual functional reduces to $\phi(\boldsymbol{\lambda}, 0, \boldsymbol{r})$ and the signal model is $\hat{x}(\boldsymbol{\lambda}, 0, \boldsymbol{r})$.

To illustrate how these results can be applied to the generalized reconstruction problem, consider the signal model and dual functional of the least-squares restoration problem subject to upper and lower bounds

$$u(\boldsymbol{r}) = \beta\,, \qquad l(\boldsymbol{r}) = \alpha\,, \qquad \text{for all} \quad \boldsymbol{r} \in K\,, \tag{2.39}$$

on the signal and a spectrum matching constraint on the noise. Then

$$h(x) = \frac{1}{2}x^2\,, \tag{2.40}$$

$$(h')^{-1}(\boldsymbol{\lambda}^{\mathrm{T}}\boldsymbol{d}(\boldsymbol{r})) = \boldsymbol{\lambda}^{\mathrm{T}}\boldsymbol{d}(\boldsymbol{r}) \tag{2.41}$$

and the signal model is

$$\hat{x}(\boldsymbol{\lambda}, 0) = \max[\min[\boldsymbol{\lambda}^{\mathrm{T}}\boldsymbol{d}(\boldsymbol{r}), \beta], \alpha]\,, \tag{2.42}$$

which is equal to $\boldsymbol{\lambda}^{\mathrm{T}}\boldsymbol{d}(\boldsymbol{r})$ with clipping at the upper and lower bounds. The dual problem is to maximize

$$\begin{aligned} D(\boldsymbol{\lambda}, 0) = &- \int_{\{\boldsymbol{r}\in K | \alpha \le \boldsymbol{\lambda}^{\mathrm{T}}\boldsymbol{d}(\boldsymbol{r}) \le \beta\}} \frac{(\boldsymbol{\lambda}^{\mathrm{T}}\boldsymbol{d}(\boldsymbol{r}))^2}{2}\, d\boldsymbol{r} \\ &- \int_{\{\boldsymbol{r}\in K | \boldsymbol{\lambda}^{\mathrm{T}}\boldsymbol{d}(\boldsymbol{r}) \le \alpha\}} \left[\frac{1}{2}\alpha^2 - \boldsymbol{\lambda}^{\mathrm{T}}\boldsymbol{d}(\boldsymbol{r})\alpha\right] d\boldsymbol{r} \\ &- \int_{\{\boldsymbol{r}\in K | \beta \le \boldsymbol{\lambda}^{\mathrm{T}}\boldsymbol{d}(\boldsymbol{r})\}} \left[\frac{1}{2}\beta^2 - \boldsymbol{\lambda}^{\mathrm{T}}\boldsymbol{d}(\boldsymbol{r})\beta\right] d\boldsymbol{r} + B_{\mathrm{s}}(-\boldsymbol{\lambda})\,. \end{aligned} \tag{2.43}$$

Table 2.1 presents a more complete list of signal models and the dual functionals to be maximized. It displays a total of 36 cases of which 24 are distinct. In three separate columns the table presents results based on least-squares, maximum entropy, and minimum cross entropy criteria. Each column is further subdivided

Table 2.1. Signal models and dual functionals for various cost criteria

Cost criterion:	Minimum energy	Maximum entropy	Minimum cross entropy
Primal functionals:	$\int_K \frac{x(\boldsymbol{r})^2}{2}\, d\boldsymbol{r}$	$-\int_K \ln[x(\boldsymbol{r})]\, d\boldsymbol{r}$	$x_K x(\boldsymbol{r}) \ln[x(\boldsymbol{r})/x'(\boldsymbol{r})]\, d\boldsymbol{r}$
Signal constraints		Signal Models and Dual Functionals	
Unconstrained	$\hat{x}(\boldsymbol{\lambda}, \boldsymbol{r}) = \boldsymbol{\lambda}^{\mathrm{T}} w(\boldsymbol{r})$ $D(\boldsymbol{\lambda}) = -\int_K \frac{x(\boldsymbol{\lambda}, \boldsymbol{r})^2}{2}\, d\boldsymbol{r} - B^*(-\boldsymbol{\lambda})$	$\hat{x}(\boldsymbol{\lambda}, \boldsymbol{r}) = -\frac{1}{\boldsymbol{\lambda}^{\mathrm{T}} w(\boldsymbol{r})}$ $D(\boldsymbol{\lambda}) = -\int_K \ln[\hat{x}(\boldsymbol{\lambda}, \boldsymbol{r})]\, d\boldsymbol{r} - B^*(-\boldsymbol{\lambda})$	$\hat{x}(\boldsymbol{\lambda}, \boldsymbol{r}) = \frac{x'(\boldsymbol{r})}{\mathrm{e}} \exp\left[\boldsymbol{\lambda}^{\mathrm{T}} w(\boldsymbol{r})\right]$ $D(\boldsymbol{\lambda}) = -\int_K \hat{x}(\boldsymbol{\lambda}, \boldsymbol{r})\, d\boldsymbol{r} - B^*(-\boldsymbol{\lambda})$
Nonnegativity Constraint	$\hat{x}(\boldsymbol{\lambda}, \boldsymbol{r}) = \max\left[\boldsymbol{\lambda}^{\mathrm{T}} w(\boldsymbol{r}), 0\right]$ $D(\boldsymbol{\lambda}) = -\int_K \frac{\hat{x}(\boldsymbol{\lambda}, \boldsymbol{r})^2}{2}\, d\boldsymbol{r} - B^*(-\boldsymbol{\lambda})$	Same as above	Same as above
Intensity Constraint	$\hat{x}(\boldsymbol{\lambda}, \mu, \boldsymbol{r}) = \boldsymbol{\lambda}^{\mathrm{T}} w(\boldsymbol{r}) + \mu$ $D(\boldsymbol{\lambda}, \mu) = -\int_K \frac{\hat{x}(\boldsymbol{\lambda}, \mu, \boldsymbol{r})^2}{2}\, d\boldsymbol{r} + \mu I_0 - B^*(-\boldsymbol{\lambda})$ s.t. $\mu \leq 0$	$\hat{x}(\boldsymbol{\lambda}, \mu, \boldsymbol{r}) = -\frac{1}{\boldsymbol{\lambda}^{\mathrm{T}} w(\boldsymbol{r}) + \mu}$ $D(\boldsymbol{\lambda}, \mu) = -\int_K \ln[\hat{x}(\boldsymbol{\lambda}, \mu, \boldsymbol{r})]\, d\boldsymbol{r} + \mu I_0 - B^*(-\boldsymbol{\lambda})$ s.t. $\mu \leq 0$	$\hat{x}(\boldsymbol{\lambda}, \mu, \boldsymbol{r}) = \frac{x'(\boldsymbol{r})}{\mathrm{e}} \exp\left[\boldsymbol{\lambda}^{\mathrm{T}} w(\boldsymbol{r}) + \mu\right]$ $D(\boldsymbol{\lambda}, \mu) = -\int_K \hat{x}(\boldsymbol{\lambda}, \mu, \boldsymbol{r})\, d\boldsymbol{r} + \mu I_0 - B^*(-\boldsymbol{\lambda})$ s.t. $\mu \leq 0$
Nonnegativity and intensity constraint	$\hat{x}(\boldsymbol{\lambda}, \mu, \boldsymbol{r}) = \max\left[\boldsymbol{\lambda}^{\mathrm{T}} w(\boldsymbol{r}) + \mu, 0\right]$ $D(\boldsymbol{\lambda}, \mu) = -\int_K \frac{\hat{x}(\boldsymbol{\lambda}, \mu, \boldsymbol{r})^2}{2}\, d\boldsymbol{r} + \mu I_0 - B^*(-\boldsymbol{\lambda})$ s.t. $\mu \leq 0$	Same as above	Same as above

into four smaller boxes corresponding to no upper and lower bound, a nonnegativity constraint, an intensity constraint, and a combination of an intensity constraint with a nonnegativity constraint on the signal. In addition, each box contains the three cases which are implied implicitly through the function $B(-\boldsymbol{\lambda})$ defined in (2.34). These cases correspond to the exact measurement matching constraint, S_e, the covariance matching constraint, S_v, and the spectrum matching constraint, S_s, on the signal.

2.3.4 Existence and Uniqueness of the Optimally Restored Signal

Unfortunately, the dual approach does not always work. This section explores issues related to the existence and uniqueness of the solutions to the primal and dual image restoration problems. It also presents some new, easily applied sufficiency conditions under which the dual approach yields the optimally restored image.

Existence. There are two ways to specify the conditions for the existence of a feasible solution. The first and most obvious way states that a feasible solution exists if and only if there is an image $x \in L^{\infty}[K]$ that satisfies the signal and noise constraints so that

$$x \in R_b\,, \qquad I(x) - I_0 \in N \quad \text{and} \quad D(x) - \boldsymbol{y} \in S\,, \tag{2.44}$$

where $N = [-\infty, 0]$. Unfortunately, this description is based on the signal to be restored, x, which is unknown. All that we have available is the blurred image y and the total intensity bound I_0. A better characterization would be based on these measurements. The study of the existence of a restored signal from the perspective of the measurements is not new. It was studied by *Lang* and *McClellan* [2.8] for the spectrum estimation problem. In spectrum estimation this is known as the extendibility problem. The treatment below is a generalization of their result to the signal restoration problem.

The description in (2.44) is equivalent to requiring that the convex set

$$D(R_b) \times I(R_b) \triangleq \{(\tilde{\boldsymbol{y}}, \tilde{I}) : \tilde{\boldsymbol{y}} = D(x)\,,\ \tilde{I} = I(x) \quad \text{for some} \quad x \in R_b\}\ , \tag{2.45}$$

and the convex set

$$S \times N + (\boldsymbol{y}, I_0) \triangleq \{(\tilde{\boldsymbol{y}}, \tilde{I}) : \quad \tilde{\boldsymbol{y}} - \boldsymbol{y}_0 \in S\,, \quad I - I_0 \in N\} \tag{2.46}$$

have a point in common, i.e.

$$\{D(R_b) \times I(R_b)\} \cap \{S \times N + (\boldsymbol{y}, I_0)\} \neq \emptyset\,. \tag{2.47}$$

The convex set $D(R_b) \times I(R_b)$ is the image of R_b in $\mathrm{R}^N \times \mathrm{R}$ due to the upper and lower bound constraints. The convex set $S \times N + (\boldsymbol{y}, I_0)$ is obtained by shifting the Cartesian product $S \times N$ of the noise set S and the negative half line N by $(\boldsymbol{y}, I_0)$. It contains the point $(\boldsymbol{y}, I_0)$. A feasible solution exists when the measurement-total intensity pair $(\boldsymbol{y}, I_0)$ is sufficiently close to $D(R_b) \times I(R_b)$ that $D(R_b) \times I(R_b)$ intersects $S \times N + (\boldsymbol{y}, I_0)$ as shown in Fig. 2.4. When the total intensity constraint

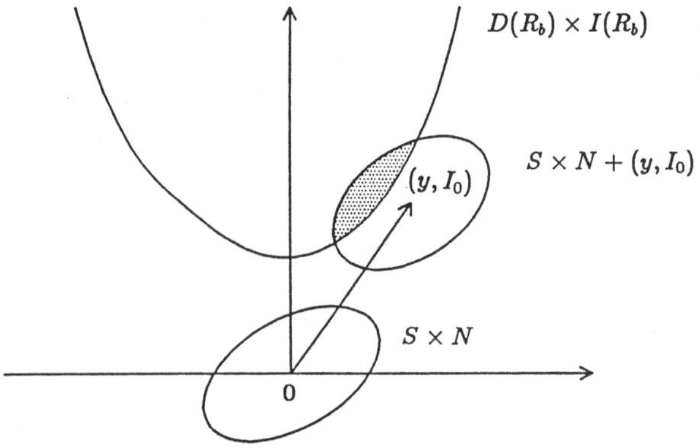

Fig. 2.4. A feasible solution exists when $(\boldsymbol{y}, I_0)$ is sufficiently close to $D(R_b)\times I(R_b)$ that $D(R_b)\times I(R_b)$ intersects $S \times N + (\boldsymbol{y}, I_0)$

is absent this condition simplifies to

$$D(R_b) \cap (S + \boldsymbol{y}) \neq \emptyset \,. \tag{2.48}$$

For example, in spectral estimation with an exact measurement matching constraint, $\boldsymbol{y}$ is the correlation vector, $S + \boldsymbol{y}$ is the point $\{\boldsymbol{y}\}$, and $D(R_b)$ is the cone E of extendible correlation vectors [2.8]. The existence condition reduces to the requirement that the correlation vector lie in the cone of extendible correlation vectors.

Uniqueness. The goal of the image restoration problem is to find the image x which minimizes $P(x)$. This criterion can be easily satisfied by restricting $P(x)$ to be a strictly convex functional of x. Because of this restriction, if the optimal solution exists, it is unique. This can be explained as follows. By the definition of a strictly convex functional, for all $\alpha \in (0,1)$, $P(x_1) < +\infty$, and $P(x_2) < +\infty$,

$$P(\alpha x_1 + (1-\alpha)x_2 < \alpha P(x_1) + (1-\alpha)P(x_2) \,. \tag{2.49}$$

If x_1 and x_2 are two distinct optimally restored signals, then $P(x_1) = P(x_2) = \inf_{x\in L^\infty[K]} P(x)$, and

$$P(\alpha x_1 + (1-\alpha)x_2) < \inf_{x\in L^\infty[K]} P(x) \,, \tag{2.50}$$

which is impossible. Therefore, x_1 and x_2 must be identical, and the optimal restored image is unique if it exists.

Although the strict convexity of the primal functional P forces the optimal restored image to be unique, there is no guarantee that it exists. For example, in finding $(x_1, x_2) \in \mathbb{R}^2$ which minimizes the negative of the entropy function

$$-\ln(x_1) - \ln(x_2) \tag{2.51}$$

such that

$$x_1 - x_2 = 0 \,, \tag{2.52}$$

and

$$x_1 \geq 0 \,, \qquad x_2 \geq 0 \,, \tag{2.53}$$

we observe that, for an arbitrary nonnegative constant α, (α, α) is a feasible solution. It satisfies the measurement matching constraint and the nonnegativity constraint, but the negative of the entropy function can be made to approach $-\infty$ by making α arbitrarily large. Therefore, the optimal solution does not exist.

In general the proof of the existence of a solution which minimizes a convex functional in an infinite dimensional vector space is very difficult. Fortunately, sufficient conditions can be found that guarantee the applicability of the dual approach.

Sufficient Conditions for the Dual Method to Work. As we have already seen, the dual approach works and the optimal restored signal exists when

1) For fixed x, the perturbed version of the primal problem, $\phi(x, \gamma, \delta)$ is a lower semi-continuous proper convex functional in γ and δ;

2) we can find a signal model $\hat{x}(\boldsymbol{\lambda}, \mu, \boldsymbol{r})$ such that

$$D(\boldsymbol{\lambda}, \mu) = \inf_{x \in L^\infty[K]} L(x, \boldsymbol{\lambda}, \mu) = L(\hat{x}(\boldsymbol{\lambda}, \mu, \boldsymbol{r}), \boldsymbol{\lambda}, \mu) \,; \tag{2.54}$$

3) the optimal values of the primal problem and the dual problem are the same, i.e.

$$\inf_{x \in L^\infty[K]} P(x) = \sup_{\boldsymbol{\lambda} \in \mathbf{R}^N, \mu \in \mathbf{R}} D(\boldsymbol{\lambda}, \mu) \,; \tag{2.55}$$

4) the optimal solution to the dual problem exists.

When these conditions are true, the optimal restored image can be obtained from the optimal solution $(\hat{\boldsymbol{\lambda}}, \hat{\mu})$ of the dual problem, and it is $\hat{x}(\hat{\boldsymbol{\lambda}}, \hat{\mu}, \boldsymbol{r})$.

A sufficient condition [2.10] for the solutions of the primal and dual problems to be the same is that (1) the objective function must be bounded below for all signals that satisfy the upper and lower bound constraints and (2) there must exist at least one signal that satisfies the constraints. The least-squares and minimum cross entropy criteria are both bounded from below. The maximum entropy criterion is also bounded from below provided that $l(\boldsymbol{r}) \geq 0$ for all $\boldsymbol{r} \in K$, and provided that the kernel $\boldsymbol{d}(\boldsymbol{r})$ satisfies two conditions. It must be a continuous function of $\boldsymbol{r}$, and it must have the property that there exists a vector $\boldsymbol{p} \in \mathrm{R}^N$ such that

$$\boldsymbol{p}^{\mathrm{T}} \boldsymbol{d}(\boldsymbol{r}) = \sum_{k=1}^{N} p_k d_k(\boldsymbol{r}) > 0 \qquad \text{for all} \quad r \in K \,. \tag{2.56}$$

Clearly, if this condition is true and an optimal restoration exists under any one of these optimization criteria, it must exist under all of them.

2.4 Numerical Implementation and Results

Many algorithms will find the parameter values which maximize the dual functional. We used several of these to compare least squares, minimum cross entropy, and maximum entropy restorations on two different simulated one-dimensional blurred signals under several sets of constraints. The next subsection discusses the implementations and the following one compares the restorations.

2.4.1 Application of Optimization Algorithms to the Dual Problem

In general, the determination of the optimal Lagrange multipliers is a constrained optimization problem, but when the bound on the integral of the restored signal is absent, the optimization becomes unconstrained. Because the constrained problem is much more difficult to manage than the unconstrained one, our attention will be restricted to the application of unconstrained convex optimization procedures to the determination of the optimal Lagrange multipliers $\hat{\boldsymbol{\lambda}} \in \mathbf{R}^N$ that minimize the negative of the dual functional $-D(\boldsymbol{\lambda})$ when the integral constraint is missing.

The optimal Lagrange multiplier vector $\hat{\boldsymbol{\lambda}}$ can be obtained using procedures from convex programming. First, an initial estimate of the Lagrange multiplier $\boldsymbol{\lambda}_0$ is found that corresponds to a finite value of $-D(\boldsymbol{\lambda}_0)$. This estimate is improved iteratively. The $(k+1)$th estimate can be determined from the kth using

$$\boldsymbol{\lambda}_{k+1} = \boldsymbol{\lambda}_k + \alpha_k \boldsymbol{d}_k \qquad (2.57)$$

for a certain step length $\alpha_k > 0$ and a certain search direction $\boldsymbol{d}_k \in \mathbf{R}^N$. Various procedures differ in how the search direction d_k and the step length α_k are generated.

When the dual functional is differentiable, the direction d_k can be constructed as a linear combination of the present or previous gradient vectors $-\boldsymbol{\nabla} D(\lambda_j)$, $j \leq k$, and the step length α_k can be selected so that the value of the objective functional decreases [2.17]. In this case the search direction d_k is called a *descent direction.* Many optimization procedures use this approach, including the steepest descent method, the conjugate gradient method, the Newton method, and the quasi-Newton methods [2.13, 18].

When the dual functional is not differentiable, the search direction $\boldsymbol{d}_k$ and the step length α_k are selected by a different strategy. In nondifferentiable optimization it does not necessarily correspond to a descent direction. It is usually selected from the subdifferential or the ε-subdifferential of the dual functional at $\boldsymbol{\lambda}_k$ [2.12]. The step length α_k may be predetermined or it may be selected at the kth iteration using the local information about the dual functional. Examples of algorithms for nondifferentiable optimization include the subgradient methods and the bundle methods [2.12]. In our own work we used more traditional algorithms which do not require gradient information such as the direction set methods of Powell. When these did not work we used the downhill simplex method which is extremely robust but slow. More detailed discussions of the direction set methods and the downhill simplex algorithm and their associated computer programs can be found in [2.13, 19].

Two additional considerations in selecting an optimization algorithm are the amount of memory it requires and the amount of computation it uses. If N is the dimension of the Lagrange multiplier, then the Newton method, the quasi-Newton methods, the bundle methods, the direction set method, and the downhill simplex algorithm all require storage space on the order of N^2. The steepest descent method, the conjugate gradient method, and the subgradient methods require storage space on the order of N. Algorithms which require N^2 words of storage may not be suitable for image restoration if $N = (256^2)$. For one-dimensional restoration problems with $N \approx 100$, on the other hand, these methods can be used.

The amount of computation that each algorithm requires also differs greatly. It depends upon how the algorithm generates its search directions and its step lengths and also upon the function being minimized. Some algorithms require more computation per iteration but fewer iterations than others and vice versa. It can be very difficult to predict which algorithm will work fastest in terms of overall CPU time. In general, however, the algorithms which use gradient information require less computation than those that do not.

2.4.2 Comparison of Restoration Methods

The least squares, minimum cross entropy, and maximum entropy optimization criteria were compared. For the least-squares method, the algorithm sought to maximize the dual functional

$$D(\boldsymbol{\lambda}, \mu) = \int_K \left[\frac{1}{2}(\hat{x}(\boldsymbol{\lambda}, \boldsymbol{r}))^2 - (\boldsymbol{\lambda}^{\mathrm{T}} \boldsymbol{d}(\boldsymbol{r}))\hat{x}(\boldsymbol{\lambda}, \boldsymbol{r})\right] d\boldsymbol{r} - B^*(-\boldsymbol{\lambda}) , \tag{2.58}$$

where $B^*(-\boldsymbol{\lambda})$ was defined in (2.33) and the signal model is

$$\hat{x}(\boldsymbol{\lambda}, \boldsymbol{r}) = \begin{cases} u(\boldsymbol{r}), & \text{if } \boldsymbol{\lambda}^{\mathrm{T}} \boldsymbol{d}(\boldsymbol{r}) > u(\boldsymbol{r}), \\ \boldsymbol{\lambda}^{\mathrm{T}} \boldsymbol{d}(\boldsymbol{r}), & \text{if } l(\boldsymbol{r}) \le \boldsymbol{\lambda}^{\mathrm{T}} \boldsymbol{d}(\boldsymbol{r}) \le u(\boldsymbol{r}), \\ l(\boldsymbol{r}), & \text{if } \boldsymbol{\lambda}^{\mathrm{T}} \boldsymbol{d}(\boldsymbol{r}) < l(\boldsymbol{r}) . \end{cases} \tag{2.59}$$

For the minimum cross entropy method, the dual problem maximizes

$$D(\boldsymbol{\lambda}, \mu) = \int_K \big[\hat{x}(\boldsymbol{\lambda}, \boldsymbol{r}) \ln[\hat{x}(\boldsymbol{\lambda}, \boldsymbol{r})/x'(\boldsymbol{r})] \\ -(\boldsymbol{\lambda}^{\mathrm{T}} \boldsymbol{d}(\boldsymbol{r}))\hat{x}(\boldsymbol{\lambda}, \boldsymbol{r})\big] \, d\boldsymbol{r} - B^*(-\boldsymbol{\lambda}) ; \tag{2.60}$$

$x'(\boldsymbol{r})$ is the prior estimate of the signal. The signal model is

$$\hat{x}(\boldsymbol{\lambda}, \boldsymbol{r}) = \begin{cases} u(\boldsymbol{r}), & \text{if } x'(\boldsymbol{r}) \exp[\boldsymbol{\lambda}^{\mathrm{T}} \boldsymbol{d}(\boldsymbol{r}) - 1] > u(\boldsymbol{r}) , \\ x'(\boldsymbol{r}) \exp[\boldsymbol{\lambda}^{\mathrm{T}} \boldsymbol{d}(\boldsymbol{r}) - 1] , & \text{if } l(\boldsymbol{r}) \le x'(\boldsymbol{r}) \exp[\boldsymbol{\lambda}^{\mathrm{T}} \boldsymbol{d}(\boldsymbol{r}) - 1] \le u(\boldsymbol{r}) , \\ l(\boldsymbol{r}), & \text{if } x'(\boldsymbol{r}) \exp[\boldsymbol{\lambda}^{\mathrm{T}} \boldsymbol{d}(\boldsymbol{r}) - 1] < l(\boldsymbol{r}) . \end{cases} \tag{2.61}$$

Under the assumptions that $0 \le l(\boldsymbol{r})$, $0 < u(\boldsymbol{r}) < \infty$ and $l(\boldsymbol{r}) < u(\boldsymbol{r})$, the dual problem corresponding to the maximum entropy criterion seeks to maximize

$$D(\boldsymbol{\lambda}, \mu) = \int_K \left[-\ln[\hat{x}(\boldsymbol{\lambda}, \boldsymbol{r})] - (\boldsymbol{\lambda}^{\mathrm{T}} \boldsymbol{d}(\boldsymbol{r}))\hat{x}(\boldsymbol{\lambda}, \boldsymbol{r}) \right] d\boldsymbol{r} - B^*(-\boldsymbol{\lambda}) \tag{2.62}$$

and the signal model is

$$\frac{1}{\hat{x}(\boldsymbol{\lambda}, \boldsymbol{r})} = \begin{cases} 1/u(\boldsymbol{r}), & \text{if } -\boldsymbol{\lambda}^{\mathrm{T}} \boldsymbol{d}(\boldsymbol{r}) < 1/u(\boldsymbol{r}), \\ -\boldsymbol{\lambda}^{\mathrm{T}} \boldsymbol{d}(\boldsymbol{r}), & \text{if } 1/l(\boldsymbol{r}) \geq -\boldsymbol{\lambda}^{\mathrm{T}} \boldsymbol{d}(\boldsymbol{r}) \geq 1/u(\boldsymbol{r}) \\ 1/l(\boldsymbol{r}), & \text{if } -\boldsymbol{\lambda}^{\mathrm{T}} \boldsymbol{d}(\boldsymbol{r}) > 1/l(\boldsymbol{r}). \end{cases} \tag{2.63}$$

In all three cases the downhill simplex method with multiple restarts was used to find the optimal $\boldsymbol{\lambda}$. Once the downhill simplex found a candidate for the optimal solution, it was used as the starting point in another search using the same method. The whole process was repeated until the optimal value of the objective function found in two successive searches changed by less than 10^{-7} %.

As a benchmark, the signals were also restored by the minimum mean-squares-error method (Wiener filtering) [2.2]. The Wiener filter assumes that the autocorrelation of the signal to be restored is known, an invalid assumption in our case. This was overcome by approximating the correlation matrix of the signal by an identity matrix multiplied by the rms value of the signal, σ_{x}. When the observation noise is white with standard deviation σ_{n}, the restored signal $x \in \mathrm{R}^M$ is given by [2.2]

$$x = D^{\mathrm{T}} \left[DD^{\mathrm{T}} + (\sigma_n/\sigma_x) I \right]^{-1} y\,, \tag{2.64}$$

where the matrix D represents the distortion operator. Unfortunately σ_{x} is also unknown. It was approximated by

$$\frac{\sigma_{\mathrm{x}}}{\sigma_{\mathrm{n}}} \approx \sqrt{\frac{1}{\sum_{i=1}^{N} \sum_{j=1}^{N} d_{ij}^2} \left(\frac{\sigma_{\mathrm{g}}^2}{\sigma_{\mathrm{n}}^2} - 1 \right)}\,. \tag{2.65}$$

Here σ_{g}^2 is the average power in the measurements, and $\sigma_{\mathrm{g}}^2/\sigma_{\mathrm{n}}^2$ is the signal-to-noise ratio.

In the first two comparisons, the signal in Fig. 2.5 a containing 128 samples was convolved with the Gaussian function,

$$\exp\left(-\frac{n^2}{32} \right), \tag{2.66}$$

which is shown in Fig. 2.5 b, to produce the blurred signal in Fig. 2.5 c. In the first comparison, 32 samples of the distorted signal were selected randomly. White Gaussian noise was added to the samples so that the 32 measurements in Fig. 2.5 d had a signal-to-noise ratio of 30 dB. In the second comparison all 128 samples were used. In both cases the goal was to restore the signal from the noisy measurements using the least-squares method, the minimum cross entropy method, and the maximum entropy method and to compare the results.

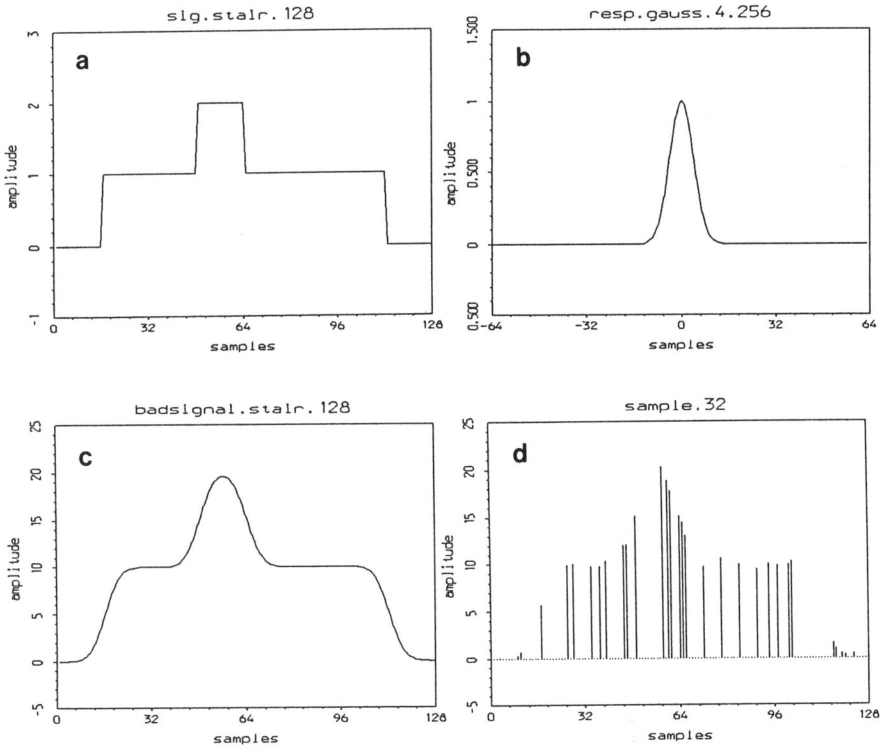

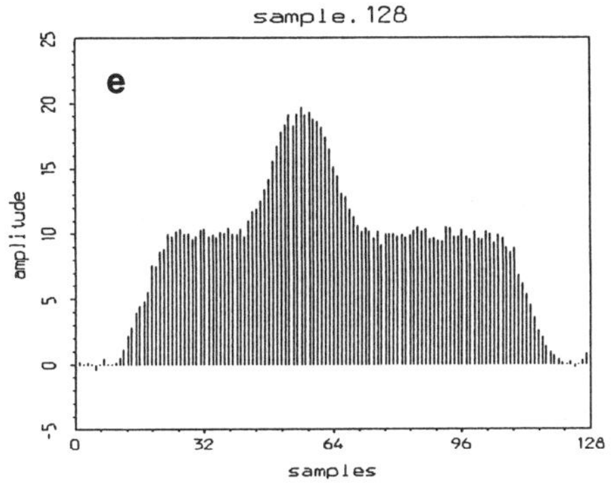

Fig. 2.5 a–e. The original signal and observations for the first two comparisons. **(a)** The original signal. **(b)** The impulse response of the blur. **(c)** The blurred signal. **(d)** 32 samples of the blurred signal with noise added. **(e)** All 128 samples of the blurred signal with noise added

In both comparisons, prior information about the signal and noise was incorporated in the restoration. This information included the fairly tight upper and lower bounds shown in Fig. 2.6, a nonnegativity constraint on the signal, a loose upper bound of 100 on the signal, and no bounds on the signal. The noise constraints included a covariance matching constraint with a 95 % confidence region on the covariance of the noise and a spectrum matching constraint which placed a 95 % confidence region on its periodogram.

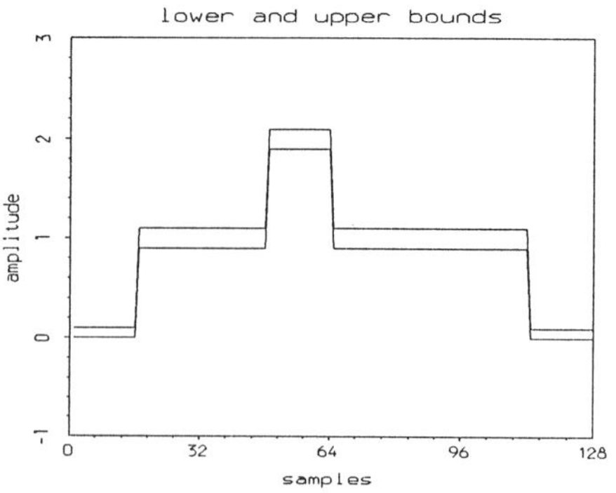

Fig. 2.6. Tight upper and lower bounds for the signal used in some of the restorations

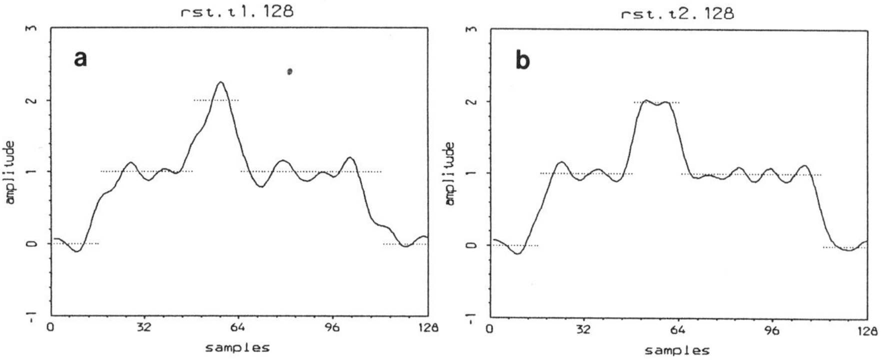

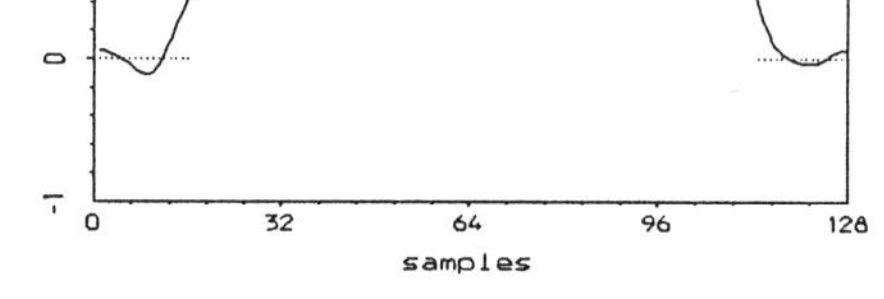

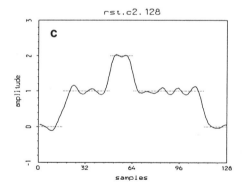

Fig. 2.7 a–c. The signals restored by Wiener filtering. (a) The signal restored from 32 randomly sampled measurements with the distortion operator approximated by a Toeplitz matrix. (b) A similar restoration made from 128 measurements. (c) The signal restored from 128 measurements with the distortion operator approximated by a circulant matrix

For comparison purposes the Wiener filtering restorations are shown in Fig. 2.7. We notice that there is little difference in the restorations from 128 samples when the Toeplitz distortion matrix is approximated by a circulant matrix. In the latter case the filter can be efficiently implemented using the discrete Fourier transform. When the restoration was made from only 32 randomly sampled measurements, the distortion matrix was not square and could not be approximated by a circulant matrix.

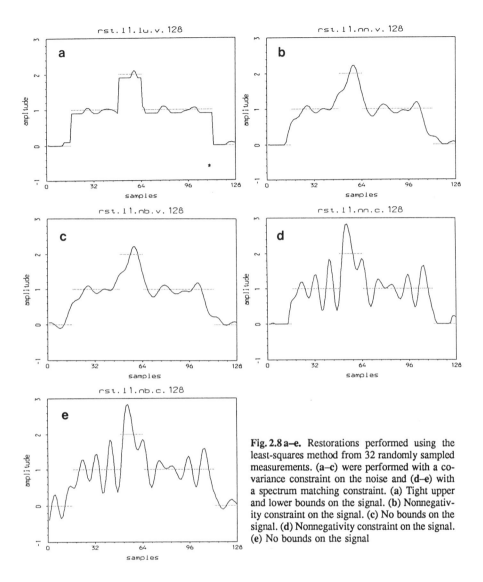

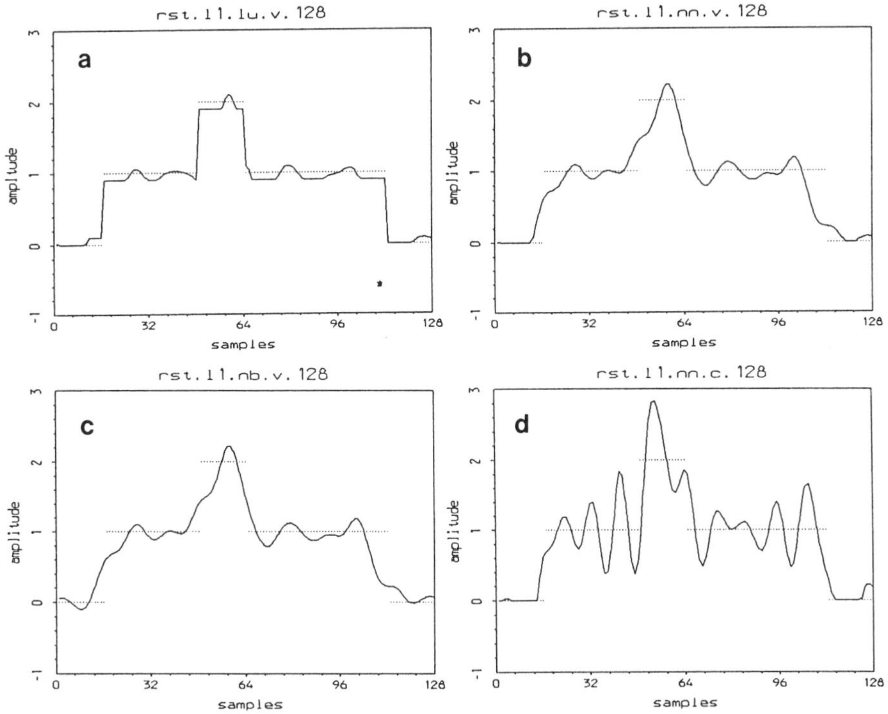

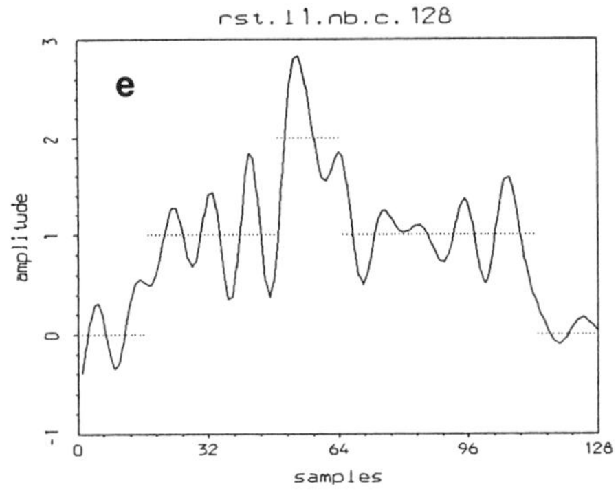

Fig. 2.8 a–e. Restorations performed using the least-squares method from 32 randomly sampled measurements. (**a–c**) were performed with a covariance constraint on the noise and (**d–e**) with a spectrum matching constraint. (**a**) Tight upper and lower bounds on the signal. (**b**) Nonnegativity constraint on the signal. (**c**) No bounds on the signal. (**d**) Nonnegativity constraint on the signal. (**e**) No bounds on the signal

Figure 2.8 shows least squares restorations for different constraints on the signal and noise. The original signal is superimposed in the form of dotted lines. We notice that the signals restored with the covariance matching constraint are significantly better than those restored with the spectrum matching constraint. We also notice that the signals that are restored with a nonnegativity constraint on the signal are essentially the same as those restored without any bounds at all. This is a reflection of the fact that for this signal, the nonnegativity constraint is not a tight one. We also see that the restoration without any bounds on the signal is similar to the Wiener restoration.

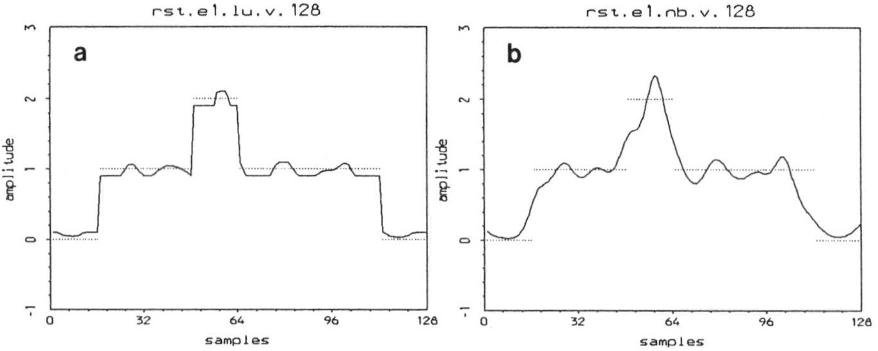

Fig. 2.9 a,b. Signals restored from 32 randomly sampled measurements using the minimum cross entropy method. A covariance constraint was applied to the noise. (**a**) Upper and lower bounds applied to the signal. (**b**) No bounds on the signal

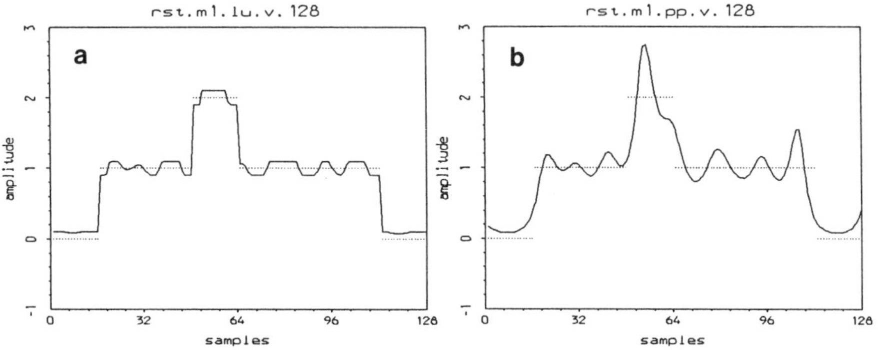

Fig. 2.10 a,b. Signals restored from 32 randomly sampled measurements using the maximum entropy method. A covariance constraint was applied to the noise. (**a**) Upper and lower bounds applied to the signal. (**b**) A large upper bound on the signal

The signals restored by the minimum cross entropy method are shown in Fig. 2.9. The prior estimate was a constant signal with a value of one. A covariance matching constraint was applied to the noise. We notice that the restoration performed with no bounds is similar to the least squares restoration with no bounds, although the minimum cross entropy restoration has slightly sharper peaks. The nonnegativity constraint was not tried since the cross entropy functional has implicitly imposed a positivity constraint on the signal. Furthermore, the spectrum matching constraints were not used because the experience from the least squares case suggested that there was nothing to be gained and the optimal Lagrange multipliers were found using the downhill simplex algorithm which was extremely slow.

The signals restored by the maximum entropy method with a covariance matching constraint on the noise are shown in Fig. 2.10. A large upper bound of 100 on the signal was used to restore the signal in Fig. 2.10 b to make the downhill simplex method numerically stable. This large upper bound had no effect on the restoration

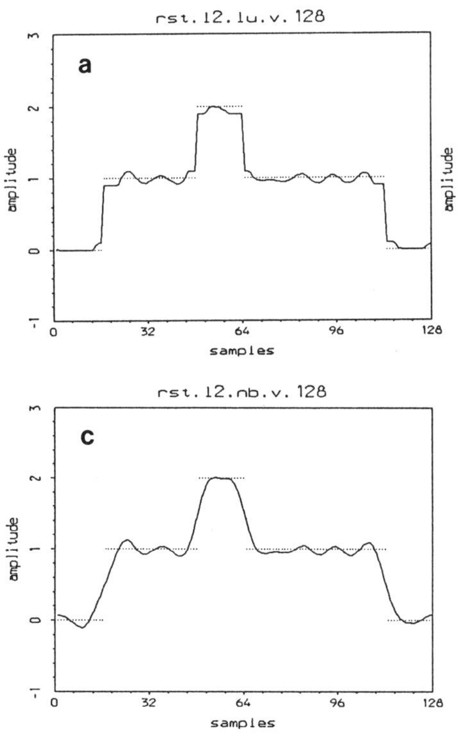

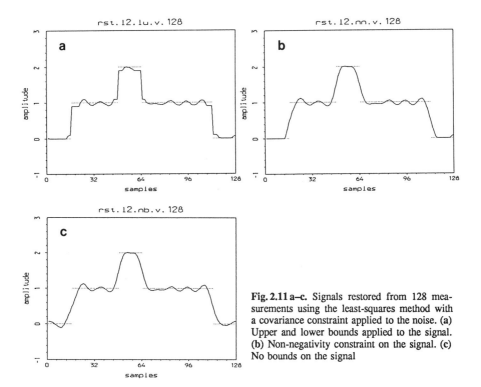

Fig. 2.11 a–c. Signals restored from 128 measurements using the least-squares method with a covariance constraint applied to the noise. (a) Upper and lower bounds applied to the signal. (b) Non-negativity constraint on the signal. (c) No bounds on the signal

and the result is the same as if no upper bound were placed on the signal. We notice that this restoration is the most peaked of all of the restorations made from these observations. Because of computational constraints maximum entropy restorations were not performed for other constraint sets.

In the second comparison, the signal was restored from all 128 measurements. The signals restored by the least-squares method with the covariance constraint on the noise are shown in Fig. 2.11. We again notice that the result due to the non-negativity constraint is similar to the restoration with no signal bounds, but it is smoother than the restoration performed using the Wiener filter.

The signals restored by the minimum cross entropy method with the prior estimate equal to 1 and with a covariance matching constraint on the noise are shown in Fig. 2.12. We notice that the signal in (b) has more overshoot at the transitions than the corresponding signal restored by the least-squares method.

The signals restored by the maximum entropy method with a covariance matching constraint on the noise are shown in Fig. 2.13. Again a large bound of 100 was applied to make the downhill simplex algorithm numerically stable without affecting the restoration. The unbounded restoration has more overshoot than the corresponding restoration with the minimum cross entropy criterion.

The third and fourth comparisons were based on the impulsive image shown in Fig. 2.14. In the third comparison the 32 randomly selected samples of the blurred

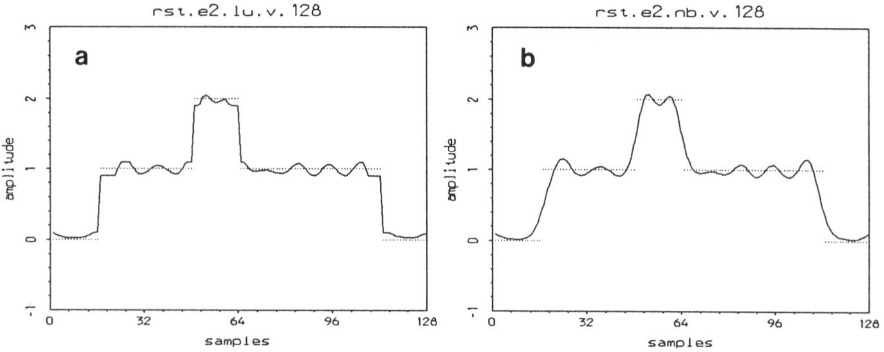

Fig. 2.12 a,b. Signals restored from 128 measurements using the minimum cross entropy method. A covariance constraint was applied to the noise. (**a**) Upper and lower bounds applied to the signal. (**b**) No bounds on the signal

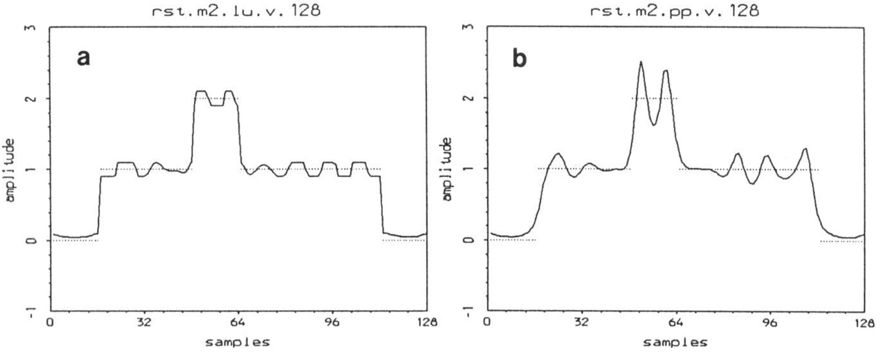

Fig. 2.13 a,b. Signals restored from 128 measurements using the maximum entropy method. A covariance constraint was applied to the noise. (**a**) Upper and lower bounds applied to the signal. (**b**) A large upper bound was placed on the signal

image shown in (d) were used and in the fourth all 128 samples shown in (e) were examined. As in the first two comparisons the signal to (white Gaussian) noise ratio was 30 dB.

The comparable restoration produced by the Wiener filter is shown in Fig. 2.15. The two dots shown over the restorations indicate the locations of the peaks in the original. We notice that there is very little difference in the restorations performed from 128 samples, and that all three of the restorations are fairly poor.

The signals restored from the 32 measurements with a covariance matching constraint on the noise for various optimization criteria are displayed in Fig. 2.16. The signals restored by the least-squares method with and without a nonnegativity constraint are very similar and they resemble the Wiener restoration. The signal restored by the minimum cross entropy method has better resolution than the least-squares restoration, but the maximum entropy restoration displays the highest resolution of all. As in the earlier maximum entropy restorations a large upper bound had to be placed on the restoration to stabilize the downhill simplex algorithm.

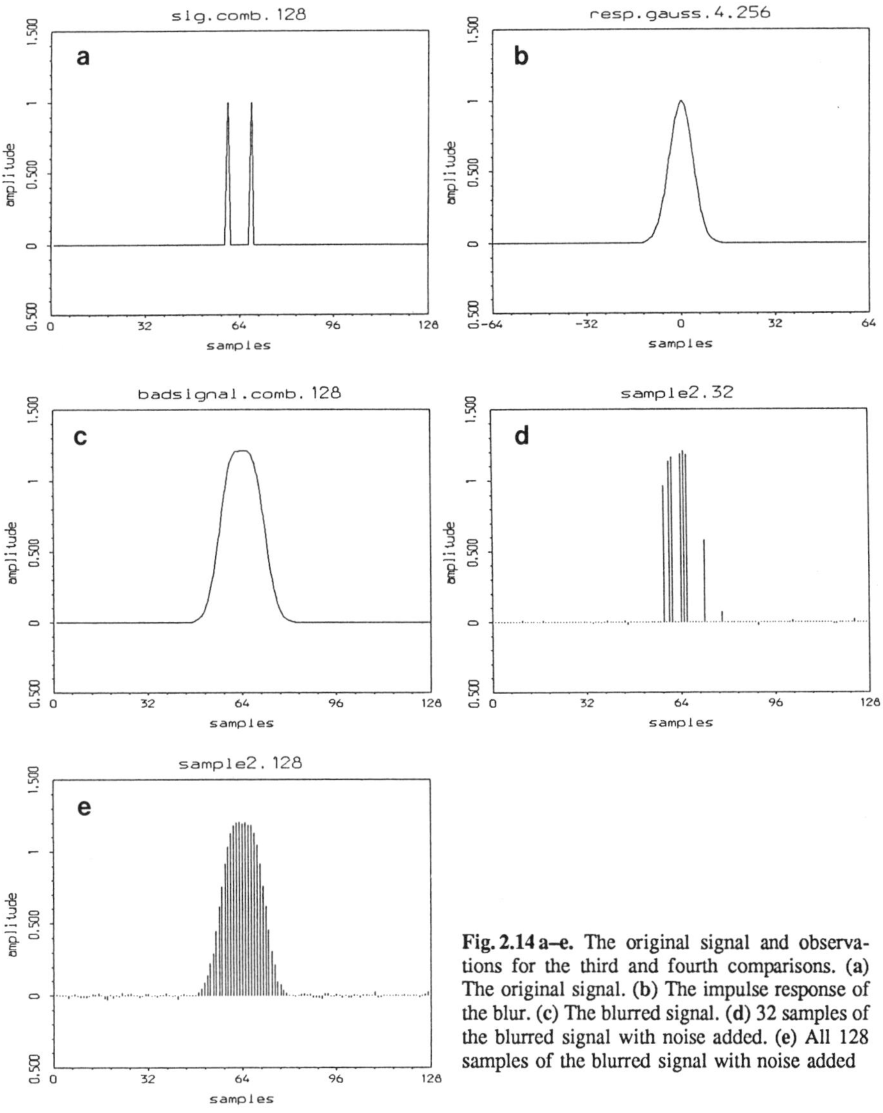

Fig. 2.14 a–e. The original signal and observations for the third and fourth comparisons. **(a)** The original signal. **(b)** The impulse response of the blur. **(c)** The blurred signal. **(d)** 32 samples of the blurred signal with noise added. **(e)** All 128 samples of the blurred signal with noise added

The restorations from the fourth comparison are shown in Fig. 2.17. All 128 measurements were used and the restorations were performed by assuming a covariance constraint on the noise. The observations are similar to the third comparison except that the quality of the restorations is higher because of the increased number of measurements. The nonnegativity constraint improved the performance of the least-squares method, but the minimum cross entropy method still performs better, and the maximum entropy method performs the best of all.

In looking over the performance of the three optimization criteria in all four comparisons, it is clear that the performance of the various methods varies. The

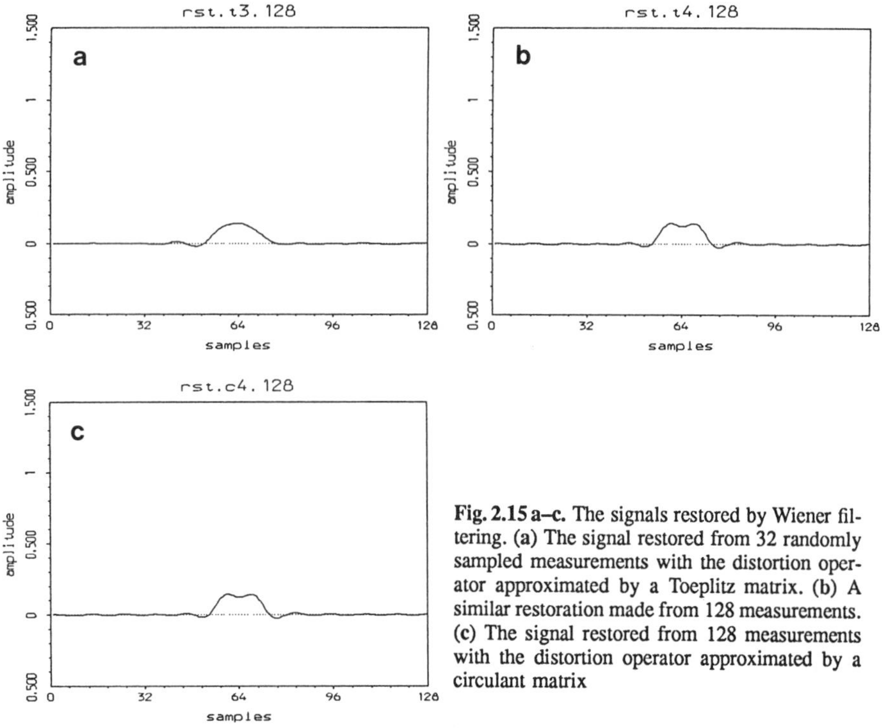

Fig. 2.15 a–c. The signals restored by Wiener filtering. (a) The signal restored from 32 randomly sampled measurements with the distortion operator approximated by a Toeplitz matrix. (b) A similar restoration made from 128 measurements. (c) The signal restored from 128 measurements with the distortion operator approximated by a circulant matrix

different criteria emphasize different aspects of the signal to be restored. In the first two comparisons the signal amplitudes are smooth and the least-squares restorations are to be preferred. In the latter two comparisons, where the signal is impulsive, the maximum entropy method gives more pleasing results. The minimum cross entropy restorations lay between these in all of the comparisons.

The non-negativity constraint on the signal can sometimes improve the restoration with the least-squares method. This is particularly the case for impulsive signals, and is perhaps not surprising, since it represents a much tighter constraint for impulsive signals than it does for smooth ones. Tight signal bounds can definitely improve performance, albeit at the expense of producing a somewhat unnatural-looking restoration. In many practical applications, however, such bounds will probably not be available.

The list below summarizes these major conclusions.

- The least-squares method is the best method for restoring smooth signals.
- The least-squares method with a covariance matching constraint on the noise gives better restorations than Wiener filtering (with the assumptions made in our implementation).
- The maximum entropy method is a good method for restoring impulsive signals which are positive.

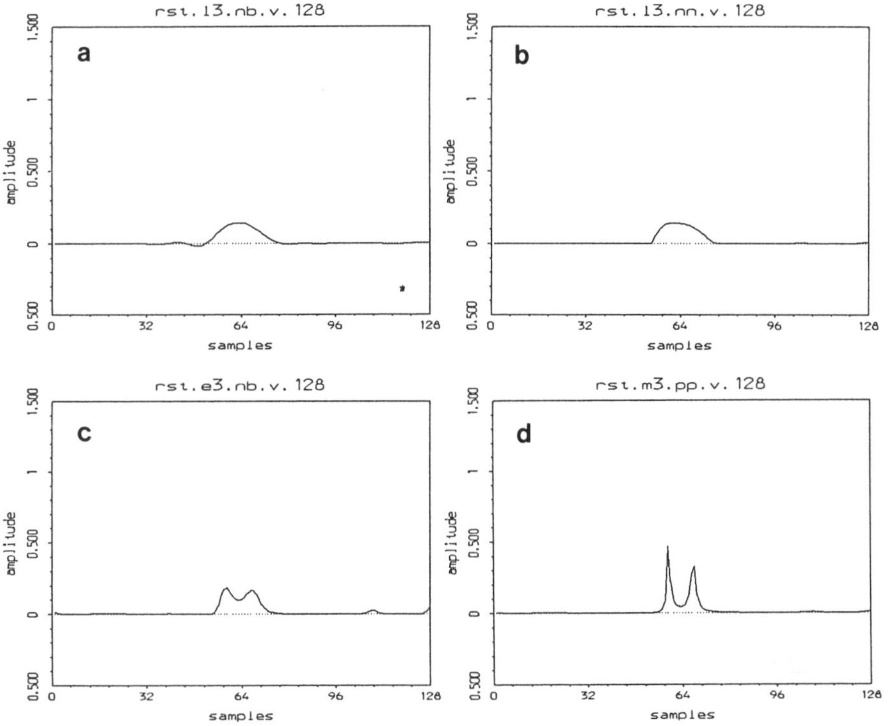

Fig. 2.16 a–d. Restorations from 32 randomly sampled measurements with a covariance matching constraint. (**a**) Least squares method with no bounds on the signal. (**b**) Least squares method with a positivity constraint. (**c**) Minimum cross entropy method with no signal bounds. (**d**) Maximum entropy method with a large upper bound on the signal

- A nonnegativity constraint on the signals improves the resolution of impulsive signals but has little effect on smooth ones.
- Good estimates of the upper and lower bounds on the signal can improve the quality of the restored signal.
- The quality of the restored signals improves as the number of measurements increases.

2.4.3 Behavior of Optimization Procedures when a Feasible Solution Does Not Exist

We saw in Sect. 2.3 that the dual approach will not work when there are no feasible solutions. What happens when this is the case? We can answer this question using a theorem based on conjugate duality. A proof of this theorem can be found in Appendix E of [2.10].

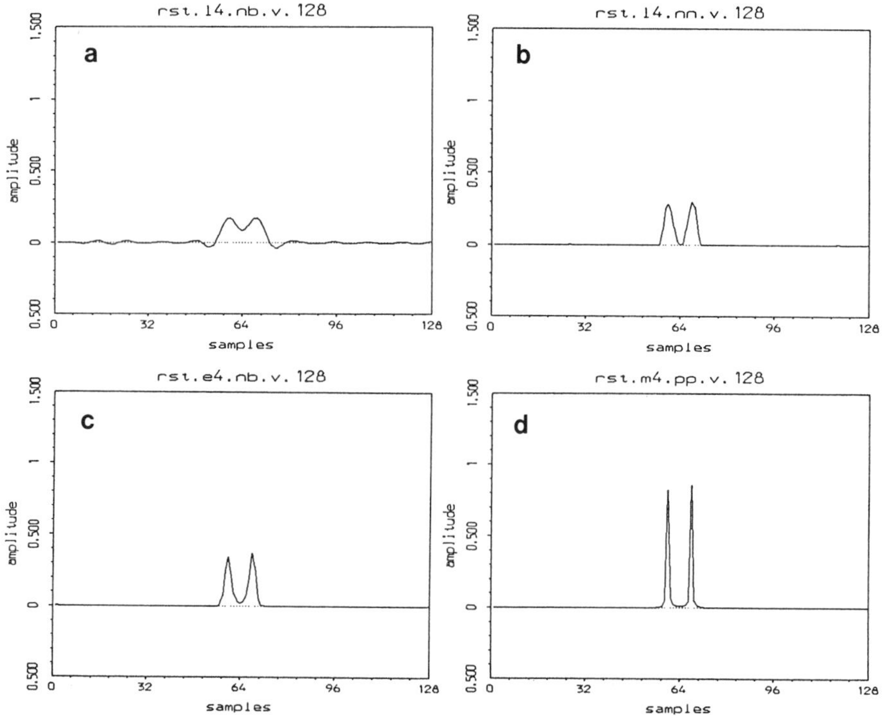

Fig. 2.17 a–d. Restorations from 128 measurements with a covariance matching constraint. (**a**) Least squares method with no bounds on the signal. (**b**) Least squares method with a positivity constraint. (**c**) Minimum cross entropy method with no signal bounds. (**d**) Maximum entropy method with a large upper bound on the signal

Theorem 1. *Given an arbitrary measurement vector and total intensity pair* $(\boldsymbol{y}, I_0)$ *in* $\mathsf{R}^N \times \mathsf{R}$, *if there is no signal* x *in* $R_b \cap R_i$ *such that* $D(x) - \boldsymbol{y} \in S$, *and if we assume that any set in* $\mathsf{R}^N \times \mathsf{R}$ *with volume zero has probability 0, then*

$$\sup\{D(\boldsymbol{\lambda}, \mu): \quad \mu \leq 0\} = \infty \tag{2.67}$$

with probability 1.

This theorem says that when the primal problem has no feasible solution, any optimization procedure applied to the dual functional $D(\boldsymbol{\lambda}, \mu)$ will almost surely diverge. The same result is true when we do not have an intensity constraint so that $\mu = 0$. In practice this divergence becomes apparent very quickly.

2.5 Cost Functionals for Sequential Restoration

It is frequently more convenient to produce updated estimates of an image as measurements are obtained than to wait until all of the measurements have been received. The quality of the current restored image can be used to tell whether more measurements are necessary and, if so, which ones might be most useful. Some convex performance functionals can be used as the basis of sequential restoration algorithms, but others cannot. This section will define two conditions – the *prior estimate consistency condition* and the *subsequent estimate consistency condition* – that a functional should satisfy to be the basis of a sequential estimation algorithm. It will be shown that the entropy and cross entropy functionals that were discussed earlier need to be modified to be useful for sequential restoration of blurred images.

2.5.1 The Prior Estimate Consistency Condition

One criterion for selecting a cost functional for image restoration when a prior estimate of the image, x^0, is available is that the restoration should equal the prior estimate if subsequent measurements do not further constrain it. This is known as the *prior estimate consistency condition*. For example, in least-squares restoration, instead of using the cost functional $\frac{1}{2}\|x\|^2$, we might choose to use the cost functional $\frac{1}{2}\|x - x^0\|^2$. If additional measurements impose no additional constraints on the restoration, this latter functional is clearly minimized by the restoration $x = x^0$, which is the prior estimate.

Several commonly used cost functionals do not pass the prior estimate consistency condition. Among these are the entropy functional

$$h_e(x) = -\int_k \ln(x(\boldsymbol{r}))\, d\boldsymbol{r} \tag{2.68}$$

and the cross entropy functional

$$h_{ce}(x) = \int_k x(\boldsymbol{r}) \ln\left(\frac{x(\boldsymbol{r})}{x^0(\boldsymbol{r})}\right) d\boldsymbol{r}\ . \tag{2.69}$$

The entropy functional does not make use of a prior estimate and, in the absence of additional measurement constraints, the cross entropy functional is minimized by the restoration $\mathrm{e}^{-1}x^0$, which is different from x^0.

2.5.2 The Subsequent Estimate Consistency Condition

The subsequent estimate consistency condition requires that an optimal sequential restoration based on a given set of measurements should produce the same result as an optimal nonsequential one. To make this statement more specific, assume at time $k-1$ that the measurements $\{y_1^0, y_2^0, \ldots, y_{N-1}^0\}$ are available[2]. These measurements have been used with the prior estimate x^0 to produce the optimally restored signal $\hat{x}^{k-1}$. At the next time instant k, an additional measurement y_N becomes available. It can be used to update the restoration in many ways. In addition to using the measurements $\{y_1^0, y_2^0, \ldots, y_N^0\}$, either the initial estimate x^0 or any one of the restored signals $(x^i), i = 1, 2, \ldots, k-1$, can be used as a prior estimate. If all

[2] At each time, we may collect more than one measurement. Therefore, we may have $N \geq k$.

of these result in the same restored signal, the functional satisfies the *subsequent estimate consistency condition.*

If the measurements of the blurred image are exact, the least-squares objective functional can be shown to satisfy the subsequent estimate consistency condition by using the least squares signal model (2.18) that was derived earlier. Let $\boldsymbol{\lambda}^1 = [\lambda_1^1, \dots, \lambda_N^1]$ denote the parameter vector at time k.

$$\hat{x}_1(\boldsymbol{\lambda}^1, \boldsymbol{r}) = (\boldsymbol{\lambda}^1)^{\mathrm{T}} w(\boldsymbol{r}) + x^0(\boldsymbol{r}) \tag{2.70}$$

$$= \sum_{i=1}^{N} \lambda_i^1 w_i(\boldsymbol{r}) + x^0(\boldsymbol{r}) \,. \tag{2.71}$$

The dual functional can be found by substituting $h_{\mathrm{ls}}[x(\boldsymbol{r})] = \frac{1}{2}[x(\boldsymbol{r}) - x^0(\boldsymbol{r})]^2$ into the general dual functional formula (2.17). For the least squares problem it takes the form

$$D_1(\boldsymbol{\lambda}^1) = -\frac{1}{2}\int_K \left[(\boldsymbol{\lambda}^1)^{\mathrm{T}} w(\boldsymbol{r}) - x^0(\boldsymbol{r})\right]^2 d\boldsymbol{r} + \frac{1}{2}\int_K [x^0(\boldsymbol{r})]^2 \, d\boldsymbol{r} + (\boldsymbol{\lambda}^1)^{\mathrm{T}} \boldsymbol{y} \,. \tag{2.72}$$

Let $\boldsymbol{\lambda}^2$ denote the optimal parameter vector when one of the earlier restorations is used as the prior estimate of the image. In this case the signal model becomes

$$\hat{x}_2(\boldsymbol{\lambda}^2, \boldsymbol{r}) = (\boldsymbol{\lambda}^2)^{\mathrm{T}} w(\boldsymbol{r}) + \left[(\boldsymbol{\lambda}^0)^{\mathrm{T}} w(\boldsymbol{r}) + x^0(\boldsymbol{r})\right] \,. \tag{2.73}$$

The parameter vector $\boldsymbol{\lambda}^0$ is the optimal parameter vector from the earlier restoration. Since $\boldsymbol{\lambda}^2$ is longer than $\boldsymbol{\lambda}^0$, for the sake of this equation $\boldsymbol{\lambda}^0$ should be considered to be extended with sufficient zeros to make these two vectors of the same length. It is now sufficient to show that that $\hat{x}_2 = \hat{x}_1$.

The dual functional corresponding to (2.73) has the form

$$D_2(\boldsymbol{\lambda}^2) = -\frac{1}{2}\int_K \left[(\boldsymbol{\lambda}^2)^{\mathrm{T}} w(\boldsymbol{r}) + (\boldsymbol{\lambda}^0)^{\mathrm{T}} w(\boldsymbol{r}) + x^0(\boldsymbol{r})\right]^2 d\boldsymbol{r} + \int_K \left[(\boldsymbol{\lambda}^0)^{\mathrm{T}} w(\boldsymbol{r}) + x^0(\boldsymbol{r})\right]^{\mathrm{T}} d\boldsymbol{r} + (\boldsymbol{\lambda}^2)^{\mathrm{T}} \boldsymbol{y} \,. \tag{2.74}$$

Its optimal solution is the same as the optimal solution of

$$D_2(\boldsymbol{\lambda}^2) + (\boldsymbol{\lambda}^0)^{\mathrm{T}} \boldsymbol{y} - \frac{1}{2}\int_K \left[(\boldsymbol{\lambda}^0)^{\mathrm{T}} w(\boldsymbol{r}) + x^0(\boldsymbol{r})\right]^2 d\boldsymbol{r} + \frac{1}{2}\int_K [x^0(\boldsymbol{r})]^2 \, d\boldsymbol{r} = D_1(\boldsymbol{\lambda}^2 + \boldsymbol{\lambda}^0) \,, \tag{2.75}$$

since $(\boldsymbol{\lambda}^0)^{\mathrm{T}} \boldsymbol{y}$ and the two integrals in this expression are constants. Comparing (2.75) with (2.72) it follows that $\boldsymbol{\lambda}^1 = \boldsymbol{\lambda}^2 + \boldsymbol{\lambda}^0$. Substituting into the signal model given by (2.71) and comparing the result with the signal model given in (2.73), it follows that the optimal restored signals obtained from the two different prior estimates are the same. Consequently, the least-squares objective function satisfies the subsequent estimate consistency condition.

Unfortunately, in general, the entropy and cross entropy functionals do not satisfy this condition. The entropy functional does not satisfy it because it does not take prior estimates into account. The cross entropy functional does not satisfy the condition unless one of the measurements constrains the integral $\int_K x(\boldsymbol{r})\,d\boldsymbol{r}$ which is the case in the power spectrum estimation and probability density estimation problems. This is because, for the minimum cross entropy functional, the signal model has the form

$$\hat{x}(\boldsymbol{r}) = x^0(\boldsymbol{r})\mathrm{e}^{(\boldsymbol{\lambda})^{\mathrm{T}} w(\boldsymbol{r})-1} \ . \tag{2.76}$$

At the kth time interval, if the prior estimate x^0 is used to restore the signal and the optimal parameters are given by $\boldsymbol{\lambda}^1$, the optimally restored signal is

$$\hat{x}^1(\boldsymbol{r}) = x^0(\boldsymbol{r})\mathrm{e}^{(\boldsymbol{\lambda}^1)^{\mathrm{T}} w(\boldsymbol{r})-1} \ . \tag{2.77}$$

If, instead, one of the previously restored signals is used as the prior estimate, the restored signal is given by

$$\hat{x}^1(\boldsymbol{r}) = \left[x^0(\boldsymbol{r})\mathrm{e}^{(\boldsymbol{\lambda}^0)^{\mathrm{T}} w(\boldsymbol{r})-1}\right] \mathrm{e}^{(\boldsymbol{\lambda}^2)^{\mathrm{T}} w(\boldsymbol{r})-1} \ . \tag{2.78}$$

Because of the constants in the exponents, these two restored images are different. Thus, the cross entropy functional does not satisfy the subsequent estimate consistency condition.

2.5.3 Modifications to the Entropy and Cross Entropy Functionals

The entropy and cross entropy functionals can be modified so that the prior and subsequent estimate consistency conditions are satisfied. Under the assumptions that the prior estimate x^0 is positive and that the measurements are exact, we can construct the modified entropy functional

$$-\int_K \ln(x(\boldsymbol{r}))\,d\boldsymbol{r} + \int_K \frac{x(\boldsymbol{r})}{x^0(\boldsymbol{r})}\,d\boldsymbol{r} \ , \tag{2.79}$$

and the modified cross entropy functional

$$\int_K x(\boldsymbol{r}) \ln\left(\frac{x(\boldsymbol{r})}{\mathrm{e}x^0(\boldsymbol{r})}\right) = \int_K x(\boldsymbol{r}) \ln\left(\frac{x(\boldsymbol{r})}{x^0(\boldsymbol{r})}\right) d\boldsymbol{r} - \int_K x(\boldsymbol{r})\,d\boldsymbol{r} \ . \tag{2.80}$$

These two cost functionals both satisfy the prior estimate consistency condition because in both cases the signal which minimizes the functional in the absence of additional measurement constraints is the prior estimate x^0. This can be seen by evaluating the gradients of these two functionals. Each of them also satisfies the subsequent estimate consistency condition. This can be shown by a procedure similar to that for the least squares criterion. This demonstration is omitted here, but can be found in [2.10].

The signal models for the modified maximum entropy and minimum cross entropy problems with exact measurement matching constraints are:

$$\hat{x}_{\mathrm{e}}(\boldsymbol{\lambda}, r) = \frac{1}{-\boldsymbol{\lambda}^{\mathrm{T}} w(\boldsymbol{r}) + 1/x^0(\boldsymbol{r})} , \tag{2.81}$$

$$\hat{x}_{\mathrm{ce}}(\boldsymbol{\lambda}, \boldsymbol{r}) = x^0(\boldsymbol{r}) \mathrm{e}^{\boldsymbol{\lambda}^{\mathrm{T}} w(\boldsymbol{r})} \, d\boldsymbol{r} + \boldsymbol{\lambda}^{\mathrm{T}} \boldsymbol{y} , \tag{2.82}$$

and the corresponding dual functionals are

$$D_{\mathrm{e}}(\boldsymbol{\lambda}) = - \int_K \ln \left(\frac{1}{-\boldsymbol{\lambda}^{\mathrm{T}} w(\boldsymbol{r}) + 1/x^0(\boldsymbol{r})} \right) d\boldsymbol{r} - \int_K d\boldsymbol{r} + \boldsymbol{\lambda}^{\mathrm{T}} \boldsymbol{y} , \tag{2.83}$$

$$D_{\mathrm{ce}}(\boldsymbol{\lambda}) = - \int_K x^0(\boldsymbol{r}) \mathrm{e}^{\boldsymbol{\lambda}^{\mathrm{T}} w(\boldsymbol{r})} \, d\boldsymbol{r} + \boldsymbol{\lambda}^{\mathrm{T}} w(\boldsymbol{r}) . \tag{2.84}$$

2.6 Relationship Between the Original and Modified Entropy and Cross Entropy Functionals

The modified functionals that were defined in the previous section are closely related to their originals. When these cost functionals are used in power spectrum estimation or probability density function estimation where one of the constraints has the form

$$y_1^0 = \int_K x(\boldsymbol{r}) \, d\boldsymbol{r} , \tag{2.85}$$

the two original functionals and their modifications produce the same optimally restored signals. This can be seen for the modified cross entropy functional, which can be written as

$$\begin{aligned} \int_K x(\boldsymbol{r}) \ln \left(\frac{x(\boldsymbol{r})}{\mathrm{e} x^0(\boldsymbol{r})} \right) d\boldsymbol{r} &= \int_K x(+\boldsymbol{r}) \ln \left(\frac{x(r)}{x^0(\boldsymbol{r})} \right) d\boldsymbol{r} - \int_K x(\boldsymbol{r}) \, d\boldsymbol{r} \\ &= \int_K x(\boldsymbol{r}) \ln \left(\frac{x(\boldsymbol{r})}{x^0(\boldsymbol{r})} \right) d\boldsymbol{r} - y_1^0 . \end{aligned} \tag{2.86}$$

The modified cross entropy functional on the left of the above equation and the original cross entropy functional on the right differ by a constant. Therefore, they give the same optimal solution when this constraint is present.

The modified form and the original form of the entropy functional are also related. This relationship can take two forms. First, when the prior estimate is $x^0(\boldsymbol{r}) = \infty$ the modified functional reduces to the original one. Second, when the prior estimate is a constant $x^0(\boldsymbol{r}) = c$, and when one of the constraints is given by (2.85), the entropy functional and its modification produce the same optimal solution. This is because

$$-\int_K \ln x(\boldsymbol{r})\,d\boldsymbol{r} + \int_K \frac{x(\boldsymbol{r})}{x^0(\boldsymbol{r})}\,d\boldsymbol{r} = -\int_K \ln x(\boldsymbol{r})\,d\boldsymbol{r} + \frac{y_1^0}{c}\,. \tag{2.87}$$

Again the modified entropy functional on the left and the original entropy functional on the right differ only by a constant.

The original forms of the entropy and cross entropy functionals may not be appropriate for the general problem of signal restoration. The cross entropy functional was derived for the problem of probability density estimation under the constraint that the integral of the probability density is equal to 1 [2.20, 21]. Without this constraint the cross entropy functional would not exist. Later, the cross entropy functional was adapted from probability density estimation and applied to the power spectrum estimation problem in various ways. One of these kept its original form and the other resulted in the entropy functional [2.22]. However, for the general image deblurring problem the situation is somewhat different; the value of the integral $\int_K x(\boldsymbol{r})\,d\boldsymbol{r}$ is not known a priori. Therefore, the original form of the entropy and cross entropy functionals have lost their meaning as measures of uncertainty.

Acknowledgement. This work was partially supported by the Joint Services Electronics Program under Contract DAAL-03-87-K-0059.

References

2.1 H. C. Andrews, B. R. Hunt: *Digital Image Restoration* (Prentice Hall, Englewood Cliffs, NJ 1977)

2.2 J. Biemond, R. L. Lagendijk, R. M. Mersereau: Proc. IEEE **78**, 856–883 (1990)

2.3 J. W. Woods: "Two-Dimensional Kalman Filtering," in *Two-Dimensional Digital Signal Processing I: Linear Filters*, ed. by T. S. Huang, Topics in Appl. Phys., Vol. 42 (Springer, Berlin, Heidelberg 1981) pp. 115–205

2.4 R. W. Schafer, R. M. Mersereau, M. A. Richards: Proc. IEEE **69**, 432–450 (1981)

2.5 B. R. Hunt: IEEE Trans. C-**22**, 805–812 (1973)

2.6 B. R. Frieden: J. Opt. Soc. Am., **62**, 511–518 (1972)

2.7 S. W. Lang, J. H. McClellan: IEEE Trans. ASSP-**30**, 880–890 (1982)

2.8 S. W. Lang, J. H. McClellan: IEEE Trans. ASSP-**31**, 349–358 (1983)

2.9 R. M. Leahy, C. E. Goutis: IEEE Trans. ASSP-**34**, 1629–1642 (1986)

2.10 C. Auyeung: "Optimal Constraint-based Signal Restoration and its Applications"; Ph.D. Thesis, Georgia Institute of Technology (1988)

2.11 D. G. Luenberger: *Optimization by Vector Space Methods* (Wiley, New York 1969)

2.12 J. Zowe: "Nondifferentiable Optimization," in *Computational Mathematical Programming*, ed. by K. Schittkowski, NATO ASI Series, Ser. F, Vol. 15 (Springer, Berlin, Heidelberg 1985) pp. 323–356

2.13 W. H. Press, B. P. Flannery, S. A. Teukolsky, W. T. Vetterling: *Numerical Recipes, the Art of Scientific Programming* (Cambridge University Press, New York 1986)

2.14 R. T. Rockafellar: *Conjugate Duality and Optimization,* (Princeton University Press, Princeton 1970)

2.15 N. Cameron: *Introduction to Linear and Convex Programming*, Australian Mathematical Society Lecture Series 1 (Cambridge University Press, Cambridge 1985)

2.16 I. Ekeland, T. Turnbull: *Infinite-dimensional Optimization and Convexity* (Chicago University Press, Chicago 1983)

2.17 L. C. W. Dixon: "Introduction to Numerical Optimization" in *Nonlinear Optimization, Theory and Algorithms* (Birkhauser, Boston 1980)
2.18 L. E. Scales: *Introduction to Non-Linear Optimization* (Springer, Berlin, Heidelberg 1985)
2.19 W. H. Press, B. P. Flannery, S. A. Teukolsky, W. T. Vetterling: *Numerical Recipes in C, the Art of Scientific Programming* (Cambridge University Press, New York 1988)
2.20 R. Ash: *Information Theory* (Wiley, New York 1965)
2.21 J. E. Shore, R. W. Johnson: IEEE Trans. IT-**26**, 26–37 (1980)
2.22 D. E. Smylie, G. K. C. Clarke, T. J. Ulrych: "Analysis of Irregularities in the Earth's Rotation" in *Methods in Computational Physics*, ed. by B. Adler, S. Fernbach, M. Rotenberg (Academic, New York 1973)

3. Hopfield-Type Neural Networks

S.-J. Yeh, H. Stark, and M.I. Sezan

With 12 Figures

The Hopfield neural network is a general purpose network structure which can be specified to function as an associative content addressable memory (ACAM), or to solve an optimization problem. Further, the ACAM can be cascaded with a perceptron network to form a Hopfield-type classifier. In the first part of this chapter, we discuss set-theoretic formulations of Hopfield-type ACAMs and classifier neural networks. The set-theoretic formulations are based on the methods of projections onto convex sets (POCS) and the generalized projections (GP). In the second part, we consider the use of the Hopfield network as an optimizer. We discuss how the Hopfield network can be configured to perform constrained least squares image restoration. We show that the network is capable of learning the value of the Lagrange multiplier associated with the regularization constraint. Finally, we present the restoration results obtained by the proposed network.

3.1 Overview

Artificial neural networks are composed of a number of nonlinear computational elements or nodes (neurons) operating in parallel and interconnected by links with variable weights. Their structure is suggested by a simplified model of biological systems. Generally speaking, the large amount of interest shown in neural networks in recent years is due to a number of features such networks possess:

- high processing capability due to massive parallelism;
- high degree of tolerance to damage to isolated nodes or links;
- strong ability to adapt to changing inputs;
- inherent non-parametric nature and much less dependence on assumptions regarding underlying distributions than their traditional counterparts (e.g., consider classifier networks).

Neural networks are frequently used as classifiers and associative content addressable memories (ACAM). In an ACAM, the memory is accessed not by an address, but rather by a possibly degraded (e.g., partially specified and/or noisy) version of the stored memory pattern. A classifier assigns an input sample to one of the predetermined classes. It should be noted that not all classifier networks are equally effective in dealing with various types of classification problems. For example, a one-layer perceptron network can be used to implement the perceptron

Springer Series in Information Sciences, Vol. 23
A.K. Katsaggelos (ed.): Digital Image Restoration

learning algorithm [3.1] when there are two classes and these are linearly separable. However, one-layer perceptron cannot solve the exclusive-or problem. This occurs, for example, when there are two classes and each class aggregates at diagonally opposite vertices on a square. The two-layer network can solve the exclusive-or problem but cannot separate classes that aggregate in non-simply connected regions; a three layer network can handle non-simply connected regions but the complexity of the regions is determined by the number of nodes etc.

Neural networks can be designed to realize basic well-known algorithms. For example, it is relatively easy to design a feed-forward network that determines which of N inputs is a maximum [3.2]. The optimum receiver for the binary symmetric channel can be realized by the Hamming network [3.3]. Simple cluster-seeking algorithms [3.4] can be realized using the Carpenter-Grossberg network [3.5]. Many other types of networks exist that are effective for different tasks [3.2].

A network of particular interest in pattern recognition and image processing is the Hopfield network [3.6–10]. The Hopfield network is a highly connected, general purpose network that can be specified to function as an ACAM [3.6–8], or to solve various optimization problems [3.9–12]. The ACAM can be cascaded with a perceptron network to form a classifier [3.3]. Our principal goals in this chapter are: to study the operation of Hopfield-type ACAMs and certain kinds of Hopfield-type classifiers from the point of view of the set-theoretic methods; and to show how the Hopfield network can be used in image restoration.

In general, because set-theoretic methods have been widely applied to signal processing problems such as image restoration and reconstruction [3.13, 14], they bring a signal processing perspective to the operational characteristics of the networks. In the particular case of the ACAM, the set-theoretic formulation provides a quantitative characterization of the stable states of the network. For instance, set-theoretic formulation enables an explanation of the origin of undesirable stable states, called 'traps', in the case of binary valued Hopfield ACAM. Taking the set-theoretic point of view, possible strategies can be proposed to avoid these traps. On the other hand, a learning algorithm for a linear, two-class perceptron classifier can be improved when it is formulated using the set-theoretic point of view. The application of a Hopfield-type optimizer network to constrained least squares image restoration has been reported in the literature by *Zhou* et al. [3.11, 12]. Here, we propose an iterative, Newton-Raphson type learning algorithm to determine the optimum value of the Lagrange multiplier associated with the image constraint. Interestingly, the learning algorithm can be implemented by a network architecture identical to the restoration network and two perceptron-type, feed-forward auxiliary networks. For learning, the neuron biases of the restoration network are adjusted to their appropriate values. Thus, the proposed network implements an alternating learning/restoration cycle. We show the feasibility of this approach through computer simulations.

3.2 Outline of the Chapter

In the next two sections (3.3.1, 2), we discuss some background material that will help to introduce the reader to fundamental ideas about the Hopfield network and set-theoretic methods. In Sects. 3.3.3, 4 we focus on the set-theoretic formulation of the Hopfield ACAM, and categorize the stable states of the network with the language of projection methods. We then consider an ACAM-perceptron network combination that functions as a classifier. We show how a very simple network, the single-layer perceptron network, can be analyzed using POCS and what advantages the POCS formulation has over the standard method (Sect. 3.3.5). The application of the Hopfield network to image restoration is discussed in Sect. 3.4. The work by *Zhou* and his colleagues [3.11, 12] in restoring gray level images degraded by space-invariant blurs and noise is reviewed. We show how Zhou's formulation can be augmented to accommodate prior knowledge and present some of our own results.

3.3 The Hopfield-Type Associative Content Addressable Memory

3.3.1 Principles of Operation

In the following, we assume that the ACAM stores N L-dimensional vectors: $\boldsymbol{x}_n \doteq [x_{n1} x_{n2} \cdots x_{nL}]^{\mathrm{T}}$, $n = 1, 2, \ldots, N$. Thus, the network has L nodes ($L \geq N$) whose states preferably converge to the library vector to be recalled when they are initialized by a degraded (e.g., partially specified and/or noisy) version of the library vector. The library vectors can be binary, e.g., $x_{ni} = \pm 1$ (the bipolar case) or continuous-valued, e.g., $-1 \leq x_{ni} \leq 1$, $i = 1, 2, \ldots, L$.

In the discrete-time, binary Hopfield ACAM [3.6], at time k, the state of the ith node, $v_i^{(k)}$, changes to its next value, $v_i^{(k+1)}$, at time $k + 1$, according to

$$v_i^{(k+1)} = \eta\left(\sum_{j=1}^{L} w_{ij}\, v_j^{(k)}\right), \qquad i = 1, 2, \ldots, N, \tag{3.1}$$

where w_{ij} corresponds to the interconnection weight between the ith and the jth node and $\eta(\cdot)$ defines the node nonlinearity. (Note that the bias input to the ith node is assumed to be zero.) For bipolar vectors, the nonlinearity $\eta(\cdot)$ is defined by

$$\eta(a) = \mathrm{sgn}(a) \doteq \begin{cases} 1, & a \geq 0 \\ -1, & a < 0, \end{cases} \tag{3.2}$$

for $a \in R$.

The interconnection weights $\{w_{ij},\ i, j = 1, 2, \ldots, L\}$ form the $L \times L$ symmetric interconnection matrix $\boldsymbol{W} \doteq [w_{ij}]$ which is defined via the *outer-product learning*

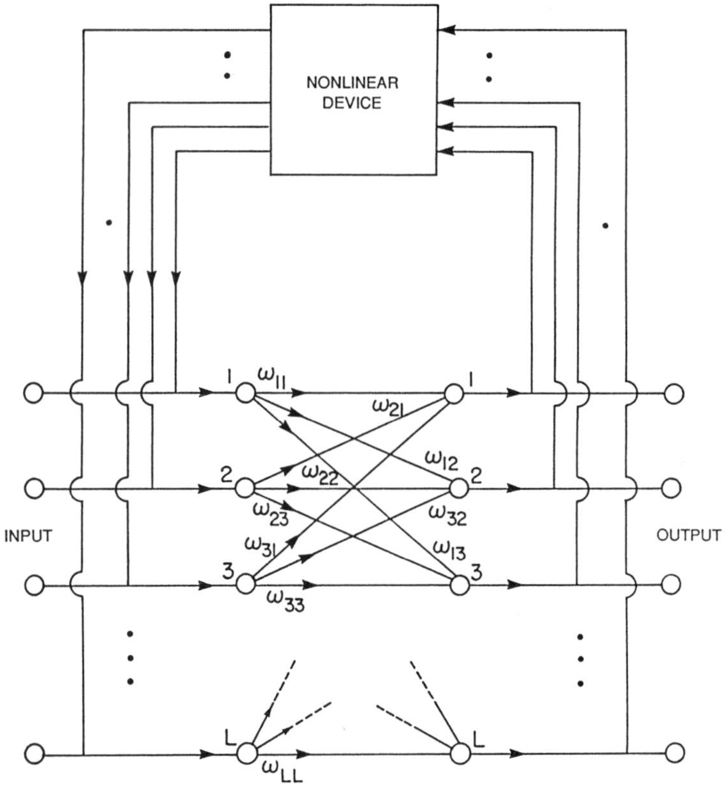

Fig. 3.1. A conceptual diagram of the Hopfield network showing linear and nonlinear operations separately: The input to each node is a weighted sum of the outputs of all neurons. The nonlinear behavior of the neurons is shown separately as a nonlinear device

rule [3.6]:

$$w_{ij} \doteq \begin{cases} \sum_{n=1}^{N} x_{ni}\, x_{nj}\,, & i \neq j \\ 0\,, & i = j\,. \end{cases} \tag{3.3}$$

That is, $\boldsymbol{W} = \boldsymbol{X}\boldsymbol{X}^{\mathrm{T}} - N\boldsymbol{I}$ where $\boldsymbol{X} \doteq [\boldsymbol{x}_1 \boldsymbol{x}_2 \ldots \boldsymbol{x}_N]$ is the matrix whose columns are the library vectors and $\boldsymbol{I}$ denotes the $L \times L$ identity matrix. Note that the *autoconnections* on the nodes are excluded due to the fact that $w_{ii} = 0$. A conceptual diagram of the network is shown in Fig. 3.1, where autoconnections are also indicated for generality. [Note that the nonlinear device in Fig. 3.1 implements some nonlinearity such as the one given by (3.2).] *Hopfield* [3.6] showed that the energy functional E defined by

$$E \doteq -\sum_{i=1}^{L}\sum_{j=1}^{L} w_{ij}\, v_i\, v_j \tag{3.4}$$

decreases monotonically upon the *update rule* given in (3.1) and that the network converges to a stable state corresponding to a local minimum of E. Note that it is this energy minimizing property of the Hopfield network that is made use of when solving optimization problems. This is discussed in Sect. 3.4 in the context of image restoration.

Gindi et al. [3.8] considered the binary Hopfield network which allows for nonzero autoconnections ($w_{ii} = N$) and showed that the stable states of the network remains the same by allowing nonzero diagonal terms in (3.3). Further, the nonzero-diagonal network was shown to outperform the original network [3.8].

It should be emphasized that in both of the zero-diagonal and the nonzero-diagonal cases, the library vectors do not necessarily form stable states. That is, the network states may not converge to themselves when they are initialized by a library vector [3.6–9]. An empirical result [3.2, 6] is that convergence to the library vector occurs with high probability if $N < 0.15L$. It is pointed out in [3.2] that it is relatively easy to select a set of N library vectors that satisfy the condition $N < 0.15L$ and yet do not exhibit self-convergence. However, these vectors usually have many elements in common. The library vectors correspond to stable states of the network if the learning rule defined in (3.3) is modified such that the interconnection matrix is given by [3.3]

$$\boldsymbol{W}' \doteq \boldsymbol{X}\left(\boldsymbol{X}^{\mathrm{T}}\boldsymbol{X}\right)^{-1}\boldsymbol{X}^{\mathrm{T}} . \tag{3.5}$$

This result will be obvious in the case of the generalized projections (GP) formulation to be discussed later.

The interconnection matrix $\boldsymbol{W}'$ was used in [3.3, 15–17] and it is identical to the interconnection matrix associated with the 'orthogonalization learning rule' discussed in [3.3] (see Appendix A). Two things to note here are (i) in the case of linearly independent vectors, the inverse $(\boldsymbol{X}^{\mathrm{T}}\boldsymbol{X})^{-1}$ always exists and (ii) in the case of orthonormal library vectors, $\boldsymbol{W}'$ reduces to $\boldsymbol{W}$ and, therefore, library vectors do correspond to stable states if they are orthonormal.

Before we discuss the set-theoretic formulations of the Hopfield-type ACAM, we briefly review the methods of POCS and GP. To the best of our knowledge, the first to establish a relationship between a particular class of ACAMs and the POCS was *Marks* [3.15, 16]. Marks proposed an ACAM network which extrapolated partially specified, continuous-valued memory patterns by alternating orthogonal projections onto two constraint sets.

3.3.2 The Methods of Projections onto Convex Sets and Generalized Projections

a) Projections onto Convex Sets. Projection onto convex sets (POCS) is an iterative signal recovery algorithm which finds a solution consistent with a number of a priori constraints. In POCS, the unknown signal $\boldsymbol{f}$ is assumed to be an element of an appropriate Hilbert space $\mathcal{H}$. Each a priori constraint restricts the solution to a closed convex set in $\mathcal{H}$. Such constraints are called 'convex-type'. Thus, for m convex-type constraints there are m corresponding closed convex sets C_i, $i = 1,2,..,m$ and $\boldsymbol{f} \in C_0 \doteq \cap_{i=1}^{m} C_i$ provided that the intersection C_0 is nonempty. Given the constraint sets C_i's and their respective projection operators $\boldsymbol{P}_i$'s, the sequence generated by

$$\boldsymbol{f}^{(k+1)} = \boldsymbol{P}_m \boldsymbol{P}_{m-1} \cdots \boldsymbol{P}_1 \boldsymbol{f}^{(k)}, \quad k = 0,1,\dots, \tag{3.6}$$

or more generally by

$$\boldsymbol{f}^{(k+1)} = \boldsymbol{T}_m \boldsymbol{T}_{m-1} \cdots \boldsymbol{T}_1 \boldsymbol{f}^{(k)}, \quad k = 0,1,\dots, \tag{3.7}$$

where $\boldsymbol{T}_i \doteq (1-\lambda_i)\boldsymbol{I}+\lambda_i \boldsymbol{P}_i$ is the relaxed projection operator ($\boldsymbol{I}$ denotes the identity operator), converges weakly to a feasible solution $\hat{\boldsymbol{f}}$ in the intersection C_0 of the constraint sets [3.18]. Note that any point in C_0 is a fixed point of the operator $\boldsymbol{P} \doteq \boldsymbol{P}_m \boldsymbol{P}_{m-1} \cdots \boldsymbol{P}_1$ as well as the operator $\boldsymbol{T} \doteq \boldsymbol{T}_m \boldsymbol{T}_{m-1} \cdots \boldsymbol{T}_1$. The parameter $\lambda_i \in (0,2)$, $i = 1,2,\dots,m$ is the relaxation parameter and for $\lambda_i = 1$, $\boldsymbol{T}_i$'s reduce to $\boldsymbol{P}_i$'s. The initialization $\boldsymbol{f}^{(0)}$ can be arbitrarily chosen from $\mathcal{H}$.

b) Generalized Projections. The generalized projection (GP) algorithm is an extension of the POCS algorithm to cases where a priori constraints are not necessarily convex-type. If one or more of the constraint sets are nonconvex, the convergence of the algorithm given in (3.6) and (3.7) is not guaranteed. However, in the case of two constraints, i.e., $m = 2$, the algorithm enjoys an important property.

Levi et al. [3.19] showed that if one or both of the sets C_1 and C_2 is nonconvex, then the algorithm retains the *set-distance error reduction* (SDER) property. At any iteration, say the kth, we have

$$Z(\boldsymbol{f}^{(k+1)}) \le Z\left(\boldsymbol{T}_1 \boldsymbol{f}^{(k)}\right) \le Z(\boldsymbol{f}^{(k)}), \quad k = 0,1,\dots, \tag{3.8}$$

where the functional Z denotes the sum of the norm distances of its argument from the sets C_1 and C_2. That is, for $\boldsymbol{y}$ arbitrary in $\mathcal{H}$,

$$Z(\boldsymbol{y}) \doteq \|\boldsymbol{P}_1 \boldsymbol{y} - \boldsymbol{y}\| + \|\boldsymbol{P}_2 \boldsymbol{y} - \boldsymbol{y}\| . \tag{3.9}$$

The SDER property holds for a wide range of relaxation parameters including the value of unity [3.19]. The value of Z can be used to monitor the dynamics of the algorithm. Note that Z attains the value of zero if a feasible solution $\hat{\boldsymbol{f}} \in C_0$ is reached.

In this study, signals are associated with vectors representing either the interconnection weights or the input/output states of the neural networks. In the case of the perceptron network, the unknown signal corresponds to the weight vector to be determined. In the case of ACAM, the output state vector of the network corresponds to the unknown signal. We assume that the vectors belong to the Hilbert space $\mathcal{H} = \mathrm{R}^L$ equipped with the usual inner product. For $\boldsymbol{y}, \boldsymbol{z} \in \mathrm{R}^L$, the inner product and norm are defined by

$$\langle \boldsymbol{y}, \boldsymbol{z} \rangle \doteq \sum_{n=1}^{L} y_n \, z_n \tag{3.10}$$

and

$$\|\boldsymbol{y}\| = \langle \boldsymbol{y}, \boldsymbol{y} \rangle^{1/2} , \tag{3.11}$$

respectively. Note that since weak convergence is equivalent to strong convergence in a finite dimensional space, the POCS algorithm is strongly convergent in $\mathbb{R}^L$.

We shall need the GP algorithm in analyzing the stable states of the Hopfield ACAM for binary-valued library vectors.

3.3.3 GP Formulation of the Binary Hopfield ACAM

The Hopfield network that operates according to the state update and learning rules given by

$$\boldsymbol{v}^{(k+1)} = \operatorname{sgn}\left(\boldsymbol{W}\boldsymbol{v}^{(k)}\right) \tag{3.12}$$

and

$$\boldsymbol{W}' = \boldsymbol{X}\left(\boldsymbol{X}^{\mathrm{T}}\boldsymbol{X}\right)^{-1}\boldsymbol{X}^{\mathrm{T}} , \tag{3.13}$$

respectively, can be formulated in terms of GP. The vector $\boldsymbol{v}^{(k)} \doteq [v_1^{(k)} v_2^{(k)} \cdots v_N^{(k)}]$ denotes the state vector and sgn($\cdot$) operates on each component of a vector as in (3.2).

We consider the following sets:

$$C_{\mathrm{sgn}} \doteq \left\{ \boldsymbol{y} \in \mathbb{R}^L : \quad y_i = \pm 1 , \ i = 1, 2, \ldots , \right\} , \tag{3.14}$$

$$C_{\mathrm{s}} \doteq \left\{ \boldsymbol{y} \in \mathbb{R}^L : \quad \boldsymbol{y} = \sum_{n=1}^{N} \alpha_n \boldsymbol{x}_n , \quad \alpha_n \in \mathbb{R} \right\} , \tag{3.15}$$

where $\boldsymbol{x}_n$, $n = 1, 2, \ldots, N$ denote the library vectors. The set C_{sgn} is the set of bipolar vectors in $\mathbb{R}^L$ and corresponds to the set of vertices of a hypercube. C_{sgn} is a closed but nonconvex set. The projection of an arbitrary $\boldsymbol{q} \doteq [q_1 q_2 \cdots q_L]^{\mathrm{T}} \in \mathbb{R}^L$ onto C_{sgn} is given by

$$\boldsymbol{P}_{\mathrm{sgn}}\boldsymbol{q} \doteq \left[\operatorname{sgn}(q_1)\operatorname{sgn}(q_2) \cdots \operatorname{sgn}(q_L)\right]^{\mathrm{T}} . \tag{3.16}$$

On the other hand, the set C_{S} is closed convex in $\mathbb{R}^L$ and defines the subspace spanned by the library vectors. The projection operator projecting onto C_{S} is given by (Appendix B)

$$\boldsymbol{P}_{\mathrm{S}}\boldsymbol{q} \doteq \boldsymbol{X}\left(\boldsymbol{X}^{\mathrm{T}}\boldsymbol{X}\right)^{-1}\boldsymbol{X}^{\mathrm{T}}\boldsymbol{q} . \tag{3.17}$$

From (3.16, 17), the state update rule (3.12) can be expressed as

$$\boldsymbol{v}^{(k+1)} = \boldsymbol{P}_{\mathrm{sgn}}\boldsymbol{P}_{\mathrm{S}}\boldsymbol{v}^{(k)} , \quad k = 0, 1, \ldots \tag{3.18}$$

which is in the form of a generalized projections algorithm. For $\boldsymbol{v}^{(0)} = \boldsymbol{x}_j$, the jth library vector, we have

$$\begin{aligned}\boldsymbol{v}^{(1)} &= \boldsymbol{P}_{\mathrm{sgn}}\boldsymbol{P}_{\mathrm{S}}\boldsymbol{x}_j \\ &= \boldsymbol{P}_{\mathrm{sgn}}\boldsymbol{x}_j \\ &= \boldsymbol{x}_j \, .\end{aligned} \tag{3.19}$$

Therefore, the library vectors correspond to stable states of the network. The state converges to itself after a single iteration when initialized by a library vector. Note that in the case of orthonormal library vectors, (3.18) is equivalent to the operation of the original Hopfield network with zero autoconnections. This analogy was also observed by *Marks* et al. [3.20].

The iteration given in (3.18) enjoys the (SDER) property: at each iteration, the sum of the norm distances of the current iterate from the sets C_{sgn} and C_{S} either decreases or stays the same, i.e.,

$$Z\left(\boldsymbol{v}^{(k+1)}\right) \leq Z\left(\boldsymbol{P}_{\mathrm{S}}\boldsymbol{v}^{(k)}\right) \leq Z\left(\boldsymbol{v}^{(k)}\right) , \tag{3.20}$$

where Z is the set-distance index defined in (3.9). It should be emphasized that the set-distance index can be used to quantitatively categorize the stable states of the network. A stable state, say $\hat{\boldsymbol{v}}$, is reached when no further change is observed in the network state. If $Z(\hat{\boldsymbol{v}}) = 0$, then $\hat{\boldsymbol{v}}$ is in the intersection $C_0 = C_{\mathrm{sgn}} \cap C_{\mathrm{S}}$. However, $\hat{\boldsymbol{v}}$ may not correspond to a library vector. That is, C_0 may contain stable states other than the library vectors.

A typical scenario is illustrated in Fig. 3.2 in the case of $N = 2$, $L = 3$ and orthogonal library vectors. The set C_{sgn} is the set of vertices of the cube and the set C_{S} is a two-dimensional subspace (a plane) in R^3. Thus, $C_0 = C_{\mathrm{sgn}} \cap C_{\mathrm{S}}$ is the set of vertices that lie on the plane. Observe that only two out of four vertices in C_0 correspond to library vectors $\boldsymbol{x}_1$ and $\boldsymbol{x}_2$. In Fig. 3.2, two cases are illustrated:

(i) the stable state vector $\hat{\boldsymbol{v}} = \hat{\boldsymbol{v}}_1$ corresponds to the library vector $\boldsymbol{x}_2$, and

(ii) the stable state vector $\hat{\boldsymbol{v}} = \hat{\boldsymbol{v}}_2$, reached with a different initialization, does *not* correspond to a library vector ('no-match'condition). The best strategy to handle the 'no-match' condition is a further research topic. A possible strategy however, which may not be the best in general, is to compute the Hamming distance between the non-matching stable state and the library vectors for all patterns and select the pattern with the minimum Hamming distance. This strategy can be implemented using the MAXNET network discussed in [3.2, 3]. In Fig. 3.2, this strategy would result in $\boldsymbol{x}_1$ in the case of $\hat{\boldsymbol{v}} = \hat{\boldsymbol{v}}_2$.

If, on the other hand, the stable state $\hat{\boldsymbol{v}}$ is such that $Z(\hat{\boldsymbol{v}}) > 0$, then $\hat{\boldsymbol{v}} \notin C_0$ and the network is said to be in a 'trap' (clearly, $\hat{\boldsymbol{v}}$ cannot be a library vector.) The trap situation can be explained by the *nonconvexity* of the set C_{sgn}. In general, the GP algorithm may undergo a trap situation due to the nonconvexity of one or more sets. A trap situation due to the nonconvexity of one set, in the case of two hypothetical sets in the plane, is illustrated in Fig. 3.3. In this case, the algorithm stabilizes on the line l, at the boundary of either C_1 or C_2. Some strategies to

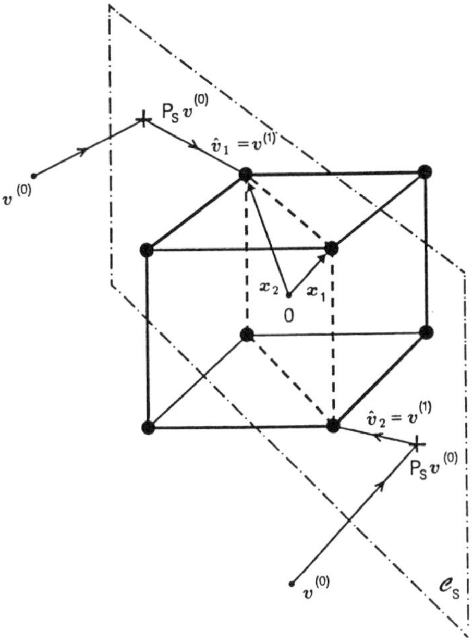

Fig. 3.2. Demonstration of the possible stable states that lie in the set intersection in the case of $N = 3$ and $L = 2$. The stable state $\hat{\boldsymbol{v}}_2 = \boldsymbol{v}^{(1)}$ reached by the network does not correspond to a library vector. However, the stable state $\hat{\boldsymbol{v}}_1 = \boldsymbol{v}^{(1)}$, reached as a result of changing the initialization point, corresponds to the library vector $\boldsymbol{x}_2$

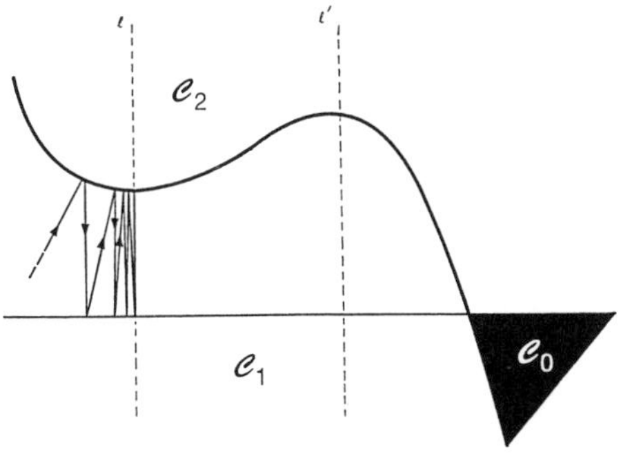

Fig. 3.3. Illustration of a trap situation occurring because of the nonconvexity of the set C_2. Note that if the algorithm has been initialized with a point that lies to the right of line l', the trap could have been avoided

get out of a trap are discussed in [3.19]. The simplest strategy to avoid a trap is to modify the initialization (e.g., by adding random noise) and repeat the process. Note that in Fig. 3.3, the trap situation can be avoided by selecting an initialization point that lies to the right of line l'. However, a quantitative and general method of avoiding traps is yet to be determined.

3.3.4 POCS Formulation of a Continuous Hopfield ACAM

We consider a direct extension of the binary-valued network to the case of continuous-valued library vectors. We assume that $-1 \leq x_{ni} \leq 1$, $n = 1, 2, \ldots, N$; $i = 1, 2, \ldots, L$. A direct continuous-valued extension of the network described in (3.12) and (3.13) can be defined as

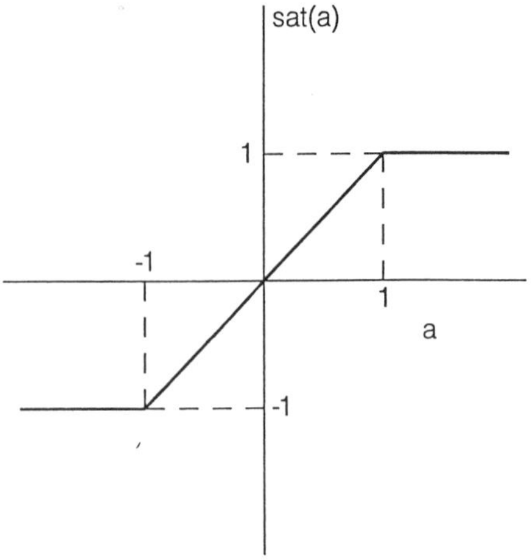

Fig. 3.4. The unity-slope saturation nonlinearity used in the continuous-valued extension of the Binary Hopfield ACAM

$$\hat{\boldsymbol{v}}^{(k+1)} = \mathrm{sat}\left(\boldsymbol{W}'\boldsymbol{v}^{(k)}\right) , \tag{3.21}$$

and

$$\boldsymbol{W}' = \boldsymbol{X}\left(\boldsymbol{X}^{\mathrm{T}}\boldsymbol{X}\right)^{-1}\boldsymbol{X}^{\mathrm{T}} , \tag{3.22}$$

where sat(·) is the unity-slope saturation nonlinearity whose action on the vector $\boldsymbol{y}^{(k)} \doteq \boldsymbol{W}'\boldsymbol{v}^{(k)}$ is defined by

$$\mathrm{sat}\left(\boldsymbol{y}^{(k)}\right) \doteq \left[\mathrm{sat}\left(y_1^{(k)}\right) \ \mathrm{sat}\left(y_2^{(k)}\right) \cdots \mathrm{sat}\left(y_L^{(k)}\right)\right] \tag{3.23}$$

and

$$\mathrm{sat}\left(y_i^{(k)}\right) \doteq \begin{cases} -1 , & y_i^{(k)} < -1 \\ y_i^{(k)} , & -1 \leq y_i^{(k)} \leq 1 \\ 1 , & y_i^{(k)} > 1 . \end{cases} \tag{3.24}$$

The sat(·) nonlinearity is illustrated in Fig. 3.4.

We consider the following sets:

$$C_{\mathrm{sat}} \doteq \left\{\boldsymbol{v} \in \mathsf{R}^L : \ -1 \leq y_i \leq 1, \quad i = 1,2,\dots L\right\} , \tag{3.25}$$

$$C_{\mathrm{S}} \doteq \left\{\boldsymbol{y} \in \mathsf{R}^L : \ \boldsymbol{y} = \sum_{n=1}^{N} \alpha_n \boldsymbol{x}_n , \quad \alpha_n \in \mathsf{R}\right\} , \tag{3.26}$$

where $\boldsymbol{x}_n$, $n = 1,2,\dots N$ are the library vectors. The set C_{sat} is a closed convex set and defines an L-dimensional hypercube. The projection of an arbitrary $\boldsymbol{q} \in \mathsf{R}^L$ onto C_{sat} is given by [3.21]

$$\boldsymbol{P}_{\mathrm{sat}}\boldsymbol{q} = \mathrm{sat}(\boldsymbol{q}) . \tag{3.27}$$

The set C_{S} is the same set defined in the binary-valued case because the learning

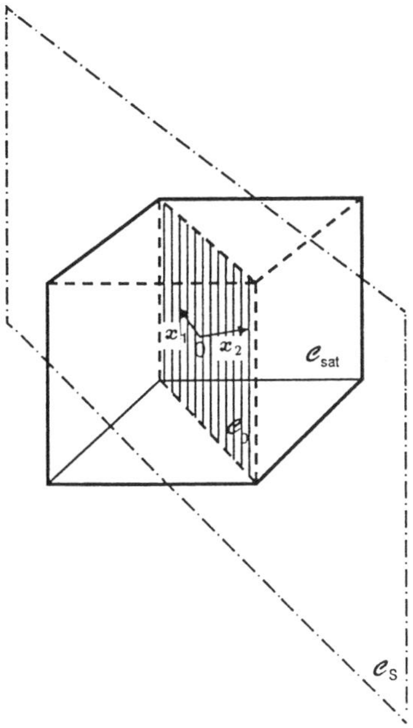

Fig. 3.5. The set of stable states in the case of the continuous-valued extension of the binary Hopfield ACAM for $N = 3$ and $L = 2$

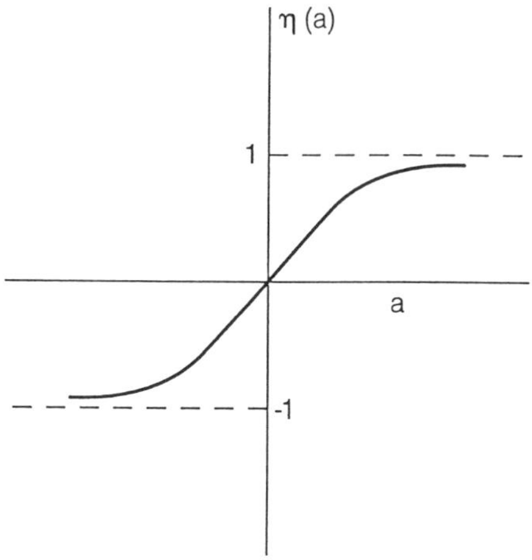

Fig. 3.6. The sigmoidal nonlinearity used in the continuous-valued, continuous-time Hopfield ACAM

rule is the same in both the binary and continuous-valued cases. Thus, from (3.17) and (3.27), the state update rule given in (3.21) can be expressed as

$$\boldsymbol{v}^{(k+1)} = \boldsymbol{P}_{\text{sat}} \boldsymbol{P}_{\text{S}} \boldsymbol{v}^{(k)}, \qquad k = 0, 1, \dots \tag{3.28}$$

which is indeed in the form of a POCS algorithm.

Therefore, for an arbitrary initialization, the network state converges to a stable state vector in $C_0 \doteq C_{\text{sat}} \cap C_{\text{S}}$. That is, the set of stable states corresponds to the set of points common to both the hypercube and the subspace spanned by the library vectors. The set C_0 is illustrated in Fig. 3.5 for the case of $N = 2$ and $L = 3$. As in the binary case, the network state may converge to a vector in C_0, which is not a library vector. In that case, the closest library vector (in the $\mathbf{R}^L$-norm sense) can be taken as the solution. Here too, the best strategy to handle the 'no-match' condition is a further research topic. Finally, note that a trap situation does not occur in the POCS formulation.

The convergence properties of the direct continuous extension is similar to Hopfield's continuous-valued, continuous-time model where he showed that the energy-minimizing stable states lie within the L-dimensional hypercube in the case of sigmoidal nonlinearity (Fig. 3.6) [3.7].

3.3.5 The Hopfield-Type Classifier: The ACAM Followed by a Perceptron

As stated earlier, a Hopfield ACAM can be modified to function as a classifier by following the Hopfield ACAM by a perceptron (Fig. 3.7). When used as an ACAM, the Hopfield network takes the degraded input at time $k = 0$ and furnishes ideally, upon convergence, one of the stored library vectors. For the Hopfield model to work as a classifier it is necessary to add a mechanism that determines which of the, say K, classes the output belongs to. This has to be done because the Hopfield network by itself is not a neural network classifier. It still requires a classification network to select which of K classes a pattern is closest to. The classification itself can be done by following the Hopfield network with a perceptron network. A Hopfield neural network classifier for K classes is shown in Fig. 3.7; there the exemplars (library vectors) are shown to be L-dimensional vectors.

The design of a perceptron depends on several factors including the choice of cost functions to be optimized. In Fig. 3.7 the input to the perceptron is the vector $\boldsymbol{x}' = [x'_1, x'_2, \ldots, x'_L]^{\mathrm{T}}$ and the output is the vector $\boldsymbol{y} = [y_1, y_2, ..., y_K]^{\mathrm{T}}$. Typically the perceptron action is described by

$$y_j = \eta\left(c_j + \sum_i w_{ij}\, x'_i\right), \qquad j = 1, 2, \ldots, K \tag{3.29}$$

where $\eta(a)$ is some nonlinear function, e.g., $\eta(a) = au(a)$, $u(a)$ being the unit step

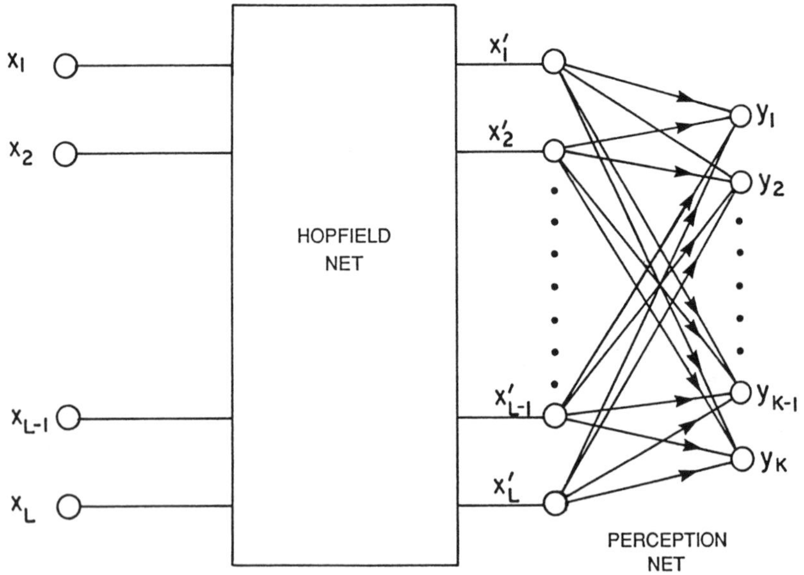

Fig. 3.7. Hopfield-type classifier: Hopfield network followed by a perceptron to perform classification into K classes

function, c_j is the bias associated with the jth output neuron, and w_{ij} are real-valued weights associated with the links. For example, suppose the cost function to be minimized is the Hamming distance, and the components of $\boldsymbol{x}'$ are ± 1's. If it is known a priori that the variability in the $\boldsymbol{x}$ vectors is caused by the statistics of the binary symmetric channel, then with

$$c_j = \Delta - L/2 \tag{3.30}$$

and

$$w_{ij} = x_i^j/2\ , \tag{3.31}$$

where x_i^j is the ith component of an exemplar of class j, only output nodes corresponding to prototypes with a Hamming distance less than Δ from the input will have positive outputs [3.3].

If the mechanism for intra-class variability is not known, then the perceptron must learn the correct weights from training samples. The algorithm for teaching the perceptron the correct weights depends on the cost function used, whether the training samples form separable classes, and the means used to extremize the cost function. In what follows we discuss a perceptron learning algorithm (PLA) for the linearly separable, two-class case.

Suppose that we have a set of N training samples, $\boldsymbol{x}_n$, $n = 1, 2, \ldots, N$, represented by L-dimensional vectors in the Euclidean space R^L equipped with the usual inner product and norm. We assume that the samples belong to two classes denoted by A and B. A PLA determines the weight vector $\boldsymbol{w}$ which defines a linear discriminant functional g as

$$g(\boldsymbol{y}) \doteq \langle \boldsymbol{w}, \boldsymbol{y} \rangle\ , \tag{3.32}$$

such that any sample $\boldsymbol{x}_j$ is classified correctly if any of the two conditions is satisfied:

$$\langle \boldsymbol{w}, \boldsymbol{x}_j \rangle > 0 \quad \text{and} \quad \boldsymbol{x}_j \in A\ ,$$
$$\langle \boldsymbol{w}, \boldsymbol{x}_j \rangle < 0 \quad \text{and} \quad \boldsymbol{x}_j \in B\ .$$

Clearly, if the samples that belong to B are replaced by their negatives, the weight vector satisfies

$$\langle \boldsymbol{w}, \boldsymbol{x}_n \rangle > 0\ , \qquad n = 1, 2, \ldots, N\ . \tag{3.33}$$

If such a weight vector exists, the classes A and B are said to be 'linearly separable'. The equation $\langle \boldsymbol{w}, \boldsymbol{x} \rangle = 0$, $\boldsymbol{x} \in \mathrm{R}^L$ defines a separating hyperplane in R^L.

The separating weight vector is, in general, not unique. The set of admissible weight vectors can be constrained by introducing a margin M. In that case (3.33) is replaced by

$$\langle \boldsymbol{w}, \boldsymbol{x}_n \rangle > M\ , \qquad n = 1, 2, \ldots, N\ . \tag{3.34}$$

If a weight vector satisfying (3.34) exists, the classes are said to be linearly separable with a margin M. Here too, the separating vector is not unique, but any solution satisfying the margin M is clearly preferred to one that offers none.

a) A Perceptron Learning Algorithm and Its POCS Formulation. A perceptron learning algorithm (PLA) for the two-class, linearly separable problem has been derived in [3.22] as a result of solving the following minimization problem:

$$\min_{\boldsymbol{w}} \left(\sum_{n \in \mathcal{N}} \frac{(\langle \boldsymbol{w}, \boldsymbol{x}_n > -M)^2}{\|\boldsymbol{x}_n\|^2} \right) \tag{3.35}$$

where $\mathcal{N}$ is the index set corresponding to the indices of misclassified samples, i.e., $\langle \boldsymbol{w}, \boldsymbol{x}_n \rangle < M$ for $n \in \mathcal{N}$. A basic iterative descent procedure on (3.35) yields [3.22]

$$\boldsymbol{w}^{(k+1)} = \boldsymbol{w}^{(k)} + \lambda_{l(k)} \frac{M - v_{l(k)}}{\|\boldsymbol{x}_{l(k)}\|^2} \boldsymbol{x}_{l(k)} , \tag{3.36}$$

where

$$v_{l(k)} \doteq \eta\left(\langle \boldsymbol{w}, \boldsymbol{x}_{l(k)} \rangle\right) , \tag{3.37}$$

$$l(k) \doteq N \text{ modulo}(k) + 1 \tag{3.38}$$

and η is a nonlinear function defined by

$$\eta(a) \doteq \begin{cases} M , & a \geq M \\ a, & a < M . \end{cases} \tag{3.39}$$

N modulo(k) denotes the remainder obtained on division of k by N and is one of the integers $0, 1, \ldots, N-1$. The parameter $\lambda_{l(k)}$ is the relaxation parameter.

Thus, learning is achieved by updating the weight vector according to (3.36–39) when a sample is misclassified. If after a number of iterations the value of the weight vector, say $\hat{\boldsymbol{w}}$, is not updated for any of the given samples, then the PLA is said to converge to $\hat{\boldsymbol{w}}$. In the case of separable classes, the iteration given in (3.36) is convergent provided that $\lambda_{l(k)} \in (0, 2)$ [3.22]. The perceptron network defined by (3.36–39) is illustrated in Fig. 3.8. The connection weight vector $\boldsymbol{w} = [w_1, w_2, \ldots, w_L]^{\mathrm{T}}$ can be determined using (3.36).

The POCS formulation can be obtained by defining the family of constraint sets C_n, $n = 1, 2, \ldots, N$:

$$C_n \doteq \left\{ \boldsymbol{y} \in \mathrm{R}^L : \ \langle \boldsymbol{y}, \boldsymbol{x}_n \rangle \geq M \right\} \tag{3.40}$$

where $\boldsymbol{x}_n$ is the nth training sample and M is the predetermined margin. For any n, the set C_n is closed convex and the corresponding projection operator $\boldsymbol{P}_n$ is defined by [3.23]

$$\boldsymbol{P}_n \boldsymbol{q} \doteq \boldsymbol{q} + \frac{M - v_n}{\|\boldsymbol{x}_n\|^2} \boldsymbol{x}_n , \tag{3.41}$$

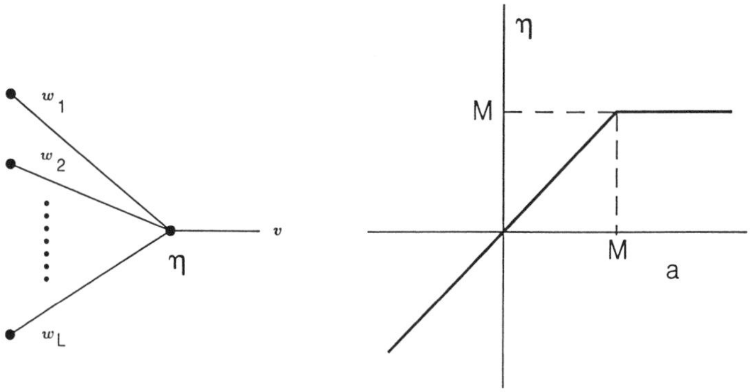

Fig. 3.8. The perceptron network for linearly separable classes

where

$$v_n \doteq \eta\big(\langle \boldsymbol{q}, \boldsymbol{x}_n \rangle\big) , \tag{3.42}$$

and $\boldsymbol{q}$ is arbitrary in R^L. The relaxed projection operator $\boldsymbol{T}_n$ is given by

$$\begin{aligned} \boldsymbol{T}_n \boldsymbol{q} &= \big(1 - \lambda_n\big)\boldsymbol{I} + \lambda_n \boldsymbol{P}_n \\ &= \boldsymbol{q} - \lambda_n \boldsymbol{q} + \lambda_n \boldsymbol{q} + \lambda_n \frac{M - v_n}{\|\boldsymbol{x}_n\|^2} \boldsymbol{x}_n \\ &= \boldsymbol{q} + \lambda_n \frac{M - v_n}{\|\boldsymbol{x}_n\|^2} \boldsymbol{x}_n \, . \end{aligned} \tag{3.43}$$

Now, if we assume that the classes are separable, a separating weight vector exists and belongs to the intersection $C_0 = \cap_{n=1}^{N} C_n$. Therefore, the sequence $\{\boldsymbol{w}^{(k)}\}$ generated by the POCS algorithm

$$\boldsymbol{w}^{(k+1)} = \boldsymbol{T}_N \boldsymbol{T}_{N-1} \cdots \boldsymbol{T}_1 \boldsymbol{w}^{(k)}, \quad k = 0, 1, \dots \tag{3.44}$$

converges to a separating vector $\hat{\boldsymbol{w}} \in C_0$. But the algorithm given in (3.44) is equivalent to that given in (3.36). In particular, one iteration cycle of the POCS algorithm (N projections) corresponds to N iterations of the PLA given in (3.36).

The POCS formulation has two important consequences:

(i) the convex projections theory allows for additional constraints to further constrain the admissible set of weight vectors,

(ii) the convex projections theory provides an optimum lower bound on the value of the relaxation parameters. (A 'good' choice of relaxation parameters increases the convergence rate).

If a desirable property of the weight vector corresponds to a convex-type constraint, it can be incorporated into the POCS-based learning algorithm. For instance, the orientation of the separating hyperplanes can be constrained such that the angle between the weight vector and the Fisher discriminant direction $\boldsymbol{w}_{\mathrm{F}}$ [3.22] does

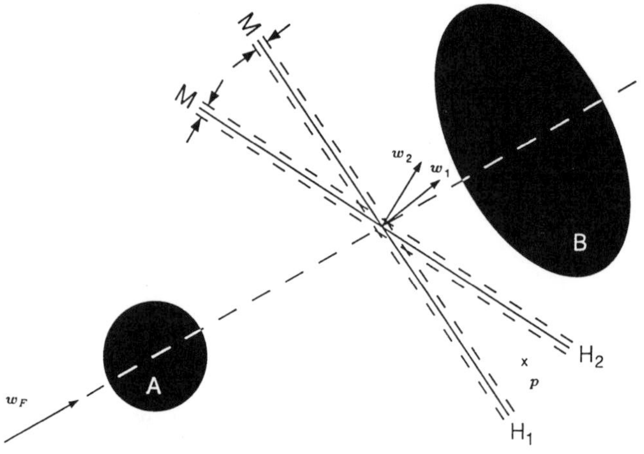

Fig. 3.9. Demonstration of the improvement in the performance of the perceptron due to an additional angle constraint. In the absence of an angle constraint, H_2 could have been a feasible separating hyperplane, in which case the point $\boldsymbol{p}$ could have been incorrectly classified to class A. However, with an appropriate angle constraint in force, H_2 cannot be a feasible solution

not exceed a predetermined value. The closed convex constraint set restricting the *cosine* of the angle between $\boldsymbol{w}$ and $\boldsymbol{w}_\mathrm{F}$ to be at least β is defined as [3.24]

$$C_\beta \doteq \left\{ \boldsymbol{y} \in \mathrm{R}^L : \frac{|\langle \boldsymbol{y}, \boldsymbol{w}_\mathrm{F} \rangle|}{\|\boldsymbol{w}_\mathrm{F}\|} \geq \beta \|\boldsymbol{y}\| \right\} . \tag{3.45}$$

The projection operator projecting onto C_β is derived in [3.24].

The rationale of the angle constraint is illustrated in the case of a hypothetical situation shown in Fig. 3.9. In Fig. 3.9 both H_1 and H_2 are valid separating hyperplanes defined by the normal weight vectors $\boldsymbol{w}_1$ and $\boldsymbol{w}_2$, respectively. The angle between $\boldsymbol{w}_1$ and $\boldsymbol{w}_\mathrm{F}$ is smaller than the angle between $\boldsymbol{w}_2$ and $\boldsymbol{w}_\mathrm{F}$. Note that the point $\boldsymbol{p}$, which intuitively is more likely to belong to class B, is correctly classified by the H_1 separating hyperplane but incorrectly classified by H_2. Without the additional angle constraint on the weight vector, H_2 would have been as likely to have been chosen as H_1 but, with the angle constraint in force, H_2 would not have been a feasible solution.

An optimum lower bound for the relaxation parameters has been derived in [3.25]. The so-called 'per-step' optimization procedure results in [3.25]

$$\lambda_n^\mathrm{opt} \geq 1 , \quad n = 1, 2, \ldots, N . \tag{3.46}$$

Thus, the allowable $(0, 2)$ range for the relaxation parameters can be constrained to the $[1, 2)$ range. *Kumaradjaja* [3.23] reported significant improvement in the convergence rate of the PLA when $\lambda_n \in [1, 2)$ as opposed to $\lambda_n \in (0, 1)$.

3.4 Image Restoration Using a Hopfield-Type Neural Network

In the previous section, Hopfield-type networks have been used to implement ACAMs. A Hopfield ACAM can be used as an image storage device in which stored images can be retrieved by their incomplete and/or distorted versions [3.26], or as a part of an image classifier. The other important application of Hopfield networks in image processing is the restoration of blurred and noisy images. This application is based on the following two facts:

1) Using the network parameters, i.e., states, interconnections and biases, one can define the energy of a Hopfield network [3.6, 7, 9]. Under certain conditions, which are discussed in the following, the energy functional always decreases upon the state update of any neuron.

2) Tikhonov-Miller type image restoration algorithms [3.27] (e.g., constrained least squares restoration) that optimize a convex objective functional subject to convex constraint(s) result in Lagrangians which are convex functionals. Thus, the stationary (zero derivative) point of the Lagrangian corresponds to its minimum.

Therefore, the key idea in using a Hopfield network for image restoration is to specify the network parameters such that the energy functional is identical to the Lagrangian of the image restoration problem. Indeed, one also needs to specify an image representation expressed in terms of the states of the neurons.

Zhou et al. [3.11, 12] have shown the feasibility of using a Hopfield network as an optimizer for image restoration. We further propose a learning algorithm that enables the network to learn the Lagrange multipliers associated with the constraints. We show that both learning and restoration can be implemented by the same network structure by changing only the external biases to the neurons.

3.4.1 Energy Reduction Property and Stable States

Hopfield [3.6, 7, 9] defined the energy function of the neural network with interconnection w_{ij} and bias b_i to each neuron to be

$$E = -\frac{1}{2}\sum_{i=1}^{L}\sum_{j=1}^{L} w_{ij}\, v_i\, v_j - \sum_{i=1}^{L} b_i\, v_i\ . \tag{3.47}$$

In his model, the neurons have no self-feedback, i.e., the autoconnections, w_{ii}, $i = 1, 2, \dots L$ are zero, and each neuron updates its state randomly in time (asynchronously) according to the hard-limit nonlinearity update rule given in (3.2), i.e.,

$$\begin{cases} \sum_{j=1}^{L} w_{ij}\, v_j + b_i \geq 0 \Rightarrow v_i^{\text{new}} = 1\ , \\ \sum_{j=1}^{L} w_{ij}\, v_j + b_i < 0 \Rightarrow v_i^{\text{new}} = 0\ , \end{cases} \tag{3.48}$$

where binary states are assumed.

Hopfield showed that if $w_{ii} = 0$ and the inter-connections are symmetric ($w_{ij} = w_{ji}$), then the energy change due to the state update of any neuron is always zero or negative. This is the so called energy reduction property. This energy landscape view and the energy reduction property are useful in solving signal processing problems since they often involve finding the extrema of some objective functions. However, the condition of zero autoconnections is usually too restrictive in applications. Actually it has been shown that the energy reduction property still holds when the autoconnections are positive [3.8, 3.28]. This fact can be observed by considering the energy change due to the update of a neuron, say the rth neuron. Let $v_r^{\text{new}} = v_r^{\text{old}} + \Delta v_r$, and $\Delta E_r = E_r^{\text{new}} - E_r^{\text{old}}$ denote the energy change due to this update. Using (3.47) and the symmetry property of interconnections we obtain

$$\Delta E_r = -(\Delta v_r)\left(\sum_{i=1}^{L} w_{ri}\, v_i^{\text{old}} + b_r\right) - \frac{1}{2} w_{rr} (\Delta v_r)^2 . \tag{3.49}$$

The first term on the right-hand side is always negative (or zero if $\sum_{i=1}^{L} w_{ri}\, v_i^{\text{old}} + b_r = 0$) because the signs of Δv_r and $\sum_{i=1}^{L} w_{ri}\, v_i^{\text{old}} + b_r$ are identical according to the update rule (3.48). The second term is always negative if $w_{rr} > 0$. Thus, the network has the energy reduction property if the autoconnections are nonnegative.

The energy reduction property guarantees that local minima in the energy landscape are stable states of the neural network. Less obvious is the answer to the question: Do stable states always correspond to local minima in the energy landscape? In other words, is there any stable state which is not a local minimum? The energy difference of a stable state and a neighbor state which differs from the stable state in the nth neuron state (say v_n for the stable state and v_n' for the neighbor state, respectively) is

$$E' - E^{\text{stable}} = -(v_n' - v_n)\left(\sum_{j=1}^{L} w_{nj}\, v_j + b_n\right) - \frac{1}{2} w_{nn} . \tag{3.50}$$

The first term $-(v_n' - v_n)(\sum_{j=1}^{L} w_{ij}\, v_j + b_n)$ is positive because the neighboring state is not reachable from the stable state. (Note that if this term were negative or zero, then an update could occur, which contradicts with the assumption of a stable state.) If w_{nn} is positive, the energy difference may still be negative, i.e., the stable state may have higher energy than one of its neighbors. If, however, w_{nn} is zero or negative, then the stable state always has lower energy than its neighbors. Therefore, we can only conclude that when the autoconnections are zero or negative, stable states always occur at local minima. However, it should be noted that in the case of strictly negative autoconnections it is also possible that the system does not reach a stable state since the energy may increase or decrease upon the update of a neuron state.

We now summarize these results about the relationship between stable states and energy local minima.

Fact 1: If $w_{ij} = w_{ji}$ and $w_{ii} \geq 0$, then any neuron-state update according to the update rule (3.48) will monotonically decrease the energy of the system. Therefore local minima of the energy function are stable states. But if there is some w_{ii} strictly positive, then stable states may not all occur at local minima.

Fact 2: If $w_{ij} = w_{ji}$ and $w_{ii} \leq 0$, then all stable states are local minima. But if there is some w_{ii} strictly negative, then the energy reduction property does not always hold if neurons are updated according to (3.48); therefore there may be local minima which do not correspond to stable states. Furthermore, the system may not always be able to reach a stable state.

Fact 3: If $w_{ij} = w_{ji}$ and $w_{ii} = 0$, then stable states and local minima are identical, and the energy reduction property holds.

In the following image restoration application, the diagonal terms w_{ii} are all negative. Hence the original update rule (3.48) does not guarantee that all local minima are stable, and therefore the energy reduction property may not hold. It is necessary to modify the update rule to enforce energy reduction during the iterations, ensuring the existence of a stable state and making local minima stable. This modified update rule will be described in the next subsection. With such a modification, local minima are forced to be stable states, and all stable states are local minima due to the fact that w_{ii} are non-positive for all i's (see Fact 2). Therefore, stable states and local minima become equivalent in this case.

3.4.2 Network Model for Image Restoration

Here, we summarize the neural network model for image restoration proposed by *Zhou* et al. [3.11, 12]. An $L \times L$ image is represented in the neural network by its gray levels. The gray level $x(i,j)$ at pixel location (i,j), $1 \leq i,j \leq L$, is represented by M binary-valued neurons in the network through a simple sum number representation scheme [3.29]

$$x(i,j) = \sum_{k=1}^{M} v_{m,k} \ , \tag{3.51}$$

where $m \doteq (i-1) \times L + j$ and $v_{m,k}$ denotes the state of the (m,k)th neuron, which is either 0 or 1. The number of neurons required to represent an $L \times L$ image is ML^2. Note that this sum number scheme has degenerate representations for image gray levels; that is, a gray level can be represented by several different combinations of neuron states. This redundancy offers the advantage of high fault-tolerance and more chances to reach a solution [3.29].

Using the lexicographic notation, the image degradation model can be written as

$$\boldsymbol{g} = \boldsymbol{D}\boldsymbol{f} + \boldsymbol{n} \ , \tag{3.52}$$

where $\boldsymbol{g}$ is the degraded image vector, $\boldsymbol{f}$ is the original image vector, $\boldsymbol{n}$ is the observation noise vector, and $\boldsymbol{D}$ is the block Toeplitz blur matrix.

A constrained least-squares estimate of the actual image is obtained as the solution of

$$\begin{array}{ll} \text{minimize} & \|\boldsymbol{D}\boldsymbol{x} - \boldsymbol{g}\|^2 \\ \text{subject to} & \|\boldsymbol{C}\boldsymbol{x}\|^2 \le \varepsilon \end{array}$$

where $\boldsymbol{x}$ denotes the lexicographical representation of an arbitrary image, and the operator $\boldsymbol{C}$ and the parameter ε are chosen such that the constraint reflects some a priori information about the actual image. Some of the commonly used operators for $\boldsymbol{C}$ are a discrete approximation of the Laplacian operator $\boldsymbol{L}$, or the identity operator $\boldsymbol{I}$. The case $\boldsymbol{C} = \boldsymbol{L}$ assumes that the actual image is 'smooth'. When $\boldsymbol{C} = \boldsymbol{L}$, the energy of the image is assumed to be bounded above by ε.

The Lagrangian of the problem can be written as

$$\begin{aligned} J(\boldsymbol{x}) &= \tfrac{1}{2}\|\boldsymbol{D}\boldsymbol{x} - \boldsymbol{g}\|^2 + \tfrac{1}{2}\gamma\left(\|\boldsymbol{C}\boldsymbol{x}\|^2 - \varepsilon\right) \\ &= \tfrac{1}{2}\boldsymbol{x}^{\mathrm{T}}\left(\boldsymbol{D}^{\mathrm{T}}\boldsymbol{D} + \gamma\boldsymbol{C}^{\mathrm{T}}\boldsymbol{C}\right)\boldsymbol{x} - \boldsymbol{x}^{\mathrm{T}}\boldsymbol{D}^{\mathrm{T}}\boldsymbol{g} + \tfrac{1}{2}\left(\|\boldsymbol{g}\|^2 - \gamma\varepsilon\right) \end{aligned} \tag{3.53}$$

where $\gamma \ge 0$ is the Lagrange multiplier. The Lagrangian is a convex functional, and therefore, in principle, the solution occurs at the minimum of J. The solution, $\hat{\boldsymbol{f}}$, satisfies the Euler equation [3.27], i.e.,

$$\hat{\boldsymbol{f}} = \left(\boldsymbol{D}^{\mathrm{T}}\boldsymbol{D} + \gamma\boldsymbol{C}^{\mathrm{T}}\boldsymbol{C}\right)^{-1}\boldsymbol{D}^{\mathrm{T}}\boldsymbol{g}\,. \tag{3.54}$$

(It can be shown that if $\boldsymbol{C}^{-1}$ exists, then $(\boldsymbol{D}^{\mathrm{T}}\boldsymbol{D} + \gamma\boldsymbol{C}^{\mathrm{T}}\boldsymbol{C})^{-1}$ also exists [3.27].)

Now, if we represent the components of the image vector $\boldsymbol{x}$ as in (3.51): $\{x_m = \sum_{k=1}^{M} v_{m,k}\}_{m=1,\dots,L^2}$, we can rewrite the Lagrangian as

$$\begin{aligned} J(\boldsymbol{x}) &= \frac{1}{2}\sum_{i=1}^{L^2}\sum_{j=1}^{L^2}\sum_{p=1}^{L^2} x_i x_j\left[d_{p,i}\,d_{p,j} + \gamma c_{p,i}\,c_{p,j}\right] - \sum_{i=1}^{L^2}\sum_{j=1}^{L^2} x_i\,d_{j,i}\,g_j \\ &= \frac{1}{2}\sum_{i=1}^{L^2}\sum_{k=1}^{M}\sum_{j=1}^{L^2}\sum_{l=1}^{M} v_{i,k}\,v_{j,l}\left[\sum_{p=1}^{L^2} d_{p,i}\,d_{p,j} + \gamma\sum_{p=1}^{L^2} c_{p,i}\,c_{p,j}\right] \\ &\quad - \sum_{i=1}^{L^2}\sum_{k=1}^{M} v_{i,k}\left[\sum_{j=1}^{L^2} d_{j,i}\,g_j\right]\,, \end{aligned} \tag{3.55}$$

where $d_{\cdot,\cdot}$ and $c_{\cdot,\cdot}$ denote the elements of the corresponding matrices, and the third term in (3.53) is dropped for simplicity because it does not affect the location of the extrema. Comparing (3.55) with the definition of the energy function (3.47), one sees that the functional to be minimized can be identified as the energy function of the network whose interconnection weight [from neuron (j,l) to neuron (i,k)] is given by

$$w_{i,k;j,l} = -\sum_{p=1}^{L^2}\left(d_{p,i}\,d_{p,j} + \gamma\,c_{p,i}\,c_{p,j}\right), \quad i,j = 1,\dots,L^2\,,\ k,l = 1,\dots,M\,, \tag{3.56}$$

and whose bias to neuron (i, k) is

$$b_{i,k} = \sum_{j=1}^{L^2} d_{j,i}\, g_j \ . \tag{3.57}$$

In this Hopfield-type neural network, the image blurring model and the constraint are encoded in the connection weights, and the degraded image is encoded in the biases applied to the neurons. It should be noted that the autoconnections $w_{i,k;i,k}$ are negative, non-zero quantities. The connections and biases of the M neurons associated with an image pixel are all the same, i.e., $w_{i,k;j,l}$ is independent of k, l, and $b_{i,k}$ is independent of k. In other words, those M neurons which are associated with the same image pixel are indistinguishable in the neural network system. In the following, we drop the subscript k and l to simplify the notation when it does not cause confusion.

3.4.3 Remarks on the Restoration Network

Due to the discrete-valued image representation (3.51), the objective functional (3.55) may have local minima as well as the global minimum, and the solution may not exactly satisfy (3.54). Thus, the network may stabilize at a 'near optimum' solution. (In appendices 3.A.1, 2 we assume that (3.54) is satisfied to make derivations mathematically tractable. Our experiments confirm that this is a reasonable assumption.) In any event, it is indeed desirable to have all local minima and stable states coincide. Since the autoconnections are negative, we have two potential problems:

(i) stable states of the network may occur at only some of the local minima (Fact 2), and

(ii) the network may not be able to reach to a stable state at all. Both of these problems are induced by the fact that the energy reduction property may not hold with negative autoconnections (Fact 1). To enforce the energy reduction property, and, at the same time, maintain the form of the energy function as in (3.55), a modification on the update rule has to be introduced. The simplest way to achieve these is to update the state of a neuron according to (3.48) only if that update will decrease the energy. That is, if

$$\Delta E_i = \Delta E_{i,k} = -\left(\Delta v_{i,k}\right)\left[\sum_{j=1}^{L^2}\sum_{l=1}^{M} w_{i,k;j,l}\, v_{j,l} + b_{i,k}\right] - \tfrac{1}{2} w_{i,k;i,k}\, (\Delta v_{i,k})^2 \leq 0 \ , \tag{3.58}$$

then the update is executed; if $\Delta E_i > 0$, then the update is not executed. In other words, the neural network has to have an inner mechanism to monitor the 'trial' energy change. This is the deterministic update rule used in [3.11, 12]. However, we have found that the condition on ΔE_i can be transformed into a condition on the total input u_i to neuron $(i, \cdot)$, the latter given by

$$u_i \doteq \sum_{j=1}^{L^2}\sum_{l=1}^{M} w_{i;j}\, v_{j,l} + b_i \ . \tag{3.59}$$

The quantity ΔE_i can be rewritten in terms of u_i as

$$\Delta E_i = -(\Delta v_i)u_i + \tfrac{1}{2}|w_{i;i}| , \tag{3.60}$$

therefore, the condition $\Delta E_i \leq 0$ is equivalent to $(\Delta v_i)u_i| \geq |w_{i;i}|/2$, and the modified update rule becomes

$$\begin{cases} |u_i| \geq |w_{i;i}|/2 \quad \text{and} \quad u_i \geq 0 \Rightarrow v_i^{\text{new}} = 1 , \\ |u_i| \geq |w_{i;i}|/2 \quad \text{and} \quad u_i < 0 \Rightarrow v_i^{\text{new}} = 0 , \\ |u_i| < |w_{i;i}|/2 \;\Rightarrow\; v_i^{\text{new}} = v_i^{\text{old}} . \end{cases} \tag{3.61}$$

It is interesting to note that this modified update rule has a natural interpretation, namely, that the magnitude of the input to a neuron has to be strong enough to trigger a change of state for that neuron.

Besides the quantization of the image gray level due to the number representation scheme, the use of the neural network model introduced another deviation from the original minimization problem formulated for image restoration. Namely, there is an intrinsic constraint on the range of magnitude for each image pixel. Note that by (3.51), the value of the gray level of each pixel, $x(i,j)$, is limited to the range $[0, M]$. The neural network is actually performing the minimization of (3.53) subject to the hidden contraint

$$0 \leq x(i,j) \leq M ,$$

for all $1 \leq i,j \leq L$. The effect of this hidden constraint on the solution has yet to be investigated further.

It has to be pointed out that, while the neural network algorithm provides an attractive implementation for constrained least-squares restoration of images, problems inherent in the least-squares solution, such as ringing due to discontinuous boundary values and/or sharp edges and noise amplification due to ill-conditioning, are still present in the neural network approach. However, because the spatial relationship between image pixels is preserved in the mapping from the image to the processing units (neurons) in the neural network, it is relatively easy to impose global or local constraints which may help reduce problems such as ringing and noise amplification. For example, boundary constraints can be applied easily by imposing the condition on neurons associated with the boundary region only. In [3.12], neurons corresponding to the boundary region of an image are clamped such that

$$\sum_{k=1}^{M} v_{i,k} = g_i , \quad i \in \text{border region} . \tag{3.62}$$

This boundary constraint helps reduce the ringing caused by unfavorable boundary values [3.30]. Also demonstrated in [3.12] are constraints imposed on specific regions other than the border region. These examples show that non-homogeneous constraints can be conveniently used in the neural net formulation. Generally speaking, the addition of more constraints makes an optimization problem more difficult;

but in the neural network approach, constraints can often be satisfied by properly programming the connection weights, or properly clamping certain set of neurons.

The Lagrange multiplier γ is critical for the network because it determines the interconnection weights. It is also critical for the solution because it balances the effects of deconvolution and regularization. In [3.11, 12], the value of γ has been empirically chosen. The value which gives the best performance for one or more cases has been experimentally obtained. The value of γ at which (3.53) is minimized is such that the resulting solution, $\hat{\boldsymbol{f}}$, satisfies [3.27]

$$\|\boldsymbol{C}\hat{\boldsymbol{f}}\|^2 = \varepsilon . \tag{3.63}$$

In the following section, we develop an algorithm to determine this (mathematically) optimum value of γ. We show that this algorithm can be implemented using the same network structure that performs the restoration. In the first phase, the network attempts restoration using an arbitrary initial value of γ. If the result does not comply with (3.63), the network goes into a *learning phase* to estimate the value of γ. Based on this current estimate, the network adjusts its connection weights and goes back to the restoration phase. The restoration/learning cycle is repeated until (3.63) is satisfied. [Note that if $\gamma = 0$, then the resulting solution is optimum only if it is feasible, i.e., $\|\boldsymbol{C}\hat{\boldsymbol{f}}\|^2 \leq \varepsilon$. In practice, however, the solution obtained by $\gamma = 0$ rarely satisfies this inequality. Thus, for all practical purposes, $\gamma > 0$ and (3.63) is satisfied at the optimum value of γ.]

3.4.4 Learning the Constraint

Unconstrained least-squares solutions are obtainable from the neural network by the modified update rule (3.61) and by setting the connection weights and bias values as in (3.56) and (3.57), with $\gamma = 0$. However, because of the ill-posedness of the problem such a solution is extremely sensitive to noise. An improved restoration can be achieved by imposing a regularization constraint of the form

$$\|\boldsymbol{C}\hat{\boldsymbol{f}}\|^2 \leq \varepsilon , \tag{3.64}$$

and solve the constrained optimization problem discussed in the previous section. Here, we are concerned with developing an algorithm to teach the network the value of the Lagrange multiplier, γ, associated with the constraint.

We first state the following important fact: The functional $\varphi(\gamma) \doteq \|\boldsymbol{C}\hat{\boldsymbol{f}}\|^2 = \|\boldsymbol{C}(\boldsymbol{D}^{\mathrm{T}}\boldsymbol{D}+\gamma\boldsymbol{C}^{\mathrm{T}}\boldsymbol{C})^{-1}\boldsymbol{D}^{\mathrm{T}}\boldsymbol{g}\|^2$ is monotonically decreasing as a function of γ for $\gamma > 0$. (This fact is proved in Appendix 3.A.3.) This implies that there is a unique value of γ such that $\varphi(\gamma) = \varepsilon$, and that value can be determined by an iterative process on γ. In the following we propose an iterative algorithm that can be implemented by the network structure that performs the restoration. Thus, the network learns the value of γ, i.e., learns the constraint.

The learning algorithm is initialized by setting the value of γ to zero or any arbitrary (positive) initial value, say γ_0. Then, the neural network is operated until a stable state, say $\boldsymbol{f}_0$, is reached [strictly speaking, the network reaches a stable state $\hat{\boldsymbol{v}}$, and by (3.51) $\sum_{k=1}^{M} \hat{v}_{i,k} = (\hat{f}_0)_i$, $i = 1, \ldots, L^2$]. We call this operation the *restoration phase*.

The connection weights $\{w_{i,k;j,l}\}$ can be represented by a matrix $\boldsymbol{W} = [w_{ij}]$ (since they are independent of k and l), and the biases $\{b_{i,k}\}$ can be represented by a vector $\boldsymbol{b} = [b_i]$. In this initial restoration phase, we have [from (3.56,57)]

$$\boldsymbol{W} = -\left(\boldsymbol{D}^{\mathrm{T}}\boldsymbol{D} + \gamma_0 \boldsymbol{C}^{\mathrm{T}}\boldsymbol{C}\right) \doteq -\boldsymbol{G}_0 \,, \tag{3.65}$$

and

$$\boldsymbol{b} = \boldsymbol{D}^{\mathrm{T}}\boldsymbol{g} \,. \tag{3.66}$$

Following the initial restoration phase, the neural network enters into the *learning phase*. The quantity $\|\boldsymbol{C}\boldsymbol{f}_0\|^2$ is calculated and compared to ε. If $\varphi(\gamma_0) = \|\boldsymbol{C}\boldsymbol{f}_0\|^2 \neq \varepsilon$, then the interconnection weights are adjusted to

$$\begin{aligned}\boldsymbol{W} &= -\left(\boldsymbol{D}^{\mathrm{T}}\boldsymbol{D} + \gamma_0 \boldsymbol{C}^{\mathrm{T}}\boldsymbol{C} + \delta\gamma_0 \boldsymbol{C}^{\mathrm{T}}\boldsymbol{C}\right) \\ &= -\boldsymbol{G}_0 - \delta\gamma_0 \boldsymbol{C}^{\mathrm{T}}\boldsymbol{C} \doteq -\boldsymbol{G}_1 \,,\end{aligned} \tag{3.67}$$

where

$$\delta\gamma_0 = \frac{1}{2} \frac{\|\boldsymbol{C}\boldsymbol{f}_0\|^2 - \varepsilon}{(\boldsymbol{C}^{\mathrm{T}}\boldsymbol{C}\boldsymbol{f}_0)^{\mathrm{T}}\boldsymbol{G}_0^{-1}(\boldsymbol{C}^{\mathrm{T}}\boldsymbol{C}\boldsymbol{f}_0)} \,. \tag{3.68}$$

The derivation of (3.68) is shown in Appendix 3.A.4. Also, note that if $\|\boldsymbol{C}\boldsymbol{f}_0\|^2 > \varepsilon$, then $\delta\gamma_0 > 0$, and if $\|\boldsymbol{C}\boldsymbol{f}_0\|^2 < \varepsilon$, then $\delta\gamma_0 < 0$, which is indeed consistent with the monotonicity of $\varphi(\gamma)$.

However, in practice the change of γ furnished by (3.68) has to be bounded to prevent unreasonable excursions that might result from the failure of the neural net to yield exactly the $\hat{\boldsymbol{f}}$ that satisfies (3.54). Recall that the neural network is subject to an additional magnitude constraint as well as quantization effects, as mentioned in the previous section. Secondly, even without the problem of approximation, generally the first-order Newton-Raphson procedure may involve changes that could be too large when the slope of the function is small at the present value of the variable, thus bringing the next estimation further away from target; in the present case, strictly following the first order estimation (3.68) may cause the value of γ in the next iteration to be negative, in which region the monotonicity of $\varphi(\gamma)$ no longer holds. We thus constrained the magnitude of $\delta\gamma$ to be no greater than the present value of γ. Incorporating the constraint on the size of change of γ and generalizing (3.67) and (3.68), the algorithm can be expressed as:

(i) Using γ_k determine $\boldsymbol{f}_k$ (restoration phase). If $\varphi(\gamma_k) = \|\boldsymbol{C}\boldsymbol{f}_k\|^2 = \varepsilon$, then $\boldsymbol{f} \doteq \boldsymbol{f}_k$ and the process is terminated. Otherwise, the learning phase (ii) is invoked.

(ii) Compute

$$\Delta = \frac{1}{2} \frac{\|\boldsymbol{C}\boldsymbol{f}_k\|^2 - \varepsilon}{\boldsymbol{f}_k^{\mathrm{T}}\boldsymbol{C}\mathrm{T}\boldsymbol{C}\boldsymbol{G}_k^{-1}\boldsymbol{C}^{\mathrm{T}}\boldsymbol{C}\boldsymbol{f}_k} \,. \tag{3.69}$$

Determine the next estimate for γ: $\gamma_{k+1} = \gamma_k + \delta\gamma_k$, where

$$\delta\gamma_k = \begin{cases} \Delta\,, & \text{if} \quad |\Delta| \leq \gamma_k/2\,; \\ \gamma_k/2\,, & \text{if} \quad |\Delta| > \gamma_k/2\,; \\ -\gamma_k/2\,, & \text{if} \quad |\Delta| < -\gamma_k/2\,. \end{cases}$$

(iii) Adjust the interconnection weights according to

$$W = -G_{k+1} \doteq G_k + \delta\gamma_k C^{\mathrm{T}} C \tag{3.70}$$

and got into the restoration phase (i).

It should be noted that the extent of the weight adjustment is determined by C. If $C = I$, we see from (3.65) that only self-connections need to be adjusted; if $C = L$, the Laplacian, the adjustment extends to connections of each neuron with neurons corresponding to neighboring pixels.

Now, we address the following question: how does the network learn? In other words, how is (3.69) computed? The term $\|Cf_k\|^2 = \langle Cf_k, Cf_k\rangle$ in the numerator of (3.69) can be determined by a perceptron-type, feed-forward network that computes the inner product of two vectors. In particular, consider the network described by (3.29). Defining $x' \doteq Cf_k$; assuming a single output neuron, i.e., $y = y_1$; setting w_{i1} equal to the ith component of Cf_k, $i = 1, 2, \ldots, L^2$; taking $c_1 = 0$; and defining $\eta(\cdot)$ to be the unity-slope linear function, the state of the output neuron, y_1 becomes equal to $\|Cf_k\|^2$. Here, we will refer to this net as the inner product network. The result is then added to $(-\varepsilon)$ by a summation amplifier to determine the numerator of (3.69). The denominator of (3.69) is equal to the inner product of two vectors: $s_1 \doteq C^{\mathrm{T}}Cf_k$ and $s_2 \doteq G_k^{-1}(C^{\mathrm{T}}Cf_k)$, and can be evaluated by the inner product network. But, first the vectors s_1 and s_2 should be determined. It is easy to see that the weights of the network described in (3.29) can be specified to perform the matrix multiplication and obtain $s_1 = C^{\mathrm{T}}Cf_k$, using zero biases, L^2 input and output nodes, and unity-slope linear functions.

To compute s_2 using the neural network, observe that s_2 satisfies the first order necessary condition, $G_k s_2 - C^{\mathrm{T}}Cf_k = 0$, of minimizing

$$\tfrac{1}{2}x^{\mathrm{T}}G_k x - x^{\mathrm{T}}C^{\mathrm{T}}f_k\,.$$

Therefore, assuming that stable state of the network approximately satisfies the necessary condition for minimization, the vector s_2 can be obtained approximately, using the same simple sum number scheme, by operating the restoration network with the same connections weights $W = -G_k$ but different biases

$$b = C^{\mathrm{T}}Cf_k\,. \tag{3.71}$$

That is, the biases are reset to the values given by (3.71) when the network enters the learning phase. Then, the network iterates and reaches to a stable state which is ideally equal to s_2. At the restoration phase, the biases are reset back to their original values (3.57). To summarize, the network learns by appropriately adjusting its biases when it enters the learning phase, and using auxiliary perceptron-like networks to compute matrix and inner products.

3.4.5 Simulation Results

To test the learning/restoration algorithm, some neural network simulations were performed on a SUN workstation. The asynchronous update of neurons was done by processing the neurons sequentially. The 'Lena' image (Fig. 3.10 A) is a 256×256 pixels square, 8 bit/pixel image. The image was blurred by a 5×5 uniform point spread function (PSF) and contaminated by additive white Gaussian noise at 30 dB signal-to-noise ratio (SNR) (Fig. 3.10 B).

In order to reduce ringing induced by unmatched boundaries (i.e., a non-periodic image) we took an eight-pixel wide boundary region and fixed the gray levels to be that of the degraded image in the boundary region. The restoration area was thus fixed to the region inside the boundary.

Figure 3.11 shows the result of the restoration without any constraint [i.e., $\gamma = 0$ in (3.53)]. The image exhibits greatly amplified noise – a standard result when the restoration is ill-conditioned. Indeed, the mean square error (mse) is now greater than that of the degraded image and the visual effect is worse as well.

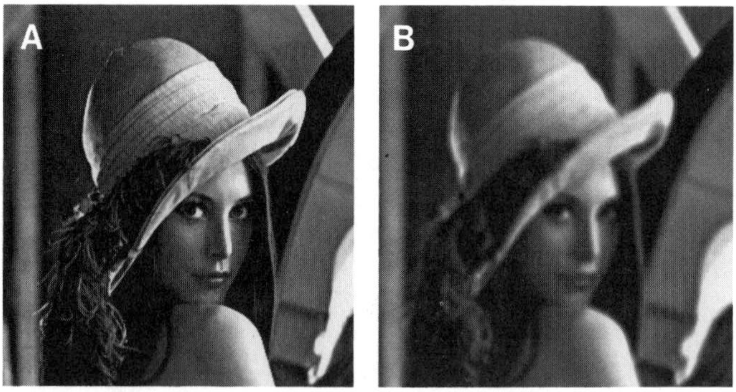

Fig. 3.10. The original and degraded images: (**A**) Original Lena image; (**B**) Degraded Lena image, blur: 5×5 uniform; noise: SNR=30 dB, additive white Gaussian

Fig. 3.11. Unconstrained restoration ($\gamma = 0$)

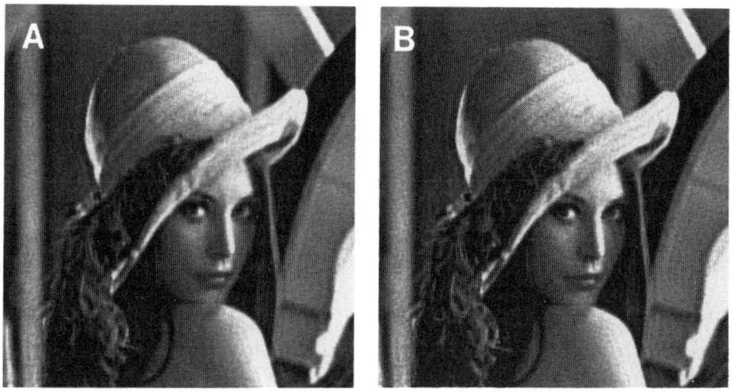

Fig. 3.12. Constrained restorations: (A) $C = I$; (B) $C = L$

Next, we applied the constraint $\|f\|^2 \le \varepsilon_1$ with $\varepsilon_1 = 12200$). In this situation, with initial γ set to 0.1, the neural network goes into three learning/restoration cycles and generates a value of $\gamma = 0.0135$. The result of the restoration after learning is shown in Fig. 3.12 A. Now we obtain a 2.41 dB mse improvement over the unprocessed image and a considerable improvement in the visual quality of the image.

In the last experiment, we applied the constraint $\|L\hat{f}\|^2 \le \varepsilon_2 = 500$ where L is the matrix associated with the Laplacian operator. In this experiment, the Laplacian kernel was the 3 × 3 window with values

$$\frac{1}{6}\begin{pmatrix} 1 & 4 & 1 \\ 4 & -20 & 4 \\ 1 & 4 & 1 \end{pmatrix} \tag{3.72}$$

Also staring with $\gamma = 0.1$ after four learning/restoration cycle, the neural network generated the value of $\gamma = 0.00898$. The resulting restoration shown in Fig. 3.12 B displays noticeable improvement over the unprocessed image.

Table 3.1 lists the mse and the degree of improvement for the various cases. These results demonstrate the feasibility of using a Hopfield-type network to both restore the image and find near-optimum restoration parameters.

Table 3.1. Experimental results

	Degraded Image	Constraint None	Constraint: $\|\hat{f}\|^2 \le \varepsilon_1$	Constraint: $\|L\hat{f}\|^2 \le \varepsilon_2$
mse	193.6	1862.2	111.1	113.8
dB improvement	0	−9.83	2.41	2.31

3.5 Summary and Conclusion

In the first part of this chapter, we generated a set-theoretic formulation of Hopfield-type neural networks. This point of view enabled us to use powerful projection methods such as generalized projections (GP) or projections onto convex sets (POCS) to analyze the dynamic behavior of these networks. In particular, the binary-valued Hopfield ACAM was analyzed using the method of GP, which enabled an explanation of the origin of undesirable states called 'traps'. On the basis of the set-theoretic formulation, possible strategies can be suggested to avoid traps. We have also formulated a continuous-valued Hopfield ACAM using POCS and characterized its stable states. An ACAM can be cascaded with a perceptron to form a Hopfield-type classifier. We showed that the single layer, linear perceptron can be described using POCS. This set-theoretic point of view enables the incorporation of prior knowledge and thereby enables an improvement in the performance of the perceptron.

In the second part of the chapter, we considered the use of the Hopfield network as an optimizer. We discussed how the network can be specified to solve a constrained least squares image restoration problem. We proposed a Newton-Raphson type algorithm to determine the value of the Lagrange multiplier associated with the image constraint. Interestingly, we have found that this algorithm can be implemented by a network which differs from the restoration network only in neuron biases, and augmented by two perceptron-type auxiliary networks. Thus, the restoration network is capable of learning the Lagrange multiplier provided that its biases are set to appropriate values and is augmented by two auxiliary perceptron-type networks. Using this architecture the optimum Lagrange multiplier can be computed by the network in an iterative fashion. One problem area is determining the appropriate value of the incremental step size in the Newton-Raphson algorithm. Future research will address this as well as other problems.

Computer experiments in which an alternating learning/restoration cycle was implemented demonstrated the feasibility of near-optimum (in the mean square error sense) constrained restoration of a blurred and noisy image.

3.A Appendices

3.A.1 Orthogonalization Learning Rule

Here, we show that the 'orthogonalization learning rule' discussed in [3.3] is equivalent to the learning rule given in (3.13). From [Ref. 3.3, p. 23],

$$\boldsymbol{W}' = \boldsymbol{X}\boldsymbol{B}^{\mathrm{T}} , \tag{3.73}$$

where $\boldsymbol{B} \doteq [\boldsymbol{b}_1 \boldsymbol{b}_2 \cdots \boldsymbol{b}_N]^{\mathrm{T}}$ is an $L \times N$ matrix whose columns are orthonormal to the library vectors, i.e., $< \boldsymbol{b}_i, \boldsymbol{x}_j >= \delta_{ij}$ and $\boldsymbol{X}$ is the $L \times N$ matrix $(L \geq N)$ formed by the library vectors. In [3.3] the matrix $\boldsymbol{B}$ is determined from

$$B = X\left(X^{\mathrm{T}}X\right)^{-1}. \tag{3.74}$$

Invoking the symmetry of $X^{\mathrm{T}}X)^{-1}$, we have

$$W' = X(X^{\mathrm{T}}X)^{-1}X^{\mathrm{T}}. \tag{3.75}$$

In the case of linearly independent library vectors, the inverse $(X^{\mathrm{T}}X)^{-1}$ always exists provided that $L \geq N$. That is, the number of stored library vectors (the network capacity) is bounded above by the dimensionality of the vectors.

3.A.2 Projection Operator of C_s

Let q be arbitrary in R^L. The projection operator P_s is defined by

$$\begin{aligned} \|q - P_s q\| &\doteq \min_{\alpha_n} \|q - \sum_{n=1}^{N} \alpha_n x_n\| \\ &= \min_{\alpha} \|q - X\alpha\| \\ &= \|q - X\hat{\alpha}\| \end{aligned} \tag{3.76}$$

where X is the $L \times N$ matrix ($L \geq N$) whose columns are the library vectors, and $\hat{\alpha}$ is the minimizing quantity. But, note that $\hat{\alpha}$ is, in fact, the least squares solution of the equation $X\alpha = q$ and, therefore, it is given by

$$\hat{\alpha} = \left(X^{\mathrm{T}}X\right)^{-1}X^{\mathrm{T}}q. \tag{3.77}$$

Hence,

$$P_s q = X\hat{\alpha} = X\left(X^{\mathrm{T}}X\right)^{-1}X^{\mathrm{T}}q. \tag{3.78}$$

3.A.3 Proof of the Monotonicity of $\varphi(\gamma)$

As defined, the function $\varphi(\gamma)$ is

$$\begin{aligned} \varphi(\gamma) &= \|C\left(D^{\mathrm{T}}D + \gamma C^{\mathrm{T}}C\right)^{-1}D^{\mathrm{T}}g\|^2 \\ &= g^{\mathrm{T}}D\left(D^{\mathrm{T}}D + \gamma C^{\mathrm{T}}C\right)^{-1}C^{\mathrm{T}}C\left(D^{\mathrm{T}}D + \gamma C^{\mathrm{T}}C\right)^{-1}D^{\mathrm{T}}g. \end{aligned} \tag{3.79}$$

Using the matrix formula

$$\frac{d}{dt}A^{-1} = -A^{-1}\left(\frac{d}{dt}A\right)A^{-1},$$

$$\frac{d}{dt}ABC = \left(\frac{d}{dt}A\right)BC + A\left(\frac{d}{dt}B\right)C + AB\left(\frac{d}{dt}C\right),$$

we obtain the derivative of $\varphi(\gamma)$ as

$$\begin{aligned}
\frac{\partial}{\partial\gamma}\varphi &= \frac{\partial}{\partial\gamma}[g^{\mathrm{T}}D(D^{\mathrm{T}}D+\gamma C^{\mathrm{T}}C)^{-1}C^{\mathrm{T}}C(D^{\mathrm{T}}D+\gamma C^{\mathrm{T}}C)^{-1}D^{\mathrm{T}}g] \\
&= g^{\mathrm{T}}D\frac{\partial}{\partial\gamma}[(D^{\mathrm{T}}D+\gamma C^{\mathrm{T}}C)^{-1}C^{\mathrm{T}}C(D^{\mathrm{T}}D+\gamma C^{\mathrm{T}}C)^{-1}]D^{\mathrm{T}}g \\
&= -2g^{\mathrm{T}}D[(D^{\mathrm{T}}D+\gamma C^{\mathrm{T}}C)^{-1}C^{\mathrm{T}}C(D^{\mathrm{T}}D+\gamma C^{\mathrm{T}}C)^{-1} \\
&\quad \times C^{\mathrm{T}}C(D^{\mathrm{T}}D+\gamma C^{\mathrm{T}}C)^{-1}]D^{\mathrm{T}}g \\
&= -2y^{\mathrm{T}}(D^{\mathrm{T}}D+\gamma C^{\mathrm{T}}C)^{-1}y\,,
\end{aligned} \tag{3.80}$$

where $y = C^{\mathrm{T}}C(D^{\mathrm{T}}D+\gamma C^{\mathrm{T}}C)^{-1}D^{\mathrm{T}}g$.

The matrix $(D^{\mathrm{T}}D+\gamma C^{\mathrm{T}}C)^{-1}$ is positive definite for positive γ. Therefore the derivative of $\varphi(\gamma)$ is negative. We thus prove that $\varphi(\gamma)$ is a monotonically decreasing function of γ in the range $\gamma > 0$.

3.A.4 Derivation of (3.68)

Let f_0 be the stable state reached at the initial restoration phase. Suppose, however, that f_0 does not satisfy the condition (3.63), i.e.,

$$\|Cf_k\|^2 \neq \varepsilon\,.$$

Therefore, we would like to modify G_0 to

$$G_1 = G_0 + \delta\gamma_0 C^{\mathrm{T}}C \tag{3.81}$$

so that the vector f_1, which denotes the stable state of the next restoration phase, satisfies condition (3.63). [Note that (3.81) reflects the effective modification of γ_0: $\gamma_1 = \gamma_0 + \delta\gamma_0$.] The problem then is to determine $\delta\gamma_0$. The quantity $\delta\gamma_0$ should be such that $\|C\hat{f}_1\|^2 = \varepsilon$.

Let $\hat{f}_0$ and $\hat{f}_1$ satisfy (3.54) with $\gamma = \gamma_0$ and $\gamma = \gamma_1$ respectively, and therefore is the analytical minima approximated by f_0 and f_1, respectively. Assuming that G_0^{-1} and G_1^{-1} exist, we have

$$\hat{f}_0 = G_0^{-1}b \tag{3.82}$$

and

$$\hat{f}_1 = (G_0 + \delta\gamma_0 C^{\mathrm{T}}C)^{-1}b\,. \tag{3.83}$$

Now, making use of the matrix inversion formula [3.32]:

$$(A+BCD)^{-1} = A^{-1} - A^{-1}B(DA^{-1}B + C^{-1})^{-1}DA^{-1}\,, \tag{3.84}$$

where A, C are invertible matrices, we obtain

$$(G_0 + \delta\gamma_0 C^{\mathrm{T}}C)^{-1} = G_0^{-1} - \delta\gamma_0 G_0^{-1}C^{\mathrm{T}}C\,(\delta\gamma_0 G_0^{-1}C^{\mathrm{T}}C + I)^{-1}\,G_0^{-1}\,. \tag{3.85}$$

If $|\delta\gamma_0| \ll 1$, then the above inverse can be approximated as

$$\left(G_0 + \delta\gamma_0 C^{\mathrm{T}}C\right)^{-1} \simeq G_0^{-1} - \delta\gamma_0 G_0^{-1}C^{\mathrm{T}}CG_0^{-1}\,. \tag{3.86}$$

Defining the function $\varphi(\gamma_1)$ as

$$\varphi(\gamma_1) \doteq \|C\hat{\boldsymbol{f}}_1\|^2\,, \tag{3.87}$$

then, using the approximation (3.86), we obtain

$$\begin{aligned}\varphi(\gamma_1) &= \boldsymbol{b}^{\mathrm{T}}\left(G_0 + \delta\gamma_0 C^{\mathrm{T}}C\right)^{-1} C^{\mathrm{T}}C\left(G_0 + \delta\gamma_0 C^{\mathrm{T}}C\right)^{-1}\boldsymbol{b} \\ &\simeq \boldsymbol{b}^{\mathrm{T}}\left(G_0^{-1} - \delta\gamma_0 G_0^{-1}C^{\mathrm{T}}CG_0^{-1}\right)C^{\mathrm{T}}C\left(G_0^{-1} - \delta\gamma_0 G_0^{-1}C^{\mathrm{T}}CG_0^{-1}\right)\boldsymbol{b} \\ &\simeq \boldsymbol{b}^{\mathrm{T}}\left(G_0^{-1}C^{\mathrm{T}}CG_0^{-1} - 2\delta\gamma_0 G_0^{-1}C^{\mathrm{T}}CG_0^{-1}C^{\mathrm{T}}CG_0^{-1}\right)\boldsymbol{b} \\ &= \hat{\boldsymbol{f}}_0^{\mathrm{T}}C^{\mathrm{T}}C\hat{\boldsymbol{f}}_0 - 2\delta\gamma_0\hat{\boldsymbol{f}}_0^{\mathrm{T}}C^{\mathrm{T}}CG_0^{-1}C^{\mathrm{T}}C\hat{\boldsymbol{f}}_0\,.\end{aligned} \tag{3.88}$$

Setting the above quantity equal to ε, we obtain

$$\delta\gamma_0 = \frac{1}{2}\,\frac{\|C\hat{\boldsymbol{f}}_0\|^2 - \varepsilon}{\hat{\boldsymbol{f}}_0^{\mathrm{T}}C^{\mathrm{T}}CG_0^{-1}C^{\mathrm{T}}C\hat{\boldsymbol{f}}_0}\,. \tag{3.89}$$

This result can be generalized to the following iterative form:

$$\delta\gamma_k = \frac{1}{2}\,\frac{\|C\hat{\boldsymbol{f}}_k\|^2 - \varepsilon}{\hat{\boldsymbol{f}}_k^{\mathrm{T}}C^{\mathrm{T}}CG_k^{-1}C^{\mathrm{T}}C\hat{\boldsymbol{f}}_k}\,, \qquad k = 0, 1, \ldots \tag{3.90}$$

from which the estimate γ_{k+1} is computed as $\gamma_{k+1} = \gamma_k + \delta\gamma_k$. This iterative process is in the form of Newton-Raphson method [3.31].

Since the assumed analytical minimum $\hat{\boldsymbol{f}}_k$'s are not available, a practical approach is to use the stable state obtained by the neural network, $\boldsymbol{f}_k$, to replace $\hat{\boldsymbol{f}}_k$ in estimating $\delta\gamma_k$.

Acknowledgement. We are grateful to Leonard Tiefel of Kodak for his valuable help in transferring images from IIT to Kodak Research Labs and in generating the hardcopies.

References

3.1. R. Rosenblatt: *Principles of Neurodynamics* (Spartan, New York 1958)

3.2. R. P. Lippmann: IEEE ASSP Mag. **4**, 4–22 (1987)

3.3. R. P. Lippmann, B. Gold, M. L. Malpass: "A comparison of Hamming and Hopfield neural nets for pattern classification", MIT Lincoln Lab., Technical Report TR-769 (1987)

3.4. J. T. Tou, R. C. Gonzalez: *Pattern Recognition Principles* (Addison Wesley, Reading, MA 1974)

3.5. G. A. Carpenter, S. Grossberg: "Neural dynamics of category learning and recognition: attention, memory consolidation, and amnesia" in *Brain Structure, Learning, and Memory*, ed. by J. Davis, R. Newburgh, E. Wegman (AAAS Symposium Series 1986)

3.6. J. J. Hopfield: Proc. Natl. Acad. Sci. USA **79**, 2554–2558 (1982)

3.7. J. J. Hopfield: Proc. Natl. Acad. Sci. USA **81**, 3088–3092 (1984)
3.8. G. R. Gindi, A. F. Gmitro, K. Parthasarthy: Appl. Opt. **27**, 129–134 (1988)
3.9. J. J. Hopfield, D. W. Tank: Science **233**, 625–633 (1986)
3.10. D. W. Tank, J. J. Hopfield: IEEE Trans. **CAS 33**, 533–541 (1986)
3.11. Y.-T. Zhou: "Artificial neural network algorithms for some computer vision problems"; Ph.D. Thesis, University of Southern California (1989)
3.12. Y. T. Zhou, R. Chellappa, A. Vaid, B.K. Jenkins: IEEE Trans. **ASSP 36**, 1141–1151 (1988)
3.13. H. Stark (ed.): *Image Recovery: Theory and Application* (Academic, Orlando 1987)
3.14. H. J. Trussell, M. R. Civanlar: IEEE Trans. **ASSP 32**, 201–212 (1984)
3.15. R. J. Marks II: Appl. Opt. **26**, 2005–2010 (1987)
3.16. R. J. Marks II, S. Oh, L. E. Atlas: IEEE Trans. **CAS 36**, 846–856 (1989)
3.17. P. M. Grant, J. P. Sage: Proc. Conf. Neural Networks for Computing, Snowbird Utah (AIP Press 1986)
3.18. D. C. Youla: "Mathematical theory of image restoration by the method of convex projections", in *Image Recovery*, ed. by H. Stark (Academic, Orlando 1987)
3.19. A. Levi, H. Stark: J. Opt. Soc. Am. **1**, 932–943 (1984)
3.20. R. J. Marks II, L. E. Atlas: "Content addressable memories: a relationship between Hopfield's neural net and an iterative matched filter", Technical Report 51887, Interactive System Design Lab., University of Washington (1987)
3.21. M. I. Sezan, H. Stark: "Applications of convex projection theory to image recovery in tomography and related areas", in *Image Recovery*, ed. by H. Stark (Academic, Orlando 1987)
3.22. R. O. Duda, P. E. Hart: *Pattern Classification and Scene Analysis* (Wiley, New York 1973)
3.23. R. Kumaradjaja: "Application of projections onto convex sets in pattern recognition", MSc. Thesis, Rensselaer Polytechnic Institute (1986)
3.24. H. Peng, H. Stark: J. Opt. Soc. Am. A **6**, 844–851 (1989)
3.25. A. Levi, H. Stark: J. Opt. Soc. Am. **73**, 810–822 (1983)
3.26. T. Kohonen: *Self-Organization and Associative Memory*, 2nd ed., Springer Ser. Information Sci. Vol. 8 (Springer, Berlin, Heidelberg 1988)
3.27. M. Bertero, C. De Mol, G. A. Viano: "Stability of inverse problems" in *Inverse Scattering Problems in Physics*, ed. by H. P. Baltes (Springer, New York 1980)
3.28. A. F. Gmitro, P. E. Keller, G. R. Gindi: Appl. Opt. **28**, 1940–1948 (1989)
3.29. M. Takeda, J. W. Goodman: Appl. Opt. **25**, 3033–3046 (1986)
3.30. J. W. Woods, J. Biemond, A. M. Tekalp: Proc. Int. Conf. Acoust., Speech and Signal Processing, Tampa (1985)
3.31. D. G. Luenberger: *Optimization by Vector Space Methods* (Wiley, New York 1977)
3.32. T. Kailath: *Linear Systems* (Prentice-Hall, Englewood Cliffs, NJ 1980) p. 656

4. Compound Gauss-Markov Models for Image Processing

F.-Ch. Jeng and J. W. Woods

With 8 Figures

This chapter is concerned with algorithms for obtaining the maximum a posteriori probability (MAP) estimate from noisy and blurred images modeled by compound Gauss-Markov random fields. We will also show how these models can be used for image textural segmentation. These compound models have several image submodels with differing characteristics along with a structure model which governs transitions between the image submodels. Compound random field models are attractive for image processing because the resulting estimates may not suffer the over-smoothing of edges that can occur when employing linear shift-invariant models. Two different compound random field models are presented in this chapter, the doubly stochastic Gaussian (DSG) and compound Gauss-Markov (CGM) random fields. Parallel MAP estimators are developed for each based on simulated annealing.

4.1 Overview

As is well known, a linear-shift invariant (LSI) model is not well-suited to image estimation, i.e. noise smoothing. The major problem is that the resulting image estimate suffers from over-smoothing of edges which are quite important to the human visual system (HVS). Partly as a result, space-variant filters have been proposed [4.1–4] wherein each pixel (or block of pixels) is filtered by a switched linear filter with the switching governed by a visibility function. The visibility function can be based on either a local variance estimate [4.2] or an average estimate of the isotropic gradient [4.1]. A more complicated visibility function which depends upon the mix of the directional components and a high frequency component was used in [4.3]. One of the problems with all these approaches is that the filter switching is rather ad hoc and cannot be justified on a theoretical basis. It would be better if the filter transitions could be related to an image model.

One way to embed a mathematical approach into the above adaptive methods is to have the models' switching controlled by a hidden random field. Toward this end, a class of models called compound Gauss-Markov models has been proposed [4.5, 6]. A compound random field consists of two levels, upper and lower. The upper level random field is the observed image, which is composed of several LSI sub-models representing a variety of local characteristics of images, e.g., edge orientation or texture. The lower or hidden level is a random field with a finite range whose purpose is to govern transitions between the observed LSI submodels.

Springer Series in Information Sciences, Vol. 23
A.K. Katsaggelos (ed.): Digital Image Restoration

The *doubly stochastic Gaussian* (DSG) *field* [4.6] possesses a conditional Gaussian, *autoregressive* (AR) upper or observed level, whose model coefficients have a causal support. They are switched by a hidden (hence lower level) 2D causal Markov chain to generate the required local edge structure. The DSG random field is a Markov random field but the observed upper level component, by itself, is not, i.e. the image data component of the DSG is not Markov.

Geman and Geman, on the other hand, used a noncausal neighborhood system in their image model [4.5]. In their nomenclature, our lower level random field becomes their line process which was defined on an interpixel grid system. Their upper level random field is a noncausal conditional Markov random field also with a finite range, i.e. a noncausal 2D Markov chain. Since they modeled images on a finite range space, they thereby excluded the Gaussian models, which are very widely used in image estimation and restoration. Generalizing their model, we have introduced an extension of the Gauss-Markov random field [4.7, 8]. Our *compound Gauss-Markov* (CGM) *model* [4.9] has continuous gray levels as an upper level observations model but retains the Gemans' lower level line process (field) as a structural model.

As mentioned above, both DSG and CGM models will be used for image estimation and restoration. Their MAP estimators will be developed by means of simulated annealing (stochastic relaxation) which was first introduced by *Geman* and *Geman* [4.5] where they presented a convergence proof for this iterative method. Their proof was confined to images that are modeled by a finite range space which, unfortunately, excludes the case of CGM models. When applying simulated annealing to our models, a proof for the convergence of simulated annealing to the MAP estimate was thus lacking. We have obtained such a proof for a broad subclass of CGM models [4.10]. This chapter will concentrate on the algorithm & experimental results of applying simulated annealing with CGM models to image estimation and restoration. Those interested in the more theoretical aspects of this work are referred to [4.10].

It is well known that simulated annealing is a computationally demanding method. Alternatively a quickly converging algorithm called *deterministic relaxation* can be used to get a local MAP estimate. This deterministic relaxation method has been called *iterated conditional mode* (ICM) in [4.11]. We also present results for this locally convergent algorithm.

Besides image estimation and restoration, a class of compound Gauss-Markov random fields is also suitable for texture discrimination. Texture is an important feature for object recognition and image analysis. Among all the methods proposed in texture discrimination, the maximum a posteriori (MAP) probability estimate based on a *multiple autoregressive* (MAR) *model* is most widely used. However, the result based on the MAR model has one major drawback: it has many isolated errors (false alarms). Here we propose a compound random field called the *doubly stochastic Gaussian* (DSG) *random field for texture discrimination* to reduce isolated errors.

One important issue only briefly addressed in this chapter is parameter identification. The parameter identification problem can be classified into two categories:

supervised and *unsupervised*. In the case of supervised problem, a training (original) image is available and parameters can be obtained based on the training image. This approach makes sense only if the images in question possess the same statistics as the training image. The other category must obtain the parameters from the degraded image itself. The solution to the unsupervised case usually leads to an EM (expectation and maximization) type approach [4.12]. In Chap. 5 of this book, *Chellappa* et al. address the parameter identification problem and propose several methods to solve it for both simple and compound Markov random fields.

We start out by first defining the two compound random fields. Then estimation problems are formulated and the various estimators are briefly described. Next, we present simulation results that provide comparisons between the various methods i.e. causal versus non-causal model, compound Gaussian versus simple Gaussian distributions, and simulated annealing versus deterministic relaxation estimators. The intention here will be to see which algorithms result in subjectively good images. We then draw conclusions about which mathematical models best match this human visual system (HVS) viewpoint. Finally, we present a version of the DSG model for texture discrimination and its simulation results.

4.2 Compound Markov Random Fields

As mentioned in the previous section, a simple shift-invariant Gaussian AR model can often lead to oversmoothing of image data. In this section, we will present two compound Markov models, the noncausal CGM and and the causal DSG, that address this problem.

A simple Gauss-Markov (GM) model can be described as follows:

$$s(m,n) = \sum_{kl \in \mathbf{R}} c_{kl} s(m-k, n-l) + w(m,n) \tag{4.1}$$

where $w(m,n)$ is a Gaussian random field satisfying the following covariance constraint:

$$E[w(m,n)w(k,l)] = \begin{cases} \sigma_w^2 & \text{if } (m,n) = (k,l) \\ -c_{m-k,n-l}\sigma_w^2 & \text{if } (m-k, n-l) \in \mathbf{R} \\ 0 & \text{otherwise} , \end{cases} \tag{4.2}$$

and $\mathbf{R}$ is shown in Fig. 4.1. A random field described by the above equation is a Markov random field with a neighborhood support $\mathbf{R}$ [4.8]. By the equivalence of Markov random fields and Gibbs distributions, we can write the joint probability density function (pdf) $p(S)$ as the Gibbs pdf:

$$p(S) = \frac{1}{Z_1} \mathrm{e}^{-U_s(S)}$$

and

$$U_s(S) \triangleq \sum_{c_s \in C_s} V_{c_s}(S) , \tag{4.3}$$

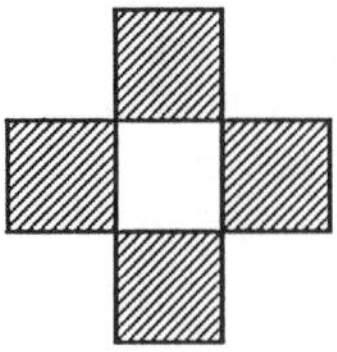

Fig. 4.1. Coefficient support region **R** of the first order model

where c_s is a clique, C_s denotes the clique system for the given Markov neighborhood system, and Z_1 is a normalizing constant which is functionally independent of S, where

$$S \triangleq \begin{pmatrix} s_{11} & s_{12} & \cdots & s_{1N} \\ s_{21} & s_{22} & \cdots & s_{2N} \\ \vdots & \vdots & \vdots & \vdots \\ s_{N1} & s_{N2} & \cdots & s_{NN} \end{pmatrix} .$$

Each $V_{c_s}(S)$ is a function on the sample space with the property that $V_{c_s}(S)$ involves only those $s(m,n)$ of S for which $(m,n) \in c_s$. In the above GM model, we have

$$V_{c_s}(S) = \frac{s^2(m,n)}{2\sigma_w^2} \quad \text{or} \quad -\frac{c_{m-k,n-l}\, s(m,n) s(k,l)}{\sigma_w^2} \quad \text{if} \quad (m-k, n-l) \in \mathbf{R} .$$

4.2.1 Compound Gauss-Markov Random Fields

We can generalize the Gemans' compound model by incorporating a conditional Gauss-Markov observations model [4.7, 8] with their line field. A CGM model consists of several conditionally Gauss-Markov submodels with an underlying structure or line field. Here

$$s(m,n) = \sum_{kl \in \mathbf{R}} c_{kl}^{l(m,n)} s(m-k, n-l) + w^{l(m,n)}(m,n) , \tag{4.4}$$

where $w^{l(m,n)}(m,n)$ is a conditionally Gaussian noise whose variance controlled by the $\boldsymbol{l}(m,n)$ and $\boldsymbol{l}(m,n)$ is a vector which consists of four nearest neighbors of the line field surrounding the pixel $s(m,n)$, with $l(m,n)$ denoting the Geman's line field. This line field takes on two values indicating whether a *bond* is broken or not. If a bond is broken between adjacent pixels, then there is little covariance between them, otherwise, a strong covariance exists.

The joint mixed probability density function (mpdf) of S, L is the Gibbs distribution

$$p(S,L) = \frac{1}{Z_2} e^{-[U_s(S|L)+U_l(L)]/T} , \tag{4.5}$$

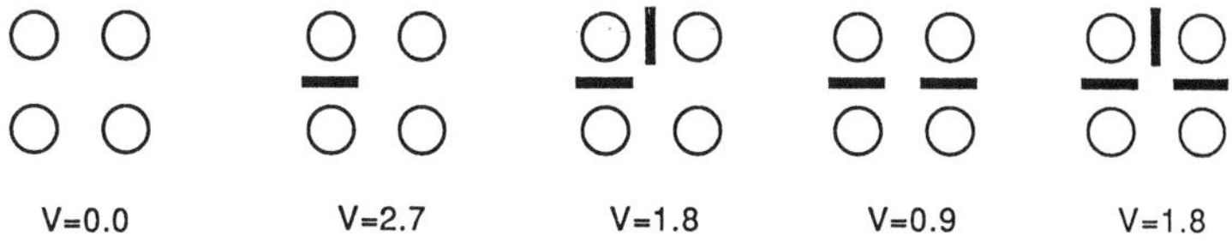

Fig. 4.2. The clique system C_l

where the constant Z_2 is independent of S, L. The variable T is a temperature parameter, U_s is defined in (4.3), and U_l is of the form

$$U_l(L) = \sum_{c_l \in C_l} V_{c_l}(L) ,$$

where

$$L \triangleq \begin{pmatrix} l_{11} & l_{12} & \cdots & l_{1N'} \\ l_{21} & l_{22} & \cdots & l_{2N'} \\ \vdots & \vdots & \vdots & \vdots \\ l_{N'1} & l_{N'2} & \cdots & l_{N'N'} \end{pmatrix}$$

and where N'^2 is the total number of points in the line field over the finite observation region.

The clique system C_l used in this chapter is the same system used in [4.5] as shown in Fig. 4.2. For a CGM model to be a valid conditional Markov random field given a realization of the line field L, there are covariance constraints on $w^{l(m,n)}(m,n)$:

$$E[w^{\underline{l}(m,n)}(m,n)w^{\underline{l}(k,l)}(k,l)]$$
$$= \begin{cases} \sigma^2_{w_{\underline{l}(m,n)}(m,n)} & \text{if } (m,n) = (k,l) \\ -c^{\underline{l}(k,l)}_{m-k,n-l}\sigma^2_{w_{\underline{l}(m,n)}(m,n)} & \text{if } (m-k, n-l) \in \mathbf{R} \\ 0 & \text{otherwise} . \end{cases} \tag{4.6}$$

By commutativity of covariance of two random variables, we have the following constraint on the model coefficients:

$$c^{\underline{l}(k,l)}_{m-k,n-l}\sigma^2_{w_{\underline{l}(m,n)}(m,n)} = c^{\underline{l}(m,n)}_{k-m,l-n}\sigma^2_{w_{\underline{l}(k,l)}(k,l)} \quad \text{if} \quad (m-k, n-l) \in \mathbf{R} \tag{4.7}$$

This constraint reduces the total number of free parameters that can be used in parameter identification. Consequently, classical unconstrained least-squares parameter identification is not applicable to CGM models.

Since the CGM model has a Gibbs probability distribution, it is a Markov random field. Depending on the functional $U_s(S|L)$, the hidden random field L, by itself, may or may not be a Markov random field. This can be seen from the following expression for the probability function $P(L)$,

$$P(L) = \frac{1}{Z_2}\int_S \mathrm{e}^{-[U_s(S|L)+U_l(L)]/T}\, dS ,$$
$$= \frac{\mathrm{e}^{-U_l(L)/T}}{Z_2}\int_S \mathrm{e}^{-U_s(S|L)/T}\, dS .$$

If $\int_S \exp[-U_s(S|L)/T]\, dS$ has the form of Gibbs probability for L, then L is a Markov random field, otherwise it is not. In general, $\int_S \exp[-U_s(S|L)/T]\, dS$ may not be a Gibbs distribution for L.

4.2.2 Doubly Stochastic Gaussian Random Fields

In the following, we will give a brief description of the DSG model. Before we describe this model, we need to introduce the 2D causal Markov chain and a corresponding AR random field [4.6].

Definition. *The* 2D *Markov chain $l(m,n)$ is called a causal Markov chain if the following condition is satisfied*

$$P\left[l(m,n)|l(i,j),(i,j) \in (i,j) < (m,n)\right]$$
$$= P\left[l(m,n)|l(i,j) : (i,j) \in \mathbf{R}_{\oplus+}(m,n)\right] \tag{4.8}$$

where $\mathbf{R}_{\oplus+}(m,n)$ is the local state support region shown in Fig.4.3 and '$(i,j) < (m,n)$' means '$i < m$ or $i = m$ and $j < n$' which is consistent with progressive image scanning. In this chapter, a 1×1-order Markov chain is used exclusively, i.e. $\mathbf{R}_{\oplus+}(m,n) = \{(m-1,n),(m+1,n-1),(m,n-1),(m-1,n-1)\}$). Thus we can write

$$P\left[l(m,n)|\underline{l}(m-1,n)\right] \triangleq P\left[l(m,n)|l(i,j) : (i,j) \in \mathbf{R}_{\oplus+}(m,n)\right] \ .$$

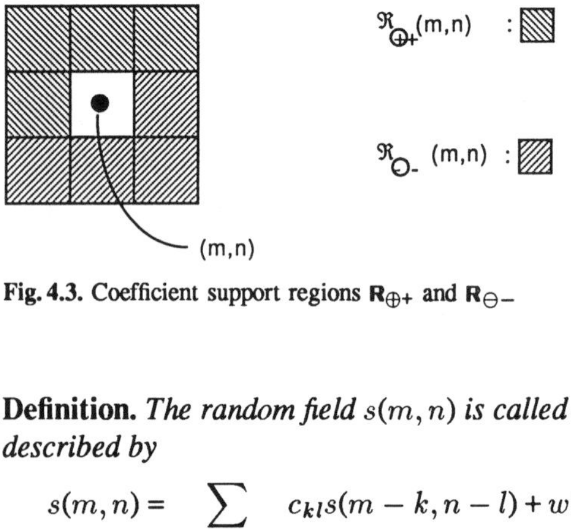

Fig. 4.3. Coefficient support regions $\mathbf{R}_{\oplus+}$ and $\mathbf{R}_{\ominus-}$

Definition. *The random field $s(m,n)$ is called a causal AR random field if it can be described by*

$$s(m,n) = \sum_{(k,l)\in\mathbf{R}_{\oplus+}} c_{kl}s(m-k,n-l) + w(m,n) \tag{4.9}$$

where $w(m,n)$ is a white noise field and $\mathbf{R}_{\oplus+} \triangleq \{(k,l) : (-k,-l) \in \mathbf{R}_{\oplus+}(0,0)\}$.

Definition. *A random field $s(m,n)$ is called a DSG random field [4.6] if it can be described as:*

$$s(m,n) = \sum_{(k,l)\in\mathbf{R}_{\oplus+}} c_{kl}^{l(m,n)}s(m-k,n-l) + w^{l(m,n)}(m,n) \tag{4.10}$$

where $l(m,n)$ is a causal Markov chain and the submodel coefficients at (m,n) in general depend upon $l(m,n)$.

The joint mpdf can be expressed as follows:

$$p(S,L) = p(S \mid L)P(L)\ .$$

Note that the formulation of the joint mpdf of the DSG model is different from the CGM model. It is easily seen by construction that the line field of the DSG model itself is a Markov random field.

4.3 Joint MAP Estimator

We wish to estimate the original image $s(m,n)$ from the degraded observations $r(m,n)$ on an $N \times N$ region:

$$r(m,n) = \sum_{k,l \in \mathbf{R}_h} h(k,l)s(m-k,n-l) + v(m,n)\ , \tag{4.11}$$

where $h(k,l)$ is a known point spread function (psf) with finite support region $\mathbf{R}_h$ and $v(m,n)$ is a zero-mean, white noise independent of $s(m,n)$ and having variance σ_v^2. In the following context, we specify the maximum a posteriori probability (MAP) criteria as used in this work.

The a posteriori joint mpdf for S and L given R can be decomposed as

$$p(S,L \mid R) = \frac{p(R|S,L)p(S,L)}{p(R)} = \frac{p(R|S)p(S \mid L)P(L)}{p(R)} \tag{4.12}$$

where the matrices S, L have been previously defined and R is defined as

$$R \triangleq \begin{pmatrix} r_{11} & r_{12} & \cdots & r_{1N} \\ r_{21} & r_{22} & \cdots & r_{2N} \\ \vdots & \vdots & \vdots & \vdots \\ r_{N1} & r_{N2} & \cdots & r_{NN} \end{pmatrix}\ .$$

Our object is to find the joint matrix estimate $\hat{S}$ and $\hat{L}$ such that

$$p(\hat{S},\hat{L} \mid R) = \max_{S,L} p(S,L \mid R)\ . \tag{4.13}$$

It can be seen that the MAP criteria leads to the need for a frame store to hold the entire image during processing. It also indirectly leads to iterative algorithms requiring massive parallelism for their efficient solution.

Since the criterion function $p(S,L \mid R)$ is nonlinear, it is extremely difficult to find the optimum solutions $\hat{S}, \hat{L}$ by any conventional method. In [4.5], a relaxation technique, called stochastic relaxation or simulated annealing, is developed to search for MAP estimates from degraded observations. In the following, we will present a version of simulated annealing appropriate for both CGM and DSG models.

Assume that $s(m,n)$ is either a CGM or a DSG random field and the observations $r(m,n)$ satisfy (4.11). Some notation is first defined for the sake of conciseness:

$$S_{(m,n)} \stackrel{\Delta}{=} \{s(k,l): \ \forall (k,l) \neq (m,n)\} \ ,$$
$$L_{(m,n)} \stackrel{\Delta}{=} \{l(k,l): \ \forall (k,l) \neq (m,n)\} \ .$$

a) CGM Case. The conditional a posteriori density function $\pi^s(m,n)$ for $s(m,n)$ given $S_{(m,n)}$, L and R is

$$\pi^s(m,n) \stackrel{\Delta}{=} p\big[s(m,n) \mid S_{(m,n)}, L, R\big] = \frac{p(S,L,R)}{\int p(S,L,R)ds(m,n)}$$
$$= \frac{p(R|S)p(S|L)P(L)}{\int p(R|S)p(S|L)P(L)ds(m,n)}$$
$$= \frac{1}{Z_3}\exp\left(-\frac{(s(m,n)-\sum_{kl} c_{kl}^{l(m,n)} s(m-k,n-l))^2}{2T\sigma^2_{w_{l(m,n)}}}\right.$$
$$\left. - \frac{\sum_{ij\in \mathbf{R}_h}\left(r(m+i,n+j)-\sum_{kl\in\mathbf{R}_h} h_{kl}s(m+i-k,n+j-l)\right)^2}{2T\sigma_v^2}\right) , \tag{4.14}$$

where Z_3 is a normalizing constant. The conditional a posteriori probability function $\pi^l(m,n)$ for $l(m,n)$ given $L_{(m,n)}$, S and R is

$$\pi^l(m,n) \stackrel{\Delta}{=} P\big[l(m,n) \mid L_{(m,n)}, S, R\big] = \frac{p(S,L,R)}{\sum_{l(m,n)} p(S,L,R)}$$
$$= \frac{p(S,L)p(R|S)}{\sum_{l(m,n)} p(S,L)p(R|S)}$$
$$= \frac{p(S,L)}{\sum_{l(m,n)} p(S,L)}$$
$$= \frac{p(s(i,j),s(i',j') \mid L)p(S_{(i,j),(i',j')}|s(i,j),s(i',j'),L)P(L)}{\sum_{l(m,n)} p(s(i,j),s(i',j') \mid L)p(S_{(i,j),(i',j')}|s(i,j),s(i',j'),L)P(L)}$$
$$= \frac{p(s(i,j),s(i',j') \mid L)P(L)}{\sum_{l(m,n)} p(s(i,j),s(i',j') \mid L)P(L)} , \tag{4.15}$$

where $l(m,n)$ is located between the two neighboring pixels $s(i,j)$, $s(i',j')$ and

$$S_{(i,j),(i',j')} \stackrel{\Delta}{=} \{s(k,l) : \forall (k,l) \neq (i,j) \quad \text{or} \quad (i',j')\} \ .$$

The dependence of $p(s(i,j),s(i',j') \mid L)P(L)$ on $l(m,n)$ can be determined from (4.5). In fact, $\pi^l(m,n)$ can be explicitly written as follows:

$$\pi^l(m,n)$$

$$= \frac{1}{Z_4} \exp \left(- \frac{\frac{s^2(i,j)}{2\sigma^2_{w_{\underline{l}(i,j)}}} - \frac{c^{\underline{l}(i',j')}_{i-i',j-j'} s(i,j)s(i',j')}{\sigma^2_{w_{\underline{l}(i,j)}}} + \frac{s^2(i',j')}{2\sigma^2_{w_{\underline{l}(i',j')}}} + \sum_{(m,n)\in c_l} V_{c_l}(L)}{T} \right),$$

where Z_4 is a normalizing constant.

b) DSG Case. The conditional a posteriori density function $\pi^s(m,n)$ for $s(m,n)$ given $S_{(m,n)}$, L and R is

$$\pi^s(m,n) = p\left[s(m,n)|S_{(m,n)}, L, R\right]$$
$$= \frac{1}{Z_5} \exp \left(- \sum_{(i,j)\in \mathbf{R}_{\ominus -}(m,n)} \left(\frac{\left(s(i,j) - \sum_{kl} c_{kl}^{l(i,j)} s(i-k, j-l)\right)^2}{2T\sigma^2_{w_{l(i,j)}}} \right) \right.$$
$$\left. - \sum_{ij\in \mathbf{R}_h} \left(\frac{\left(r(m+i, n+j) - \sum_{kl\in \mathbf{R}_h} h_{kl} s(m+i-k, n+j-l)\right)^2}{2T\sigma_v^2} \right) \right),$$

where Z_5 is a normalizing constant and the support region $\mathbf{R}_{\ominus -}(m,n)$ is specified in Fig. 4.3. The conditional a posteriori probability function $\pi^l(m,n)$ for $l(m,n)$ given $L_{(m,n)}$, S and R is

$$\pi^l(m,n) = P\left[l(m,n)|L_{(m,n)}, S, R\right]$$
$$= \frac{p(S,L,R)}{\sum_{l(m,n)} p(S,L,R)} = \frac{p(S,L)p(S|R)}{\sum_{l(m,n)} p(S,L)p(S|R)}$$
$$= \frac{p(S|L)P(L)}{\sum_{l(m,n)} p(S|L)P(L)} . \tag{4.16}$$

Recall that

$$p(S|L) = \prod_{(i,j)} p\big(s(i,j)|\{s(k,l) : (k,l) \in \mathbf{R}_{\oplus +}(i,j)\}, l(i,j)\big)$$

and

$$P(L) = P\left(l(i,j)|\,\{l(k,l) : (k,l) \in \mathbf{R}_{\oplus +}(i,j)\}\right) .$$

Inserting these two equations into (4.16), we have

$$\pi^l(m,n) = \frac{1}{Z_6} p\left(s(m,n)|\,\{s(k,l) : (k,l) \in \mathbf{R}_{\oplus +}(m,n)\}\;, l(m,n)\right)$$
$$\times P\left(l(m,n)|\,\{l(k,l) : (k,l) \in \mathbf{R}_{\oplus +}(m,n)\}\right) , \tag{4.17}$$

where Z_6 is a normalizing constant. The remaining term in (4.17), $p(s(m,n)|\{s(k,l) : (k,l) \in \mathbf{R}_{\oplus +}(m,n)\}, l(m,n))$ can be expressed as:

$$p\left(s(m,n)\middle|\left\{s(k,l):(k,l)\in \mathbf{R}_{\oplus+}(m,n)\right\},l(m,n)\right)$$

$$=\frac{1}{\sqrt{2\pi T\sigma^2_{w_{l(m,n)}}}}\exp\left\{-\frac{\left[s(m,n)-\sum_{kl}c_{kl}^{l(m,n)}s(m-k,n-l)\right]^2}{2T\sigma^2_{w_{l(m,n)}}}\right\}.$$

4.3.1 Simulated Annealing Approach

The simulated annealing method can be implemented in a sequential or parallel manner. We first describe sequential simulated annealing, which is appropriate for raster scanning of the image. We keep the temperature constant for each sweep of the image and reduce the temperature only after the complete sweep (or iteration) of the image. Since $\pi^s(m,n)$ and $\pi^l(m,n)$ both depend on T, we henceforth denote them by $\pi_t^s(m,n)$ and $\pi_t^l(m,n)$ respectively.

a) Sequential Simulated Annealing Algorithm. The sequential simulated annealing algorithm can be described as follows: Let (m_t,n_t), $t=1,2,\ldots,$ be the sequence in which the sites are visited for updating.

1) Set $t=0$ and assign an initial configuration denoted as S_{-1}, L_{-1} and an initial temperature $T(0)=1$.
2) The evolution $L_{t-1}\longrightarrow L_t$ of the hidden system can be obtained by sampling the next point of the hidden system from the raster-scanning scheme based on the conditional probability mass function $\pi_t^l(m_t,n_t)$ and keeping the rest of L_{t-1} unchanged.
3) Set $t=t+1$. Go back to Step 2 until a complete sweep of the field L is finished.
4) The evolution $S_{t-1}\longrightarrow S_t$ of the observed system can be obtained by sampling the new value of the observations $s(m_t,n_t)$ based on the conditional pdf $\pi_t^s(m_t,n_t)$ and keeping the rest of S_{t-1} unchanged.
5) Set $t=t+1$. Go back to Step 4 until a complete sweep of the whole image is achieved.
6) Goto step 2 until $t>t_f$, where t_f is a specified integer.

The following theorem from [4.10] guarantees that simulated annealing converges to the MAP estimate if the stated conditions are satisfied.

Theorem 1. *If the following conditions are satisfied:*

(a) $\sum_{kl}|c_{kl}^{l}|=\varrho<1 \quad \forall \underline{l}$,

(b) *Let* $T(t)\longrightarrow 0$ *as* $t\longrightarrow\infty$, *and*

(c) $T(t)\geq C/\log(1+k(t))$,

then for any starting configuration S_{-1}, L_{-1}, *we have*

$$p(S_t, L_t \mid S_{-1}, L_{-1}, R) \longrightarrow \pi_0(S, L), \quad as \quad t \longrightarrow \infty, \tag{4.18}$$

where $\pi_0(\cdot,\cdot)$ *is the uniform distribution over the MAP solutions and* $k(t)$ *is the sweep iteration number at time* t.

b) Parallel Simulated Annealing Algorithm. As pointed out in [4.5, 13], stochastic relaxation converges very slowly to the MAP estimate because of the logarithmic temperature cooling schedule. Now, in [4.5], it was suggested that simulated annealing can be implemented in an asynchronous parallel machine to speed up the processing. However, an asynchronous machine may be rather difficult to implement and use compared to a single-instruction multiple-data (SIMD) machine. Here we present a coding scheme for implementation of simulated annealing on an SIMD machine as has been suggested by *Murray* et al. in [4.14], *see also* [4.15]. The total speed-up depends on the size of the neighborhood of the Markov random field. In theory, we can have $2N^2/k$ speed-up if we have enough processors where N^2 is the total number of pixels in the image and k is the size of the neighborhood of the Markov random field. We describe this maximally parallel "coding scheme" next.

Instead of updating one pixel at each iteration, we can partition the entire image into disjoint regions (called *coding regions*) so that pixels which belong to the same region are conditionally independent given the data of all the other regions. The total number of coding regions depends on the size of the neighborhood support of the image model, hence the speed-up factor given above. Since the pixels in the same coding region are conditionally independent, we can update them simultaneously at each iteration by using the previous iteration result in the sequential simulated annealing procedure. A parallel version of our simulated annealing procedure can thus be described as:

1) Set $t = 0$ and assign an initial configuration denoted as S_{-1}, L_{-1}, an initial temperature $T(0) = 1$ and the disjoint coding regions for S denoted as $\Gamma_1^s, \Gamma_2^s, \ldots, \Gamma_{\alpha_1}^s$ and the disjoint coding regions for L denoted as $\Gamma_1^l, \Gamma_2^l, \ldots, \Gamma_{\alpha_2}^l$. Here, we assume that α_1 and α_2 are the total number of coding regions for S and L respectively.

2) The evolution $L_{t-1} \longrightarrow L_t$ of the line field can be obtained by sampling the new value of the coding region $\Gamma_{i_t}^l$ of the structure image L_t based on the conditional probability mass function $\pi_t^l(m,n)\ \forall(m,n) \in \Gamma_{i_t}^l$, where $\Gamma_{i_t}^l$ is the coding region visited at time t.

3) Set $t = t + 1$. Go back to Step 2 until the whole line field is finished.

4) The evolution $S_{t-1} \longrightarrow S_t$ of the image can be obtained by sampling the new value of the coding region $\Gamma_{i_t}^s$ of the image S_t based on the conditional density function $\pi_t^s(m,n)\ \forall(m,n) \in \Gamma_{i_t}^s$, where $\Gamma_{i_t}^s$ is the coding region visited at time t.

5) Set $t = t + 1$ and assign a new value to $T(t + 1)$ after each complete sweep of the image and go forward to the next step, otherwise keep the temperature unchanged and go back to the previous step.

6) Go to step 2 until $t > t_f$, where t_f is a specified integer.

The following theorem from [4.16] guarantees that this parallel processing version of simulated annealing will converge to the MAP estimate under the stated conditions.

Theorem 2. *If the following conditions are satisfied:*

(a) $\sum_{kl} | c_{kl}^{l} | = \varrho < 1 \quad \forall \underline{l}$,

(b) $T(t) \longrightarrow 0 \quad$ *as* $\quad t \longrightarrow \infty$, $\quad$ *and*

(c) $T(t) \geq C / \log[1 + k(t)]$,

then for any starting configuration S_{-1}, L_{-1}, *we have*

$$p(S_t, L_t \mid S_{-1}, L_{-1}, R) \longrightarrow \pi_0(S, L), \quad \textit{as} \quad t \longrightarrow \infty . \tag{4.19}$$

4.3.2 Deterministic Search for the MAP Estimate

Instead of using a stochastic approach, we can use a deterministic method to search for a local optimal point instead of a global one. This deterministic algorithm is an extension of the iterated conditional mode of [4.11] to the continuous valued, compound Gauss Markov random fields. An advantage of deterministic relaxation is that the convergence is much faster than that of simulated annealing on a sequential machine. The disadvantage is the local nature of the optimum achieved. The algorithm can be described as follows: Let (m_t, n_t), $t = 1, 2, \ldots$ be the sequence in which the sites are visited for updating.

1) Start at any initial point S_0 and L_0 and set the temperature T to 1 throughout the whole algorithm and set $t = 1$. Set $\varepsilon > 0$.

2) The evolution $L_{t-1} \longrightarrow L_t$ of the hidden system can be obtained by maximizing the functional $\pi^l(m_t, n_t)$ and keeping the rest of L_{t-1} unchanged.

3) Set $t = t + 1$. Go back to Step 2 until a complete sweep of the field L is finished.

4) The evolution $S_{t-1} \longrightarrow S_t$ of the observed system can be obtained by maximizing the functional $\pi^s(m_t, n_t)$ while keeping the rest of S_{t-1} unchanged.

5) Set $t = t + 1$. Go back to Step 4 until a complete sweep of the whole image is achieved.

6) Go to Step 2 until

$$| p(S_t, L_t \mid R) - p(S_{t-1}, L_{t-1} \mid R) | < \varepsilon . \tag{4.20}$$

7) Finally, set $\hat{S} = S_t$, $\hat{L} = L_t$.

Among the above five steps, only steps 2 and 3 need further explanation. The new value $l(m_t, n_t)$ in Step 2 can be obtained by exhaustive search since $l(m_t, n_t)$ can take on only a small number of values. In distinction, since $\pi^s(m_t, n_t)$ is a quadratic form of $s(m_t, n_t)$, the new value $s(m_t, n_t)$ in Step 3 can be easily obtained by taking a derivative of $\pi^s(m_t, n_t)$ and setting it to zero.

It is clearly seen that such a new choice of values for S & L at (m_t, n_t) always increases the value of the likelihood function, i.e.

$$p(S_t, L_t \mid R) \geq p(S_{t-1}, L_{t-1} \mid R) . \tag{4.21}$$

In general, the deterministic search converges faster than simulated annealing, but not necessarily to the the global optimal MAP estimate. As in Sect. 4.3.1 a parallel version of deterministic search is possible.

4.4 Parameter Identification and Simulation Results

In this section we will describe the practical way to obtain parameters which has been employed in our simulations. Also experimental results of image estimation and restoration will be presented.

4.4.1 Parameter Identification

Various parameters, such as model coefficients and transition probabilities, are needed before we can implement these filtering algorithms. Since these parameters are not often available, we must estimate them from the data. Here we try to estimate these parameters from training data that may be prototypical of the expected noisy images. Using four orientation directional edge operators scanning through the training image (the original image is used here), we partition this image into six disjoint regions. Each region corresponds to a different submodel which will be used to model that part of the image. After obtaining a model configuration, i.e. the hidden structure of the whole image, we can use *maximum likelihood* (ML) identification techniques to estimate the various submodels' coefficients.

For the causal DSG case, we can obtain ML identification by using the classic *least squared error* parameter identification method within each disjoint structural region. For the noncausal CGM case, the situation is more complicated and the difficulty is twofold. First, the ML identification for a noncausal Gauss-Markov model is not the classic least-squares problem [4.7]. A method called the "coding scheme" has been widely used. However, this method is not efficient in that only 50 % of the data is used. Also the result is not unique since many different coding schemes exist. In [4.7], a consistent estimation method was proposed for the noncausal Gauss-Markov model. This scheme is quite similar to least-square error identification. We adopt this method for parameter identification in the CGM case. Second, due to the covariance constraints on the submodel coefficients (4.7), the set of coefficients obtained through the above identification procedures will be not consistent in general. There are two ways around this difficulty. One of them is to modify the identification results from the least-squares method to make the solutions consistent. Another way is to heuristically assign a set of consistent model coefficients that seems reasonable, much as was done in [4.5]. Here we use this latter ad hoc approach to obtain the consistent set of model coefficients needed for our simulations.

The transition probabilities for the lower-level Markov chain of the DSG random field can be obtained by using the ML identification technique given the model configuration of the image. It turns out that *histogram estimation* is the optimal solution. For the line field in the CGM model, we use the same Gibbs distribution as in [4.5].

4.4.2 Experimental Results

In this section, we present some simulation results and compare them with Wiener filtering results and also with deterministic relaxation. All simulations use first order image models. For image estimation (i.e. no blurring), white Gaussian noise was added to our intensity data at the signal-to-noise ratio (SNR) = 10 dB. Figure 4.4 shows estimation results for the DSG model and is arranged as follows: (A) shows the input image (degraded image), (B) shows the linear filtering (Wiener filter) result, (C) shows the simulated annealing result with 200 iterations, and (D) shows a deterministic search result with 25 iterations. The estimation results for the CGM model are shown in Fig. 4.5.

It is clearly seen that the estimate results from both compound Gauss-Markov models provide better visual quality, i.e. sharper edges and cleaner flat regions, than the simple Gaussian models. Although the deterministic relaxation results have some degree of degradation compared with those of simulated annealing, they are still superior to those of the simple Gaussian models, with the DSG model getting into more difficulties, perhaps because of its large number of transition probabilities.

Comparing the simulated annealing results for the DSG model (Fig. 4.5 C) and the CGM model (Fig. 4.6 C), the results are visually quite similar, with the DSG-based estimate showing a bit more detail and the CGM-based estimate apparently a bit smoother. However, this visual difference could easily be accounted for by differences in the model coefficients, transition probabilities, line-field parameters, and model orders.

Simulations for image restoration, i.e. deblurring, were also performed. The blurring function was the 5×5 uniform blur. Figure 4.6 shows the estimate results for the DSG model restored with BSNR = 20 dB. The restoration results based on the CGM model from the same blurred and noisy image are shown in Fig. 4.7.

Here, the differences among the restoration results for the various models become much stronger. The compound models provide sharper images without the noise amplification that results in the LSI Gauss-Markov based estimates. Comparing the two compound models, we find that the DSG model-based results appear somewhat better than the first-order CGM based estimates. Both compound models

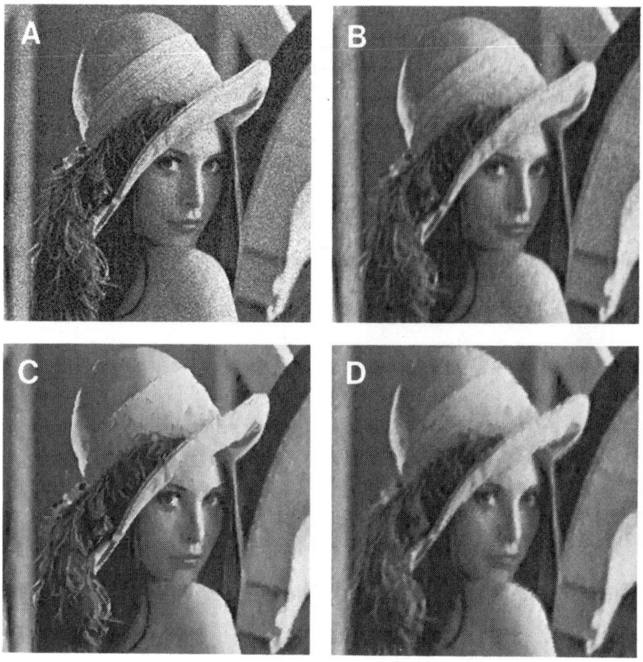

Fig. 4.4.
(**A**) Noisy image with SNR = 10 dB; (**B**) Wiener filter result for the NSHP model with SNR = 10 dB; (**C**) Simulated annealing result for the DSG model at 200 iterations; (**D**) Deterministic relaxation result for the DSG model at 25 iterations

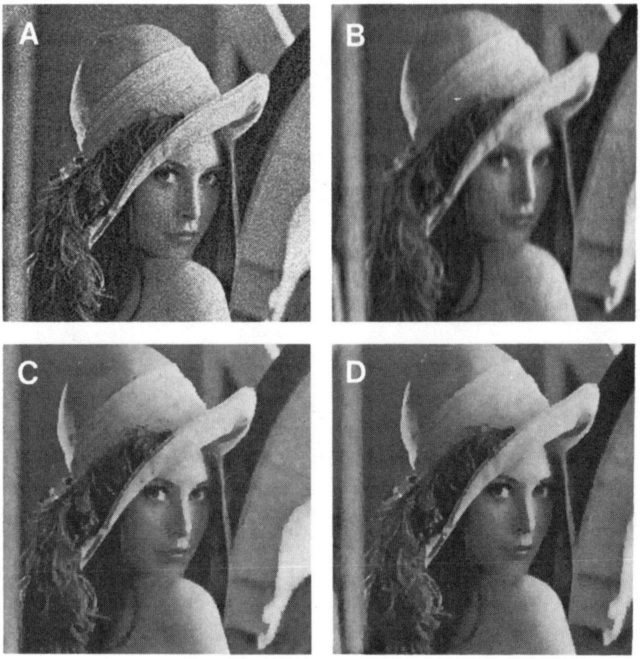

Fig. 4.5.
(**A**) Noisy image with SNR = 10 dB; (**B**) Wiener filter result for Gauss-Markov model with SNR = 10 dB; (**C**) Simulated annealing result for the CGM model at 200 iterations; (**D**) Deterministic relaxation result for the CGM model at 25 iterations

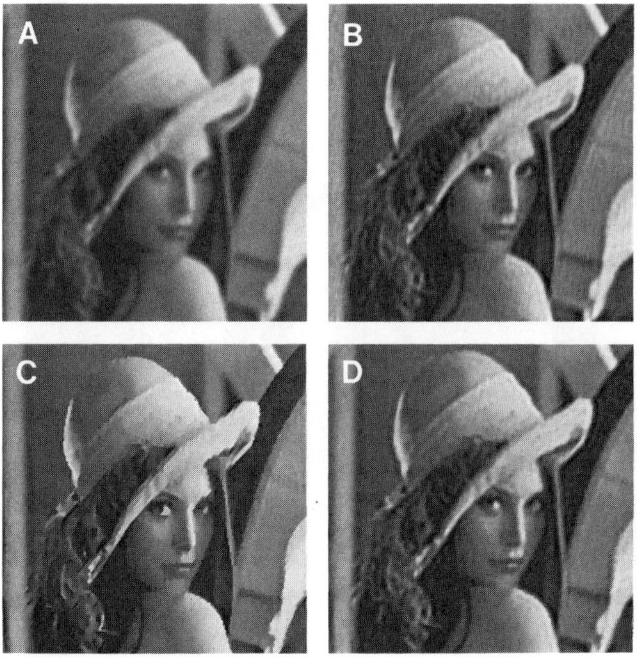

Fig. 4.6.
(**A**) Blurred and noisy image with BSNR = 20 dB; (**B**) Wiener filter result for the NSHP model with SNR = 20 dB; (**C**) Simulated annealing result for the DSG model at 200 iterations; (**D**) Deterministic relaxation result for the DSG model at 25 iterations

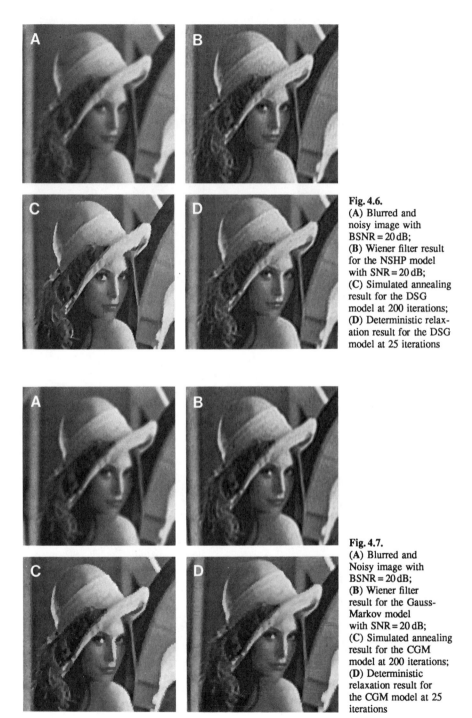

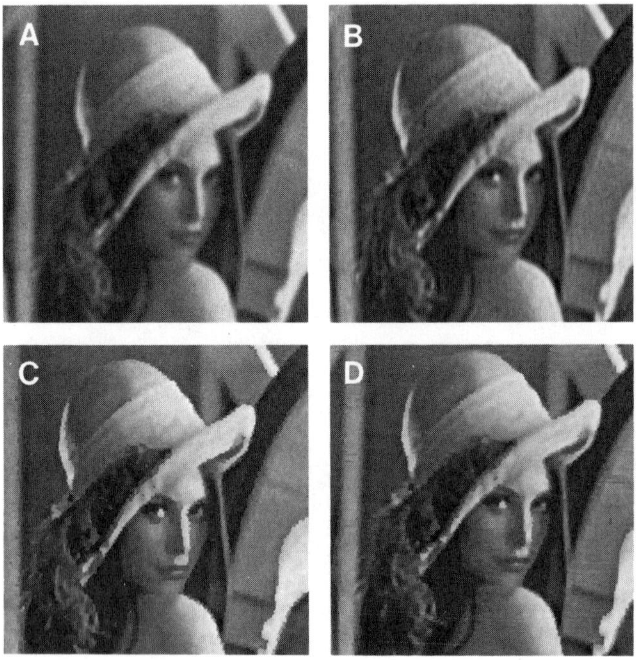

Fig. 4.7.
(**A**) Blurred and Noisy image with BSNR = 20 dB; (**B**) Wiener filter result for the Gauss-Markov model with SNR = 20 dB; (**C**) Simulated annealing result for the CGM model at 200 iterations; (**D**) Deterministic relaxation result for the CGM model at 25 iterations

allow the restoration to proceed with strong noise reduction in fairly flat regions of the image, yet still retain sharp edge restoration. The Wiener filter results clearly suffer from an inability to deal with these twin problems.

4.5 Texture Segmentation

Many algorithms based on the statistical approach have been proposed to solve texture discrimination problems. Among all methods used in the statistical approach, the multiple autoregressive (MAR) model method is the most widely used. However, the result obtained from the MAR model has one major drawback, that is, many isolated spots (false alarms) exist. Most researchers avoid this difficulty by using a small window around the pixel and making a decision not only based on the model itself but also on the model distribution within this window. In order to avoid using this ad hoc method, we propose a solid mathematical model to perform this task and also avoid the drawback occurring in MAR models. The idea of this model is that the value of the model itself is also regarded as a random field with a specific distribution. This distribution usually reflects the a priori information we know about the model distribution of the target image. By doing this, we have again constructed a compound random field which possesses two components or levels.

4.5.1 Mathematical Models for Texture Segmentation

For texture discrimination, we can think of the lower level field as the texture class and the upper level field as the observed image. Because of its ease in the problem of parameter estimation, due to its causal structure, we use only the DSG model for texture segmentation.

We assume that $\tilde{s}(m,n) \stackrel{\Delta}{=} s(m,n) - E[s(m,n)]$ satisfies (4.10) and that $w^{l(m,n)}(m,n)$ is a white Gaussian noise field with zero mean. Moreover, the mean $E[s(m,n)]$ only depends on $l(m,n)$. Due to the NSHP causality, the probability mass function for the lower level field L is

$$P(L) = \prod_{mn} P_l(m,n)$$

and the condition probability density function for the upper level field S given the lower level field L is

$$p(S|L) = \prod_{mn} p_s(m,n)$$

where

$$P_l(m,n) \stackrel{\Delta}{=} P\left(l(m,n)|(l(m+k,n+l) : (k,l) \in \mathbf{R}_{\oplus+})\right) \quad ,$$

$$p_s(m,n) \stackrel{\Delta}{=} p\left(s(m,n)|l(m,n), \left(l(m+k,n+l), s(m+k,n+l) : (k,l) \in \mathbf{R}_{\oplus+}\right)\right) \; .$$

We use the following functional form for the conditional probability mass function of $l(m,n)$

$$P_l(m,n) \stackrel{\triangle}{=} \frac{1}{Z} \exp \left[-\beta \sum_{k,l \in \mathbf{R}_{\oplus +}} \delta \left(l(m,n) - l(m+k, n+l) \right) / T \right] ,$$

where Z is a normalizing constant, β is a clustering constant and

$$\delta \left(l(m,n) - l(m',n') \right) = \begin{cases} 1 & \text{if } l(m,n) = l(m',n') \\ 0 & \text{otherwise} . \end{cases}$$

The above functional form has a clustering property, i.e. if the majority of neighboring pixels of $l(m,n)$ belong to a certain texture, then $l(m,n)$ has a higher probability of belonging to this texture than the others. Note that if β is zero, then the DSG model becomes an MAR model.

4.5.2 Supervised and Unsupervised Algorithms

There are two methods of feature extraction – the supervised mode and the unsupervised mode. In the supervised mode, we know the class of each training sample. In our case, the AR coefficients of each texture class (which can be extracted by

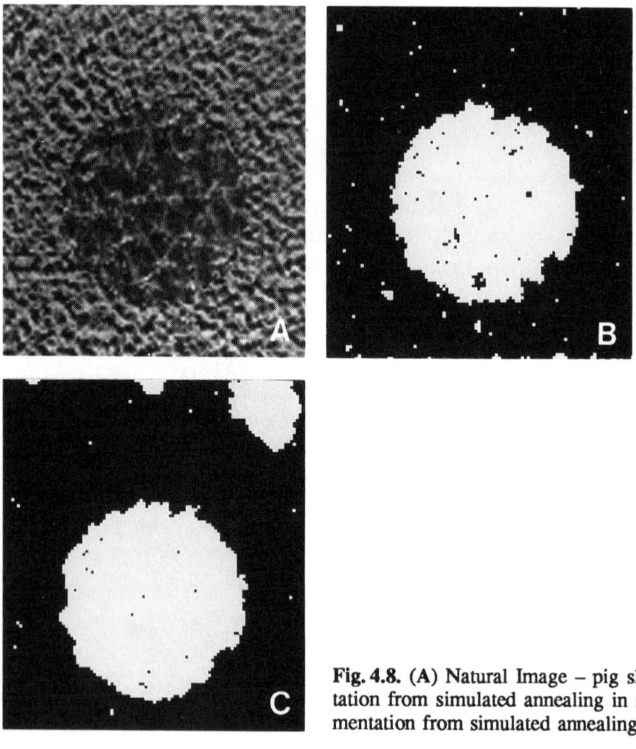

Fig. 4.8. (A) Natural Image – pig skin on paper; (B) Segmentation from simulated annealing in supervised mode; (C) Segmentation from simulated annealing in unsupervised mode

a least square error fitting) are known in advance. For the unsupervised mode, the class of each training sample is unknown. Then features must be obtained by using a clustering technique. In our case, the model parameters can be obtained by first dividing the whole image into several blocks, then performing parameter identification for each block and finally using a *K-means* algorithm to obtain the model parameters for each class, thereby treating the coefficients and means from each block as feature vectors [4.17].

4.5.3 Experimental Results

The above segmentation procedures were applied to a natural image. The clustering constant β is 0.5. Figure 4.8 A shows a natural texture image made up of two different textures from the Brodatz collection. The background is a chapter texture and the inner circle is a pig-skin texture. The image size is 128×128. The window size for the K-means algorithm is 8×8. Figure 4.8 B shows the segmentation results obtained from simulated annealing with 200 iterations in the supervised mode. Figure 4.8 C shows the segmentation results obtained from simulated annealing with 200 iterations in the unsupervised mode. The segmentation results obtained from simulated annealing have a high percentage of correct classification and almost no isolated errors for the cases of both supervised and unsupervised algorithms.

4.6 Conclusions

In this chapter, we have developed compound Gauss-Markov random fields for image modeling and presented their MAP estimators for image estimation and restoration. Corresponding to the causal and noncausal approaches, we proposed two different compound Gauss-Markov fields to model images, i.e. DSG and CGM models. The nice features of compound random fields are that the upper level field can provide a description of the local characteristics for each pixel while the lower level field provides the mechanism for model transitions to represent local structure. Therefore, compound models can more faithfully reflect this property of real images, and hence, processing results based on these compound models can be markedly better. In fact, our simulation results have shown that compound Gauss-Markov models do provide much better visual results (preserving edges with little remaining noise) than can LSI models.

Due to the complexities of the compound Gauss-Markov models, it is in general hard to find an analytic solution for the MAP estimate. An appropriate version of simulated annealing for the compound Gauss-Markov models has been developed and applied to obtain the MAP estimates. Since Gaussian random fields have non-compact range spaces, a proof of convergence of simulated annealing was needed for the compound Gauss-Markov models. We have established the convergence results of simulated annealing for a broad class of compound Gauss-Markov models in the estimation case. Due to the extensive computation of simulated annealing, a "coding" version for parallel implementation and a suboptimal solution, i.e. a deterministic relaxation were developed to speed up the processing.

Regarding causal and noncausal modeling approaches, the experiments show that both approaches perform similarly for image estimation and restoration. However, parameter identification for the causal models (DSG) is much easier than the noncausal models (CGM).

References

4.1 J. F. Abramatic, L. M. Silverman: "Nonlinear Restoration of Noisy Images," *IEEE Trans. Pattern Anal. Machine Intell.* PAMI-**4**, 141–149 (1982)

4.2 F. C. Jeng, J. W. Woods: "Inhomogeneous Gaussian Image Models for Image Estimation and Restoration," *IEEE Trans. Acoust., Speech, and Signal Process.* ASSP-**36**, 1305–1312 (1988)

4.3 H. E. Knutsson, R. Wilson, G. H. Granlund: "Anisotropic Nonstationary Image Estimation and Its Applications: Part I-Restoration of Noisy Images," *IEEE Trans. Commun.* COM-**31**, 388–397 (1983)

4.4 S. A. Rajala, R. J. P. DeFigueiredo: "Adaptive Nonlinear Image Restoration by a Modified Kalman Filtering Approach," *IEEE Trans. Acoust., Speech, and Signal Process.* ASSP-**29**, 1033–1042 (1981)

4.5 S. Geman, D. Geman: "Stochastic Relaxation, Gibbs Distributions, and the Bayesian Restoration of Images," *IEEE Trans. Pattern Anal. Machine Intell.* PAMI-**6**, 721–741 (1984)

4.6 J. W. Woods, S. Dravida, R. Mediavilla: "Image Estimation Using Doubly Stochastic Gaussian Random Field Models," *IEEE Trans. Pattern Anal. Machine Intell.* PAMI-**9**, 245–253 (1987)

4.7 R. L. Kashyap, R. Chellappa: "Estimation and Choice of Neighbors in Spatial-Interaction Models of Images," *IEEE Trans. Inform. Theory* IT-**29**, 60–72 (1983)

4.8 J. W. Woods: "Two-dimensional Discrete Markovian Fields,"*IEEE Trans. Inform. Theory* IT-**18**, 232–240 (1972)

4.9 F. C. Jeng, J. W. Woods: "Image Estimation by Stochastic Relaxation in the Compound Gaussian Case," *Proceedings ICASSP 1988* (New York, 1988) pp. 1016–1019

4.10 F. C. Jeng, J. W. Woods: "Simulated Annealing in Compound Gauss-Markov Random Fields," *IEEE Trans. Inform. Theory* IT-**36**, 94–101 (1990)

4.11 J. Besag: "On the Statistical Analysis of Dirty Pictures", *J. Royal Statistics Soc. B* **48**, 259–302 (1986)

4.12 A. P. Dempster, N. M. Laird, D. B. Rubin: "Maximum Likelihood from Incomplete Data via the EM Algorithm," *Ann. Royal Statistical Soc.* 1–38 (1978)

4.13 S. Kirkpatrick, C. D. Gelatt, M. P. Vecchi: "Optimization by Simulated Annealing," *Science* **220** 671–680 (1983)

4.14 D. W. Murray, A. Kashko, H. Buxton: "A Parallel Approach to the Picture Restoration Algorithm of Geman and Geman on an SIMD Machine," *Image and Vision Comput.* **4**, 133–142 (1986)

4.15 H. Derin, C. S. Won: "A Parallel Image Segmentation Algorithm Using Relaxation with Varying Neighborhoods and its Mapping to Array Processors, " *Computer Vision, Graphics, and Image Process.* CVGIP-**40**, 54–78 (1987)

4.16 F. C. Jeng: "Compound Gauss-Markov Random Fields for Image Estimation and Restoration," *Ph. D. Thesis,* Rensselaer Polytechnic Institute, Troy, NY (1988)

4.17 J. Zhang, J. W. Modestino: "A Model Fitting Approach to Cluster Validation with Application to Stochastic Model-Based Image Segmentation," in *Proceedings of ICASSP 1988* (New York, 1988)

5. Image Estimation Using 2D Noncausal Gauss-Markov Random Field Models

R. Chellappa, T. Simchony, and Z. Lichtenstein

With 8 Figures

This chapter is concerned with the representation and applications of 2D noncausal Gauss Markov random field (GMRF) models and their extensions to image estimation in the presence of additive Gaussian or multiplicative noise. We first present the GMRF and Compound GMRF models, originally developed by Woods. Then estimation methods for GMRF model parameters are discussed. Specifically, we consider the coding, pseudolikelihood and constrained maximum likelihood methods for the GMRF model. A variation of the popular Expectation Maximization (EM) is presented for the estimation of parameters in the Compound GMRF model. The usefulness of these methods is illustrated using real images.

We consider two image estimation applications. The first application is estimation of gray level images modeled by GMRF models and corrupted by film grain noise. The degradation involves nonlinear transformation and multiplicative noise. We take a Bayesian approach using the GMRF as the prior distribution and compute the maximum a posteriori (MAP) estimate, using either a stochastic or deterministic relaxation technique. The second application is estimation of gray level images modeled by compound GMRF models and corrupted by additive Gaussian noise. A *deterministic* algorithm for obtaining a near-optimal MAP estimate is presented. The deterministic algorithm which is an extension of the graduated non convexity (GNC) algorithm is able to find the approximate MAP estimate in a small number of iterations. As a by product, the line process configuration determined by the MAP estimate produces an accurate edge map. Real image results are given to illustrate the applications.

5.1 Preliminaries

In the analysis and processing of 2D images one encounters a large amount of data. In a typical image estimation problem, it is not uncommon to work with images defined on grids of dimensions 256×256 or 512×512. To enable efficient processing of this data, it would be preferable to have an underlying model that explains the dominant statistical characteristics of the given data. Subsequent processing of the images can be efficiently done using the models fitted to the images. A typical image is represented by a 2D array of numbers, the gray level variations defined over a rectangular or square lattice. One of the important characteristics of such data is the special nature of the statistical dependence of the gray level at

Springer Series in Information Sciences, Vol. 23
A.K. Katsaggelos (ed.): Digital Image Restoration

a lattice point on those of its neighbors. One way of characterizing the statistical dependence among the neighboring pixels is to represent $x(s)$ as a linear weighted combination of $\{x(s+\tau), \tau \in N\}$ and additive noise, where N is known as the neighbor set and does not contain $(0,0)$. Specific restrictions on the members of the neighbor set N yield representations familiar in image processing literature. For example, the popular "causal models" are obtained when N is defined as a subset of the set $\{(i,j) : i \leq 0, j \leq 0, (i,j) \neq (0,0)\}$. One can generalize the causal models to obtain the class of "unilateral" models by including more neighbors, but still preserving the recursive structure of the image processing algorithms. The unilateral models result when N is a subset of the non symmetric half plane S^+ defined recursively in [5.1]. Unlike in a 1D discrete stochastic process, where the existence of a preferred direction is inherently assumed, no such preferred ordering is appropriate for a 2D discrete lattice on which an image is defined. Thus it is possible that $x(s)$ is dependent on neighboring pixels in all directions leading to noncausal or bilateral representation. The simplest noncausal model is obtained when $x(s)$ is dependent on its east, west, north, and south neighbors. One can consider more general representations by including the diagonal neighbors and so on.

In this chapter we are first concerned with a particular class of 2D noncausal models known as the Gaussian Markov random field (GMRF) models. Let $\{x(s), s \in \Omega\}, \Omega = \{s = (i,j); 1 \leq i, j \leq M\}$ be the original, noise free image gray level data. It is postulated that this data is generated by an appropriate 2D (noncausal) GMRF model. The 2D GMRF models characterize the statistical dependency among pixels by requiring that

$$p\big(x(s)|x(r), r \neq s\big) = p\big(x(s)|x(s+\tau), \tau \in N\big) , \tag{5.1}$$

where N is an appropriate symmetric neighbor set. For instance $N = \{(0,1), (0,-1), (-1,0), (1,0)\}$ corresponds to the simplest GMRF model and by including more neighbors, we can construct higher order GMRF models. Since GMRF models are defined only for symmetric neighbor sets, often N is equivalently characterized using an asymmetrical neighbor set N^*; i.e., if $\tau \in N^*$ then $-\tau \notin N^*$ and $N = (\tau : \tau \in N^*) U (-\tau : \tau \in N^*)$.

In real images, the estimation of gray levels requires the ability of the estimate to preserve the sharpness of edges, which play an important role in human interpretation of images. Linear filters [5.2, 3], as well as minimum mean squared error or maximum a posteriori estimation using the homogeneous GMRF model for the intensity, tend to smear the edges. To avoid this problem, a class of models called the compound GMRF was suggested in [5.4]. The reader is referred to Chap. 4 for detailed discussion on these models. The model suggested is a GMRF coupled with a line process. In this model, the structure of the line process determines the value of the GMRF model coefficients. The GMRF model parameters are required to satisfy a symmetry constraint, and the choice of the parameters for a given line configuration remains an open problem. We consider a simplified compound GMRF model that is a member of the class of models proposed in [5.4]. In our formulation, the line process breaks the correlation between neighboring pixels, when the gray level jump is above a threshold. The model can be viewed as an extension of the weak membrane model [5.5] used for surface interpolation and edge detection. The GMRF breaks when edges occur, which in turn creates homogeneous GMRF patches separated by the line process.

Since the introduction of GMRF models in the literature [5.6–8], there has been considerable interest in using GMRF models for image estimation, image classification, synthesis and coding. Prior to any practical application of GMRF models, two major problems have to be tackled, viz. the estimation of parameters in GMRF models and the choice of appropriate N for the given image. We discuss several estimation methods for the GMRF model representation. The compound GMRF model presents a new problem in parameter estimation. Since we have to estimate the GMRF parameters only in the homogeneous parts of the image, we present a method based on the EM algorithm.

To illustrate the usefulness of GMRF models for image processing applications, algorithms for image estimation are discussed for the case of an image degraded by a multiplicative noise and nonlinear trasnformation. We adopt a Bayesian approach and use the GMRF model for computing the MAP estimate. Obtaining the MAP estimate involves maximization of a very complicated nonconvex function. We first experiment with a deterministic relaxation (DR) method using the line search extension of the conjugate gradient algorithm [5.9]. Although this method may sometimes yield acceptable results, it may converge to a local maximum, if the initial conditions are not chosen properly.

We then present a stochastic relaxation (SR) algorithm to ensure convergence to the global MAP estimate. We use the Metropolis algorithm [5.10–12] which can sample from the conditional distribution, without requiring the explicit distribution.

Since the image pixels can take only finitely many gray level values (256), this introduces quantization due to the use of a continuous GMRF model. It is shown that as the number of gray levels increases the MAP solution we find using the quantized SR algorithm converges in probability to the continuous MAP solution. Owing to the modeling assumption, the relaxation algorithms require the estimates of GMRF model parameters. Assuming that a prototype of the original image is available, we have used a constrained conjugate gradient algorithm [5.9] to obtain the maximum likelihood (ML) estimate of the GMRF parameters. Examples of estimation of gray level images corrupted by 10 and 5 dB multiplicative lognormal noise implemented using SR, DR, and greedy algorithms [5.13] are given.

In the case of the compound GMRF model and the MAP estimate, we show how the problem can be formulated so that a deterministic algorithm based on GNC principle [5.5] can be used to find a good approximation to the global minimum of the cost function. To obtain the global MAP estimate for an image obeying a compound GMRF model and corrupted by additive Gaussian noise, *Jeng* and *Woods* [5.4] use simulated annealing. This stochastic algorithm is slow, and cannot in practice obey the theoretical requirement on the initial temperature. We use a modified version of the GNC algorithm [5.5]. The algorithm is deterministic and good results are obtained in less then 100 iterations. We have used the algorithm on a real image and obtained good restoration results. The configuration of the line process is determined by the MAP estimate. It provides an accurate estimate of the image edges without any additional cost.

5.2 Model Representation

5.2.1 The GMRF Model

Suppose that the original image $\{x(s)\}$ is defined on a finite lattice $\Omega = \{s = (i,j) : 1 \leq i,j \leq M\}$. We partition this finite lattice Ω into mutually exclusive and totally inclusive subsets Ω_B, the boundary set, and Ω_I, the interior set:

$$\begin{aligned}\Omega_B &= \{s = (i,j) : s \in \Omega \quad \text{and} \quad (s+\tau) \notin \Omega \\ &\qquad \text{for at least one} \quad \tau \in N\} \;, \\ \Omega_I &= \Omega - \Omega_B \;,\end{aligned}$$

where N is a symmetric neighbor set related to the asymmetric neighbor set N^* as $N = \{s : s \in N^*\} \cup \{-s : s \in N^*\}$. Specific assumption on $\{x(s), s \in \Omega_B\}$ leads to finite lattice representations [5.14].

Assume that the original image $\{x(s)\}$ is wide sense stationary, with mean $x_m(s) = E[x(s)]$, and obeys the GMRF model [5.8, 6] defined on Ω_I. Then

$$x(s) - x_m(s) = \Theta^t\left(x_s - x_{m,s}\right) + e(s) \tag{5.2}$$

where $\Theta = \text{col}[\theta_\tau, \tau \in N^*]$, $\boldsymbol{x}_s = \text{col}[x(s+\tau) + x(s-\tau), \tau \in N^*]$, and $\boldsymbol{x}_{m,s} = \text{col}[x_m(s+\tau) + x_m(s-\tau), \tau \in N^*]$. In (5.2), the stationary Gaussian noise sequence $e(s)$ has the following correlation properties:

$$\begin{aligned}E[e(s)e(r)] &= -\nu\theta_{s-r} \quad & (s-r) \in N \\ &= \nu & s = r \\ &= 0 & \text{otherwise}\end{aligned} \tag{5.3}$$

where ν is the variance of $e(s)$. Using (5.2) and (5.3) one can show that [5.8], $\{\boldsymbol{x}(s), s \in \Omega\}$ obeys a 2D Markov property, i.e. $p(x(s)|$ all $x(r), r \neq s) = p(x(s)|x(s+\tau), \tau \in N)$.

The GMRF model considered in this section is noncausal, i.e., the intensity $x(s)$ at site s is a function of the neighbors of s in all directions. The GMRF model are characterized by conditional densities of the form [5.6, 8]

$$p\left(x(s)|\boldsymbol{x}_s\right) = \frac{1}{\sqrt{2\pi\nu}} \exp\left\{-\frac{1}{2\nu}\left[x(s) - x_m(s) - \Theta^{\mathrm{T}}\left(x_s - x_{m,s}\right)\right]^2\right\} \;. \tag{5.4}$$

Using the vector-matrix notation, (5.2) and (5.3) can then be written as

$$B(\Theta)\left(x - x_m\right) = e \;, \tag{5.5}$$

$$E\left[ee^{\mathrm{T}}\right] = \nu B(\Theta) , \tag{5.6}$$

respectively, where $B(\Theta)$ is a block-Toeplitz matrix and $\boldsymbol{x}_m = \mathrm{col}[x_m(s), s \in \Omega_I]$. Assuming $B(\Theta)^{-1}$ exists, from (5.5) and (5.6) we obtain the covariance matrix of the original image as

$$Q_x = E\left[\left(x - x_m\right)\left(x - x_m\right)^{\mathrm{T}}\right] = \nu B(\Theta)^{-1} . \tag{5.7}$$

The probability density function of $\boldsymbol{y}$ can then be written as

$$p(\boldsymbol{x}) = \left\{ \frac{1}{(2\pi)^{M^2} \det(\nu B(\Theta)^{-1})} \right\}^{1/2} \times \exp\left\{ -\frac{1}{2\nu}\left(x - x_m\right)^{\mathrm{T}} B(\Theta)\left(x - x_m\right) \right\} . \tag{5.8}$$

We consider the toroidal boundaries case, where $B(\Theta)$ is a $M^2 \times M^2$ block-circulant symmetric matrix. A necessary and sufficient condition to ensure bounded input bounded output stability in this case is

$$\left(1 - 2\Theta^{\mathrm{T}}\Phi_s\right) > 0 , \qquad \forall s \in \Omega \tag{5.9}$$

where

$$\Phi_s = \mathrm{col}\left[\cos\left(\frac{2\pi}{M} s^{\mathrm{T}}\tau\right), \tau \in N^*\right] . \tag{5.10}$$

5.2.2 The Compound GMRF Model

In order to model piecewise constant information, coupled Markov fields consisting of an Ising model to present the homogeneous part and a line process to model the abrupt transitions were first presented in [5.10]. Extensions to piecewise continuous surface models using compound GMRF were presented in [5.4]. The compound GMRF model is an extension of the weak membrane model defined by *Blake* and *Zissermann* [5.5], and used for surface interpolation as well as edge detection. In this section we extend the weak membrane model to a compound GMRF and line process model.

We define the following conditional distribution for the compound GMRF model:

$$p\left(x(s) | x(s+\tau), x(s-\tau), l(s,\tau), l(s-\tau,\tau), \tau \in N^*\right) = \frac{\mathrm{e}^{-U(x(s)|x(s+\tau),x(s-\tau),l(s,\tau),l(s-\tau,\tau), \tau \in N^*)}}{Z}$$

where N^* is the set of shift vectors corresponding to the neighborhood of the GMRF model. The line process notation is illustrated in Fig. 5.1.

For a second order GMRF model $N^* = \{(0,1),(1,0),(1,1),(-1,1)\}$. Thus,

$$U\left(x(s) | x(s+\tau), x(s-\tau), l(s,\tau), l(s-\tau,\tau), \tau \in N^*\right)$$

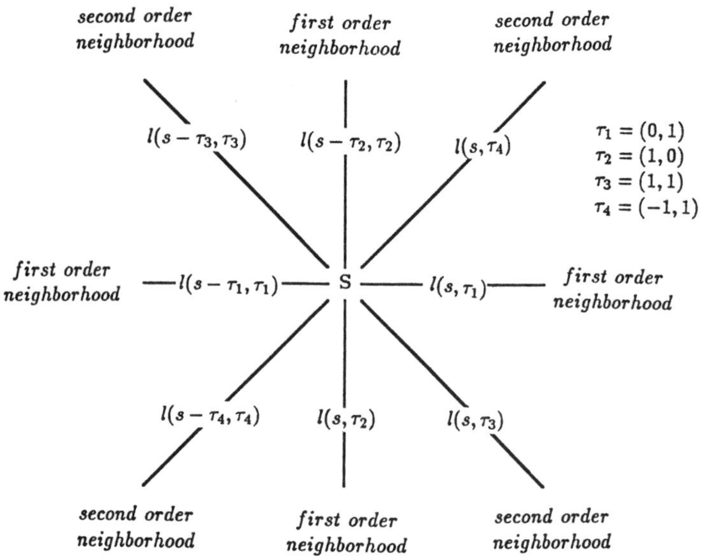

Fig. 5.1. The line process notation for a second order model

$$= \frac{1}{2\nu}\left[\sum_{\tau\in N^*} \Theta_\tau \left[(x(s) - x(s+\tau))^2 (1 - l(s,\tau))\right.\right.$$

$$\left.\left. + (x(s) - x(s-\tau))^2 (1 - l(s-\tau,\tau))\right] \left(+(1 - \sum_{\tau\in N^*} 2\Theta_\tau\right) x(s)^2\right] .$$

The line process is now defined on the edges that connect the nodes (the grid points) that are neighbors of a given pixel.

The prior probability of the line process is

$$p\left(l(s,\tau_i) | l(r,\tau),\ r\in\Omega,\ \tau\in N^*,\ (r,\tau)\neq(s,\tau_i)\right)$$

$$= \frac{e^{-U(l(s,\tau_i)|l(r,\tau),\ r\in\Omega,\ \tau\in N^*,\ (r,\tau)\neq(s,\tau_i))}}{Z}$$

where

$$U\left(l(s,\tau_i) | l(r,\tau),\ r\in\Omega,\ \tau\in N^*,\ (r,\tau)\neq(s,\tau_i)\right) = \beta l(s,\tau_i) .$$

Recall that for a zero mean GMRF model [5.6]

$$U\left(x(s) | x(s+\tau), x(s-\tau),\ \tau\in N^*\right)$$

$$= \frac{1}{2\nu}\left(x(s) - \sum_{\tau\in N^*} \Theta_\tau \left[x(s+\tau) + x(s-\tau)\right]\right)^2 .$$

It can be shown that the conditional distribution of the compound GMRF model is equal to the GMRF model when $l(s,\tau) = 0$, $l(s-\tau,\tau) = 0$, $\forall\tau\in N^*$. We shall assume that $\Theta_\tau > 0$, $\forall\tau\in N^*$ which is almost always the case for the first order neighborhoods. The corresponding joint distribution of the compound GMRF is

$$p(x,l) = \frac{e^{-U(x,l)}}{Z}$$

where

$$U(\boldsymbol{x},\boldsymbol{l}) = \sum_{s\in\Omega}\left\{\sum_{\tau\in N^*}\Theta_\tau\left[\frac{1}{2\nu}[x(s)-x(s+\tau)]^2(1-l(s,\tau))+\beta l(s,\tau)\right]\right.$$

$$\left.+\frac{1}{2\nu}\left(1-\sum_{\tau\in N^*}2\Theta_\tau\right)x(s)^2\right\} .$$

One can see that if $x(s) - x(s+\tau)$ is bigger then a threshold, it is cheaper to break the connection and introduce an edge in the same way it is done in the weak membrane formulation. The global energy corresponding to the compound GMRF model with additive white noise is:

$$U(\boldsymbol{x},\boldsymbol{l}|\boldsymbol{y}) = \sum_{s\in\Omega}\left(\frac{[y(s)-x(s)]^2}{2\sigma^2}+\frac{(1-\sum_{\tau\in N^*}2\Theta_\tau)x(s)^2}{2\nu}\right.$$

$$\left.+\sum_{\tau\in N^*}\Theta_\tau\left\{\frac{1}{2\nu}[x(s)-x(s+\tau)]^2[1-l(s,\tau)]+\beta l(s,\tau)\right\}\right)$$

$$=\frac{1}{2\sigma^2}\sum_{s\in\Omega}\left\{[y(s)-x(s)]^2+\lambda^2\left(1-\sum_{\tau\in N^*}2\Theta_\tau\right)x(s)^2\right.$$

$$\left.+\sum_{\tau\in N^*}\Theta_\tau\left\{\lambda^2[x(s)-x(s+\tau)]^2[1-l(s,\tau)]+\alpha l(s,\tau)\right\}\right\} , \quad (5.11)$$

where $\lambda^2 = \sigma^2/\nu$, $\alpha = 2\beta\sigma^2$.

Equation (5.11) corresponds to the model $y(s) = x(s) + n(s)$, where $n(s)$ is additive Gaussian noise with zero mean and variance σ^2.

5.3 Estimation in GMRF Models

In any practical application of GMRF models, two problems have to be tackled. Firstly, given the structure of the model, methods for estimating the parameters of the model must be found, and secondly, the structure of the appropriate model itself must be estimated. By first assuming that the neighbor set N of the GMRF model is known, we discuss several estimation schemes for GMRF models. The problem of choosing appropriate GMRF model for the given data is considered in [5.15]. In general, due to the fact that the Jacobian of the transformation matrix $B(\Theta)$ in (5.8) is not unity, but a complicated function of Θ for GMRF models, the likelihood function is difficult to evaluate for infinite lattice GMRF models. However, for the special case of finite lattice GMRF models, one can evaluate the Jacobian of the tranformation matrix and hence the likelihood function [5.16]. The resulting likelihood function is usually a non quadratic function of the parameters requiring the use of numerical optimization algorithms. To avoid the difficulty of obtaining the likelihood function in a general case, an estimation scheme, known as the coding method, was developed by *Besag* [5.6]. However, the coding estimate is not as efficient as the ML estimate as it only uses part of the given data [5.16]. A least square (LS) estimate whose efficiency lies between that of the coding and ML estimates for Gaussian GMRF models was independently developed in [5.15].

5.3.1 Coding Method

Assume that the noise free image $\{x(s)\}$ obey the GMRF model in (5.4). Consider the case of GMRF model with $N^* = \{(0,1),(1,0)\}$, characterized by $\Theta = \mathrm{col}[\Theta_\tau, \tau \in N^*]$. The conditional distribution $p(x(s)|x(s+\tau)$, all $\tau \in N)$ is of the form,

$$p\left(x(s)|x(s+\tau),\, \tau \in N\right) = \frac{1}{(2\pi\nu)^{1/2}} \exp\left\{ -\frac{1}{2\nu}\left[x(s) - \sum_{\tau \in N} \Theta_\tau x(s+\tau)\right]^2 \right\} .$$

We define Ω_0 to be a subset of Ω such that the sites associated with it, given the observed values at all other sites, are mutually independent. Then the conditional likelihood for this subset has a simple form and the coding estimate Θ_C is given by

$$\Theta_\mathrm{C} = \left[\sum_{\Omega_0} \boldsymbol{q}(s)\boldsymbol{q}^\mathrm{T}(s)\right]^{-1} \left(\sum_{\Omega_0} \boldsymbol{q}(s)x(s)\right)$$

where

$$\boldsymbol{q}(s) = \mathrm{col}\left[x(s+\tau) + x(s-\tau), \tau \in N^*\right] ,$$

and Ω_0 is a subset of Ω (every other site of Ω skipped). The coding scheme yields another estimate similar to Θ_C, say Θ'_C, with the sum being evaluated over Ω–Ω_0. One of the main disadvantages of this method is that the estimates thus obtained are not efficient [5.16] due to the partial utilization of the data.

5.3.2 A Consistent Estimation Scheme

Consider the estimates

$$\tilde{\Omega} = \left[\sum_{\Omega_\mathrm{I}} \boldsymbol{q}(s)\, \boldsymbol{q}^\mathrm{T}(s)\right]^{-1} \left(\sum_{\Omega_\mathrm{I}} \boldsymbol{q}(s)x(s)\right) \tag{5.12}$$

$$\tilde{\nu} = \frac{1}{M^2} \sum_{\Omega_\mathrm{I}} \left[x(s) - \tilde{\Omega}^\mathrm{T} \boldsymbol{q}(s)\right]^2 \tag{5.13}$$

where Ω_I is the region of Ω containing the interior pixels. The estimate $\tilde{\Omega}$ obtained is an improvement over Θ_C. The statistical properties of this estimate are derived in [5.15]. Specifically, in [5.15] the asymptotic mean square convergence was proved. An asymptotic expression for the covariance of the estimator was also derived for the general GMRF model. The asymptotic variance for the first order isotropic

GMRF model was compared to that of the coding and ML estimates. This estimate now known as the pseudolikelihood estimate was originally proposed by *Besag* [5.17]. Subsequently, its efficiency was compared to those of the coding and ML estimates in a note [5.18], for the first order isotropic GMRF model. Consistency of the pseudolikelihood estimate has also been established in [5.19].

5.3.3 Maximum Likelihood Estimation of Parameters

The ML estimates are obtained by minimizing the function [5.6, 20],

$$(-2/M^2)\log p(x|\Theta,\nu) = \frac{1}{(2\pi)^2}\int[\log S(\omega,\Theta)]d\omega + (1/\nu)\left[C_0 - 2\sum_{\tau\in N^*}\Theta_\tau C_\tau\right] + \log 2\pi \tag{5.14}$$

where

$$S(\omega,\Theta) = \frac{\nu}{(1-2\sum_{\tau\in N^*}\Theta_\tau\cos\omega^{\mathrm{T}}\cdot\tau)} \tag{5.15}$$

and C_τ are the sample correlations

$$C_\tau = \frac{1}{M^2}\sum_{s\in\Omega} x(s)x(s+\tau)\ . \tag{5.16}$$

The estimates obtained by minimizing (5.14) should satisfy

$$\left(1-2\sum_{\tau\in N^*}\Theta_\tau\cos\omega^{\mathrm{T}}\cdot\tau\right) > 0 \tag{5.17}$$

for the model to be stable. The ML estimate $\hat{\Theta}$ thus obtained also satisfy

$$\frac{1}{4\pi^2}\int\cos(\omega^{\mathrm{T}}\cdot\tau)S(\omega,\hat{\Theta})d\omega = C_\tau\ . \tag{5.18}$$

The usefulness of the correlation matching property is in developing a GMRF model based approach for 2D maximum entropy power spectrum (MEPS) estimation. Using the correlation matching property and the fact that the 2D MEPS has a structure similar to that of the GMRF spectrum, a model based approach has been developed [5.21] for 2D MEPS estimation.

The ML estimation scheme may not be practical for image and signal processing applications involving large values of M. By using special boundary conditions, computational load can be reduced as discussed in [5.16, 21–23]. Realistically, to minimize (5.14) one has to use a constraint minimization approach because the parameters have to satisfy (5.17). Recently, we have used a modified version of the line search extension of the conjugate gradient method, with the restart procedure suggested in [5.9] for this problem. Every time the search reaches a point out of the constraint set, we add a big penalty term to the evaluated likelihood function to guarantee that the optimal step calculated in each iteration keeps the parameters inside the constraint set. For any given value of $\Theta, \nu(\Theta)$ is computed directly using the equation

$$\frac{\partial \log p(x|\Theta,\nu)}{\partial \nu} = 0 \Rightarrow \nu(\Theta) = \frac{C_0 - 2\sum_{\tau\in N^*}\Theta_\tau C_\tau}{M^2} .$$

Let $f(\Theta) = -\log p(x|\Theta, \nu(\Theta))$ then the modified line search algorithm can be summarized as follows:

Algorithm 1

- *Step 1.* **For** $k = 1$
  a) Given Θ^1 from the scaled LS estimates compute $G_1 = \nabla f(\Theta^1)$.
  b) **Set** $t = 1$, $D_1 = -G_1$
  c) Choose ζ (orthogonality parameter).
  d) **Go to** step 3

- *Step 2.* **For** $k + 2, \cdots, n$:
  a) Compute $G_k = \nabla f(\Theta^k)$.
  b) **If** $|G_{k-1}^{\mathrm{T}} G_k| / |G_k^{\mathrm{T}} G_k| \geq \zeta$ **then** $t = k - 1$.
  c) **Set** $\beta_k = G_k^{\mathrm{T}}(G_k - G_{k-1}) / D_{k-1}^{\mathrm{T}}(G_k - G_{k-1})$
  d) **If** $k = t + 1$ **then**
  set $\gamma_k = 0$ and compute D_k, where $D_k = -G_k + \beta_k D_{k-1} + \gamma_k D_t$
  go to step 3
  else
  compute γ_k and D_k where $\gamma_k = G_k^{\mathrm{T}}(G_{t+1} - G_t) / D_t^{\mathrm{T}}(G_{t+1} - G_t)$ (now check that the search direction D_k is sufficiently downhill)
  if $D_k^{\mathrm{T}} G_k \leq -0.8 G_k^{\mathrm{T}} G_k$ **continue, else set** $t = k - 1$ and **go to** 2.*d*

- *Step 3.*
  a) **Set** $\Theta^{k+1} = \Theta^k + \alpha_k D_k$ where α_k minimizes $f(\Theta^k + \alpha D_k)$. The optimal step is calculated using a univariate search based on the values of $f(\Theta^k + \alpha D_k)$ for different values of α. Every time $\Theta^k + \alpha D_k$ violates any of the M^2 constraints in (5.17) we add a big penalty to the evaluated $f(\Theta^k + \alpha D_k)$ to guarantee that Θ^{k+1} will satisfy the constraints.
  b) **If** the terminating condition holds **stop, else go** back **to** step 2.

Experimental results using this algorithm are given in Sect. 5.4.4.

5.3.4 Parameter Estimation for the Compound Model

The compound GMRF model presents a new problem in parameter estimation. We would like to estimate the GMRF parameters only in the homogeneous regions that do not include edges. The problem is that even if the edge locations are known, removing the adjacent pixels from the rectangular domain we started with leaves a highly irregular domain, which is cumbersome to work with. Furthermore, in the case of ML estimation, the irregularity of the domain makes it impossible to write a closed form expression for the likelihood function, even if toroidal assumptions are made. Instead, we suggest an algorithm based on the EM algorithm [5.24]. For the time being we present the algorithm for estimating the parameters from the original image. We believe that the method can be extended to estimation techniques such as bias compensated least squares (BCLS) [5.25] based on the noisy image. More on applications of the EM algorithm for blur estimation and image restoration may be found in Chap. 6.

The idea behind the algorithm is that we ignore the intensity data in strips centered at the edges, and replace this data by the conditional mean of the GMRF model, given the model parameters and the neighboring pixels intensity data. The conditional mean is calculated using a relaxation method, i.e. for the first order neighborhood we repeatedly set

$$\begin{aligned} x^{k+1}(i,j) = {} & \Theta_x\left(x^k(i+1,j) + x^k(i-1,j)\right) \\ & + \Theta_y\left(x^k(i,j+1) + x^k(i,j-1)\right) . \end{aligned} \tag{5.19}$$

Note that we modify the intensity only in the strips centered at the edges. The iterations are bound to converge, since the stability requirement of the GMRF model parameters ensures that the eigenvalues of the iteration matrix are smaller than 1. Once we have computed the conditional mean, we perform an estimation step based on LS or ML on the smoothed image. We use the estimated parameters to calculate a new conditional mean for the pixels in the edge vicinity, which in turn are used for a new parameter estimation step. We use the GNC edge detector [5.5] to find the location of the edges in the image. In future, we intend to combine the image and parameters estimation. The results we obtain with this algorithm differ significantly from the results obtained directly from the original image. For example, the estimated model variance is much smaller, although the image variance is reduced only slightly. The results show the importance of suppressing the effect of the edges on the parameter estimation. The algorithm is summarized as follows:

Algorithm 2

- 1. Get an initial estimate for the model parameters, using the LS technique on the original image.
- 2. Find the image edges' locations using the GNC algorithm [5.5].
- 3. By using the current estimate of the model parameters, find the conditional mean of the intensity in a strip, four pixels wide, centered at the edge by using the relaxation equation (5.19). (The E step)

- 4. Calulate a new parameter estimate on the smoothed image obtained in step 3 using algorithm 1. (The M step)
- 5. **If** the change in the parameters is small enough – **stop, else go** back **to** step 3.

We experimented with this algorithm on real images and obtained good results [5.26].

5.4 Relaxation Algorithms for MAP Estimation

In this section, we consider the actual MAP estimation procedure, using the GMRF formulation. Given the distribution of the corrupting noise, we write the conditional density of the degraded image conditioned on the original image. The degradation we consider in this work is a nonlinear transformation corrupted by multiplicative lognormal noise. This degradation model corresponds to film grain noise [5.27]. We assume that the original image is generated by a 2D noncausal GMRF model [5.6, 8] with unknown parameters. This assumption enables us to write the probability density function of the original image as a function of the parameters of the GMRF model. Assuming that a prototype of the original image is available, we use the ML technique [5.16, 20, 21] to obtain estimates of the GMRF model parameters from the original image. Thus, the MAP algorithm is written in terms of the GMRF model parameter estimates.

Obtaining the MAP estimate involves maximization of a very complicated function. For a 64×64 image with gray levels in the range 1–256, the dimensionality of the solution space is extremely large, making an exhaustive search for the MAP estimate computationally extensive. We first experiment with a DR method, using the line search extension of the conjugate gradient algorithm [5.9]. Although this method may sometimes yield acceptable results, it may converge to a local maximum, if the initial conditions are not chosen properly.

We then present a SR algorithm to ensure convergence to the global MAP estimate. The conditional distribution $p(x(s)|x(s), x(s+\tau), \tau \in N)$ involves 256 different states corresponding to different levels of $x(s)$. It is inefficient to calculate the explicit conditional distribution necessary for the Gibbs sampler method suggested in [5.10] because the computation should be repeated in every iteration due to the changes in the neighborhood $x(s+\tau), \tau \in N$. We use the Metropolis algorithm [5.10–12], which can sample from this distribution, without requiring the explicit distribution. The Metropolis algorithm requires only the ratio between the probability of the current state and the one suggested to replace it. We can easily calculate this ratio and obtain an efficient algorithm.

The SR algorithm generates a sequence of images which converges in probability to the global MAP estimate. This sequence evolves by local changes in the pixel gray level. Convergence to a local maximum is avoided by permitting random changes that actually decrease the posterior density function. The rate at which convergence is approached, is based on an annealing process [5.10] characterized by a global control parameter T called the temperature. Since the image pixels can take only finitely many gray level values (256), this introduces quantization effects due to the use of a continuous GMRF model. It is first shown that the quantization process defines a discrete Gibbs measure, which is maximized by the SR algorithm of the Metropolis type, for which convergence has been established in [5.12]. We then show that as the number of gray levels is increased, the discrete measure converges in distribution to the continuous measure, and that the MAP solution which we find using the quantized SR algorithm converges in probability to the continuous MAP solution. Owing to the modeling assumption, the relaxation algorithms require the estimates of GMRF model parameters. Assuming that a prototype of the original image is available, we have used a constrained conjugate gradient algorithm [5.9] to obtain the ML estimate of the GMRF parameters. Examples of estimation of gray level images corrupted by 10 and 5 dB multiplicative lognormal noise implemented using SR, DR, and greedy algorithms [5.13] are given.

5.4.1 Image and Noise Models

The image model is the GMRF model considered in (5.4). We consider the following model for image intensity degraded by film grain noise originally proposed in [5.27]:

$$y(s) = cx(s)^{-\gamma} \exp(-v(s)) = cx(s)^{-\gamma} v_1(s) \tag{5.20}$$

where $v(s)$ is a Gaussian random variable with zero mean and variance σ_v^2, c is a multiplication factor and γ defines the nonlinear mapping from the original intensity to the observed image intensity. Hence, v_1 is a multiplicative noise process and obeys a lognormal statistics,

$$p\big(v_1(s)\big) = \frac{1}{\sqrt{2\pi\sigma_v^2} v_1(s)} \exp\left[-\frac{(\log v_1(s))^2}{2\sigma_v^2}\right] .$$

For a specified $\boldsymbol{x}$, the variations in $\boldsymbol{y}$ are given by $\boldsymbol{v} = \mathrm{col}[v_1(s) = y(s)/cx(s)^{-\gamma},\ s \in \Omega]$. Since $v_1(s)$ is a white lognormal noise variable, we can express the conditional density function $p(\boldsymbol{y}|\boldsymbol{x})$ as

$$p(\boldsymbol{y}|\boldsymbol{x}) = \frac{1}{(2\pi\sigma_v^2)^{M^2/2} \prod_{s\in\Omega} y(s)} \times \exp\left\{-\frac{1}{2\sigma_v^2} \sum_{s\in\Omega} \left[\log\left(\frac{y(s)}{cx(s)^{-\gamma}}\right)\right]^2\right\} . \tag{5.21}$$

Chapter 8 presents a Wiener filter for the deconvolution of blurred photographic images corrupted by multiplicative noise.

Knowing the statistical properties of the original image $\boldsymbol{x}$ and the degradations, one can construct the a posteriori density function $p(\boldsymbol{x}|\boldsymbol{y})$ from the observation $\boldsymbol{y}$.

Bayes rule leads to the a posteriori density

$$p(\boldsymbol{x}|\boldsymbol{y}) = \frac{p(\boldsymbol{y}|\boldsymbol{x})p(\boldsymbol{x})}{p(\boldsymbol{y})} \tag{5.22}$$

where $\boldsymbol{x}$ is the original image we wish to estimate. The MAP estimate is obtained by maximizing the a posteriori density function $p(\boldsymbol{x}|\boldsymbol{y})$ to find the most probable value of $\boldsymbol{x}$. Since the observation $\boldsymbol{y}$ is given, $p(\boldsymbol{y})$ can be treated as a constant, and we have

$$p(\boldsymbol{x}|\boldsymbol{y}) = Kp(\boldsymbol{y}|\boldsymbol{x})p(\boldsymbol{x}) \tag{5.23}$$

where constant K is equal to $1/p(\boldsymbol{y})$.

Using (5.8, 21, 23) and taking logarithms, we get

$$\begin{aligned}\ln p(\boldsymbol{x}|\boldsymbol{y} &= \ln K - \tfrac{1}{2}\ln\left\{(2\pi)^{M^2}\det\left[\nu B(\Theta)^{-1}\right]\right\} \\ &\quad - \frac{1}{2\nu}\left(\boldsymbol{x}-\boldsymbol{x}_m\right)^t B(\Theta)\left(\boldsymbol{x}-\boldsymbol{x}_m\right) - \tfrac{1}{2}\ln\left(2\pi\sigma_\nu^2\right)^{M^2} \\ &\quad - \frac{1}{2\sigma_v^2}\sum_{s\in\Omega}\left[\log\left(\frac{y(s)}{cx(s)^\gamma}\right)\right]^2 - \sum_{s\in\Omega}\ln y(s)\,.\end{aligned} \tag{5.24}$$

We find the MAP estimate by locating the maximum of the right-hand side in (5.24). We first used the line search extension of the conjugate gradient algorithm by *Powell* [5.9]. Since the function to be maximized in (5.24) is nonconvex this algorithm may very well converge to a local maximum. The results are described in Sect. 5.4.4.

5.4.2 Stochastic Relaxation

We now present the SR algorithm designed to find the global MAP estimate. The algorithm simulates *annealing*, a procedure by which certain chemical system are driven to their minimum energy-highly regular states [5.10].

The SR algorithm is based on the Gibbs structure of the posterior density. Using the Gibbs-MRF equivalence, one can easily note that $p(\boldsymbol{x}|\boldsymbol{y})$ is Gibbs [5.6, 10]. The annealing process is equivalent to sampling from the local density function [5.10, 28]

$$p_T\left(x(s)|y(s),\boldsymbol{x}_s\right) = \frac{\exp[-\frac{1}{T}U^P(x(s)|y(s),\boldsymbol{x}_s)}{Z_T} \tag{5.25}$$

where T is the temperature, and $U^P(x(s)|y(s),\boldsymbol{x}_s)$ is the sum of all energy terms that correspond to cliques that include $x(s)$. Thus, we need to derive an expression for $p(x(s)|y(s),\boldsymbol{x}_s)$. For the film grain noise degradation model in (5.20), we can express the conditional density function $p(y(s)|x(s))$ as

$$p(y(s)|x(s)) = \frac{1}{\sqrt{2\pi\sigma_v^2 y(s)}}\exp\left\{-\frac{1}{2\sigma_v^2}\left[\log\left(\frac{y(s)}{cx(s)^{-\gamma}}\right)\right]^2\right\}\,. \tag{5.26}$$

Using (5.4) and (5.26), we have

$$p\left(x(s)|y(s), \boldsymbol{x}_s\right) = \frac{K}{2\pi\sqrt{\nu\sigma_v^2 y(s)}} \exp\left\{-\left[\frac{1}{2\nu}\left[(x(s) - x_m(s)\right.\right.\right.$$

$$\left.\left. - \sum_{\tau\in N} \Theta_\tau\left(x(s+\tau) - x_m\right)\right)\right]^2$$

$$\left.\left. + \frac{1}{2\sigma_v^2}\left(\log\left(\frac{y(s)}{cx(s)^{-\gamma}}\right)\right)^2\right]\right\} . \tag{5.27}$$

The SR algorithm simulates an annealing process, using the following steps:

1. Find an initial estimate. In our experiments we considered the nosiy image and a 0 dB white Gaussian noise images as the initial estimates. We found that the choice of the initial estimates did not have any significant effect on the quality of the restored image, even when we started with initial temperature that was much smaller than the one required by the theory.
2. Given the initial image, sample from the non-stationary density $p_T(\boldsymbol{x}|\boldsymbol{y})$ using the Metropolis algorithm [5.11], which is based on the local characteristics of the posterior density function in (5.27).

The algorithm samples for each pixel from its non-stationary density $p_T(x(s)|y(s), \boldsymbol{x}_s)$. For the raster scan approach taken in this work, the procedure is as follows: For a given image pixel at step k, say $x^{(k)}(s)$ (in the first iteration $k = 1$), we randomly choose another gray level, say $z^{(k)}(s)$ according to

$$z^{(k)}(s) = x^{(k)}(s) + \alpha_k(s) \tag{5.28}$$

where $\alpha_k(s)$ is a zero mean Gaussian random variable with standard deviation $\sigma(k)$. The optimal variance should be the same as the variance of the non-stationary distribution from which we are sampling. Since we were not able to derive the exact one, we used instead

$$\sigma(k) = \frac{\sigma_0}{1 + 0.025k} ,$$

satisfying a monotonic decreasing function of the number of iterations, where σ_0 is the initial standard deviation of the Gaussian random variable. Next, we quantize the new pixel value ot the nearest integer value in the [1,256] interval. As the algorithm converges we shrink the variance of α_k to allow more changes in each iteration, which in turn accelerates the convergence of the algorithm. Experimental results show that $\sigma_0 = 10$ is a reasonable choice. If the indicated move puts the gray level outside the interval [1,256] it reenters the interval from the opposite side [5.11]. The pixel $x^{(k+1)}(s)$ is decided by computing the energy change $\Delta\mathcal{E} = \mathcal{E}(z^{(k)}(s)) - \mathcal{E}(x^{(k)}(s))$ and the quantity

$$q = \frac{p_T(z^{(k)}(s)|y(s), \boldsymbol{x}_s)}{p_T(x^{(k)}(s)|y(s), \boldsymbol{x}_s)}$$
$$= \frac{K \exp\{-[\mathcal{E}(z^{(k)})/T(k)]\}}{K \exp\{-[\mathcal{E}(x^{(k)})/T(k)]\}} = \exp\left\{-\frac{\Delta\mathcal{E}}{T(k)}\right\} . \tag{5.29}$$

If $q > 1$, the move to $z^{(k)}(s)$ is allowed and the pixel is updated at s as $x^{(k+1)}(s) = z^{(k)}(s)$, whereas, if $q \leq 1$, the transition is made with probability q. Thus, we choose a random number ξ uniformly in the interval [0,1] and set $x^{(k+1)}(s) = z^{(k)}(s)$ if $\xi \leq q$, and $x^{(k+1)}(s) = x^{(k)}(s)$ if $\xi > q$.

After finishing a full sweep of the picture (going through all the pixels and updating their gray levels according to the algorithm), we update the temperature:

$$T(k) = \frac{T_0}{\log(1+k)} , \quad k = 1, 2, 3, \dots , \tag{5.30}$$

where k is the number of full sweeps that are completed. Since the theoretical value of T_0 is too large for practical implementation, we tried different values of T_0 in our experiments.

5.4.3 Quantization Effects

In the following, we use the notation x_s to denote $x(s)$ and drop the dependence on $\boldsymbol{y}$ in $U^P(.|\boldsymbol{y})$. The random step in the Metropolis algorithm introduces quantization to the nearest integer value. Using the MRF-Gibbs equivalence theorem, we see that the quantization defines a discrete Gibbs measure with the following conditional probabilities:

$$P(x_s|y_s, \boldsymbol{x}_s) = \frac{K_d \, \mathrm{e}^{-\mathcal{E}(x_s)}}{2\pi\sqrt{\nu\sigma^2}} \tag{5.31}$$

where

$$\mathcal{E}(x(s)) = \frac{1}{2\nu}\left[x(s) - x_m(s) - \sum_{\tau\in N}\Theta_\tau\left(x(s+\tau) - x_m(s+\tau)\right)\right]^2$$
$$+ \frac{1}{2\sigma_n^2}\left(\log\left(\frac{y(s)}{cx(s)^{-\gamma}}\right)\right)^2 + \ln(y(s)) \tag{5.32}$$

and

$$K_d = \frac{2\pi\sqrt{\nu\sigma^2}}{\sum_{x_s=1}^{256} \mathrm{e}^{-\mathcal{E}(x_s)}} . \tag{5.33}$$

Note that all pixel gray level take integer values in [1,256]. Since the positivity condition is satisfied in our model, we obtain the discrete joint probability as [5.6]

$$\frac{P_D(\boldsymbol{x}|\boldsymbol{y})}{P_D(\mathbf{1}|\boldsymbol{y})} = \prod_{s=1}^{M^2} \frac{P(x_s|1, 1, \cdots, 1, 1, x_{s+1}, \cdots, x_{M^2}, \boldsymbol{y})}{P(1|1, 1, \cdots, 1, 1, x_{s+1}, \cdots, x_{M^2}, \boldsymbol{y})} \tag{5.34}$$

where $\mathbf{1}$ denotes the vector of length M^2 whose elements are all 1. That implies

$$P_D(\boldsymbol{x}|\boldsymbol{y}) = P_D(\mathbf{1}|\boldsymbol{y}) \prod_{s=1}^{M^2} \exp\left\{-\left[U_s^P(1,1,\cdots,1,1,x_s,x_{s+1},\cdots,x_{M^2}) - U_s^P(1,1,\cdots,1,x_{s+1},\cdots,x_{M^2})\right]\right\} \tag{5.35}$$

where $U_s^P(\boldsymbol{x}) = \mathcal{E}(x_s)$ are given in (5.32). The above equation gives the structure of the joint probability measure for the discrete Gibbs model taking values in [1,256] at each pixel. An important point to note is the fact that $P_D(\mathbf{1}|\boldsymbol{y})$ is a normalizing factor of the form

$$P_D(\mathbf{1}|\boldsymbol{y}) = \frac{\exp[-U^P(\mathbf{1})]}{\sum_{\boldsymbol{x}|x_s=1\ldots256} \exp[-U^P(\boldsymbol{x})]} \;. \tag{5.36}$$

One can also see that the structure of $p_C(\boldsymbol{x}|\boldsymbol{y})$ – the density function in the continuous case is

$$p_C(\boldsymbol{x}|\boldsymbol{y}) = p_C(\mathbf{1}|\boldsymbol{y}) \prod_{s=1}^{M^2} \exp\left\{-\left[U_s^P(1,1,1,\cdots,1,x_s,x_{s+1},\cdots,x_{M^2}) - U_s^P(1,1,1,\cdots,1,x_{s+1},\cdots,x_{M^2})\right]\right\}$$

where

$$p_C(\mathbf{1}|\boldsymbol{y}) = \frac{\exp[-U^P(\mathbf{1})]}{\int_{x\in\mathbf{R}^{M^2}} \exp[-U^P(x)]\,dx} \;,$$

which implies

$$P_D(\boldsymbol{x}|\boldsymbol{y}) = K p_C(\boldsymbol{x}|\boldsymbol{y}) \;, \quad \forall \boldsymbol{x} \text{ such that } P_D(\boldsymbol{x}|\boldsymbol{y}) \neq 0 \;. \tag{5.37}$$

As the quantized version of the Metropolis algorithm maximizes $P_D(\boldsymbol{x}|\boldsymbol{y})$, the convergence of the discrete algorithm follows [5.12]. What remains to be proved is the convergence of the discrete distribution to the continuous resulting from the use of GMRF models for the representation of images. Also remaining to be proved is the relationship between the MAP solution of the discrete problem (owing to implementation) and the continuous problem (owing to our representation).

The answers to these questions are given in the following theorems:

Theorem 1. *The Gibbs measures obtained by discretizing the possible gray levels converge to the Gibbs measure corresponding to the continuous model.*

More precisely define the discrete density function, depending on $\boldsymbol{y}$

$$P_{D,L} : \mathbf{R}^{\Omega} \to (0\ 1) \tag{5.38}$$

for a model obeying

$$\forall s \in \Omega\ x(s) = \frac{k}{\sqrt{L}} \;, \quad \text{for some} \quad k \in [-L,\cdots,L] \;,$$

[$2L+1$ is the number of gray levels taken by $x(s)$]. In (5.38), L is included in the subscript to explicitly indicate the dependence on the number of gray levels $2L+1$.

From (5.35),

$$P_{D,L}(\boldsymbol{x}|\boldsymbol{y}) = P_{D,L}(\mathbf{1}|\boldsymbol{y}) \prod_{s=1}^{M^2} \exp\left\{-\left[U_s^P(1,1,\cdots,1,x_s,x_{s+1},\cdots,x_{M^2}) - U_s^P(1,1,\cdots,1,1,x_{s+1},\cdots,x_{M^2})\right]\right\},$$

where

$$P_{D,L}(\mathbf{1}|\boldsymbol{y}) = \frac{\exp[-U^P(1)]}{\sum_{x|y_s=k/\sqrt{L},\, k=-L,\dots,L} \exp[-U^P(x)]} .$$

Let F: $\mathbf{R}^{\Omega} \to [0\ 1]$, F^L: $\mathbf{R}^{\Omega} \to [0\ 1]$ be the cumulative distribution functions of the continuous and the discrete models respectively. Then $F^L \to F$, everywhere.

Proof. See Appendix 5.A.1 at the end of the chapter.

Theorem 2. *Let x'_L be a location of a global maximum of $P_{D,L}(\boldsymbol{x}|\boldsymbol{y})$. If $\boldsymbol{x}'_{L_i} \to \tilde{\boldsymbol{x}}$, then $\tilde{\boldsymbol{x}} \in M$ – the set of locations of global maximum of $p_C(\boldsymbol{x}|\boldsymbol{y})$.*

It should be noted that by using the annealing process, we find the configurations that correspond to the global maximum of $P_{D,L}(\boldsymbol{x}|\boldsymbol{y})$. We now show that if these configurations converge to a limit, then, the limit is a configuration that corresponds to a global maximum of the a posteriori density function of the continuous model.

Proof. See Appendix 5.A.2 at the end of the chapter.

5.4.4 Experimental Results

The results presented here are for two different types of real images, the first is a girls' face (Fig. 5.2. A) and the second is an outdoor scene (Fig. 5.5 A). First we estimated the GMRF parameters for a second order neighborhood using Algorithm 1 as described in Sect. 5.3.3. The GMRF model parameters were estimated from the original non-noisy images. The global estimate of the mean was subtracted from the image. The least square (LS) estimates [5.15] of a second order GMRF model were then computed with a free boundary assumption. It was found that the LS estimates $\tilde{\Theta}$ were unstable, i.e., some of the eigenvalues of the transformation matrix $B(\tilde{\Theta})$ were found to be negative. The LS estimates were rescaled by multiplying the vector $\tilde{\Theta}$ by $\psi = 0.499/\max_{s\in\Omega}\sum_{\tau_i\in N^*}\Theta_{\tau_i}\Phi_{s,\tau_i}$ where $\Phi_{s,\tau_i} = \cos(2\pi s^{\mathrm{T}}\tau_i/M)$, and

$$N^* = \{\tau_1, \tau_2, \dots, \tau_{|N^*|/2}\} = \{(0,1), (1,0), (-1,1), (1,1)\}$$

are the shift vectors corresponding to the second order GMRF model, to ensure that the parameters satisfy

$$\left(1 - 2\sum_{\tau_i\in N^*} \Theta_{\tau_i}\Phi_{s,\tau_i}\right) > 0 , \quad \forall s \in \Omega . \tag{5.39}$$

The rescaled estimates were then used as the initial conditions for the maximum

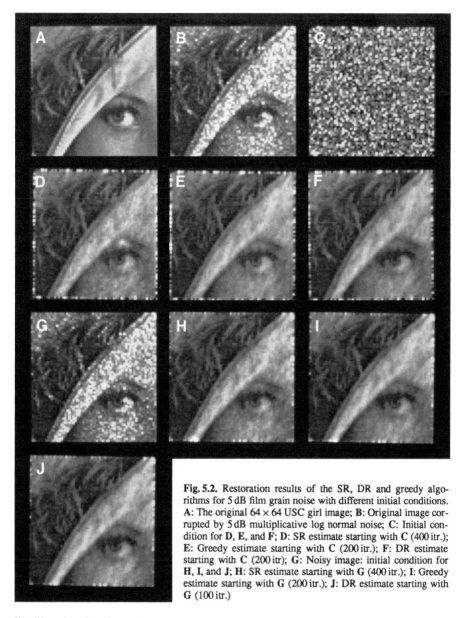

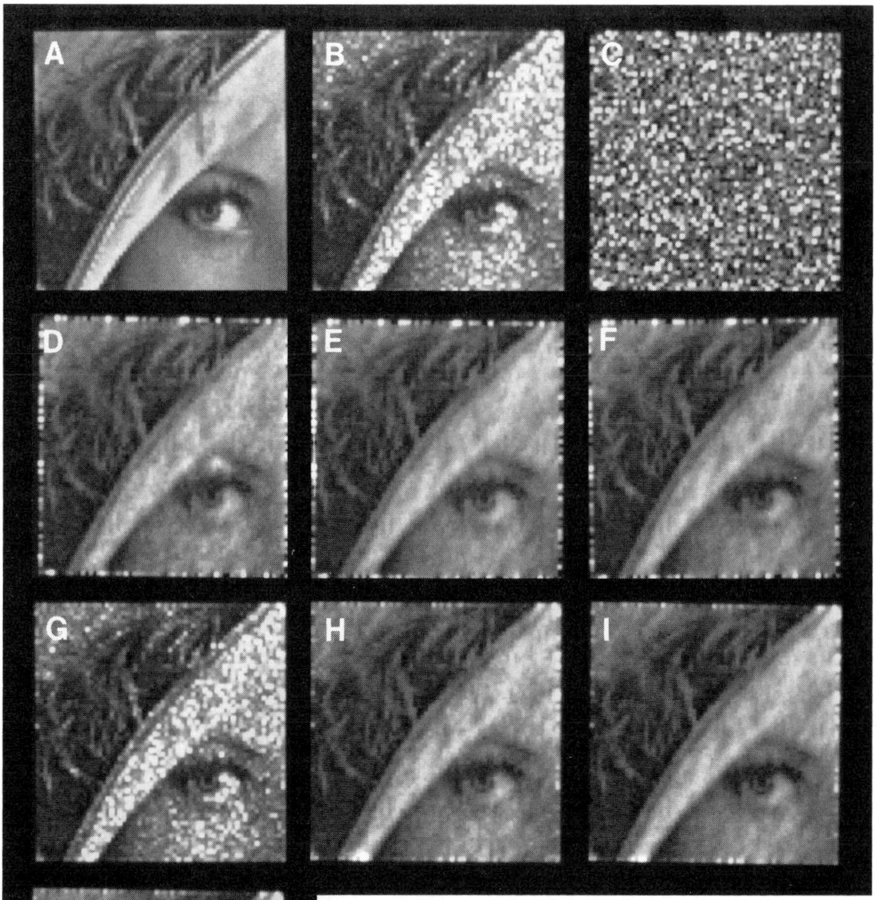

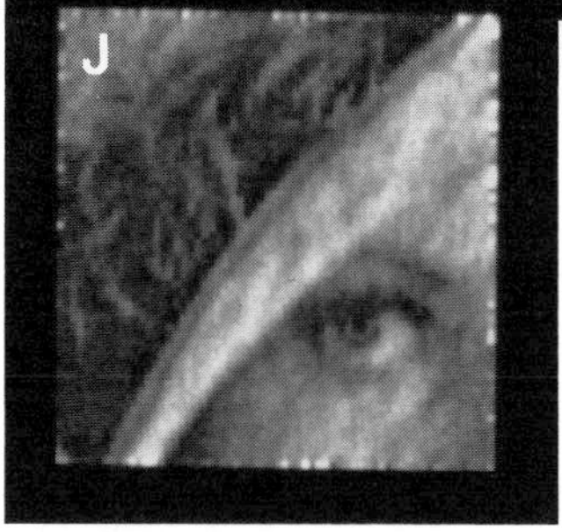

Fig. 5.2. Restoration results of the SR, DR and greedy algorithms for 5 dB film grain noise with different initial conditions. **A**: The original 64×64 USC girl image; **B**: Original image corrupted by 5 dB multiplicative log normal noise; **C**: Initial condition for **D**, **E**, and **F**; **D**: SR estimate starting with **C** (400 itr.); **E**: Greedy estimate starting with **C** (200 itr.); **F**: DR estimate starting with **C** (200 itr); **G**: Noisy image: initial condition for **H**, **I**, and **J**; **H**: SR estimate starting with **G** (400 itr.); **I**: Greedy estimate starting with **G** (200 itr.); **J**: DR estimate starting with **G** (100 itr.)

likelihood estimation (MLE) algorithm. The numerical values of the estimates are listed in the tables below.

From the results, one can see that the variance estimated using MLE is much higher than the variance estimated using LS estimate. The noisy images were created from the original images by first making a nonlinear transformation on each pixel, and later multiplying it with a noise variable. The SNR was computed as follows,

Table 5.1. Parameter estimation results for Fig. 5.2 A

	initial conditions	minimum scaling	MLE
Θ_1	0.0957	0.0918	0.1051
Θ_2	0.3835	0.3678	0.3192
Θ_3	−0.1333	−0.1279	−0.0597
Θ_4	0.1594	0.1528	0.1353
ν	239.50	244.38	332.73
$f(\Theta)$		15574	14995

$$y(s) = x(s)\mathrm{e}^{-v(s)} = x(s)v_1(s) \tag{5.40}$$

where $v(s)$ is a Gaussian random variable with zero mean and variance σ_v^2 and the probability density function (PDF) of $v_1(s)$ is

$$p\big(v_1(s)\big) = \frac{1}{\sqrt{2\pi}\sigma_v v_1(s)} \exp\left\{-\frac{[\log v_1(s)]^2}{2\sigma_v^2}\right\}$$

with mean

$$m_{v_1} = \mathrm{e}^{\sigma_v^2/2}$$

and variance

$$\sigma_{v_1}^2 = \mathrm{e}^{\sigma_v^2}\left(\mathrm{e}^{\sigma_v^2} - 1\right) .$$

Now define

$$y(s) = x(s)m_{v_1} + x(s)\left(v_1 - m_{v_1}\right) \stackrel{\text{def}}{=} \tilde{x}(s) + n(s) ,$$

$$\mathrm{SNR} = 10\log\left(\frac{\sigma_{\tilde{x}}^2}{\sigma_n^2}\right) .$$

In our experiments $m_{v_1} \to 1$ so that

$$\mathrm{SNR} \simeq 10\log\left[\frac{\sigma_x^2}{\left(\sigma_x^2 + m_x^2\right)\sigma_{vl}^2}\right] .$$

We compared the performance of the SR algorithm with the greedy and the deterministic relaxation algorithms. In all the experiments the noise variance is assumed to be known. In this experiment we did not perform the nonlinear degradation and the image was corrupted only by multiplicative noise with SNR of 5 dB. The results of the experiment are shown in Fig. 5.2. The MAP estimates after 400 iterations of the SR algorithm did not converge yet. Since the theoretical value of T_0 is extremely large, we used lower values for T_0. The results in Fig. 5.2 were obtained with $T_0 = 1$. The number of iterations that are required for convergence of the greedy and the deterministic algorithms are considerably less than that of

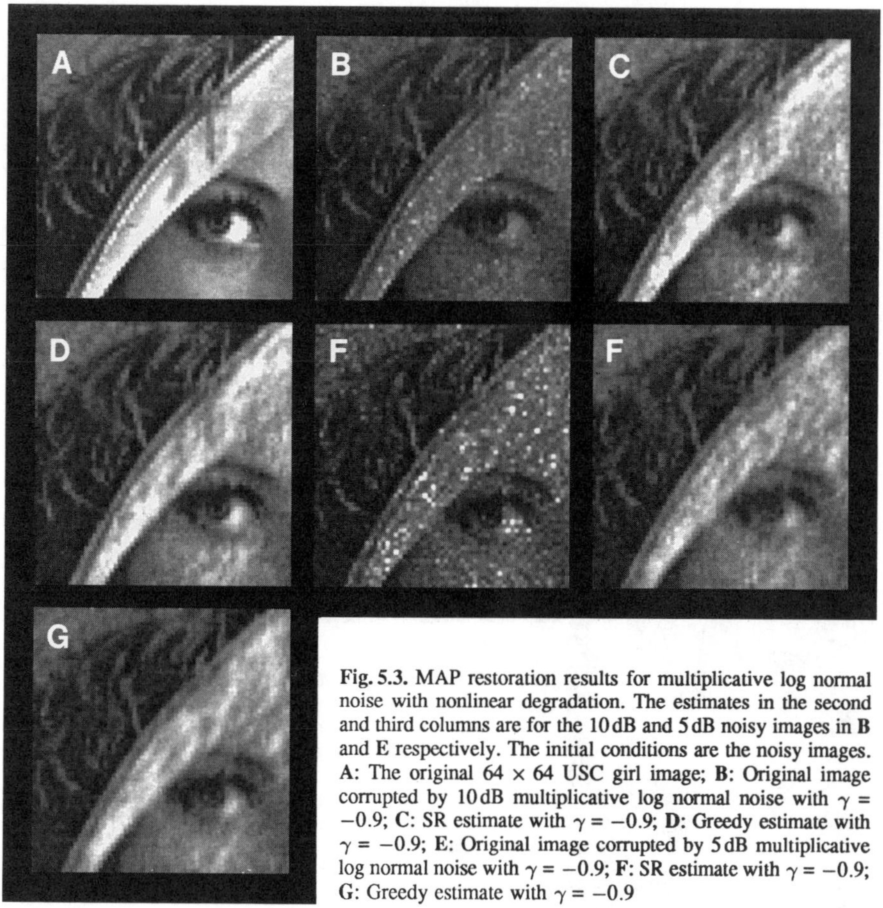

Fig. 5.3. MAP restoration results for multiplicative log normal noise with nonlinear degradation. The estimates in the second and third columns are for the 10 dB and 5 dB noisy images in **B** and E respectively. The initial conditions are the noisy images. A: The original 64 × 64 USC girl image; **B**: Original image corrupted by 10 dB multiplicative log normal noise with $\gamma = -0.9$; C: SR estimate with $\gamma = -0.9$; **D**: Greedy estimate with $\gamma = -0.9$; E: Original image corrupted by 5 dB multiplicative log normal noise with $\gamma = -0.9$; **F**: SR estimate with $\gamma = -0.9$; G: Greedy estimate with $\gamma = -0.9$

SR. The results shown here are after 200 iterations, except for the deterministic algorithm that converged after 100 iterations when started with the noisy image. The greedy algorithm randomly chooses a possible new value for the updated pixel, and updates the pixel's value to the new value if the new configuration corresponds to a lower Gibbs energy. This algorithm is bound to converge since the chain of configurations we obtain has decreasing Gibbs energies which are bounded from below by the ground state energy. Note that the algorithm is not deterministic because the step size is chosen randomly. In the deterministic relaxation, we used the conjugate gradient search with optimal step and the restart procedure suggested by *Powell* [5.9]. Both the greedy and the deterministic algorithms may not converge to the global minimum, since the energy function in non-convex. However, we could not simulate convergence to a wrong result. The results for two different initial conditions are shown in Fig. 5.2.

There is a small difference in the estimation results when we introduce nonlinear degradation. The results for images with 10 dB and 5 dB noise, with $\gamma = -0.9$ and

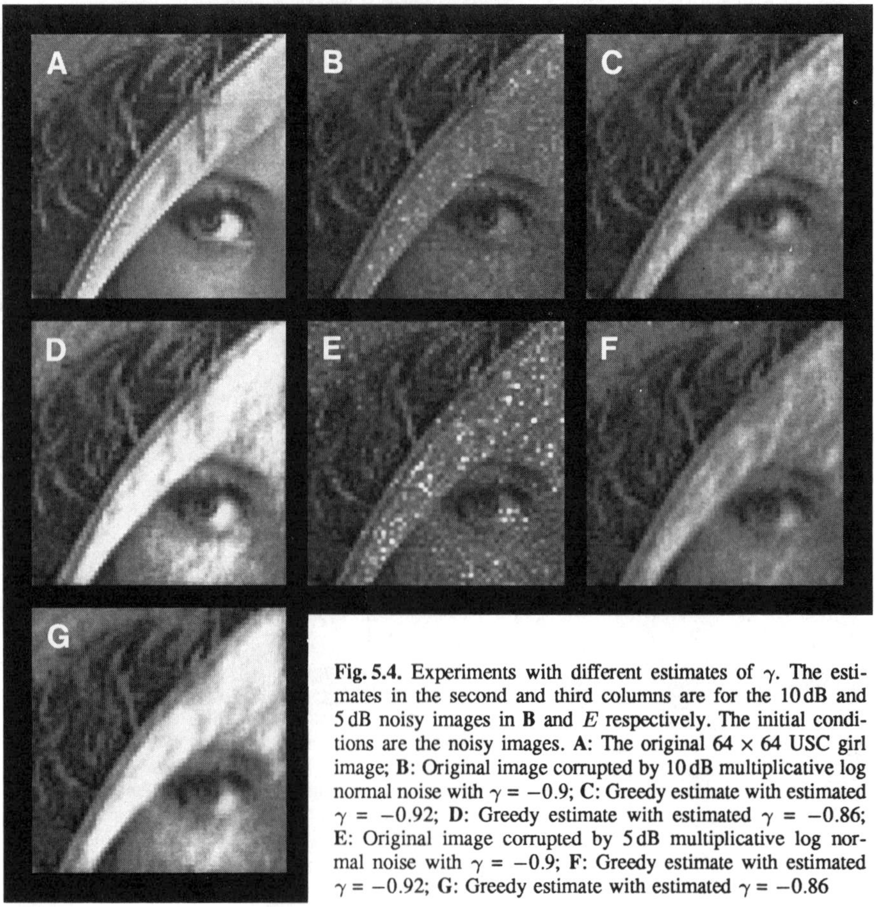

Fig. 5.4. Experiments with different estimates of γ. The estimates in the second and third columns are for the 10 dB and 5 dB noisy images in **B** and E respectively. The initial conditions are the noisy images. **A**: The original 64 × 64 USC girl image; **B**: Original image corrupted by 10 dB multiplicative log normal noise with $\gamma = -0.9$; **C**: Greedy estimate with estimated $\gamma = -0.92$; **D**: Greedy estimate with estimated $\gamma = -0.86$; E: Original image corrupted by 5 dB multiplicative log normal noise with $\gamma = -0.9$; **F**: Greedy estimate with estimated $\gamma = -0.92$; **G**: Greedy estimate with estimated $\gamma = -0.86$

estimated γ also equal to $-09.$ are shown in Fig. 5.3. Since γ may not be known, it is shown in Fig. 5.4 that exact knowledge of γ is not necessary. The effect of the change is mainly in the brightness of the restored image, which can be examined and fixed easily. In Figs. 5.5, 6 the results for the outdoor scene are shown. This scene has a lot of fine details and large areas with constant intensity.

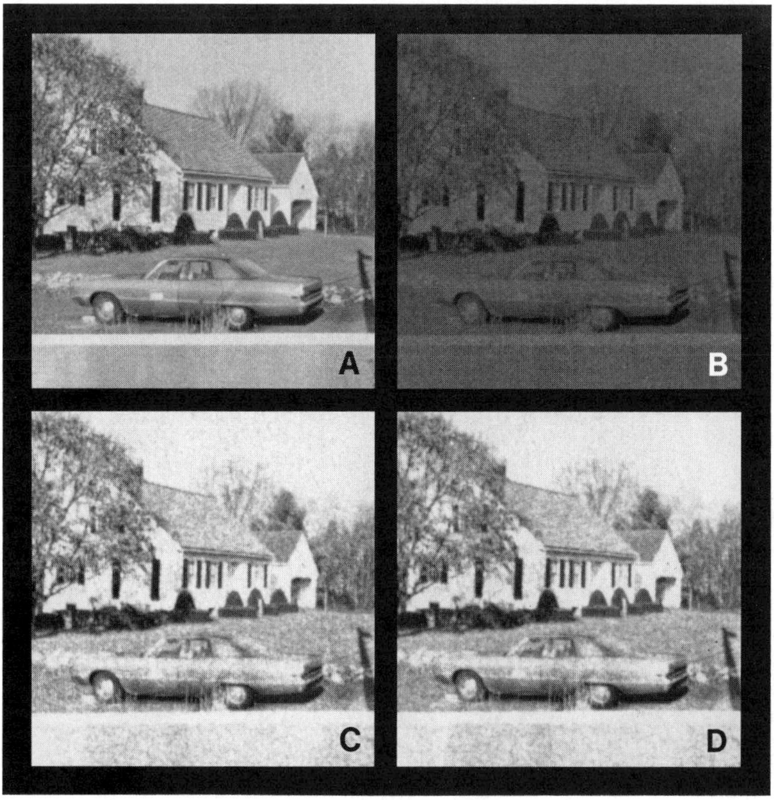

Fig. 5.5. Restoration of an outdoor scene with 10 dB noise and nonlinear degredation. **A**: Original 256 × 256 outdoor scene; **B**: Image corrupted by 10 dB noise and $\gamma = -0.9$; **C**: SR estimate after 400 itr. with estimated $\gamma = -0.87$; **D**: Greedy estimate after 200 itr. with estimated $\gamma = -0.87$

Table 5.2. Parameter estimation results for Fig. 5.5 A

	initial conditions	minimum scaling	MLE
Θ_1	0.3474	0.3457	0.2646
Θ_2	0.3973	0.3953	0.3406
Θ_3	−0.1393	−0.1386	−0.0239
Θ_4	−0.1039	−0.1034	−0.0813
ν	184.49	184.55	251.83

Fig. 5.6. Restoration of an outdoor scene with 5 dB noise and nonlinear degredation. **A**: Original 256 × 256 outdoor scene; **B**: Image corrupted by 5 dB noise and $\gamma = -0.95$; **C**: SR estimate after 400 itr. with estimated $\gamma = -0.925$; **D**: Greedy estimate after 200 itr. with estimated $\gamma = -0.925$

5.5 GNC Algorithm for MAP Estimation of Images Modeled by Compound GMRF

One can see the similarity between the global energy function corresponding to the posterior density in equation (5.11) and the global energy that *Blake* and *Zisserman* suggested should be minimized in the weak membrane formulation [5.5]. We recall that the global energy function that was sugested in [5.5] is of the form:

$$E = \sum_{i,j} (x_{i,j} - y_{i,j})^2 + \sum_{i,j} \left[\lambda^2 (x_{i,j} - x_{i-1,j})^2 (1 - l_{ij}) + \alpha l_{ij}\right]$$
$$+ \sum_{i,j} \left[\lambda^2 (x_{i,j} - x_{i,j+1})^2 (1 - m_{ij}) + \alpha m_{ij}\right] .$$

The weak membrane model is a special case of the compound GMRF model with a first order neighborhood system, isotropic parameters $\Theta_x = \Theta_y = 0.25$ and appropriate scaling of γ and α. Blake and Zisserman have developed the GNC algorithm to find the global minimum of the weak membrane cost function. We modify the GNC algorithm to obtain an algorithm which is able to find a near global MAP solution for the compound GMRF model. For simplicity in the formulation we restrict our attention to a first order compound GMRF model. For the first order compound GMRF model we can write:

$$\begin{aligned} U(\boldsymbol{x}, \boldsymbol{l}, \boldsymbol{m}|\boldsymbol{y}) = \sum_{i,j\in\Omega} \frac{1}{2\sigma^2}\Big\{ &\left(y_{i,j} - x_{i,j}\right)^2 \\ &+ \gamma^2\left(1 - 2(\Theta_x + \Theta_y)\right)x_{ij}^2 \\ &+ \Theta_x\left[\lambda^2\left(x_{i,j} - x_{i-1,}\right)^2\left(1 - l_{i,j}\right) + \alpha l_{i,j}\right] \\ &+ \Theta_y\left[\lambda^2\left(x_{i,j} - x_{i,j+1}\right)^2\left(1 - m_{i,j}\right) + \alpha m_{i,j}\right]\Big\} \end{aligned}$$

where $l_{i,j}, m_{i,j}$ activate the line process in the x and y directions respectively. We can write the posterior energy function in the form:

$$\begin{aligned} U = \frac{1}{2\sigma^2}\Big\{ D &+ \sum_{ij}\Theta_x h_{\alpha,\lambda}\left(x_{i,j} - x_{i-1,j}, l_{ij}\right) \\ &+ \sum_{ij}\Theta_y h_{\alpha,\lambda}\left(x_{i,j} - x_{i,j+1}, m_{ij}\right)\Big\}, \end{aligned} \tag{5.41}$$

where

$$D = \sum_{ij}\left(x_{i,j} - y_{i,j}\right)^2\lambda^2\left(1 - 2(\Theta_x + \Theta_y)\right)x_{i,j}^2 \tag{5.42}$$

and

$$h_{\alpha,\lambda}(t, l) = \lambda^2(t)^2(1 - l) + \alpha l\ .$$

Note that $(1 - 2(\Theta_x + \Theta_y)) > 0$ because of the positivity requirement of the spectral density of the GMRF model. The problem is thus reduced to the following optimization problem,

$$\begin{aligned} \min_{\{x_{ij}\}}\Big\{\frac{1}{2\sigma^2}\Big[D &+ \min_{\{l_{ij}\}}\Big(\sum_{ij}\Theta_x h_{\alpha,\lambda}\left(x_{i,j} - x_{i-1,j}, l_{ij}\right)\Big) \\ &+ \min_{\{m_{ij}\}}\Big(\sum_{ij}\Theta_y h_{\alpha,\lambda}\left(x_{i,j} - x_{i,j+1}, m_{ij}\right)\Big)\Big]\Big\}. \end{aligned}$$

As D does not involve l_{ij}, m_{ij}, minimization over l_{ij}, m_{ij} can be performed and one is then left with minimization with respect to x_{ij},

$$\min_{\{x_{ij}, l_{ij}, m_{ij}\}} U = \min_{\{x_{ij}\}}\Big\{\frac{1}{2\sigma^2}\Big[D + \sum_{ij}\Theta_x g_{\alpha,\lambda}\left(x_{i,j} - x_{i-1,j}\right)$$

$$+\sum_{ij} \Theta_y g_{\alpha,\lambda}\big(x_{i,j} - x_{i,j+1}\big)\Big]\Big\}$$

where

$$g_{\alpha,\lambda}(t) = \min_{l\in\{0,1\}} h_{\alpha,\lambda}(t,l) = \min\big(\lambda^2(t)^2, \alpha\big) .$$

Following [5.5] we look for a convex approximation U^* to U. The convexity of U^* is guaranteed by requiring that it has a posive definite Hessian matrix $H = \partial^2 U^*/\partial x_{i,j}\partial x_{k,l}$. Suppose g^* is designed to satisfy

$$\forall t\; g^{*\prime\prime}(t) \geq -c^*$$

where $c^* > 0$. Then the "worst case" of H occurs when

$$\forall i,j\; g^{*\prime\prime}\big(x_{i,j} - x_{i,j+1}\big) = -c^* \quad \text{and} \quad g^{*\prime\prime}\big(x_{i,j} - x_{i-1,j}\big) = -c^*$$

so that

$$H = \big[2 + 2\lambda^2\big(1 - 2(\Theta_x + \Theta_x)\big)\big]I - c^* R .$$

The matrix R is a symmetric tri-diagonal block-Toeplitz matrix:

$$R = \begin{bmatrix} Q & -\Theta_x I & & \\ -\Theta_x I & Q & -\Theta_x I & \\ & -\Theta_x I & Q & -\Theta_x I \\ & & -\Theta_x I & Q \end{bmatrix}$$

$$Q = \begin{bmatrix} 2\Theta_x + 2\Theta_y & -\Theta_y & & \\ -\Theta_y & 2\Theta_x + 2\Theta_y & -\Theta_y & \\ & -\Theta_y & 2\Theta_x + 2\Theta_y & -\Theta_y \\ & & -\Theta_y & 2\Theta_x + 2\Theta_y \end{bmatrix} .$$

To prove that H is positive definite, it is sufficient to show that the largest eigenvalue $\mathcal{E}_{\max}$ of R satisfies $\mathcal{E}_{\max} \leq 2 + 2\lambda^2[1 - 2(\Theta_x + \Theta_y)]/c^*$.

The eigenvalues $\mathcal{E}_{i,j}$, $i,j \in (0 \cdots M-1)$ of R can be found using the sine transform [5.29].

$$\mathcal{E}_{i,j} = \Theta_x\left(2 - 2\cos\frac{2\pi i}{M}\right) + \Theta_y\left(2 - 2\cos\frac{2\pi j}{M}\right) .$$

So that $\max \mathcal{E}_{i,j} = 4(\Theta_x + \Theta_y)$, thus to guarantee convexity c^* must satisfy

$$c^* \leq \frac{1 + \lambda^2(1 - 2(\Theta_x + \Theta_y))}{2(\Theta_x + \Theta_y)} .$$

Following [5.5], we construct the best quadratic approximation g^* with a given bound $-c^*$ on its second derivative, satisfying the extra condition: $\forall t\; g^*(t) \leq g(t)$

$$g^*_{\alpha,\lambda}(t) = \begin{cases} \lambda^2(t)^2\,, & |t| < q \\ \alpha - c^*(|t| - r)^2/2\,, & q \leq |t| < r \\ \alpha\,, & |t| \geq r \end{cases}$$

where

$$r^2 = \alpha\left(\frac{2}{c^*} + \frac{1}{\lambda^2}\right)\,, \quad q = \frac{\alpha}{\lambda^2 r}\,.$$

Thus, we obtain the convex approximation for U:

$$U^* = \frac{1}{2\sigma^2}\left[D + \sum_{ij} \Theta_x g^*_{\alpha,\lambda}(x_{ij} - x_{i-1,j}) + \sum_{ij} \Theta_y g^*_{\alpha,\lambda}(x_{i,j} - x_{i,j+1})\right]\,. \tag{5.43}$$

A one parameter family of cost functions $U^{(P)}$ is then defined by replacing g^* in (5.43) by $g^{(P)}$ · $g^{(P)}$ is similar to g^* except that c^* is replaced by a variable c, that varies with P. Therefore

$$U^{(P)} = \frac{1}{2\sigma^2}\left[D + \sum_{ij} \Theta_x g^{(P)}_{\alpha,\lambda}(x_{i,j} - x_{i-1,j}) + \sum_{ij} \Theta_y g^{(P)}_{\alpha,\lambda}(x_{i,j} - x_{i,j+1})\right] \tag{5.44}$$

with

$$g^{(P)}_{\alpha,\lambda}(t) = \begin{cases} \lambda^2(t)^2\,, & |t| < q \\ \alpha - c(|t| - r)^2/2\,, & q \leq |t| < r \\ \alpha\,, & |t| \geq r \end{cases}$$

where $c = c^*/P$, $r^2 = \alpha(2/c + 1/\lambda^2)$, and $q = \alpha/\lambda^2 r$.

The GNC algorithm begins by minimizing $U^{(P=1)} = U^*$. Then P is decreased from 1 to 0, which makes $g^{(P)}$ change steadily from g^* to g. For every value of P we minimize $U^{(P)}$ starting with the last configuration corresponding to the previous P (local minimum of $U^{(2P)}$). We suggest that minimization of $U^{(P)}$ can be efficiently performed using the optimal step conjugate gradient algorithm.

5.5.1 Experimental Results

The original airport image corrupted by 5 dB and 10 dB additive white Gaussian noise was filtered using the modified GNC algorithm. The GMRF parameters were estimated from the original image using Algorithm 2. In the image estimation part, the noisy image was used as an initial condition for the algorithm. The results were obtained using at most 25 iterations for each value of P. For some values of P the algorithm converged in less then 20 iterations.

In the first experiment we restored an image corrupted by 10 dB additive white Gaussian noise. The edge threshold was chosen to be $h = 20$, and the noise variance

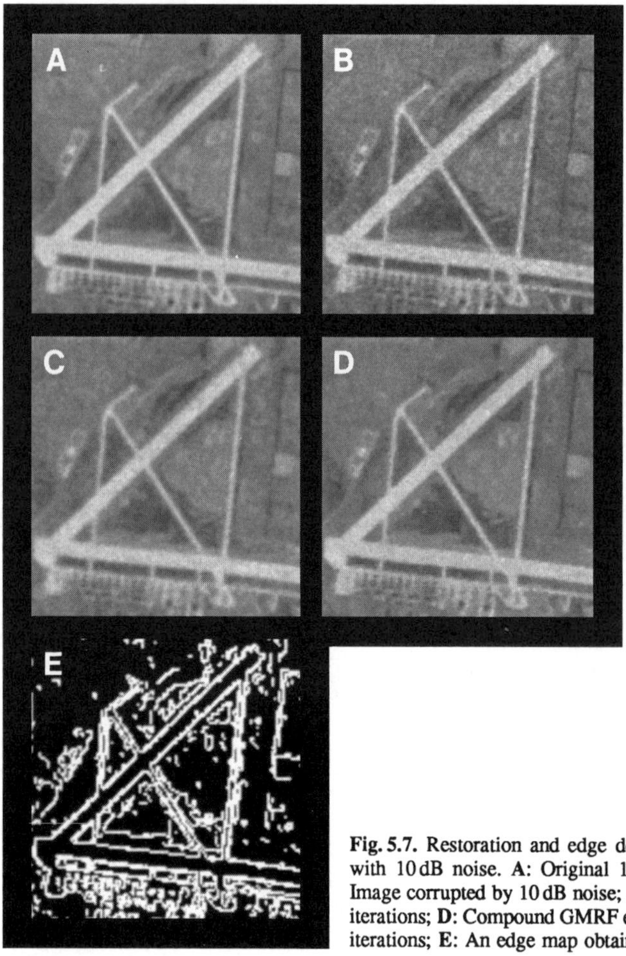

Fig. 5.7. Restoration and edge detection on an airport image with 10 dB noise. **A**: Original 128 × 128 airport image; **B**: Image corrupted by 10 dB noise; **C**: GMRF estimate after 100 iterations; **D**: Compound GMRF estimate using GNC after 100 iterations; **E**: An edge map obtained from the GNC algorithm

was assumed to be known. The results after 100 iterations are presented in Fig. 5.7. We then repeated the experiment for the 5 dB additive white Gaussian noise case. In this experiment h was set to 25. The results are presented in Fig. 5.8. The results we obtained for 10 dB noise are very good. The estimates include all the information in the original image and in addition we obtain a precise edge map. We compare the results obtained assuming a GMRF model for the image intensity, and show that the image estimates are substantially blurred. In the 5 dB case the results are

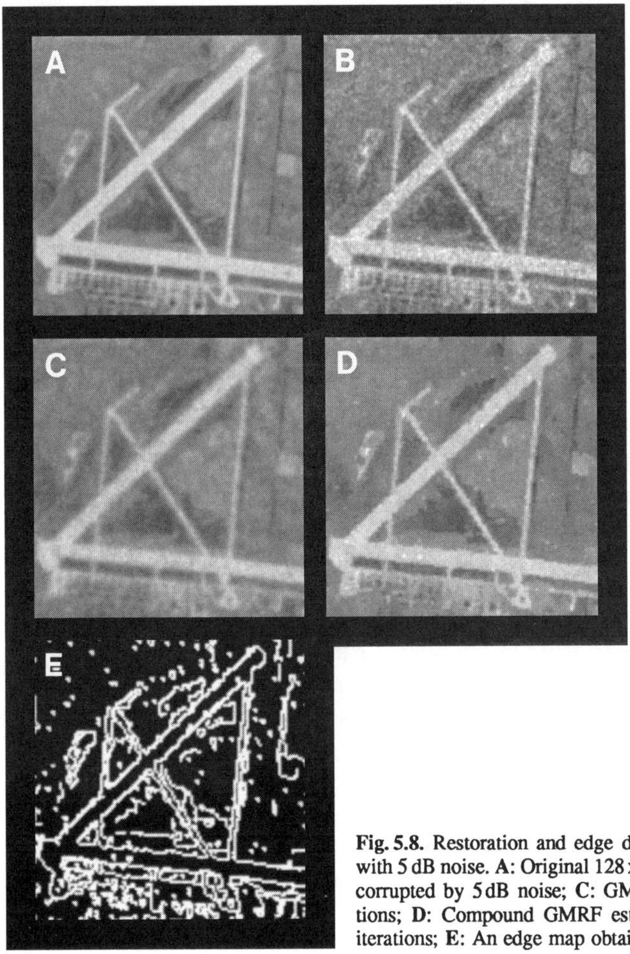

Fig. 5.8. Restoration and edge detection on an airport image with 5 dB noise. A: Original 128 × 128 airport image; B: Image corrupted by 5 dB noise; C: GMRF estimate after 100 iterations; D: Compound GMRF estimate using GNC after 100 iterations; E: An edge map obtained from the GNC algorithm

also good, though a few noisy points were isolated by the line process. This is an inherent problem, owing to the simple line process used in this model. It can partially be overcome by increasing λ. One can also modify the line process to include an energy term that will inhibit the formation of such edges as in [5.10]. In a recent work [5.30], the GNC algorithm has been modified to incorporate a more sophisticated line process which appears to alleviate the problem of isolated points.

5.A Appendices

5.A.1 Proof of Theorem 1

Define

$$\mathsf{R}_L^{\Omega} = \left\{ z | z_s = \frac{k}{\sqrt{L}} \,, \quad \text{for some} \quad k \in [-L, \cdots, L] \right\} \,, \tag{5.A.1}$$

$$B_L = \left[-\sqrt{L} \,,\, \sqrt{L} \right]^{M^2} \,, \tag{5.A.2}$$

$$\mathsf{R}_x = \left\{ z | \forall s \in \Omega \,,\, z_s \le x_s \,,\, \boldsymbol{x} \in \mathsf{R}^{M^2} \right\} .$$

For simplicity we drop the dependence on $\boldsymbol{y}$ in p_c and $P_{D,L}$. We first note that as $\|\boldsymbol{x}\| \to \infty$ $p_C(\boldsymbol{x}|\boldsymbol{y}) \to 0$ exponentially. Also, $p_C(\boldsymbol{x}|\boldsymbol{y})$ is continuous. Consequently, for any compact set of the form $B_L \cap \mathbf{R}_{\boldsymbol{x}}$ the Riemann integral

$$\int_{B_L \cap \mathbf{R}_x} p_C(\boldsymbol{z}) d\boldsymbol{z}$$

exists, and can be approximated uniformly by a Riemann sum

$$\sum_{\boldsymbol{z}_L \in \mathbf{R}_L^{\Omega} \cap \mathbf{R}_x} K_L^* p_C(\boldsymbol{z}_L)$$

where K_L^* is the unit volume corresponding to the above discretization.

Given $\boldsymbol{x}$ and $\varepsilon > 0$ pick L_0, $\sqrt{L_0} \ge \|\boldsymbol{x}\|$ so $L \ge L_0$ implies

$$\int_{B_{L_0}} p_C(\boldsymbol{z})\, d\boldsymbol{z} > 1 - \varepsilon$$

$$\sum_{\boldsymbol{z}_L \in \mathbf{R}_L^{\Omega} \cap B_{L_0}} K_L p_C(\boldsymbol{z}_L) > 1 - \varepsilon$$

and $\forall \boldsymbol{v} \in B_L$

$$\left| \int_{B_{L_0} \cap \mathbf{R}_v} p_C(\boldsymbol{z})\, d\boldsymbol{z} - \sum_{\boldsymbol{z}_L \in \mathbf{R}_L^{\Omega} \cap \mathbf{R}_v \cap B_{L_0}} K_L^* p_C(f \boldsymbol{z}_L) \right| < \varepsilon$$

where R_v is analogous to R_x. Now for $L \ge L_0$,

$$\left| F^L(\boldsymbol{x}|\boldsymbol{y}) - F(\boldsymbol{x}|\boldsymbol{y} \right|$$

$$\le \left| F^L(\boldsymbol{x}|\boldsymbol{y}) - \int_{B_{L_0} \cap \mathbf{R}_x} p_C(\boldsymbol{z})\, d\boldsymbol{z} \right| + \left| \int_{\boldsymbol{z} \notin B_{L_0}} p_C(\boldsymbol{z})\, d\boldsymbol{z} \right|$$

$$\begin{aligned}
&\le \left| \sum_{z_L \in \mathbf{R}_L^\Omega \cap \mathbf{R}_x} P_{D,L}(z_L) - \int_{B_{L_0} \cap \mathbf{R}_x} p_C(z)\,dz \right| + \varepsilon \\
&= \left| \sum_{z_L \in \mathbf{R}_L^\Omega \cap \mathbf{R}_x \cap B_{L_0}} K_L p_C(z_L) - \int_{B_{L_0} \cap \mathbf{R}_x} p_C(z)\,dz \right| \\
&\quad + \left| \sum_{z_L \in \mathbf{R}_L^\Omega \setminus B_{L_0}} K_L p_C(z_L) \right| + \varepsilon, \\
&\le \left| \sum_{z_L \in \mathbf{R}_L^\Omega \cap \mathbf{R}_x \cap B_{L_0}} (K_L - K_L^*)\, p_C(z_L) \right| \\
&\quad + \left| \sum_{z_L \in \mathbf{R}_L^\Omega \cap \mathbf{R}_x \cap B_{L_0}} K_L^* p_C(z_L) - \int_{B_{L_0} \cap \mathbf{R}_x} p_C(z)\,dz \right| + 2\varepsilon \\
&\le \left| \sum_{z_L \in \mathbf{R}_L^\Omega \cap B_{L_0}} (K_L - K_L^*)\, p_C(z_L) \right| + 3\varepsilon \\
&\le \left| \sum_{z_L \in \mathbf{R}_L^\Omega \cap B_{L_0}} K_L p_C(z_L) - \int_{B_{L_0}} p_C(z)\,dz \right| \\
&\quad + \left| \int_{B_{L_0}} p_C(z)\,dz - \sum_{z_L \in \mathbf{R}_L^\Omega \cap B_{L_0}} K_L^* p_C(z_L) \right| + 3\varepsilon \\
&\le |1 - (1-\varepsilon)| + 4\varepsilon < 5\varepsilon\,.
\end{aligned}$$

□

5.A.2 Proof of Theorem 2

Recall from (5.37) that

$$P_{D,L}(\boldsymbol{x}|\boldsymbol{y}) = K_L p_C(\boldsymbol{x}|\boldsymbol{y}),\ \forall \boldsymbol{x} \quad \text{such that} \quad P_{D,L}(\boldsymbol{x}|\boldsymbol{y}) \neq 0\,.$$

The annealing process converges in probability to the MAP solution of $P_{D,L}(\boldsymbol{x}|\boldsymbol{y})$.

Let

$$M = \left\{\boldsymbol{x}' | p_C(\boldsymbol{x}'|\boldsymbol{y}) \ge p_C(\boldsymbol{x}|\boldsymbol{y})\ \forall \boldsymbol{x} \in R^S\right\}\,.$$

M is not empty and compact since as $\|\boldsymbol{x}\| \to \infty$ $p_C(\boldsymbol{x}) \to 0$, and on a compact set a continuous function reaches its maximum. Let

$$\begin{aligned}
M_L &= \left\{\boldsymbol{x}'_L \in \mathrm{R}_L^\Omega | P_{D,L}(\boldsymbol{x}'_L|\boldsymbol{y}) \ge P_{D,L}(\boldsymbol{x}_L|\boldsymbol{y})\ \forall \boldsymbol{x}_L \in \mathrm{R}_L^\Omega\right\} \\
&= \left\{\boldsymbol{x}'_L \in \mathrm{R}_L^\Omega | p_C(\boldsymbol{x}'_L|\boldsymbol{y}) \ge p_C(\boldsymbol{x}_L|\boldsymbol{y})\ \forall \boldsymbol{x}_L \in \mathrm{R}_L^\Omega\right\}
\end{aligned}$$

where R_L^Ω was defined in (5.A.1). Note that since R_L^Ω is finite, we have $M_L \neq \emptyset$. Next $\forall L$ we choose an arbitrary $\boldsymbol{x}'_L$ from M_L to form a sequence. We show that all the limits of all subsequences of the sequence $\{\boldsymbol{x}'_L\}_{L=1\cdots\infty}$ are in M.

For simplicity we use $p(\boldsymbol{x})$ for $p_C(\boldsymbol{x}|\boldsymbol{y})$.

Define: $\forall \varepsilon > 0$

$$A^\varepsilon = \{\boldsymbol{x}|p(\boldsymbol{x}) \geq p(\boldsymbol{x}') - \varepsilon \quad \text{for any} \quad \boldsymbol{x}'\varepsilon M\} .$$

Since p is continuous A^ε is closed and $\bigcap_{\varepsilon>0} A^\varepsilon = M$.

Now $p(\boldsymbol{x})$ is uniformly continuous $\Rightarrow \forall\varepsilon > 0 \ \exists\delta > 0$ such that

$$\bigcup_{\boldsymbol{x}\in M} B_\delta(\boldsymbol{x}) \subset A^\varepsilon .$$

Since M is compact and any $\boldsymbol{x} \in B_L$ [B_L defined in (5.A.2)] is within $1/\sqrt{L}$ of some point in R_L^Ω $\exists$ L_0 s.t. $\forall L > L_0$, $\forall \boldsymbol{x} \in M$.

$$B_\delta(\boldsymbol{x}) \cap R_L^\Omega \neq \emptyset$$
$$\Rightarrow \boldsymbol{x}'_L \in M_L \rightarrow p(\boldsymbol{x}'_L) \geq p(\boldsymbol{x}) - \varepsilon .$$

Now if $\boldsymbol{x}'_{L_i} \rightarrow \tilde{\boldsymbol{x}}$ then

$$p(\tilde{\boldsymbol{x}}) = \lim p(\boldsymbol{x}'_{L_i}) > p(\boldsymbol{x}') - \varepsilon .$$

Since ε is arbitrary, $p(\tilde{\boldsymbol{x}}) = p(\boldsymbol{x}')$, i.e. $\tilde{\boldsymbol{x}} \in M$. □

Acknowledgments. This research was partially supported by the NSF Grant No. MIP-84-51010 and matching funds from IBM, AT&T, and Hughes Aircraft Company. The second author was also supported by ECI Telecom. The authors thank Anand Rangarajan for his helpful comments.

References

5.1 D.M. Goddman, M.P. Ekstrom: IEEE Trans. AC-**25**, 58–62 (1980)
5.2 A.K. Jain, J.R. Jain: IEEE Trans. AC-**23**, 817–833 (1978)
5.3 R. Chellappa, R.L. Kashyap: IEEE Trans. ASSP-**30**, 461–472 (1982)
5.4 F.C. Jeng, J.W. Woods: "Image estimation by stochastic relaxation in the compound Gaussian case", in Proc. IEEE Inter. Conf. ASSP (1988)
5.5 A. Blake, A. Zisserman: *Visual Reconstruction* (MIT Press, Cambridge 1987)
5.6 J. Besag: J. Roy. Stat. Soc. B-**36**, 192–236 (1974)
5.7 Y.A. Rosanov: Theory Prob. Appl.-**XII**, 381–391 (1967)
5.8 J.W. Woods: IEEE Trans. IT-**18**, 232–240 (1972)
5.9 M.J.D. Powell: Math. Program. **12**, 241–254 (1977)
5.10 S. Geman, D. Geman: IEEE Trans. PAMI-**6**, 721–741 (1984)
5.11 N. Metropolis et al.: J. Chem. Phys. **21**, 1087–1091 (1953)
5.12 B. Gidas: J. Stat. Phys. **39**, 71–131 (1985)
5.13 H. Derin, C.S. Won: Computer Vision Graphics and Image Processing **40**, 54–78 (1987)
5.14 R.L. Kashyap: "Random field models on finite lattices for finite images", in Proc. of the Conf. on information sciences and system, Johns Hopkins University, (1981) pp. 215–220

5.15 R. L. Kashyap, R. Chellappa: IEEE Trans. IT-**29**, 60–72 (1983)
5.16 P. A. P. Moran, J. E. Besag: Bometrika **62**, 555–562 (1975)
5.17 J. Besag: The Statistician **24**, 179–195 (1975)
5.18 J. Besag: Biometrika **64**, 616–618 (1977)
5.19 S. Geman, C. Graffigne: "Markov random fields image models and their application to computer vision", in Proc. of the International Congress of Mathematicians (1986) pp. 1496–1517
5.20 H. Kunsch: Z. Wahr. Ver. Geb. **58**, 401–421 (1981)
5.21 G. Sharma, R. Chellappa: IEEE Trans. IT-**31**, 90–99 (1985)
5.22 R. Chellappa: "Two-dimensional discrete Gaussian Markov random field models for image processing", in *Progress in Pattern Recognition 2*, ed. by L. N. Kanal, A. Rosenfeld (North-Holland, New York 1985)
5.23 Y. H. Hu, R. Chellappa, S. Y. Kung: IEEE Trans. ASSP-**31**, 836–841 (1983)
5.24 A. P. Dempster, N. M. Laird, D. B. Rubin: J. Roy. Stat. Sco. B-**39** (1977)
5.25 H. Kaufman et al.: IEEE Trans. AC-**28**, 745–755 (1983)
5.26 T. Simchony, R. Chellappa, Z. Lichtenstein: "Graduated nonconvexity algorithm for image estimation using compound Gauss Markov field models", Tech. Rpt. USC-SIPI 128, Signal and Image Process. Inst., University of Southern California (August 1988)
5.27 B. R. Hunt: Proc. IEEE **63**, 693–708 (1975)
5.28 J. Besag: J. Roy. Stat. Soc. B-**48**, 259–302 (1986)
5.29 A. K. Jain: IEEE Trans. PAMI-**1**, 356–365 (1979)
5.30 A. Rangarajan, R. Chellappa: "Generalized Graduated Non-Convexity Algorithm for Maximum A Posteriori Image Estimation", Tech. Rpt. USC-SIPI 149, Signal and Image Process. Inst., University of Southern California (December 1989)

6. Maximum Likelihood Identification and Restoration of Images Using the Expectation-Maximization Algorithm

A. K. Katsaggelos and K.-T. Lay

With 13 Figures

In this chapter the problem of identifying the image and blur parameters and restoring a noisy-blurred image is addressed. In the process of restoration, by using some a priori knowledge of the degradation mechanism, attempt is made to reconstruct or recover a degraded image such that it is as close as possible (based on a certain criterion) to its undegraded (or original) version. Most of the work on restoration in the literature was done under the assumption that the blurring process (usually modeled as a linear space-invariant system (LSI) and specified by its point spread function (PSF)) is exactly known. However, this may not be the actual case in practice since we do not usually have enough knowledge about the mechanism of the degradation process. Therefore, the estimation of the parameters that characterize the degradation operation needs to be based on the available noisy and blurred data. Specifying the blurring process by its PSF, the blur identification problem is formulated as the maximum likelihood (ML) estimation of the PSF. Modeling the original image and the additive noise as zero-mean Gaussian processes, the ML estimates of their covariance matrices are also computed. We derive explicit expressions for the estimation of the relevant unknown parameters, with the use of an iterative approach for finding ML estimates called the Expectation-Maximization (EM) algorithm. In applying the EM algorithm, a set of complete data has to be chosen. In this chapter three possible choices of complete data are investigated. However, only one of these choices results in the simultaneous identification of the blur and image parameters and the restoration of the image, thus justifying the term complete data. Assuming that the blur PSF is known, we obtain the form of an iterative Wiener restoration filter. Finally, we present the restoration results obtained by the proposed algorithms with simulated and photographically blurred images.

6.1 Overview

Images are recorded to depict useful information. Unfortunately, a recorded image will almost certainly be a degraded version of an original image due to the imperfections of physical imaging systems. It is desired that by restoration, an estimate of the original image be obtained from the observed (i.e. the recorded) image. Most of the work on image restoration which appears in the literature [6.1, Chap. 1 of this book] is done based on the assumption that the blur function which degrades the original image is exactly known from knowledge of the imaging system. In practice,

Springer Series in Information Sciences, Vol. 23
A. K. Katsaggelos (ed.): Digital Image Restoration

however, we usually do not have enough knowledge about the mechanism of the degradation process. Therefore, the degradation that an image has suffered must be estimated prior to restoration based on the available observed image, which is noisy and blurred. Modeling the blurring process by an LSI system, the blur identification problem becomes the estimation of its unknown PSF.

The earliest work on blur identification concentrated on estimating PSFs of specific functional form. However, the applicability of these techniques is limited to identifying PSFs that have zeros only on the unit bi-circle [6.1]. The identification problem then was the search for the location of these zeros in the frequency domain. In more recent work [6.2, 3], the image and blur model identification problem is specified as an estimation of two-dimensional (2D) autoregressive moving-average (ARMA) parameters. *Tekalp* et al. [6.2] computed the maximum likelihood estimates of these ARMA parameters by first decomposing the PSF into four causal quarterplane convolutional factors and then identifying each of these factors recursively. *Biemond* et al. [6.3] showed that the 2D ARMA identification can be done in parallel, where each of the parallel channels requires the identification of an one-dimensional (1D) complex ARMA process. *Lagendijk* et al. [6.4] and *Katsaggelos* et al. [6.5] formulated the blur identification and image restoration problem as a constrained ML and least-squares problem, respectively. The resulting nonlinear minimization problem was solved by iterative gradient-aided search methods. A priori knowledge about the blur and the image model was incorporated into the iterations. In Chap. 7 by *Angwin* and *Kaufman* adaptive ML estimation techniques are used for identifying the parameters of nonstationary image and blur models.

In this chapter, we derive iterative algorithms for image model and blur identification and image restoration. One advantage of iterative techniques is that they are free from the causality restriction and offer the possibility of incorporating prior knowledge about the original blur and image model into the identification and restoration procedure. More specifically, the image and the observation noise are modeled as multivariate Gaussian processes. Then the method of maximum likelihood estimation is applied to find the parameters which characterize the Gaussian processes. Direct maximization of the likelihood function is difficult because of its high nonlinearity with respect to these parameters. An iterative approach for computing maximum likelihood estimates, called the EM algorithm [6.6], is exploited to find these parameters [6.7–9]. In the application of the EM algorithm, a set of complete data has to be chosen properly. In this chapter, three possible choices of complete data are investigated. Due to the assumption that the image process is stationary and the blurring process is LSI, the image covariance and distortion matrices are block circulant. Thus, the problem under consideration is solved in the discrete frequency domain and simple iterative expressions are derived. If the original image is part of the complete data, its estimate which represents the restored image is computed in the E-step of the EM iterations. Thus the identification and restoration are achieved at the same time during the course of an EM iteration. One of the choices of complete data does not incorporate restoration; instead it results in the effect of noise smoothing. However, only one of the three choices of complete data results in the simultaneous identification of the blur and image parameters and the restoration of the image, thus justifying the term complete data. The other two choices are shown for completeness of the presentation. As a byproduct of this analysis, the form of an iterative Wiener restoration filter is derived, under the assumption that the blur PSF is known.

This chapter is organized as follows. In the next section, the image and blur models are described. In Sect. 6.3 the identification of the unknown parameters is formulated as a ML estimation problem. In Sect. 6.4, a review of the EM algorithm is first presented, and the particular form of the EM algorithm for the problem under consideration is obtained. In Sect. 6.5, identification/restoration algorithms are derived based on three different choices of complete data. In Sect. 6.6, modifications of the proposed algorithms are addressed. Experiments with simulated and photographically blurred images are shown in Sect. 6.7 and Sect. 6.8 concludes this chapter.

6.2 Image and Blur Models

In this work we assume that the original image, denoted by $x(i,j)$, $i=0,\dots,N-1$, $j=0,\dots,N-1$, or by the $N^2\times 1$ vector $\boldsymbol{x}$ in lexicographically ordered form [6.1], is modeled as a realization of a random process which is Gaussian with zero-mean. Its probability density function (pdf) is equal to

$$f_X(\boldsymbol{x}) = |2\pi\Lambda_X|^{-1/2}\exp\left\{\frac{-1}{2}\boldsymbol{x}^{\mathrm{H}}\Lambda_X^{-1}\boldsymbol{x}\right\}\ , \tag{6.1}$$

where Λ_X is the covariance matrix of $\boldsymbol{x}$, ^{H} denotes the Hermitian (i.e. conjugate transpose) of a matrix and a vector, and $|\cdot|$ denotes the determinant of a matrix. A special case of this representation is when $x(i,j)$ satisfies the equation

$$x(i,j) = \sum_{(p,q)\in S_A} a(p,q)x(i-p,j-q)+u(i,j)\ , \tag{6.2}$$

or in lexicographically ordered form,

$$\boldsymbol{x} = A\boldsymbol{x}+\boldsymbol{u}\ , \tag{6.3}$$

where $\{a(p,q)\}$ are the prediction coefficients, S_A is the finite causal image model support and $u(i,j)$ is a zero-mean homogeneous Gaussian distributed white noise process, which is independent of $x(i,j)$. The coefficients $\{a(p,q)\}$ are chosen in such a way that (6.3) represents a stable system [6.10]. Then the image covariance matrix is equal to

$$\Lambda_X = (I-A)^{-1}\Lambda_U(I-A)^{-\mathrm{H}}\ , \tag{6.4}$$

where $\Lambda_U=\sigma_U^2 I$ is the covariance matrix of $\boldsymbol{u}$. The inverse of $(I-A)$ exists due to the causality of the support S_A.

The observed image $y(i,j)$, $i = 0, \ldots, N-1$, $j = 0, \ldots, N-1$, is modeled as the output of a 2D LSI system with PSF $\{d(p,q)\}$. The output of the LSI system is corrupted by additive zero-mean Gaussian noise $v(i,j)$ with covariance matrix Λ_V, which is uncorrelated with $x(i,j)$. That is, the observed image $y(i,j)$ is expressed as

$$y(i,j) = \sum_{(p,q)\in S_D} d(p,q)x(i-p, j-q) + v(i,j) , \tag{6.5}$$

where S_D is the finite support region of the distortion filter. The support region S_D can have any shape. In other words, there are no constraints imposed on S_D, such as, for example, the requirement that $\{d(p,q)\}$ represents a causal minimum phase system, imposed by recursive identification methods [6.2]. In matrix/vector form, (6.5) can be rewritten as

$$\boldsymbol{y} = D\boldsymbol{x} + \boldsymbol{v} . \tag{6.6}$$

Equations (6.2) and (6.5) can be written in the discrete frequency domain according to the convolution theorem. Since the discrete Fourier transform (DFT) will be used in implementing convolution, we assume that (6.2) and (6.5) represent circular convolution. 2D sequences can be padded with zeros in such a way that the result of the linear convolution equals that of the circular convolution [6.11], or the observed image can be preprocessed around its boundaries so that (6.2) and (6.5) are consistent with the circular convolution of $\{a(p,q)\}$ with $\{x(p,q)\}$ and $\{d(p,q)\}$ with $\{x(p,q)\}$, respectively [6.12]. Then matrices A and D in (6.3) and (6.6), respectively, can be assumed to be block circulant [6.1].

6.3 ML Parameter Identification

The assumed image and blur models are specified in terms of the deterministic parameters $\phi = \{\Lambda_X, \Lambda_V, D\}$ or $\phi_{AR} = \{A, \sigma_U^2, \Lambda_V, D\}$. The image identification and restoration problem at hand is then the identification of these parameters and the determination of an image as close as possible to the original one, given the observed image $\boldsymbol{y}$. A maximum likelihood approach is followed next in carrying out the task. The following presentation refers to the identification of ϕ. The identification of ϕ_{AR} will be considered in a later section.

6.3.1 Formulation

Since $\boldsymbol{x}$ and $\boldsymbol{y}$ are uncorrelated, the observed image $\boldsymbol{y}$ is also Gaussian with pdf equal to

$$f_Y(\boldsymbol{y}) = |2\pi(D\Lambda_X D^{\mathrm{H}} + \Lambda_V)|^{-1/2} \exp\left\{\frac{-1}{2}\boldsymbol{y}^{\mathrm{H}}\left(D\Lambda_X D^{\mathrm{H}} + \Lambda_V\right)^{-1}\boldsymbol{y}\right\} , \tag{6.7}$$

where the inverse of the matrix $(D\Lambda_X D^{\mathrm{H}} + \Lambda_V)$ is assumed to be defined since covariance matrices are symmetric positive definite. To emphasize that $f_Y(\boldsymbol{y})$ is parameterized, we rewrite it as $f_Y(\boldsymbol{y};\phi)$. The ML estimation of the parameter set ϕ is the determination of ϕ_{ML} which maximizes the logarithm of the likelihood function $f_Y(\boldsymbol{y};\phi)$. That is,

$$\phi_{\mathrm{ML}} = \arg\left\{\max_{\{\phi\}} f_Y(\boldsymbol{y};\phi)\right\} = \arg\left\{\max_{\{\phi\}} \log f_Y(\boldsymbol{y};\phi)\right\} . \tag{6.8}$$

Taking the logarithm of (6.7) and disregarding constant additive and multiplicative terms, the maximization of the log-likelihood function becomes the minimization of the function $L(\phi)$, given by

$$L(\phi) = \log\left|D\Lambda_X D^{\mathrm{H}} + \Lambda_V\right| + \boldsymbol{y}^{\mathrm{H}}\left(D\Lambda_X D^{\mathrm{H}} + \Lambda_V\right)^{-1}\boldsymbol{y} , \tag{6.9}$$

where it is assumed that $\log|D\Lambda_X D^{\mathrm{H}} + \Lambda_V|$ is defined. By studying the function $L(\phi)$ it is clear that if no structure is imposed on the matrices D, Λ_X and Λ_V, the number of unknowns involved is very large. With so many unknowns and only one observation (i.e. $\boldsymbol{y}$), the ML identification problem becomes unmanageable. Furthermore, the estimate of $\{d(p,q)\}$ is not unique, because the ML approach to image and blur identification uses only second order statistics of the blurred image, since all pdfs are assumed to be Gaussian. More specifically, the second order statistics of the blurred image do not contain information about the phase of the blur and therefore, the phase of the ML solution for the blur is in general undetermined. In order to obtain a unique solution to the ML image and blur identification and restoration problem, additional information about the unknown parameters needs to be incorporated into the solution process.

6.3.2 Constraints on the Unknown Parameters

The structure we are imposing on Λ_X and Λ_V results from the commonly used assumptions in the field of image restoration [6.1]. First we assume that the additive noise $\boldsymbol{v}$ is white, with variance σ_V^2, that is,

$$\Lambda_V = \sigma_V^2 I , \tag{6.10}$$

where I is the identity matrix. Further we assume that the random process $\boldsymbol{x}$ is stationary which results in Λ_X being a block Toeplitz matrix [6.1]. A block Toeplitz matrix is asymptotically equivalent to a block circulant matrix as the dimension of the matrix becomes large [6.13]. For average size images, the dimensions of Λ_X are very large indeed; therefore, the block circulant approximation is a valid one. Associated with Λ_X is the 2D sequences $\{l_X(p,q)\}$. The matrix D in (6.6) is also block circulant, as was mentioned earlier. Block circulant matrices can be diagonalized with a transformation matrix W constructed from discrete Fourier kernels [6.14]. More specifically, it holds that

$$\Lambda_X = W Q_X W^{-1} , \tag{6.11}$$

and

$$D = WQ_DW^{-1}\,. \tag{6.12}$$

All matrices W, Q_X and Q_D are of size $N^2 \times N^2$. Q_X and Q_D are diagonal matrices with elements, the raster scanned 2D DFT values of the 2D sequences $\{l_X(p,q)\}$ and $\{d(p,q)\}$, denoted respectively by $S_X(m,n)$ and $\Delta(m,n)$. Due to the particular form of W^{-1}, the product $W^{-1}\boldsymbol{\beta}$, where $\boldsymbol{\beta}$ is an $N^2 \times 1$ vector obtained by stacking an $N \times N$ 2D sequence $\beta(i,j)$, is the stacked 2D DFT of $\beta(i,j)$.

Due to the assumptions expressed by (6.10–12), (6.9) can be written in the frequency domain as

$$L(\phi) = \sum_{m=0}^{N-1}\sum_{n=0}^{N-1}\left\{\log\left(|\Delta(m,n)|^2 S_X(m,n) + \sigma_V^2\right) + \frac{|Y(m,n)|^2}{|\Delta(m,n)|^2 S_X(m,n) + \sigma_V^2}\right\}, \tag{6.13}$$

where $Y(m,n)$ is the 2D DFT of $y(i,j)$. Equation (6.13) more clearly demonstrates the already mentioned non-uniqueness of the ML blur solution, since only the magnitude of $\Delta(m,n)$ appears in $L(\phi)$. If the blur is zero-phase, as is the case with D modeling atmospheric turbulence with long exposure times and mild defocussing ($\{d(p,q)\}$ is a 2D Gaussian sequence in this case), then a unique solution may be obtained. Non-uniqueness of the estimation of $\{d(p,q)\}$ can in general be avoided by enforcing the solution to satisfy a set of constraints. Most PSFs of practical interest can be assumed to be symmetric, i.e. $d(p,q) = d(-p,-q)$. In this case the phase of the DFT of $\{d(p,q)\}$ is zero or $\pm\pi$. Unfortunately, uniqueness of the ML solution is not always established by the symmetry assumption, due primarily to the phase ambiguity. Therefore, additional constraints may alleviate this ambiguity. Such additional constraints are the following:

(i) The PSF coefficients are nonnegative,
(ii) the support S_D is finite, and
(iii) the blurring mechanism preserves energy [6.1], which results in

$$\sum_{(i,j)\in S_D} d(i,j) = 1\,. \tag{6.14}$$

6.4 ML Identification via the EM Algorithm

The likelihood function $L(\phi)$ in (6.9) or (6.13) is nonlinear with respect to ϕ. Therefore, analytic solutions for ϕ can not be found in general and numerical optimization techniques need to be employed. Gradient based techniques were considered in [6.4, 5] and recursive techniques were developed in [6.2]. In this work, an iterative approach, called the EM algorithm, is applied for obtaining an estimate of ϕ. The algorithm is outlined in the next section.

6.4.1 The EM Algorithm in Review

The EM algorithm is a general iterative approach for solving ML identification problems. As the name implies, the EM algorithm consists of two steps – the expectation step (E-step) and the maximization step (M-step). It was first proposed by *Dempster* et al. [6.6] in 1977. Many effective estimation algorithms in various signal processing applications have been derived based on the EM algorithm [6.15–19].

In applying the EM algorithm, the observation $\boldsymbol{y}$ represents the incomplete data and a set of complete data $\boldsymbol{z}$ has to be chosen properly. The term "incomplete data" implies the existence of two sample spaces Ω_Y and Ω_Z and a many-to-one mapping from Ω_Z to Ω_Y. The observed data $\boldsymbol{y}$ is a realization from Ω_Y. The corresponding $\boldsymbol{z}$ in Ω_Z is not observed directly, but only indirectly through $\boldsymbol{y}$. The choice of the complete data may not be unique. For this and the following section, let us denote by θ the set of the unknown parameters and $f_Y(\boldsymbol{y};\theta)$ the likelihood function to be maximized. In the E-step of the EM algorithm, the conditional expectation of $\log f_Z(\boldsymbol{z};\theta)$, conditioned upon the observed data $\boldsymbol{y}$ and the current estimate of the relevant parameters, is computed, where $f_Z(\boldsymbol{z};\theta)$ is the pdf of the complete data; in the M-step, this expectation is maximized. In compact form, the EM algorithm can be expressed as the alternate computation of the following two equations

$$\theta^{(p+1)} = \arg\left\{\max_{\{\theta\}} Q\left(\theta;\theta^{(p)}\right)\right\} , \tag{6.15}$$

and

$$\begin{aligned} Q\left(\theta;\theta^{(p)}\right) &= E\left[\log f_Z(\boldsymbol{z};\theta)|\boldsymbol{y};\theta^{(p)}\right] \\ &= \int_{\Omega_{Z|\boldsymbol{y}}} f_{Z|Y}\left(\boldsymbol{z}|\boldsymbol{y};\theta^{(p)}\right)\log f_Z(\boldsymbol{z};\theta)\,d\boldsymbol{z} , \end{aligned} \tag{6.16}$$

where $\theta^{(p)}$ is the estimate of θ at the p-th iteration step and the integration is over all possible values of $\boldsymbol{z}$ that may produce the observed result $\boldsymbol{y}$, denoted by $\Omega_{Z|\boldsymbol{y}}$. Equation (6.16) and (6.15) correspond to the E-step and the M-step, respectively. By using the EM algorithm, $f_Y(\boldsymbol{y};\theta)$ converges to a stationary point, if $Q(\theta;\theta^{(p)})$ is continuous in both θ and $\theta^{(p)}$ [6.6, 20]. The maximization in (6.15) ensures that $f_Y(\boldsymbol{y};\theta)$ is monotonically nondecreasing. The EM algorithm is an attractive alternative to the direct maximization of $f_Y(\boldsymbol{y};\theta)$ if the solution to (6.15) can be found relatively easily. However, since the EM algorithm does not necessarily drive the likelihood function to converge to the global maximum of $f_Y(\boldsymbol{y};\theta)$, the choice of the starting point $\theta^{(0)}$ can affect the estimation significantly.

A slightly modified version of the EM algorithm was also proposed in [6.6]. The modification is on (6.15). That is, the maximization in (6.15) is replaced by any operation which makes $Q(\theta;\theta^{(p+1)})$ greater than $Q(\theta;\theta^{(p)})$, while retaining the form of (6.16), resulting in the generalized EM (GEM) algorithm. The GEM algorithm is useful if increasing $Q(\theta;\theta^{(p)})$ is much easier than maximizing $Q(\theta;\theta^{(p)})$. The GEM algorithm has a similar convergence performance to the EM algorithm, except that the former is slower. For the image identification and restoration problem, however, it turns out that the maximization of $Q(\theta;\theta^{(p)})$ can be done explicitly. Therefore, the use of the GEM algorithm is not explored further. Before we apply the EM algorithm to the identification/restoration problem, its relation to the method of alternating optimization is discussed.

6.4.2 Alternating Optimization of Cross Entropy

The EM algorithm belongs to a general class of algorithms of alternating minimization. A purely mathematical treatment of this approach is given by *Csiszar* and *Tusnady* [6.21]. In describing the alternating minimization approach, it is shown that the EM algorithm can be derived from the minimization of the cross entropy between two pdfs. In this presentation, we follow the work by *Miller* and *Snyder* [6.22].

Suppose that the a priori density $f_Z(\boldsymbol{z})$ is given, and the maxent density $\hat{q}(\boldsymbol{z})$ (i.e. the density which results in maximum entropy) is sought such that $E(\hat{q}, f_Z)$ is no less than $E(q, f_Z)$ for all $q(\boldsymbol{z})$, where $q(\boldsymbol{z})$ is a pdf. In other words, the maximization of $E(q, f_Z)$ with respect to $q(\boldsymbol{z})$ is required, where

$$E(q, f_Z) = -\int_{\Omega_Z} q(\boldsymbol{z}) \log \frac{q(\boldsymbol{z})}{f_Z(\boldsymbol{z})}\, d\boldsymbol{z} , \tag{6.17}$$

and

$$\Omega_Z = \{\boldsymbol{z} : f_Z(\boldsymbol{z}) \neq 0\} . \tag{6.18}$$

Clearly the maximization of $E(q, f_Z)$ is equivalent to the minimization of $-E(q, f_Z)$, which is termed *cross entropy* in the literature. Let us assume that $f_Z(\boldsymbol{z})$ represents the pdf of the complete data. We show next how the observed data $\boldsymbol{y}$ can be used as a constraint in the maximization of $E(q, f_Z)$. The observed (or incomplete) data $\boldsymbol{y}$ is assumed to be related to the complete data $\boldsymbol{z}$ by

$$\boldsymbol{y} = h(\boldsymbol{z}) . \tag{6.19}$$

The incomplete data $\boldsymbol{y}$ restricts the admissible domain of $\boldsymbol{z}$ which may produce $\boldsymbol{y}$ (i.e. $\Omega_{Z|\boldsymbol{y}}$). That is, the incomplete data $\boldsymbol{y}$ specifies the domain over which the maxent density has support, with the constraint

$$\int_{\Omega_{Z|\boldsymbol{y}}} q(\boldsymbol{z})\, d\boldsymbol{z} = 1 . \tag{6.20}$$

From Jensen's inequality [6.23], the density $q(\boldsymbol{z})$ maximizing $E(q, f_Z)$ subject to the constraint in (6.20) becomes

$$\hat{q}(\boldsymbol{z}) = \frac{f_Z(\boldsymbol{z};\theta)}{\int_{\Omega_{Z|\boldsymbol{y}}} f_Z(\boldsymbol{z};\theta)\, d\boldsymbol{z}} , \quad \text{for} \quad \boldsymbol{z} \in \Omega_{Z|\boldsymbol{y}} , \tag{6.21}$$

where the pdf of $\boldsymbol{z}$ (i.e. f_Z) has been written as $f_Z(\boldsymbol{z};\theta)$ to emphasize that it is parameterized by θ, the set of the unknown parameters. Noting that the conditional density of $\boldsymbol{z}$ given $\boldsymbol{y}$ (denoted by $f_{Z|Y}(\boldsymbol{z}|\boldsymbol{y};\theta)$) is zero for $\boldsymbol{z} \notin \Omega_{Z|\boldsymbol{y}}$ and that

$f_{Z|Y}(\boldsymbol{z},\boldsymbol{y};\theta) = f_Z(\boldsymbol{z};\theta)$ for $\boldsymbol{z} \in \Omega_{Z|\boldsymbol{y}}$, $\hat{q}(\boldsymbol{z})$ in (6.21) is precisely $f_{Z|Y}(\boldsymbol{z}|\boldsymbol{y};\theta)$. Therefore, the conditional and maxent densities are identical.

With the method of maximum likelihood estimation, the log-likelihood function (i.e. $\log f_Y(\boldsymbol{y};\theta)$) is to be maximized. For $z \in \Omega_{Z|\boldsymbol{y}}$ the log-likelihood can be written as

$$\log f_Y(\boldsymbol{y};\theta) = \log f_Z(\boldsymbol{z};\theta) - \log f_{Z|Y}(\boldsymbol{z}|\boldsymbol{y};\theta) . \tag{6.22}$$

The evaluation of the expectation of the expressions in (6.22) with respect to $f_{Z|Y}(\boldsymbol{z}|\boldsymbol{y};\theta)$ results in the following function to be maximized,

$$\log f_Y(\boldsymbol{y};\theta) = -\int_{\Omega_{Z|\boldsymbol{y}}} f_{Z|Y}(\boldsymbol{z}|\boldsymbol{y};\theta) \log \frac{f_{Z|Y}(\boldsymbol{z}|\boldsymbol{y};\theta)}{f_Z(\boldsymbol{z};\theta)}\, d\boldsymbol{z} . \tag{6.23}$$

Because of the equivalence between the conditional and maxent densities, the log-likelihood to be maximized becomes

$$\log f_Y(\boldsymbol{y};\theta) = \max_{\{q\}} \left\{ -\int_{\Omega_{Z|\boldsymbol{y}}} q(\boldsymbol{z}) \log \frac{q(\boldsymbol{z})}{f_Z(\boldsymbol{z};\theta)}\, d\boldsymbol{z} \right\} , \tag{6.24}$$

and the ML estimate of θ is equal to

$$\theta_{\mathrm{ML}} = \arg \left\{ \max_{\{\theta\}} \left[\max_{\{q\}} E\big(q, f_Z(\boldsymbol{z};\theta)\big) \right] \right\} . \tag{6.25}$$

Now it follows directly that θ_{ML} can be obtained by the following alternating optimization,

$$\theta_{\mathrm{ML}} = \arg \left\{ \max_{\{\theta\}} \left[\int_{\Omega_{Z|\boldsymbol{y}}} \hat{q}(\boldsymbol{z}) \log f(\boldsymbol{z};\theta)\, d\boldsymbol{z} \right] \right\} \tag{6.26}$$

and

$$\hat{q}(\boldsymbol{z}) = \mathrm{den} \left\{ \max_{\{q\}} \left[-\int_{\Omega_{Z|\boldsymbol{y}}} q(\boldsymbol{z}) \log \frac{q(\boldsymbol{z})}{f_Z(\boldsymbol{z};\theta)}\, d\boldsymbol{z} \right] \right\} , \tag{6.27}$$

where the notation den$\{\cdot\}$ denotes probability density. Recall that in the EM algorithm the maximization of the function $Q(\theta;\theta^{(p)})$ in (6.16) is sought, which is precisely (6.26) with $\hat{q}(\boldsymbol{z}) = f_{Z|Y}(\boldsymbol{z}|\boldsymbol{y};\theta^{(p)})$. In the mean time, note that (6.27) is satisfied by choosing $\hat{q}(\boldsymbol{z}) = f_{Z|Y}(\boldsymbol{z}|\boldsymbol{y};\theta^{(p)})$. Therefore the alternating maximization of (6.26) and (6.27) reduces to the maximization of (6.16), which represents the EM algorithm.

6.4.3 The EM Algorithm in the Linear Gaussian Case

In this section the form of the EM algorithm for the case when the mapping in (6.19) is linear and the random fields involved are Gaussian, is presented. Let H denote the linear noninvertible transformation, which relates the complete and incomplete data, according to

$$y = Hz \,. \tag{6.28}$$

The particular form of H depends on the possible choices of complete data. Since it is assumed that y is a zero-mean Gaussian process, z is also zero-mean Gaussian with pdf equal to

$$f_Z(z) = |2\pi \Lambda_Z|^{-1/2} \exp\left\{ \frac{-1}{2} z^{\mathrm{H}} \Lambda_Z^{-1} z \right\} \,. \tag{6.29}$$

The conditional pdf of z given y is also Gaussian [6.24] with conditional mean equal to

$$\mu_{Z|y} = E[z|y] = \Lambda_{ZY} \Lambda_Y^{-1} y = \Lambda_Z H^{\mathrm{H}} \left(H \Lambda_Z H^{\mathrm{H}} \right)^{-1} y \,, \tag{6.30}$$

and conditional covariance equal to

$$\begin{aligned} \Lambda_{Z|y} &= E[z z^{\mathrm{H}} | y] = \Lambda_Z - \Lambda_{ZY} \Lambda_Y^{-1} \Lambda_{YZ} \\ &= \Lambda_Z - \Lambda_Z H^{\mathrm{H}} \left(H \Lambda_Z H^{\mathrm{H}} \right)^{-1} H \Lambda_Z \,, \end{aligned} \tag{6.31}$$

where the relations $\Lambda_Y = H \Lambda_Z H^{\mathrm{H}}$, $\Lambda_{YZ} = H \Lambda_Z$ and $\Lambda_{ZY} = \Lambda_Z H^{\mathrm{H}}$ have been used. Rewriting $f_Z(z)$ as $f_Z(z; \phi)$ and taking its logarithm, we have

$$\begin{aligned} \log f_Z(z; \phi) &= \frac{-1}{2} \log |2\pi \Lambda_Z| + \frac{-1}{2} z^{\mathrm{H}} \Lambda_Z^{-1} z \\ &= K - \frac{1}{2} \left\{ \log |\Lambda_Z| + z^{\mathrm{H}} \Lambda_Z^{-1} z \right\} \,, \end{aligned} \tag{6.32}$$

where $\phi = \{\Lambda_Z\}$ and K is a constant independent of ϕ. Substituting (6.32) into (6.16), we obtain

$$\begin{aligned} Q(\phi; \phi^{(p)}) &= K - \frac{1}{2} \left\{ E\left[\log |\Lambda_Z| | y; \phi^{(p)} \right] + E\left[z^{\mathrm{H}} \Lambda_Z^{-1} z | y; \phi^{(p)} \right] \right\} \\ &= K - \frac{1}{2} \left\{ \log |\Lambda_Z| + \mathrm{tr}\left(\Lambda_Z^{-1} C_{Z|y}^{(p)} \right) \right\} \,, \end{aligned} \tag{6.33}$$

where $\mathrm{tr}(A)$ denotes the trace of a matrix A, $C_{Z|y}^{(p)} = E[z z^{\mathrm{H}} | y; \phi^{(p)}] = \Lambda_{Z|y}^{(p)} + \mu_{Z|y}^{(p)} \mu_{Z|y}^{(p)\mathrm{H}}$, $\mu_{Z|y}^{(p)} = E[z | y; \phi^{(p)}]$ and $\Lambda_{Z|y}^{(p)} = E[(z - \mu_{Z|y})(z - \mu_{Z|y})^{\mathrm{H}} | y; \phi^{(p)}]$. From (6.33), it is obvious that maximizing $Q(\phi; \phi^{(p)})$ is equivalent to minimizing

$$F(\phi; \phi^{(p)}) = \log |\Lambda_Z| + \mathrm{tr}\left(\Lambda_Z^{-1} C_{Z|y}^{(p)} \right) \,. \tag{6.34}$$

In other words, the EM algorithm in the linear Gaussian case reduces to the minimization of $F(\phi; \phi^{(p)})$. Substituting the expression for $C_{Z|y}^{(p)}$ into (6.34), $F(\phi; \phi^{(p)})$ becomes

$$F(\phi; \phi^{(p)}) = \log |\Lambda_Z| + \mathrm{tr}\left(\Lambda_Z^{-1} \Lambda_{Z|y}^{(p)} \right) + \mu_{Z|y}^{(p)H} \Lambda_Z^{-1} \mu_{Z|y}^{(p)} \,. \tag{6.35}$$

That is, the E-step of the algorithm is the computation of $F(\phi; \phi^{(p)})$ in (6.35) with the use of the expressions in (6.30, 31), while the M-step of the algorithm is described by the following equation

$$\phi^{(p+1)} = \arg\left\{\min_{\{\phi\}} F(\phi;\phi^{(p)})\right\} . \tag{6.36}$$

In our formulation of the identification/restoration problem the original image is not one of the unknown parameters in the set ϕ. However, as it will be shown in the next section, the restored image will be obtained in the E-step of the iterative algorithm.

6.5 The EM Iterations for the ML Estimation of ϕ

The last step to be taken in implementing the EM algorithm is the determination of the linear mapping H in (6.28). Clearly (6.6) can be rewritten as

$$\boldsymbol{y} = [0 \quad I]\begin{bmatrix}\boldsymbol{x}\\ \boldsymbol{y}\end{bmatrix} = [D \quad I]\begin{bmatrix}\boldsymbol{x}\\ \boldsymbol{v}\end{bmatrix} = [I \quad I]\begin{bmatrix}D\boldsymbol{x}\\ \boldsymbol{v}\end{bmatrix} , \tag{6.37}$$

where 0 and I represent the $N^2 \times N^2$ zero and identity matrices, respectively. Therefore, according to (6.37), there are three candidates for representing the complete data, namely, $\{\boldsymbol{x},\boldsymbol{y}\}$, $\{\boldsymbol{x},\boldsymbol{v}\}$ and $\{D\boldsymbol{x},\boldsymbol{v}\}$. All three cases are analyzed in the following. However, as it will be shown, only the choice of $\{\boldsymbol{x},\boldsymbol{y}\}$ as the complete data fully justifies the term "complete data", since it results in the simultaneous identification of all unknown parameters and the restoration of the image.

With the assumption of block circulant structures of relevant matrices, which was justified in Sect. 6.3.2, the evaluation of (6.35) can be performed in the frequency domain as is shown next. The three choices of complete data represented by (6.37) for the application of the EM algorithm to this particular blur identification and image restoration problem are investigated and compared.

6.5.1 $\{\boldsymbol{x},\boldsymbol{y}\}$ as the Complete Data

Choosing the original and observed images as the complete data, the expressions $H = [0 \; I]$ and $z = [\boldsymbol{x}^{\mathrm{H}} \; \boldsymbol{y}^{\mathrm{H}}]^{\mathrm{H}}$ are obtained according to (6.28) and (6.37). The covariance matrix of $\boldsymbol{z}$ takes the form

$$\Lambda_Z = E[\boldsymbol{z}\boldsymbol{z}^{\mathrm{H}}] = \begin{bmatrix}\Lambda_X & \Lambda_X D^{\mathrm{H}}\\ D\Lambda_X & D\Lambda_X D^{\mathrm{H}} + \Lambda_V\end{bmatrix} , \tag{6.38}$$

and its inverse is equal to [6.25]

$$\Lambda_Z^{-1} = \begin{bmatrix}\Lambda_X^{-1} + D^{\mathrm{H}}\Lambda_V^{-1}D & -D^{\mathrm{H}}\Lambda_V^{-1}\\ -\Lambda_V^{-1}D & \Lambda_V^{-1}\end{bmatrix} . \tag{6.39}$$

Substituting (6.38, 39) into (6.30, 31, 35), (6.35) can be rewritten as

$$F(\phi;\phi^{(p)}) = \log|\Lambda_X| + \log|\Lambda_V| + \mathrm{tr}\left\{\left(\Lambda_X^{-1} + D^{\mathrm{H}}\Lambda_V^{-1}D\right)\Lambda_{X|y}^{(p)}\right\}$$
$$+ \mu_{X|y}^{(p)\mathrm{H}}\left(\Lambda_X^{-1} + D^{\mathrm{H}}\Lambda_V^{-1}D\right)\mu_{X|y}^{(p)} - 2y^{\mathrm{H}}\Lambda_V^{-1}D\mu_{X|y}^{(p)} + y^{\mathrm{H}}\Lambda_V^{-1}y \tag{6.40}$$

where

$$\mu_{X|y}^{(p)} = \Lambda_X^{(p)}D^{(p)\mathrm{H}}\left(D^{(p)}\Lambda_X^{(p)}D^{(p)\mathrm{H}} + \Lambda_V^{(p)}\right)^{-1} y\,, \tag{6.41}$$

and

$$\Lambda_{X|y}^{(p)} = \Lambda_X^{(p)} - \Lambda_X^{(p)}D^{(p)\mathrm{H}}\left(D^{(p)}\Lambda_X^{(p)}D^{(p)\mathrm{H}} + \Lambda_V^{(p)}\right)^{-1} D^{(p)}\Lambda_X^{(p)}\,. \tag{6.42}$$

Due to the constraints on the unknown parameters described in Sect. 6.3.2, (6.40) can be written in the discrete frequency domain, as follows (for details see Appendix A),

$$F(\phi;\phi^{(p)}) = N^2\log\sigma_V^2 + \frac{1}{\sigma_V^2}\sum_{m=0}^{N-1}\sum_{n=0}^{N-1}$$
$$\times\left\{|\Delta(m,n)|^2\left(S_{X|y}^{(p)}(m,n) + \frac{1}{N^2}|M_{X|y}^{(p)}(m,n)|^2\right)\right.$$
$$\left. + \frac{1}{N^2}\left(|Y(m,n)|^2 - 2\,\mathrm{Re}\left[Y^*(m,n)\Delta(m,n)M_{X|y}^{(p)}(m,n)\right]\right)\right\}$$
$$+\sum_{m=0}^{N-1}\sum_{n=0}^{N-1}\left\{\log S_X(m,n) + \frac{1}{S_X(m,n)}(S_{X|y}^{(p)}(m,n)\right.$$
$$\left. + \frac{1}{N^2}|M_{X|y}^{(p)}(m,n)|^2)\right\}\,, \tag{6.43}$$

where

$$M_{X|y}^{(p)}(m,n) = \frac{\Delta^{(p)*}(m,n)S_X^{(p)}(m,n)}{|\Delta^{(p)}(m,n)|^2 S_X^{(p)}(m,n) + \sigma_V^{2(p)}}Y(m,n)\,, \tag{6.44}$$

$$S_{X|y}^{(p)}(m,n) = \frac{S_X^{(p)}(m,n)\sigma_V^{2(p)}}{|\Delta^{(p)}(m,n)|^2 S_X^{(p)}(m,n) + \sigma_V^{2(p)}}\,, \tag{6.45}$$

and $\mathrm{Re}\,[\cdot]$ denotes the real part of a complex number. In (6.43), $Y(m,n)$ is the 2D DFT of the observed image $y(i,j)$ and $M_{X|y}^{(p)}(m,n)$ is the 2D DFT of the unstacked vector $\mu_{X|y}^{(p)}$ into an $N \times N$ array. Taking the partial derivatives of $F(\phi;\phi^{(p)})$ with respect to $S_X(m,n)$ and $\Delta(m,n)$ and setting them equal to zero, we obtain the solutions that minimize $F(\phi;\phi^{(p)})$, which represent $S_X^{(p+1)}(m,n)$ and $\Delta^{(p+1)}(m,n)$. They are equal to

$$S_X^{(p+1)}(m,n) = S_{X|y}^{(p)}(m,n) + \frac{1}{N^2}|M_{X|y}^{(p)}(m,n)|^2\,, \tag{6.46}$$

$$\Delta^{(p+1)}(m,n) = \frac{1}{N^2}\frac{Y(m,n)M_{X|y}^{(p)*}(m,n)}{S_{X|y}^{(p)}(m,n) + \frac{1}{N^2}|M_{X|y}^{(p)}(m,n)|^2}\,, \tag{6.47}$$

where $M^{(p)}_{X|y}(m,n)$ and $S^{(p)}_{X|y}(m,n)$ are computed by (6.44) and (6.45). Substituting (6.47) into (6.43) and then minimizing $F(\phi;\phi^{(p)})$ with respect to σ_V^2, we obtain

$$\sigma_V^{2(p+1)} = \frac{1}{N^2}\sum_{m=0}^{N-1}\sum_{n=0}^{N-1}\left\{|\Delta^{(p+1)}(m,n)|^2\left(S^{(p)}_{X|y}(m,n)+\frac{1}{N^2}|M^{(p)}_{X|y}(m,n)|^2\right)\right.$$
$$\left.+\frac{1}{N^2}\left(|Y(m,n)|^2 - 2\mathrm{Re}\left[Y^*(m,n)\Delta^{(p+1)}(m,n)M^{(p)}_{X|y}(m,n)\right]\right)\right\}. \tag{6.48}$$

According to (6.44) the restored image (i.e. $M^{(p)}_{X|y}(m,n)$) is the output of a Wiener filter, based on the available estimate of ϕ, with the observed image as input.

6.5.2 $\{\boldsymbol{x},\boldsymbol{v}\}$ as the Complete Data

Choosing $\{\boldsymbol{x},\boldsymbol{v}\}$ as the complete data, $H=[D\quad I]$ and $\boldsymbol{z}=[\boldsymbol{x}^{\mathrm{H}}\quad \boldsymbol{v}^{\mathrm{H}}]^{\mathrm{H}}$. Because $\boldsymbol{x}$ and $\boldsymbol{v}$ are uncorrelated, the covariance matrix of $\boldsymbol{z}$ is equal to

$$\Lambda_Z = \begin{bmatrix}\Lambda_X & 0\\ 0 & \Lambda_V\end{bmatrix}, \tag{6.49}$$

and its inverse is equal to

$$\Lambda_Z^{-1} = \begin{bmatrix}\Lambda_X^{-1} & 0\\ 0 & \Lambda_V^{-1}\end{bmatrix}. \tag{6.50}$$

Substituting (6.49,50) into (6.30,31,35) and expressing $F(\phi;\phi^{(p)})$ in the frequency domain, as was done in the previous section, (6.35) can be rewritten as

$$F(\phi;\phi^{(p)}) = N^2\log\sigma_V^2 + \frac{1}{\sigma_V^2}\sum_{m=0}^{N-1}\sum_{n=0}^{N-1}\left\{\left(S^{(p)}_{V|y}(m,n)+\frac{1}{N^2}|M^{(p)}_{V|y}(m,n)|^2\right)\right\}$$
$$+\sum_{m=0}^{N-1}\sum_{n=0}^{N-1}\left\{\log S_X(m,n)+\frac{1}{S_X(m,n)}\left(S^{(p)}_{X|y}(m,n)\right.\right.$$
$$\left.\left.+\frac{1}{N^2}|M^{(p)}_{X|y}(m,n)|^2\right)\right\}, \tag{6.51}$$

where $S^{(p)}_{X|y}(m,n)$, $M^{(p)}_{X|y}(m,n)$, $S^{(p)}_{V|y}(m,n)$ and $M^{(p)}_{V|y}(m,n)$ are the 2D DFT values of the conditional covariances and conditional means of $\boldsymbol{x}$ and $\boldsymbol{v}$ given $\boldsymbol{y}$, respectively. $M^{(p)}_{X|y}(m,n)$ and $S^{(p)}_{X|y}(m,n)$ are computed by (6.44) and (6.45), respectively, while $M^{(p)}_{V|y}(m,n)$ and $S^{(p)}_{V|y}(m,n)$ are computed by the following two equations,

$$M^{(p)}_{V|y}(m,n) = \frac{\sigma_V^{2(p)}}{|\Delta^{(p)}(m,n)|^2 S^{(p)}_X(m,n)+\sigma_V^{2(p)}}Y(m,n), \tag{6.52}$$

$$S_{V|y}^{(p)}(m,n) = \frac{|\Delta^{(p)}(m,n)|^2 S_X^{(p)}(m,n)\sigma_V^{2(p)}}{|\Delta^{(p)}(m,n)|^2 S_X^{(p)}(m,n) + \sigma_V^{2(p)}} . \tag{6.53}$$

Note that the estimation of D (or equivalently, $\Delta(m,n)$) can not be obtained by minimizing (6.51) since $\Delta(m,n)$ does not appear in this equation. In order to estimate D, a separate minimization must be carried out. For convenience of exposure, let us divide the set of unknown parameters ϕ into two sets ϕ_1 and ϕ_2, where $\phi_1 = \{\Lambda_V, \Lambda_X\}$ and $\phi_2 = \{D\}$. Then the functional to be minimized in (6.51) should be specified as $F(\phi_1; \phi^{(p)})$. Setting the partial derivatives of $F(\phi_1; \phi^{(p)})$ with respect to σ_V^2 and $S_X(m,n)$ equal to 0, the solutions which minimize $F(\phi_1; \phi^{(p)})$ are equal to

$$S_X^{(p+1)}(m,n) = S_{X|y}^{(p)}(m,n) + \frac{1}{N^2}|M_{X|y}^{(p)}(m,n)|^2 , \tag{6.54}$$

$$\sigma_V^{2(p+1)} = \frac{1}{N^2}\sum_{m=0}^{N-1}\sum_{n=0}^{N-1}\left(S_{V|y}^{(p)}(m,n) + \frac{1}{N}|M_{V|v}^{(p)}(m,n)|^2\right) . \tag{6.55}$$

In evaluating (6.54) and (6.55) at the $(p+1)$th iteration step, with the use of (6.44, 45, 52, 53), an estimate of $\Delta(m,n)$ at the pth step is required. Such an estimate can be obtained by minimizing

$$J\left(D; \phi_1^{(p)}\right) = \log|D\Lambda_X^{(p)}D^{\mathrm{H}} + \Lambda_V^{(p)}| + \boldsymbol{y}^{\mathrm{H}}\left(D\Lambda_X^{(p)}D^{\mathrm{H}} + \Lambda_V^{(p)}\right)^{-1}\boldsymbol{y} . \tag{6.56}$$

Expressed in the frequency domain, $J(D; \phi_1^{(p)})$ becomes

$$J(\Delta(m,n); \phi_1^{(p)}) = \sum_{m=0}^{N-1}\sum_{n=0}^{N-1} \log\left(|\Delta(m,n)|^2 S_X^{(p)}(m,n) + \sigma_V^{2(p)}\right) + \frac{\frac{1}{N^2}|Y(m,n)|^2}{|\Delta(m,n)|^2 S_X^{(p)}(m,n) + \sigma_V^{2(p)}} . \tag{6.57}$$

By setting the partial derivative with respect to $\Delta(m,n)$ equal to zero, we obtain

$$|\Delta^{(p)}(m,n)|^2 = \begin{cases} \frac{\frac{1}{N^2}|Y(m,n)|^2 - \sigma_V^{2(p)}}{S_X^{(p)}(m,n)}, & \text{if } \frac{1}{N^2}|Y(m,n)|^2 > \sigma_V^{2(p)} \\ 0, & \text{otherwise} . \end{cases} \tag{6.58}$$

From (6.58) we observe that only the magnitude of $\Delta^{(p)}(m,n)$ is available, as was mentioned earlier. A similar observation can be made for (6.47), according to which the phase of $\Delta(m,n)$ is equal to the phase of $\Delta^{(0)}(m,n)$. Note that the estimation of ϕ is done through the alternation of (6.54, 55) and (6.58).

The effect of mixing the optimization procedure into the EM algorithm has not been completely analyzed theoretically. That is, the convergence properties of the EM algorithm do not necessarily hold, although both the applications of (6.54, 55) and (6.58) increase the likelihood function. However, based on the experimental results the algorithm derived in this section always converges to a stationary point;

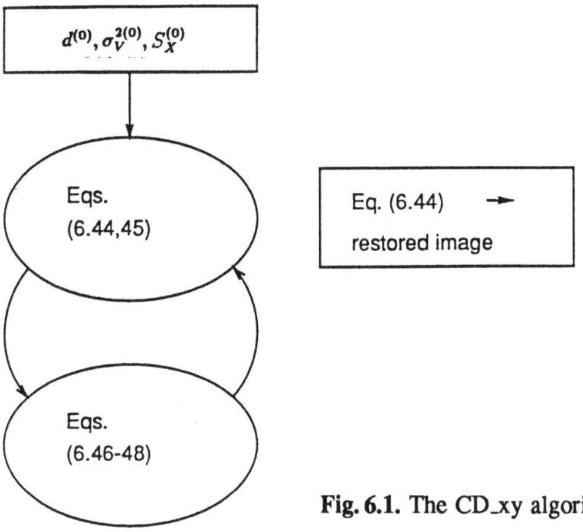

Fig. 6.1. The CD_xy algorithm

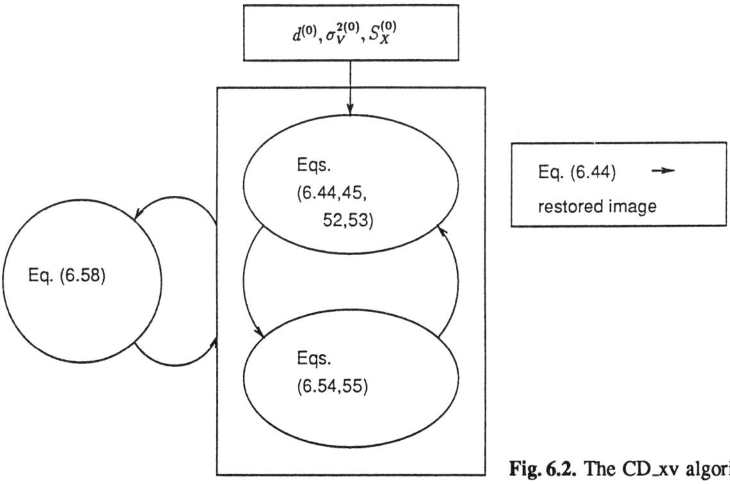

Fig. 6.2. The CD_xv algorithm

furthermore, the results are comparable to the ones obtained with the algorithm of Sect. 6.5.1.

The algorithms developed in Sects. 6.5.1 and 6.5.2 are shown in block diagram form, in Figs. 6.1 and 6.2, respectively. For convenient referencing, the algorithms derived in Sects. 6.5.1 and 6.5.2 are respectively referred to as the CD_xy and CD_xv algorithms.

6.5.3 $\{D\boldsymbol{x}, \boldsymbol{v}\}$ as the Complete Data

The third choice of the complete data is $\boldsymbol{z} = [(D\boldsymbol{x})^{\mathrm{H}}, \boldsymbol{v}^{\mathrm{H}}]^{\mathrm{H}}$. In this case, D and $\boldsymbol{x}$ can not be estimated separately, since various combinations of D and $\boldsymbol{x}$ can result in the same $D\boldsymbol{x}$. The two quantities D and $\boldsymbol{x}$ are lumped into one quantity $\boldsymbol{t} = D\boldsymbol{x}$.

The observed image $\boldsymbol{y}$ can then be expressed as

$$y = [I \quad I] \begin{bmatrix} t \\ v \end{bmatrix} . \tag{6.59}$$

Because $\boldsymbol{x}$ and $\boldsymbol{v}$ are uncorrelated, $\boldsymbol{t}$ and $\boldsymbol{v}$ are also uncorrelated. The autocovariance matrix of $\boldsymbol{z}$ is equal to

$$\Lambda_Z = \begin{bmatrix} \Lambda_T & 0 \\ 0 & \Lambda_V \end{bmatrix} , \tag{6.60}$$

and its inverse is equal to

$$\Lambda_Z^{-1} = \begin{bmatrix} \Lambda_T^{-1} & 0 \\ 0 & \Lambda_V^{-1} \end{bmatrix} . \tag{6.61}$$

Substituting the relevant quantities (i.e. H, Λ_Z and Λ_Z^{-1}) into (6.30,31), we have

$$\boldsymbol{\mu}_{T|\boldsymbol{y}}^{(p)} = \Lambda_T^{(p)}(\Lambda_T^{(p)} + \Lambda_V^{(p)})^{-1}\boldsymbol{y} , \tag{6.62}$$

$$\boldsymbol{\mu}_{V|\boldsymbol{y}}^{(p)} = \Lambda_V^{(p)}(\Lambda_T^{(p)} + \Lambda_V^{(p)})^{-1}\boldsymbol{y} , \tag{6.63}$$

$$\Lambda_{T|\boldsymbol{y}}^{(p)} = \Lambda_T^{(p)} - \Lambda_T^{(p)}(\Lambda_T^{(p)} + \Lambda_V^{(p)})^{-1}\Lambda_T^{(p)} , \tag{6.64}$$

$$\Lambda_{V|\boldsymbol{y}}^{(p)} = \Lambda_V^{(p)} - \Lambda_V^{(p)}(\Lambda_T^{(p)} + \Lambda_V^{(p)})^{-1}\Lambda_V^{(p)} . \tag{6.65}$$

Minimizing $F(\phi;\phi^{(p)})$ in the frequency domain as was done in the two previous subsections, the EM iterations reduce to

$$\sigma_V^{2(p+1)} = \frac{1}{N^2}\sum_{m=0}^{N-1}\sum_{n=0}^{N-1}\left(S_{V|\boldsymbol{y}}^{(p)}(m,n) + \frac{1}{N^2}|M_{V|\boldsymbol{y}}^{(p)}(m,n)|^2\right) , \tag{6.66}$$

and

$$S_T^{(p+1)}(m,n) = S_{T|\boldsymbol{y}}^{(p)}(m,n) + \frac{1}{N^2}|M_{T|\boldsymbol{y}}^{(p)}(m,n)|^2 , \tag{6.67}$$

where $S_{T|\boldsymbol{y}}^{(p)}(m,n)$, $M_{T|\boldsymbol{y}}^{(p)}(m,n)$, $S_{V|\boldsymbol{y}}^{(p)}(m,n)$ and $M_{V|\boldsymbol{y}}^{(p)}(m,n)$ are the 2D DFT values of the quantities in (6.62–65). Based on the current estimate of ϕ, the signal after noise smoothing is the conditional mean of $\boldsymbol{t}$ given $\boldsymbol{y}$ (i.e. $M_{T|\boldsymbol{y}}^{(p)}(m,n)$), which is computed from the equation

$$M_{T|\boldsymbol{y}}^{(p)}(m,n) = \frac{S_T^{(p)}(m,n)}{S_T^{(p)}(m,n) + \sigma_V^{2(p)}} Y(m,n) . \tag{6.68}$$

6.5.4 Iterative Wiener Filtering

In this subsection, we deviate somewhat from the original formulation of the identification problem by assuming that the blur function is known. The problem then at hand is the restoration of the noisy-blurred image. Although there are a large number of approaches that can be followed in this case, as can be seen in Chap. 1, the Wiener filtering approach represents a commonly used choice. However, in Wiener filtering knowledge of the power spectrum of the original image (S_X) and the additive noise (S_V) is required. A standard assumption is that of ergodicity according to which ensemble averages are approximated by spatial averages. Even in this case, the estimation of the power spectrum of the original image has to be based on the observed noisy-blurred image, since the original image is not available. Assuming that the noise is white, its variance σ_V^2 needs also to be estimated from the observed image. Approaches, according to which the power spectrum of the original image is computed from images with similar statistical properties, have been suggested in the literature [6.1]. However, a reasonable idea is to successively use the Wiener-restored image as an improved prototype for updating the unknown S_X and σ_V^2. This idea is precisely implemented by the algorithm in Sect. 6.5.1.

More specifically, now that the blur function is known, (6.47) is removed from the EM iterations. Thus, (6.46) and (6.48) are used to estimate S_X and σ_V^2, respectively, while (6.44) is used to compute the Wiener-filtered image. The starting point $S_X^{(0)}$ for the Wiener iteration can be chosen to be equal to

$$S_X^{(0)} = \hat{S}_Y \,, \tag{6.69}$$

where $\hat{S}_Y$ is an estimate of the power spectral density of the observed image. The value of $\sigma_V^{2(0)}$ can be determined from flat regions in the observed image, since this represents a commonly used approach for estimating the noise variance. With the iterative Wiener restoration filter, a restored image is obtained, based on the most likely parameters which gave rise to the obtained image $\boldsymbol{y}$.

6.6 Modified Forms of the Proposed Algorithm

In this section, we first present the form of the CD_xy algorithm when an AR image model is used. Then the equivalent form of the CD_xy algorithm in the spatial domain is shown. Finally, various ways for parameterizing the blur PSF are suggested. Possible advantages and disadvantages of these forms of the CD_xy algorithm are discussed.

6.6.1 ML Estimation of ϕ_{AR}

As was mentioned in Sect. 6.3 the identification/restoration problem can be formulated as the ML estimation of the parameter set $\phi_{\mathrm{AR}} = \{A, \sigma_U^2, \Lambda_V, D\}$, where A and σ_U^2 are the parameters specifying the AR image model, as explained in Sect. 6.2. Then in this case, Λ_X in (6.4) can be rewritten as

$$\Lambda_X = \sigma_U^2 B^{-1} B^{-\mathrm{H}} \,, \tag{6.70}$$

where $B = (I - A)$ and $\Lambda_U = \sigma_U^2 I$. Since A is a block circulant matrix, B is also block circulant and it is uniquely specified by the sequence $b(i,j) = \delta(i,j) - a(i,j)$, where $\delta(i,j)$ is the 2D impulse. Substituting (6.70) into the equations for Λ_Z and Λ_Z^{-1} in Sect. 6.5.1, the expression in (6.43) becomes equal to

$$
\begin{aligned}
F(\phi;\phi^{(p)}) = {} & N^2 \log \sigma_U^2 + N^2 \log \sigma_V^2 \\
& + \sum_{m=0}^{N-1}\sum_{n=0}^{N-1} \log \frac{1}{|\tilde{b}(m,n)|^2} \\
& + \sum_{m=0}^{N-1}\sum_{n=0}^{N-1} \left\{ \left(\frac{|\tilde{b}(m,n)|^2}{\sigma_U^2} + \frac{|\Delta(m,n)|^2}{\sigma_V^2} \right) S_{X|y}^{(p)}(m,n) \right. \\
& + \frac{1}{N^2} \left[\left(\frac{|\tilde{b}(m,n)|^2}{\sigma_U^2} + \frac{|\Delta(m,n)|^2}{\sigma_V^2} \right) |M_{X|y}^{(p)}(m,n)|^2 \right. \\
& - \frac{2}{\sigma_V^2} \mathrm{Re}\left[Y^*(m,n)\Delta(m,n)M_{X|y}^{(p)}(m,n) \right) \\
& \left. \left. \frac{1}{\sigma_V^2} |Y(m,n)|^2 \right] \right\}
\end{aligned}
\tag{6.71}
$$

where $\tilde{b}(m,n)$ is the 2D DFT of $b(i,j)$. Setting the partial derivatives of $F(\phi;\phi^{(p)})$ with respect to σ_U^2 and $\tilde{b}(m,n)$ equal to zero, the following EM iterations are obtained

$$
\sigma_U^{2(p+1)} = \frac{1}{N^2} \sum_{m=0}^{N-1}\sum_{n=0}^{N-1} |\Delta(m,n)|^2 \left(S_{X|y}^{(p)}(m,n) + \frac{1}{N^2} |M_{X|y}^{(p)}(m,n)|^2 \right) , \tag{6.72}
$$

and

$$
|\tilde{b}^{(p+1)}(m,n)|^2 = \frac{\sigma_U^{2(p)}}{S_{X|y}^{(p)}(m,n) + \frac{1}{N^2}|M_{X|y}^{(p)}(m,n)|^2} , \tag{6.73}
$$

where $S_{X|y}^{(p)}(m,n)$ and $M_{X|y}^{(p)}(m,n)$ are computed from (6.44) and (6.45), respectively, with $S_X^{(p)}(m,n) = \sigma_U^2|\tilde{b}(m,n)|^2$. The equations for the computation of $\Delta^{(p+1)}(m,n)$ and $\sigma_V^{2(p+1)}$ are the same as in Sect. 6.5.1 ((6.47) and (6.48), respectively). It is worth noting that according to (6.73) only the magnitude of the frequency response of the filter $\{b(i,j)\}$ is obtained. Therefore, a unique determination of the prediction coefficients is not possible, without providing information about the phase, as is in the case of the identification of the blur.

6.6.2 Spatial Domain Iteration

In this section, we present an equivalent form of the CD_xy algorithm in the spatial domain. By combining (6.46) and (6.47), (6.47) can be rewritten as

$$
S_X^{(p+1)}(m,n)\Delta^{(p+1)}(m,n) = \frac{1}{N^2} Y(m,n) M_{X|y}^{(p)*}(m,n) . \tag{6.74}
$$

Taking the inverse discrete Fourier transform (IDFT) of both sides, the above equation becomes

$$\gamma_X^{(p+1)}(i,j) \star d^{(p+1)}(i,j) = \frac{1}{N^2} y(i,j) \star \mu_{X|y}^{(p)}(-i,-j)\,, \tag{6.75}$$

where $\gamma_X^{(p+1)}(i,j) = \text{IDFT}\{S_X^{(p+1)}(m,n)\}$ and $\star$ denotes 2D convolution. Expressing the convolution operation explicitly, (6.75) is rewritten as

$$\begin{aligned} &\sum_{r=0}^{N-1}\sum_{q=0}^{N-1} \gamma_X^{(p+1)}(i-r,j-q) d^{(p+1)}(r,q) \\ &= \frac{1}{N^2}\sum_{r=0}^{N-1}\sum_{q=0}^{N-1} y(i-r,j-q)\mu_{X|y}^{(p)}(-r,-q) \\ &\approx E\left[y(i-r,j-q)\mu_{X|y}^{(p)}(-r,-q)\right] \stackrel{\triangle}{=} \gamma_{y\mu}^{(p)}(i,j)\,. \end{aligned} \tag{6.76}$$

In other words, $d^{(p+1)}(i,j)$ can be obtained by solving the following set of linear equations

$$\sum_{r=0}^{N-1}\sum_{q=0}^{N-1} \gamma_X^{(p+1)}(i-r,j-q)d^{(p+1)}(r,q) - \gamma_{y\mu}^{(p)}(i,j) = 0\,, \quad i,j = 0,\ldots,N-1\,. \tag{6.77}$$

If information about S_D, the support region of D, is available, (6.77) can be reduced to

$$\sum_{(r,q)\in S_D} \gamma_X^{(p+1)}(i-r,j-q)d^{(p+1)}(r,q) - \gamma_{y\mu}^{(p)}(i,j) = 0\,, \quad i,j = 0,\ldots,N-1\,. \tag{6.78}$$

In general, (6.78) represents an overdetermined set of linear equations, and $\{d(r,q)\}$ represents the minimum norm least squares solution. Clearly, (6.78) is suitable for identifying regionally varying blurs. Furthermore, (6.78) is suitable for incorporating a priori information about the blur into the identification procedure, as was done in [6.4, 5]. This way, the set of feasible solutions is further restricted, and the phase ambiguity in estimating $\{d(r,q)\}$ may be resolved. Similarly, the spatial domain counterpart of (6.46) is equal to

$$\gamma_X^{(p+1)}(i,j) = \gamma_{X|y}^{(p)}(i,j) + \gamma_{\mu\mu}^{(p)}(i,j)\,. \tag{6.79}$$

where $\gamma_{\mu\mu}^{(p)}(i,j) \stackrel{\triangle}{=} E[\mu_{X|y}^{(p)}(i-r,j-q)\mu_{X|y}^{(p)}(-r,-q)]$. As to $\sigma_V^{2(p+1)}$ and $b(i,j)$, they can also be computed in the spatial domain, by taking the IDFT of the right hand side of (6.48) and (6.73), respectively. Equations similar to the spatial domain iterations presented in this section were obtained in [6.26]. A disadvantage of the spatial domain approach may be the requirement for knowing the support regions S_D and S_A in advance.

6.6.3 Parameterization of the Image and Blur Models

In the previous sections, the only structure imposed on the blur function was that D was a block circulant matrix. Although due to this and the assumptions of Sect. 6.3.2 maximization of the likelihood function $f_Y(\boldsymbol{y};\phi)$ becomes feasible in the frequency domain, the number of independent variables is still very large, since it is equal to the number of elements in $\{\Delta(m,n)\}, 0 \le m,n \le N-1$. With such a large number of unknown parameters, it is expected that many stationary points of $f_Y(\boldsymbol{y};\phi)$ exist. Therefore, since the EM algorithm converges to a stationary point, the corresponding value of the likelihood function may be far below the global maximum. One approach to alleviate this problem is to reduce the number of stationary points, which can be achieved by the parameterization of the PSF of the blur. Such an approach is also discussed in Chap. 7.

In practice, the PSF to be estimated can be parameterized if information about the type or class of the blurring process is available. Some types of blurs which can be specified with a small number of parameters are listed below :

- Pill-box blur (the 1D motion blur is a special case of this):

$$d(i,j;L_i,L_j) = \begin{cases} \frac{1}{K}, & \text{if } |i| \le L_i \text{ and } |j| \le L_j \\ 0, & \text{otherwise} \end{cases} . \tag{6.80}$$

- Out-of-focus blur:

$$d(i,j;R) = \begin{cases} \frac{1}{K}, & \text{if } (i^2+j^2) \le R^2 \\ 0, & \text{otherwise} \end{cases} . \tag{6.81}$$

- Gaussian blur (modeling the distortion due to atmospheric turbulence):

$$d(i,j;\sigma^2) = K \exp\left\{\frac{-(i^2+j^2)}{2\sigma^2}\right\} \tag{6.82}$$

  where K is selected so that (6.14) is satisfied.

One feasible choice for the parameterization of image models is the AR modeling (6.2) with finite model support S_D. Another commonly adopted choice is to assume that the autocorrelation function of the original image has the form of a separable exponentially decaying function, that is [6.10]

$$\gamma_X(i,j) = \sigma_X^2 \varrho_1^{|i|} \varrho_2^{|j|} , \tag{6.83}$$

where ϱ_1 and ϱ_2 are the vertical and horizontal coefficients and σ_X^2 is the variance of the image field.

With parameterization, the number of unknowns involved in evaluating $\log f_Y(\boldsymbol{y})$ can be reduced to the order of ten. Numerical methods (e.g. gradient-based searching) can then be applied to optimize the likelihood function. Although with parameterization the image and blur identification problem becomes considerably more stable, the structure of the blur PSF and the image model need to be known.

6.7 Experimental Results

Experimental results with simulated and photographically blurred images are described in this section. The algorithms proposed in Sect. 6.5 were tested. Convergence thresholds were set for $\sigma_V^{2(p)}$, $S_X^{(p)}$ and $\Delta^{(p)}$ for terminating the EM iterations. That is, if $\xi_v^{(p)} = |v^{(p)} - v^{(p-1)}|/|v^{(p-1)}| < \delta$, $v \in \{\sigma_V^2, S_X, \Delta\}$, where $\delta = 10^{-4}$ was used, the iterations are terminated. Equation (6.44) was used to compute the restored image. An arbitrary value (preferably somewhat larger than the true value of σ_V^2) was chosen as $\sigma_V^{2(0)}$, the initial value of the estimate of σ_V^2. The Blackman-Tukey algorithm [6.27] was used to compute S_Y, an estimate of the power spectral density of $\boldsymbol{y}$, which in turn was used as $S_X^{(0)}$, in both the CD_xy and CD_xv cases. We know that the EM algorithm has the drawback that it converges to a stationary point of the likelihood function. Therefore, it is reasonable to conjecture that if the initial guess for the PSF (i.e. $d^{(0)}$) is sufficiently good, then the algorithm has a better chance to converge to the true values. This conjecture was verified, by rerunning the CD_xy algorithm with different initial conditions $d^{(0)}$, such as a 2D impulse, a decaying exponential function and a 3×3 pill-box function, as is further explained later. In all cases no knowledge was assumed about the support of the PSF, thus representing a major advantage of the proposed algorithm. The above conjecture was also used in reinforcing the finite support constraint for the PSF. That is, after convergence of the EM iteration was reached, the estimate of $d(i,j)$ was truncated, normalized and used as $d^{(0)}(i,j)$ in restarting a new iteration cycle (i.e. another run of the EM iterations until convergence). In truncating the PSF, the rule was applied that if two adjacent values of the estimates of $\{d(i,j)\}$ were different by at least an order of magnitude, the smaller one was disregarded. In the following the number of iteration cycles is denoted by I_c while the number of iterations at the ith iteration cycle is denoted by $I_p(i)$. In comparing the various blur identification results, the following figure of merit was used

$$\varepsilon = \frac{||d - \hat{d}||}{||d||} = \frac{\sqrt{\sum_{(i,j)\in S_D \cup S_{\hat{D}}} |d(i,j) - \hat{d}(i,j)|^2}}{\sqrt{\sum_{(i,j)\in S_D} |d(i,j)|^2}}, \tag{6.84}$$

where $\{d(i,j)\}$ and $\{\hat{d}(i,j)\}$ denote the original and the estimated PSFs with S_D and $S_{\hat{D}}$ their respective regions of support.

Figure 6.3 shows the original cameraman image. Figure 6.4 A shows a degraded version of Fig. 6.3. The PSF is 2D Gaussian, with values as shown in Table 6.1, and the signal-to-noise ratio (SNR) is equal to 50 dB. The restored image by applying the CD_xy algorithm is shown in Fig. 6.4 B and the values of the estimated blur with the number of iterations run are shown in Table 6.2. The values of $d(i,j)$ not shown in Table 6.2 (i.e. outside the 5×5 support region), were at least an order of magnitude smaller than the smallest value appearing in Table 6.2 and thus truncated. A general observation with this approach is that increased sharpness in the restored image is traded with noise amplification, as we increase the number of iteration cycles. This effect can be seen in Figs. 6.5 and 6.6. Figure 6.5 A shows the

Table 6.1. Values of the 2D Gaussian PSF

$d(i,j)$	j: -2	-1	0	1	2
i: -2	0.0030	0.0133	0.0219	0.0133	0.0030
-1	0.0133	0.0596	0.0983	0.0596	0.0133
0	0.0219	0.0983	0.1621	0.0983	0.0219
1	0.0133	0.0596	0.0983	0.0596	0.0133
2	0.0030	0.0133	0.0219	0.0133	0.0030

Table 6.2. Estimated PSF for Fig. 6.4 A by the CD_xy algorithm
$\varepsilon = 0.2426$

$d(i,j)$	j: -2	-1	0	1	2
i: -2	0.0056	0.0171	0.0262	0.0171	0.0056
-1	0.0171	0.0786	0.1205	0.0786	0.0171
0	0.0262	0.1205	0.1971	0.1205	0.0262
1	0.0171	0.0786	0.1205	0.0786	0.0171
2	0.0056	0.0171	0.0262	0.0171	0.0056

$I_c = 1$; $I_p(1) = 18$

Fig. 6.3. Original cameraman image

degraded cameraman image with SNR = 30 dB and blur PSF as shown in Table 6.1. The restored image at the end of one iteration cycle is shown in Fig. 6.5 B. Figure 6.5 C shows another restoration, after four iteration cycles. The estimated values of the $\{d(i,j)\}$ are shown in Table 6.3. Figure 6.6 A shows the degraded cameraman image, with SNR = 50 dB and blur PSF the truncated 1D Gaussian function shown

Fig. 6.4. (A) Noisy blurred image; 2D Gaussian blur, SNR = 50 dB. (B) Restored image of (a) by the CD_xy algorithm

Table 6.3. Estimated PSF for Fig. 6.5 A by the CD_xy algorithm

$\varepsilon = 0.6104$

$d(i,j)$	j: −2	−1	0	1	2
i: −2	−0.0023	0.0193	0.0268	0.0193	−0.0023
−1	0.0158	0.0942	0.0883	0.0942	0.0158
0	0.0136	0.0844	0.3199	0.0844	0.0136
1	0.0158	0.0942	0.0883	0.0942	0.0158
2	−0.0023	0.0193	0.0268	0.0193	−0.0023

$I_c = 4$; $I_p(1) = 18$, $I_p(2) = 16$
$I_p(3) = 16$, $I_p(4) = 13$

in Table 6.4. The restored images after one and three iteration cycles are shown respectively in Figs. 6.6 B and 6.6 C. The estimated values of $\{d(i,j)\}$ corresponding to Fig. 6.6 C are shown in Table 6.5. As is clear from these values the estimated PSF can be considered to be 1D, although no information about its type and its support region was incorporated into the algorithm. A photographically blurred image (courtesy of Kodak Research Laboratories) is shown next in Fig. 6.7 A. The CD_xy algorithm was applied to it; the restored image is shown in Fig. 6.7 B. As in previous experiments, sharpness in the restored image has been traded with noise amplification.

The CD_xv algorithm was tested next. The restoration of Fig. 6.4 A is shown in Fig. 6.8 and the values of the estimated blur in Table 6.6. As was done previously, the values of $\{d(i,j)\}$ not shown in the table were very small and thus truncated.

Fig. 6.5. (A) Noisy blurred image; 2D Gaussian blur, SNR = 30 dB. Restored images of (A) by the CD_xy algorithm. (B) one iteration cycle; (C) four iteration cycles

Table 6.4. Values of the 1D Gaussian PSF

$d(i,j)$	j: −4	−3	−2	−1	0	1	2	3	4
i: 0	0.0052	0.0298	0.1039	0.2199	0.2824	0.2199	0.1039	0.0298	0.0052

The restoration of Fig. 6.6 A is shown in Fig. 6.9 and the estimated blur in Table 6.7. Finally, the restoration of Fig. 6.7 A is shown in Fig. 6.10. In Tables 6.6 and 6.7 the quantities specifying the number of iterations are I_t and $I_e(j)$, where I_t is the number of alternations of (6.54, 55) and (6.58) and $I_e(j)$ is the number of the EM iterations (i.e. (6.54, 55)) at the jth alternation of (6.54, 55) and (6.58).

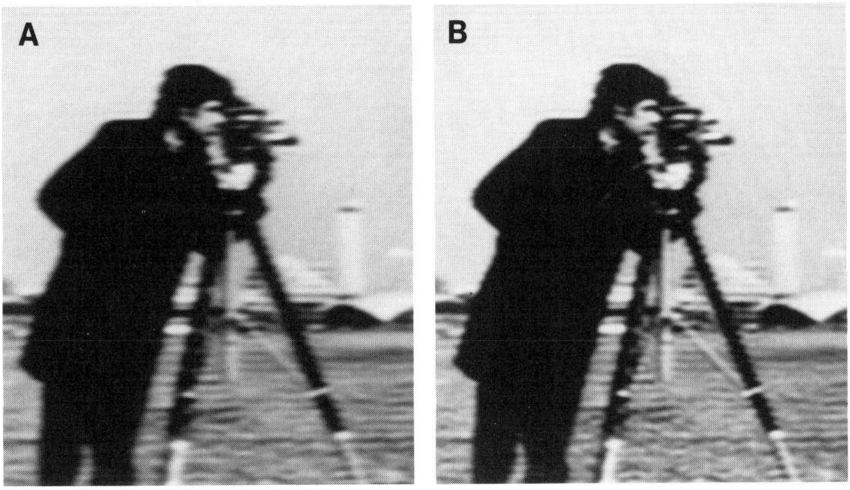

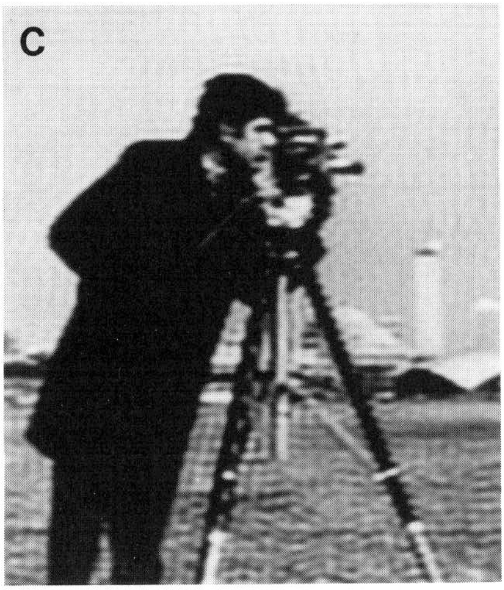

Fig. 6.6. (**A**) Noisy blurred image; 1D Gaussian blur, SNR = 50 dB. Restored images of (**A**) by the CD_xy algorithm: (**B**) one iteration cycle; (**C**) three iteration cycles

Table 6.5. Estimated PSF for Fig. 6.6 A by the CD_xy algorithm

$\varepsilon = 0.5751$

$d(i,j)$	j: -4	-3	-2	-1	0	1	2	3	4
i: -1	-0.0079	-0.0067	0.0028	0.0184	0.0276	0.0184	0.0028	-0.0067	-0.0079
0	0.0108	0.0211	0.0881	0.2080	0.2725	0.2080	0.0881	0.0211	0.0108
1	-0.0079	-0.0067	0.0028	0.0184	0.0276	0.0184	0.0028	-0.0067	-0.0079

$I_c = 3$; $I_p(1) = 18$, $I_p(2) = 16$, $I_p(3) = 9$

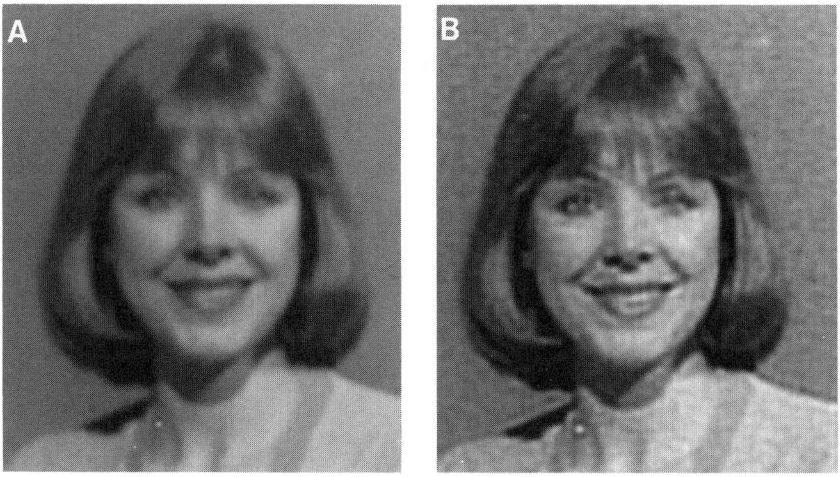

Fig. 6.7. (A) A photographically blurred image. (B) Restored image of (A) by the CD_xy algorithm

Fig. 6.8. Restored image of Fig. 6.4 A by the CD_xv algorithm

Fig. 6.9. Restored image of Fig. 6.6 A by the CD_xv algorithm

Table 6.6. Estimated PSF for Fig. 6.4 A by the CD_xv algorithm
$\varepsilon = 0.5751$

$d(i,j)$	j: -1	0	1
i: -1	0.0705	0.1491	0.0705
0	0.1377	0.2853	0.1377
1	0.0705	0.1491	0.0705

$I_t = 4$; $I_e(1) = 12$, $I_e(2) = 13$,
$I_e(3) = 10$, $I_e(4) = 11$

Fig. 6.10. Restored image of Fig. 6.7 A by the CD_xv algorithm

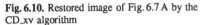

Fig. 6.11. Restored image of Fig. 6.4 A by the CD_xy algorithm and $d^{(0)}$ given by (6.85)

Table 6.7. Estimated PSF for Fig. 6.6 A by the CD_xv algorithm

$\varepsilon = 0.2082$

$d(i,j)$	j: −2	−1	0	1	2
i: 0	0.0801	0.2455	0.3487	0.2455	0.0801

$I_t = 6$; $I_e(1) = 23$, $I_e(2) = 14$, $I_e(3) = 17$, $I_e(4) = 12$, $I_e(5) = 12$, $I_e(6) = 9$

In all previous experiments, the 2D impulse was used as initial guess for the PSF. In verifying the effect of the initial guess on the solutions, as discussed above, the CD_xy algorithm was applied to Fig. 6.4 a with the initial choice

$$d^{(0)}(i,j) = 2^{-(i+j)}/6.25 \qquad -2 \leq i,j \leq 2\,, \tag{6.85}$$

which better resembles a Gaussian blur than the 2D impulse function. The restored image is shown in Fig. 6.11 and the estimated blur is shown in Table 6.8. Comparing the restored images in Figs. 6.4 B and 6.11 and the estimated blurs in Tables 6.2 and 6.8, we see that with a better starting point, the EM algorithm generates a better result, based on the visual quality of the images and the parameter ε. We also experimented with the choice of a 3×3 pill-box as $d^{(0)}$. The restored image is shown in Fig. 6.12 and the estimated blur is shown in Table 6.9. The estimated values of d in Table 6.9 are somewhat better than those in Table 6.2, since the 3×3 pill-box is closer in the mean square sense to the actual blur than the 2D impulse function.

Table 6.8. Estimated PSF for Fig. 6.4 A by the CD_xy algorithm and $d^{(0)}$ given by (6.85)

$\varepsilon = 0.1801$

$d(i,j)$	j: -2	-1	0	1	2
i: -2	0.0167	0.0201	0.0202	0.0201	0.0167
-1	0.0182	0.0580	0.0871	0.0580	0.0182
0	0.0163	0.0837	0.1324	0.0837	0.0163
1	0.0182	0.0580	0.0871	0.0580	0.0182
2	0.0167	0.0201	0.0202	0.0201	0.0167

$I_c = 3$; $I_p(1) = 12$, $I_p(2) = 8$, $I_p(3) = 8$

Table 6.9. Estimated PSF for Fig. 6.4 A by the CD_xy algorithm and $d^{(0)}$ a 3×3 pill box

$\varepsilon = 0.2347$

$d(i,j)$	j: -2	-1	0	1	2
i: -2	0.0203	0.0269	0.0254	0.0269	0.0103
-1	0.0228	0.0786	0.1132	0.0786	0.0228
0	0.0186	0.1099	0.1686	0.1099	0.0228
1	0.0228	0.0786	0.1132	0.0786	0.0228
2	0.0203	0.0269	0.0254	0.0269	0.0103

$I_c = 4$; $I_p(1) = 28$, $I_p(2) = 15$,
$I_p(3) = 16$, $I_p(4) = 10$

Fig. 6.12. Restored image of Fig. 6.4 A by the CD_xy algorithm and $d^{(0)}$ a 3×3 pill box

Based on our experiments we have made the following observation:

(a) By rerunning the EM iterations sharpness in the restored image is traded with noise amplification.

(b) Proper incorporation of constraints improves the image restoration and parameter identification results, significantly.

(c) The estimated σ_V^2 is usually smaller than the actual one. This results in a sharper but more noisy restored image than the Wiener restored image with the true values for $\{d(i,j)\}$, σ_V^2 and S_X.

(d) The restoration results are very sensitive to variations in the values of the PSF, while they are quite insensitive to variations in the values of σ_V^2 and S_X, as was also reported in [6.2].

(e) Based on the quality of the restored images and the accuracy of the estimated PSF, it seems that the performance of the algorithm with $\{\boldsymbol{x}, \boldsymbol{y}\}$ as the complete data is better than the performance of the algorithm with $\{\boldsymbol{x}, \boldsymbol{v}\}$ as the complete data. This is primarily due to the fact that in the case where $\{\boldsymbol{x}, \boldsymbol{v}\}$ is used as the complete data, decomposition of the unknown parameters into two sets (i.e. $\{\Lambda_X, \Lambda_V\}$ and $\{D\}$) is unavoidable.

Finally the iterative Wiener filter described in Sect. 6.5.4 was used in restoring noisy-blurred images. The restorations of Fig. 6.4 A by the iterative Wiener filter are shown in Figs. 6.13 A and 6.13 B, for 3 and 10 iterations, respectively. For comparison purposes, the Wiener restoration of Fig. 6.4 A based on the true values of the relevant parameters is shown in Fig. 6.13 C. Since the original undistorted image is available in a simulation environment, the performance of the restoration can be evaluated by measuring the improvement in SNR, $\eta^{(p)}$, after p iterations. It

Table 6.10. An Experiment of iterative Wiener filtering

p	$\eta^{(p)}$(in dB)
1	4.72
2	4.94
3	5.24
4	5.56
5	5.87
6	6.16
7	6.42
8	6.65
9	6.83
10	6.96
η_{WF}:	7.17

Fig. 6.13. (**A**) Restored image of Fig. 6.4 A; iterative Wiener filter; 3 iterations; (**B**) Restored image of Fig. 6.4 A; iterative Wiener filter; 10 iterations; (**C**) Restored image of Fig. 6.4 A; Wiener filter

is defined by

$$\eta^{(p)} = \frac{\|\boldsymbol{y} - \boldsymbol{x}\|^2}{\|\boldsymbol{\mu}_{X|\boldsymbol{y}}^{(p)} - \boldsymbol{x}\|^2} , \tag{6.86}$$

where $\|\cdot\|$ denotes the norm of a vector and $\boldsymbol{x}$ represents the original undistorted image. The values of $\eta^{(p)}$ and η_{WF}, which represents the improvement in SNR when S_X and σ_V^2 are available, are shown in Table 6.10. From our experiments we observed that the iterative Wiener filter is more effective for high SNRs in the sense that $\eta^{(p)}$ increases with p and finally approaches η_{WF}.

6.8 Conclusions

In this chapter, we have proposed iterative algorithms, based on different choices of complete data, for the identification of the blur and image parameters and the restoration of a noisy blurred image. The algorithms obtain the maximum likelihood estimates of the unknown parameters with the use of the EM algorithm. Explicit expressions of the EM iterations are obtained in the discrete frequency domain. The restored image is computed in the E-step of the EM algorithm. One of the advantages of the proposed algorithm is that no knowledge about the type of the distortion or its support region needs to be incorporated into the iteration. In most of our experiments the iteration was initialized with a 2D impulse, although other initial guesses of the PSF were tested, for comparison purposes. Another advantage of the EM iterations is that a priori knowledge about the blur and image can be incorporated into the identification/restoration process. The experimental results corresponding to the different choices of complete data are compared. It turns out that the choice of $\{\boldsymbol{x}, \boldsymbol{y}\}$ as the complete data seems to result in a more effective algorithm.

Modified forms of the proposed algorithm were also presented. One such form is obtained by representing the image field by an AR model, instead of its covariance matrix Λ_X. If the process driving the AR process is Gaussian, then the same iterations are obtained, since the image covariance matrix is described in terms of the AR coefficients. The identification/restoration iterations were derived in the discrete frequency domain. Its equivalent form in the spatial domain was also shown. Although it may be easier to incorporate additional knowledge about the blur and the AR coefficients into the spatial form of the iteration, exact knowledge of the support of $\{d(i,j)\}$ and $\{a(i,j)\}$ is required. Furthermore, the appropriate number of equations to be used in solving the unknown blur and model parameters needs to be chosen. The algorithms presented in this chapter have also been applied to the identification/restoration of multi-channel images (i.e., color images), as reported in [6.28].

The parametric statistical model used for the original image is quite powerful and has found many applications in the area of image processing [6.1]. Clearly, the main reason for its use, in cases where the assumed multivariate Gaussian behavior may not be borne out by the data or the physical reality of the problem, is its mathematical tractability. Both assumptions of zero mean and stationarity for the original image result in an image model being able to describe only the gross or global properties of a class of images. Therefore, the development of efficient algorithms for identification and restoration based on an image model with nonstationary mean and/or covariance is currently under investigation. Such algorithms are expected to provide better restoration results at an additional computational expense.

6.A Appendix: Detailed Derivation of Eqs. (6.43–45)

According to (6.42), $\Lambda_{X|y}^{(p)}$ is a block circulant matrix, because $\Lambda_X^{(p)}$ and $D^{(p)}$ are block circulant. Therefore, we have

$$\Lambda_{X|y}^{(p)} = W Q_{X|y}^{(p)} W^{-1} , \tag{6.A 1}$$

where $Q_{X|y}^{(p)}$ is a diagonal matrix with elements $S_{X|y}^{(p)}(m,n)$. Since all matrices in (6.42) are block circulant, the following equation holds

$$W Q_{X|y}^{(p)} W^{-1} = W Q_X^{(p)} W^{-1} - W Q_X^{(p)} Q_D^{(p)H} \times \left(Q_D^{(p)} Q_X^{(p)} Q_D^{(p)H} + \sigma_V^2 I \right)^{-1} Q_D^{(p)} Q_X^{(p)} W^{-1} , \tag{6.A 2}$$

where the fact that $W^{\mathrm{H}} = (1/N^2) W^{-1}$ has been applied. Therefore,

$$Q_{X|y}^{(p)} = Q_X^{(p)} - Q_X^{(p)} Q_D^{(p)\mathrm{H}} \left(Q_D^{(p)} Q_X^{(p)} Q_D^{(p)\mathrm{H}} + \sigma_V^2 I \right)^{-1} Q_D^{(p)} Q_X^{(p)} , \tag{6.A 3}$$

or equivalently in the frequency domain,

$$S_{X|y}^{(p)}(m,n) = \frac{S_X^{(p)}(m,n) \sigma_V^{2(p)}}{|\Delta^{(p)}(m,n)|^2 S_X^{(p)}(m,n) + \sigma_V^{2(p)}} ,$$

which represents (6.45). Similarly (6.41) can be written in the frequency domain as shown below,

$$\boldsymbol{\mu}_{X|y}^{(p)} = W Q_X^{(p)} Q_D^{(p)\mathrm{H}} \left(Q_D^{(p)} Q_X^{(p)} Q_D^{(p)\mathrm{H}} + \sigma_V^2 I \right)^{-1} W^{-1} \boldsymbol{y} . \tag{6.A 4}$$

Premultiplying both sides by W^{-1}, we obtain

$$M_{X|y}^{(p)} = W^{-1} \boldsymbol{\mu}_{X|y}^{(p)} = Q_X^{(p)} Q_D^{(p)\mathrm{H}} \left(Q_D^{(p)} Q_X^{(p)} Q_D^{(p)\mathrm{H}} + \sigma_V^2 I \right)^{-1} Y , \tag{6.A 5}$$

or equivalently in the frequency domain,

$$M_{X|y}^{(p)}(m,n) = \frac{\Delta^{(p)*}(m,n) S_X^{(p)}(m,n)}{|\Delta^{(p)}(m,n)|^2 S_X^{(p)}(m,n) + \sigma_V^{2(p)}} Y(m,n) ,$$

which represents (6.44).

With similar operations applied on (6.40) (i.e. diagonalization of block circulant matrices), (6.40) becomes

$$F(\phi; \phi^{(p)}) = \log |Q_X| + \log |\sigma_V^2 I| + \mathrm{tr} \left\{ \left(Q_X^{-1} + \frac{1}{\sigma_V^2} Q_D^{\mathrm{H}} Q_D \right) Q_{X|y}^{(p)} \right\} + \boldsymbol{\mu}_{X|y}^{(p)\mathrm{H}} W \left(Q_X^{-1} + \frac{1}{\sigma_V^2} Q_D^{\mathrm{H}} Q_D \right) W^{-1} \boldsymbol{\mu}_{X|y}^{(p)} - 2 \frac{1}{\sigma_V^2} \boldsymbol{y}^{\mathrm{H}} W Q_D W^{-1} \boldsymbol{\mu}_{X|y}^{(p)} + \frac{1}{\sigma_V^2} \boldsymbol{y}^{\mathrm{H}} W W^{-1} \boldsymbol{y} , \tag{6.A 6}$$

where the fact that $|W\Psi W^{-1}| = |\Psi|$ and $\mathrm{tr}\{W\Psi W^{-1}\} = \mathrm{tr}\{\Psi\}$ for any matrix Ψ has been used. Since Q_X, $[Q_X^{-1} + (1/\sigma_V^2)Q_D^{\mathrm{H}}Q_D]$ and $Q_{X|y}^{(p)}$ are diagonal, it is straightforward to rewrite (6.A 6) as

$$\begin{aligned}F(\phi;\phi^{(p)}) = {} & N^2\log\sigma_V^2 + \frac{1}{\sigma_V^2}\sum_{m=0}^{N-1}\sum_{n=0}^{N-1}\Bigg\{|\Delta(m,n)|^2 \\ & \times\left(S_{X|y}^{(p)}(m,n) + \frac{1}{N^2}|M_{X|y}^{(p)}(m,n)|^2\right) \\ & + \frac{1}{N^2}\left(|Y(m,n)|^2 - 2\mathrm{Re}\left[Y^*(m,n)\Delta(m,n)M_{X|y}^{(p)}(m,n)\right]\right)\Bigg\} \\ & + \sum_{m=0}^{N-1}\sum_{n=0}^{N-1}\Bigg\{\log S_X(m,n) + \frac{1}{S_X(m,n)} \\ & \times\left(S_{X|y}^{(p)}(m,n) + \frac{1}{N^2}|M_{X|y}^{(p)}(m,n)|^2\right)\Bigg\},\end{aligned}$$

which represents (6.43).

Acknowledgment. This material is based upon work supported in part by NSF under Grant No. MIP-8614217.

References

6.1 H. C. Andrews, B. R. Hunt: *Digital Image Restoration* (Prentice-Hall, Englewood Cliffs, NJ 1977)
6.2 A. M. Tekalp, H. Kaufman, J. W. Woods: IEEE Trans. ASSP-**34**, 963–972 (1986)
6.3 J. Biemond, F. G. van der Putten, J. W. Woods: IEEE Trans. CAS-**35**, 385–392 (1988)
6.4 R. L. Lagendijk, A. K. Katsaggelos, J. Biemond: "Iterative Identification and Restoration", in Proc. IEEE Intern. Conf. ASSP (1988) pp. 992–995
6.5 A. K. Katsaggelos, R. L. Lagendijk, J. Biemond: "Constrained Iterative Identification and Restoration of Images", in Proc. EUSIPCO-88 (1988) pp. 1585–1588
6.6 A. D. Dempster, N. M. Laird, D. B. Rubin: J. Roy. Stat. Soc. **B39**, 1–37 (1977)
6.7 K. T. Lay, A. K. Katsaggelos: "Simultaneous Identification and Restoration of Images Using Maximum Likelihood Estimation and the EM Algorithm", 26th Annual Allerton Conf. Comm., Control and Computing, pp. 661–662 (1988)
6.8 K. T. Lay, A. K. Katsaggelos: "Maximum Likelihood Image Identification and Restoration Based on the EM Algorithm", in Proc. Conf. on Info. Sci. and Sys. (March 1989) pp. 656–662
6.9 K. T. Lay, A. K. Katsaggelos: Opt. Eng. **29**, 436–445 (1990)
6.10 A. K. Jain: *Fundamentals of Digital Image Processing* (Prentice-Hall, Englewood Cliffs, NJ 1989)
6.11 D. E. Dudgeon, R. M. Mersereau: *Multidimensional Digital Signal Processing* (Prentice-Hall, Englewood Cliffs, NJ 1984)
6.12 J. W. Woods, J. Biemond, A. M. Tekalp: "Boundary Value Problem in Image Restoration", in Proc. ICASSP (1985) pp. 18.11.1–18.11.4
6.13 R. M. Gray: IEEE Trans. IT-**18**, 725–730 (1985)
6.14 B. R. Hunt: IEEE C-**22**, 805–812 (1973)
6.15 M. Feder: "Statistical Signal Processing using a class of Iterative Estimation Algorithms", Ph.D. dissertation, MIT Tech. Rep. no. 532 (1987)
6.16 M. Feder, E. Weinstein: IEEE Trans. ASSP-**36**, 477–489 (1988)
6.17 M. Segal, E. Weinstein: Proc. IEEE **76**, 1388–1390 (1988)
6.18 M. V. Ranganath, A. P. Dhawan, N. Mullanni: IEEE Tran. MI-7, 273–277 (1988)

6.19 B. R. Musicus, J. S. Lim: "Maximum Likelihood Parameter Estimation of Noisy Data", in Proc. ICASSP (1979) pp. 224–227
6.20 C. F. Wu: Ann. Statistics **11**, 95–103 (1983)
6.21 I. Csiszar, G. Tusnady: Statistics and Decisions, Supplement Issue **1**, 205–237 (1984)
6.22 M. I. Miller, D. L. Snyder: Proc. IEEE **75**, 892–907 (1987)
6.23 R. E. Blahut: *Principles and Practice of Information Theory* (Addison-Wesley, Reading, MA 1987)
6.24 J. M. Mendel: *Lessons in Digital Estimation Theory* (Prentice-Hall, Englewood Cliffs, NJ 1987)
6.25 T. Kailath : *Linear Systems* (Prentice-Hall, Englewood Cliffs, NJ 1980)
6.26 R. L. Lagendijk, J. Biemond, D. E. Boekee: "Blur Identification Using the Expectation-Maximization Algorithm", ICASSP (1989) pp. 1397–1400
6.27 S. M. Kay: *Modern Spectral Estimation – Theory and Application* (Prentice-Hall, Englewood Cliffs, NJ 1988)
6.28 K. T. Lay: "Maximum Likelihood Iterative Image Identification and Restoration", Ph.D. dissertation, Department of EECS, Northwestern University (1991)

7. Nonhomogeneous Image Identification and Restoration Procedures

D. L. Angwin and H. Kaufman

With 12 Figures

The need for an implementable procedure for identifying spatially varying image models and restoring images has prompted the development of a reduced order model Kalman filter (ROMKF). The ROMKF, presented in this chapter, in conjunction with the maximum likelihood parameter identification technique leads to an adaptive restoration procedure that directly takes into account the spatially varying nature of both the image and degradation models.

We begin this chapter with an introduction to the image restoration problem in Sect. 7.1. Then, in Sect. 7.2 we present the ROMKF, whose development was motivated by the need for a reduction in computation of existing Kalman filtering techniques. The ROMKF is utilized in the implementation of the maximum likelihood parameter identification method described in Sect. 7.3. Finally, since spatially invariant models are inappropriate for modeling real world images, in Sect. 7.4 we discuss the incorporation of nonstationary models and the use of the ROMKF/maximum likelihood technique for adaptive restoration and parameter identification.

7.1 Image Modeling

Images recorded in electronic or photographic medium are often degraded due to recording system imperfections. These degradations may be caused by a variety of circumstances including diffraction effects, optical system aberrations, camera or object motion, a defocussed lens, and atmospheric turbulence. In addition, to these blurring effects, the recorded image is also corrupted by noise from the recording medium due to the randomness of the film grain or photoelectric effects. Measurement errors due to the accuracy of the recording system, transmission errors, and digitization also degrade the image further.

In general, the goal of image restoration is to model these degradations, then estimate the original scene, given the degraded recorded data. In practical situations, generally very little, if anything, is known about the characteristics of the recording system, and the degradations must be estimated from the degraded data itself. This topic is addressed later in Sect. 7.3. We first introduce models for the degraded observations and the original image.

The degradations are classified into two categories: spatial degradations causing blur and random point degradations introducing noise. Assuming a linear image

Springer Series in Information Sciences, Vol. 23
A. K. Katsaggelos (ed.): Digital Image Restoration

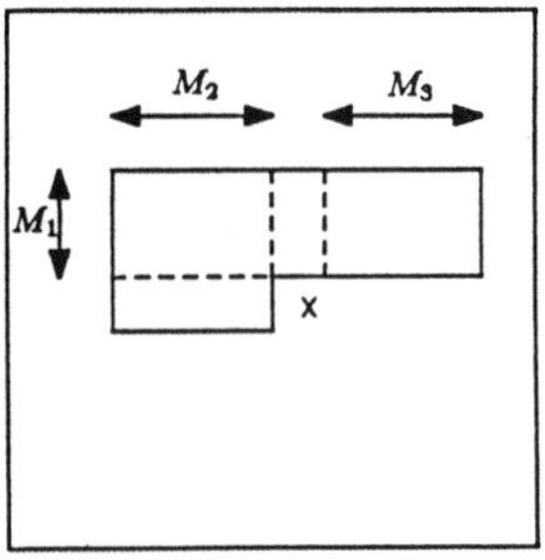

Fig. 7.1. $M_1 \times M_2 \times M_3$ nonsymmetric half-plane model support

formation system [7.1] we can represent the observed image by

$$\boldsymbol{y}(i,j) = \sum_{m,n \in R_1} d(m,n;i,j)\boldsymbol{s}(i-m,j-n) + \boldsymbol{v}(i,j) \tag{7.1}$$

where $\boldsymbol{y}(i,j)$ represents the intensity of the pixels of the degraded image, $\boldsymbol{s}(i,j)$ represents the original image, $d(m,n;i,j)$ is referred to as the point spread function with R_1 denoting its support. The observation noise $\boldsymbol{v}(i,j)$ is assumed to be a zero-mean signal-independent Gaussian process with variance σ_v^2.

In addition to these assumptions, we also assume a lossless image formation system. By this we imply that the total energy of the original image (object) is preserved in the recording and that the lens or imaging system does not absorb or generate optical energy. This is translated mathematically as

$$\sum_{m,n \in R_1} d(m,n;i,j) = 1 \qquad \forall (i,j) \; . \tag{7.2}$$

As discussed by *Jain* [7.2], it is appropriate to model the original image as the output of an autoregressive (AR) process driven by a white Gaussian noise process $w(i,j)$ with variance σ_w^2 described by

$$\boldsymbol{s}(i,j) = \sum_{k,l \in R_{\oplus +}} a(k,l;i,j)\boldsymbol{s}(i-k,j-l) + \boldsymbol{w}(i,j) \; , \tag{7.3}$$

where $R_{\oplus +}$ indicates the $M_1 \times M_2 \times M_3$ nonsymmetric half-plane (NSHP) model support illustrated in Fig. 7.1 and described by

$$R_{\oplus +} = \{k,l | [1 \le k \le M_2, 0 \le l \le M_1] \cup [-M_3 \le k \le 0, 1 \le l \le M_1]\} \; . \tag{7.4}$$

The $a(k,l;i,j)$ are referred to as the image model parameters and $w(i,j)$ is often referred to as the plant noise process.

If we assume that the image and the degradation processes are wide-sense stationary, i.e.

$$\begin{aligned} a(k,l;i,j) &= a_{kl} \quad \forall (i,j) \\ d(m,n;i,j) &= d_{mn} \quad \forall (i,j) \; , \end{aligned} \tag{7.5}$$

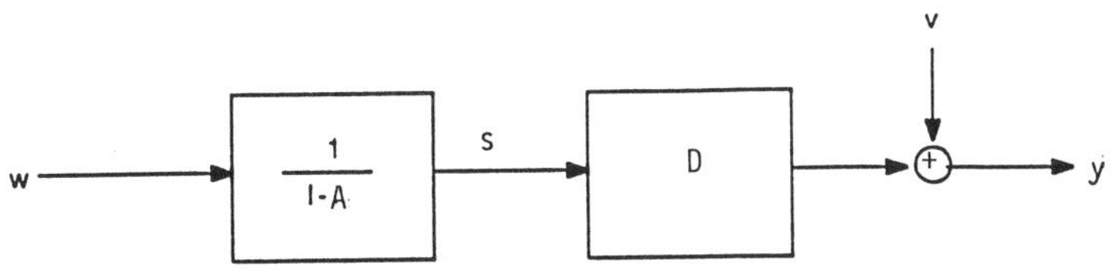

Fig. 7.2. Input-output diagram

then we can obtain an input-output description of the system described by Fig. 7.2 and

$$y(i,j) = \sum a_{kl} y(i-k, j-l) + \sum d_{mn} w(i-m, j-n) \\ - \sum a_{kl} v(i-k, j-l) + v(i,j) \,. \tag{7.6}$$

The observed image corresponds to noisy observations of a 2D autoregressive moving-average (ARMA) process. Therefore, in the absence of observation noise, this input-output relation is an ARMA process with the AR coefficients corresponding to the image model and the MA coefficients corresponding to the PSF model.

7.2 Kalman-Type Filtering for Restoration

The Kalman filter has been used extensively for image restoration [7.3–9]. Early work in 2D recursive filtering was presented by *Habibi* [7.10] for image estimation (no blur). A 1D Kalman filtering approach was used to restore images by *Nahi* [7.11] for image estimation and by *Aboutalib* and *Silverman* [7.12] for linear motion blur. They extended this approach to the case of general motion blur in [7.13].

Since it was desirable to use 2D models to describe the image and the degradation PSF or blurring operator, further consideration was given to the use of 2D Kalman filtering. The main hurdle was the development of an appropriate state-space representation which was manageable in terms of computation and storage. *Woods* with *Radewan* [7.9] and with *Ingle* [7.8] derived a scalar Kalman filter based on the NSHP model described by (7.3) and one direction of recursion propagating through the image in a raster scan format. Because this particular state-space representation requires a state of large dimension, they also presented two approximations, a "reduced update" filter and a strip filter, to reduce the computational load. *Murphy* and *Silverman* [7.7] described a vector Kalman filter which restores an image a line at a time. This method was also computationally intensive so they also proposed two suboptimal procedures. *Biemond* et al. [7.4] presented a fast parallel Kalman filtering approach based on the one-dimensional DFT and circulant approximations to Toeplitz matrices. *Suresh* and *Shenoi* [7.14], and *Wu* [7.18] derived Kalman filters based on a state-space representation using 2D *Roesser* models [7.15]. More recently *Mahalanabis* and *Xue* [7.16] presented a fast Kalman filter based on a 2D Chandrasekhar filtering algorithm [7.17]. In the implementation of these filters, it is assumed that the PSF of the blur, the image model, and the noise statistics are known prior to filtering. The image and blur processes are also assumed spatially wide-sense stationary resulting in models which are constant throughout an entire image.

In this chapter we would like to progress beyond these assumptions and determine the parameters for the spatially varying models of (7.1) and (7.3) from the available observed image data. One of the attributes of the Kalman filter, since it is implemented in the spatial domain, is the ability to incorporate changing (nonstationary) parameters with ease. Each of the Kalman filtering approaches described in this section is restrictive due to the inability to incorporate spatially varying parameters except in a limited sense [7.4, 7, 14, 16, 18] or restricted due to a large level of computation [7.8, 9, 16]. The maximum likelihood parameter identification algorithm, presented in [7.19] and Sect. 7.3, requires repetitive restorations of the image to compute the likelihood function as the parameters vary. Particularly, the high order state-space models employed by [7.9, 16] would make parameter identification and adaptive filtering computationally intensive.

These restrictions motivated the development of the Reduced Order Model Kalman filter (ROMKF), a low order state-space model based Kalman filter, with consequently, a low level of computation. This feature makes it useful with maximum likelihood parameter identification scheme presented in the next section. It also retains all of the advantages of the Kalman filter for adaptive filtering.

In Sect. 7.2.1, we review the Kalman filter in the context of the image restoration problem. In Sect. 7.2.2, we introduce and discuss the ROMKF. In Sect. 7.2.3, we compare the ROMKF with the Reduced Update Kalman filter (RUKF) [7.8, 9] and the 2D Chandrasekhar Kalman filter [7.16], with concluding comments in Sect. 7.2.4.

7.2.1 The 2D Kalman Filter for Image Restoration

The Kalman filter is based on a state-space model of a system, described in 1D by:

$$\boldsymbol{x}(i) = \boldsymbol{A}\boldsymbol{x}(i-1) + \boldsymbol{B}\boldsymbol{w}(i) + \boldsymbol{E}\boldsymbol{u}(m) \tag{7.7}$$

$$\boldsymbol{y}(m) = \boldsymbol{D}\boldsymbol{x}(i) + \boldsymbol{v}(i)\ . \tag{7.8}$$

With the extension to 2D as in [7.9] we still have only one direction of recursion:

$$\boldsymbol{x}(i,j) = \boldsymbol{A}\boldsymbol{x}(i-1,j) + \boldsymbol{B}\boldsymbol{w}(i,j) + \boldsymbol{E}\boldsymbol{u}(i,j) \tag{7.9}$$

$$\boldsymbol{y}(i,j) = \boldsymbol{D}\boldsymbol{x}(i,j) + \boldsymbol{v}(i,j)\ . \tag{7.10}$$

In these equations $\boldsymbol{x}(i,j)$ is the signal state vector at pixel (i,j), $\boldsymbol{w}(i,j)$ is the random process accounting for uncertainty in the state models, $\boldsymbol{y}(i,j)$ is the observation of the received signal, $\boldsymbol{v}(i,j)$ is the observation or measurement noise, and A, B, D, and E are system matrices. A is often referred to as the state transition matrix. It is assumed that $\boldsymbol{v}(i,j)$ and $\boldsymbol{w}(i,j)$ are uncorrelated white Gaussian zero-mean noise processes with covariances σ_v^2 and Q_w respectively.

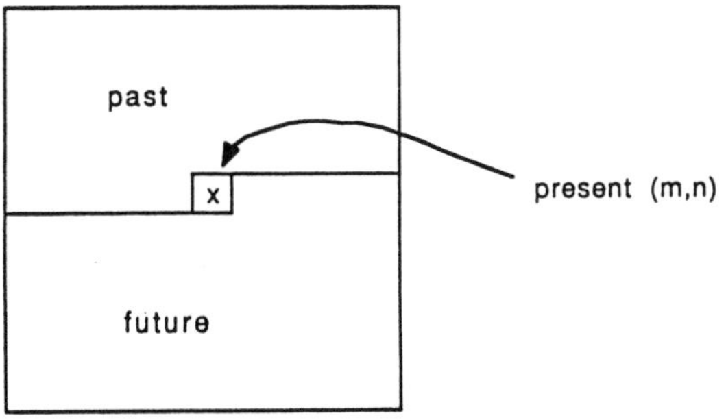

Fig. 7.3. Raster scan ordering of pixels

We have referred to "one direction of recursion" for (7.9) and will refer to "horizontal direction of recursion" for (7.11). This is misleading since we have 2D data. What is meant is that recursions progress normally in one direction (i), horizontally in this case, until reaching the image boundary. Then, to transition across the boundary, the horizontal index (i) is reset to the beginning of the row and the vertical index (j) is incremented. Recursions then progress normally in one direction until the next boundary. Suitable boundary conditions are required, and will be discussed later.

In order to use the Kalman filter for image restoration, we must formulate the problem as in (7.9, 10). The recursive nature of the Kalman filter compels the use of a causal image model. Causality implies that filter outputs can not precede inputs. The 2D image data can be ordered such that the notion of past, present, and future can be defined. This ordering could be arbitrary, however, it is customary to order the pixels in a raster scan format, left to right, top to bottom. The past, present, and future pixels are defined with respect to the present pixel (i,j), shown in Fig. 7.3. For this ordering, the NSHP model is causal and appropriate for our use.

Using a horizontal direction of recursion and an image $N_h \times N_v$ pixels, horizontal and vertical dimensions respectively, the state $\boldsymbol{x}$ at pixel (i,j) can be described [7.9] as

$$
\begin{aligned}
\boldsymbol{x}(i,j) = [&s(i,j), s(i-1,j), \ldots, s(1,j);\\
&s(N_h, j-1), \ldots, s(1, j-1);\\
&\vdots\\
&s(N_h, j-M_1), \ldots, s(i-M_2, j-M_1);\\
&b(1-M_2, j-M_1+1), \ldots, b(0, j-M_1+1);\\
&\vdots\\
&b(1-M_2, N_v), \ldots, b(0, N_v);\\
&b(N_h+1, j-M_1) \ldots, b(N_h+M_3, j-M_1)\\
&\vdots\\
&b(N_h+1, N_v-1) \ldots, b(N_h+M_3, N_v-1)]^T
\end{aligned}
\qquad (7.11)
$$

where $b(\cdot,\cdot)$ are boundary pixels. This state is pictured in Fig. 7.4.

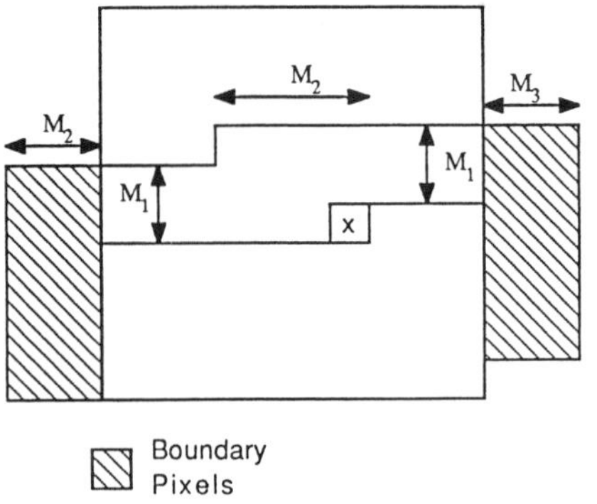

Fig. 7.4. State model support

The Kalman filter is a linear filter implemented in 2 steps: prediction and update. The filter equations are presented in detail in Appendix A. Although the filter is linear, the computation of the filter gain is nonlinear and requires the solution of the Riccati equation, resulting in a large amount of computation. The number of computations required per recursion is of the order $O(T^2)$ where T is the dimension of the state. The size of this vector (7.11) is of the order $O(M_1 N_h)$ and is of variable dimension. With the state dimension proportional to the image width, the number of computations required per recursion can grow quite large for images with practical resolutions, *i.e.*, 1024×1024 pixels. The major burdens of the Kalman filter with the state defined by (7.11) are the storage and computational requirements of the error covariance prediction and update (7.A6, A7). In order to reduce the computations to a manageable level, several approximations have been introduced [7.4–9, 14, 16, 18]. The most practical of these are [7.8, 9, 16]; however, these use the large dimensioned state defined in (7.11). The reduction of the computation and storage is the motivation behind the development of the ROMKF presented next.

We have noted that the disadvantages of [7.8, 9, 16] stem from the definition of the state. In the following section, we present an alternative state definition with a substantially lower dimension. The approximation made to reduce the state size is local to the model supports of (7.1) and (7.3). This ROMKF is more suitable than [7.8, 9, 16] for the parameter identification and adaptive filtering algorithms described in Sects. 7.3, 4.

7.2.2 The ROMKF

a) The Filter. In this section, we detail the Reduced Order Model Kalman Filter (ROMKF) which uses an approximation to reduce the state of (7.11) to a more manageable dimension. We use the 1D state-space representation of (7.9) and (7.10). For simplicity in this discussion, we will assume that the blur PSF support is contained within the $M_1 \times M_2 \times M_3$ NSHP support of the image model (7.3).

With the ordering of the pixels as defined by a raster scan, the models of (7.1) and (7.3) logically lead to the state definition of (7.11). However, these models only utilize a small number of pixels, from the previous rows of the image. These

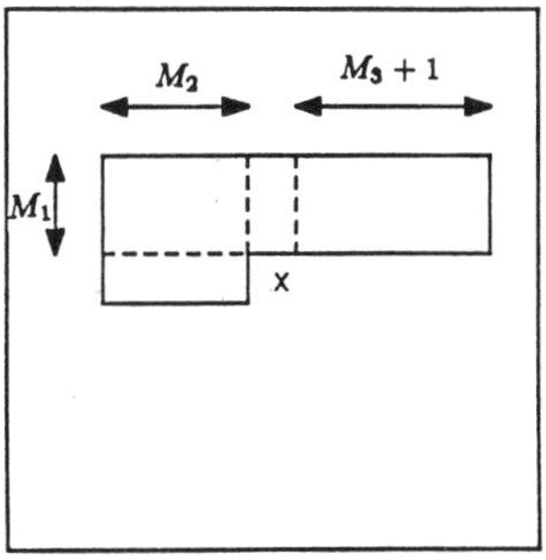

Fig. 7.5. ROMKF state support

are the pixels in the model supports, a $M_1 \times M_2 \times M_3$ NSHP neighborhood. The other pixels in the state of (7.11) are used to track the state elements.

We propose to include in the state only those pixels required to represent the image models of (7.1) and (7.3). However, since we must formulate a state difference representation in the form of (7.9), it is necessary to make approximations for pixels just to the right of the $M_1 \times M_2 \times M_3$ model support. We introduce the following reduced order state vector

$$\begin{aligned} \boldsymbol{x}(i,j) = [&s(i,j), s(i-1,j), \ldots, s(i-M_2,j);\\ &s(i-M_2,j-1), s(i-M_2+1,j-1), \ldots, s(i+M_3+1,j-1);\\ &\vdots\\ &s(i-M_2,j-M_1), s(i-M_2+1,j-M_1), \ldots, s(i+M_3+1,j-M_1)]^{\mathrm{T}} . \end{aligned} \tag{7.12}$$

This state support is also pictured in Fig. 7.5. The basis of the ROMKF is the approximation of the pixels located in the state, $\boldsymbol{x}(i,j)$, which can not be represented in terms of $\boldsymbol{x}(i-1,j)$. We approximate these values by their most recent estimates with the uncertainty represented in a noise term. This is described by

$$s(i+M_3+1, n-k) = \hat{s}(i+M_3+1, n-k) + w_k(i,j)\,, \quad \text{for} \quad k = 1, \ldots, M_1 \tag{7.13}$$

where $\hat{s}(\cdot,\cdot)$ indicates the best available estimate of the image and w_k is the noise term included to account for uncertainty in this approximation. By "best available" estimate, we are referring to the most recent update of the pixels (7.13) available at the time that pixel (i,j) is filtered. This approximation is incorporated into the deterministic input term $\boldsymbol{u}(i,j)$ in (7.9).

The ROMKF is then the implementation of the optimal Kalman filter for this reduced state. The dimension of this state representation is significantly reduced from the representation using (7.11). The order of the computation is also reduced. The state support for the general ROMKF is pictured in Fig. 7.5 and the state dimension is $\mathrm{O}(M_1(M_2 + M_3))$. The dimension of this state is proportional to the number of elements in the union of the model supports, as opposed to the image width as in (7.11). The Kalman filter implemented with this state definition progresses in a raster scan format as described in the previous section. At the end of each image line, the line index (n) is incremented and the column index (m) is reset. At both boundaries, left and right, it is necessary to include boundary pixels in the state.

The ROMKF approximation may be clarified with an example. Consider the image estimation problem (no blur),

$$d_{m,n}(i,j) = \begin{cases} 0 & (i,j) \neq (0,0) \\ 1 & (i,j) = (0,0) \end{cases} \tag{7.14}$$

and a $1 \times 1 \times 1$ NSHP model:

$$\begin{aligned} s(i,j) = & \, a_{11} s(i-1,j-1) + a_{01} s(i,j-1) + a_{-11} s(i+1,j-1) \\ & + a_{10} s(i-1,j) + w_0(i,j) \, . \end{aligned} \tag{7.15}$$

The reduced state is represented by

$$\boldsymbol{x}(i,j) = [s(i,j-1) \; s(i+1,j-1) \; s(i+2,j-1) \; s(i-1,j) \; s(i,j)]^{\mathrm{T}} \, . \tag{7.16}$$

The remainder of the system, in the notation of (7.9) and (7.10), is described by

$$\boldsymbol{A} = \begin{bmatrix} 0 & 1 & 0 & 0 & 0 \\ 0 & 0 & 1 & 0 & 0 \\ 0 & 0 & 0 & 0 & 0 \\ 0 & 0 & 0 & 0 & 1 \\ a_{11} & a_{01} & a_{-11} & 0 & a_{10} \end{bmatrix} \tag{7.17}$$

$$\boldsymbol{D} = [0 \;\; 0 \;\; 0 \;\; 0 \;\; 1] \tag{7.18}$$

$$\boldsymbol{B} = \begin{bmatrix} 0 & 0 & 1 & 0 & 0 \\ 0 & 0 & 0 & 0 & 1 \end{bmatrix}^{\mathrm{T}} \tag{7.19}$$

$$\boldsymbol{E} = [0 \;\; 0 \;\; 1 \;\; 0 \;\; 0]^{\mathrm{T}} \, . \tag{7.20}$$

For this example, pixel $s(i+2,j-1)$ can be approximated by its most recent estimate, i.e.,

$$s(i+2,j-1) = \hat{s}(i+2,j-1) + w_1(i,j) \, . \tag{7.21}$$

The noise term $w_1(i,j)$ is included to account for the uncertainty of the approximation.

b) Technical Aspects of the ROMKF. A discussion topic pertinent to the introduction of this filter representation is its optimality. A Kalman filter built upon the linear dynamic system described by (7.9) and (7.10), based on the assumption of Gaussian distributed random processes, results in state estimates with minimum mean-square error. Therefore, the ROM Kalman filter is an optimal filter in the sense that it minimizes the mean-square error given the modeling assumptions of (7.1,3), and (7.13).

As in the modeling of any system, if there are inaccuracies or errors in the models, the filter output is no longer optimum. It would be erroneous to suggest that a model such as (7.3) can accurately describe a "real life" image. Therefore, even if a filter has a sound theoretical basis given a particular image model, when applied to a practical case, the estimate will never be truly optimal due to modeling errors. The ROM Kalman filter is stable and the gains, defined by (7.A5–A7), converge to steady-state. The specific conditions for stability and convergence to steady-state are given in [7.20], and will be subsequently discussed in more detail.

Although stationary models may adequately describe small regions of an image, they do not suitably describe an entire image. Thus, the use of nonstationary parameters should improve the models and provide better restoration results. It is in the use of nonstationary models that the ROMKF should have its strength. With varying models, the Kalman gain, (7.A5–A7) must be updated. This is accomplished easily and efficiently using the ROMKF, due to the low dimensionality of the error covariances [$\boldsymbol{P}_a$ and $\boldsymbol{P}_b$ in (7.A7) and (7.A6)]. This is discussed in more detail in Sect. 7.4.

For most practical images, the image model parameters $a(k,l;i,j)$ and the blur model parameters $d(m,n;i,j)$ are unknown. However, these parameters describe the system and must be determined a priori to the implementation of the Kalman filter. As discussed in Sect. 7.3, the ROMKF can be used in conjunction with a maximum likelihood parameter identification technique to determine these parameters.

For implementation of the ROMKF, appropriate handling of the boundary is necessary for initial conditions and the transition of the state across the boundary from the end of one scan line to the beginning of the next. The size of the boundary is related to the supports of the image and PSF models. The boundary region is pictured in Fig. 7.6. There are several ways to assign boundary values [7.4, 8, 21]:

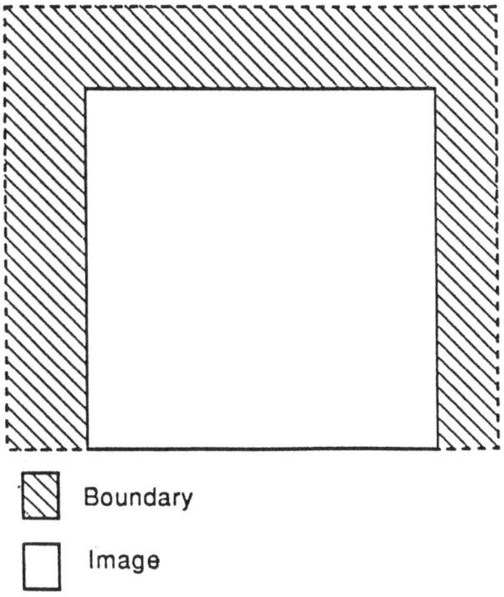

Fig. 7.6. Boundary region

- Boundary values can be given random values with mean and variance the same as the image.
- Boundary values may be fixed at the image mean.
- Boundary values may be assigned the value of the nearest row or column of image data. The values can be repeated as necessary to satisfy the boundary requirements.
- A circulant matrix approximation can be made for the image as in [7.4, 21]. The image is thought of as a cylinder instead of a flat array, with the boundary values linearly interpolated between the end pixel of one scan line to the beginning pixel of the next.

For these methods the image is augmented by boundary values, where the shaded boundary region (Fig. 7.6) is exterior to the image. Another alternative, used in the experiments in this chapter, is to decrease the effective size of the image by using image pixels as boundary conditions. The result is that the boundary region is not restored. This decreases the restored image size with the decrease dependent on the size of the model supports. However, for the relatively small model supports used in simulations, the decrease is not noticeable. This is easy to implement and suits the purpose of our experiments. For restoration of images in which the model supports are larger than a few pixels, it would be appropriate to chose one of the previously described methods.

We have examined the stability and performance of the ROMKF. First, as discussed in [7.20], the Kalman filter state model is asymptotically stable when the eigenvalues of the state transition matrix, $\boldsymbol{A}(i,j)$, have magnitude less than unity. This also implies that the prediction error covariance (7.A6) converges to a steady-state value for any nonnegative symmetric initial condition, i.e., the solution to the steady-state Riccati equation (7.A13).

Using the approximation of (7.13), one of the eigenvalues of the state transition matrix will be a_{10} and the rest will be zero. Therefore, if $|a_{10}|$ is constrained to be less than unity, then the ROMKF will be stable and converge to steady-state with this approximation. This can be stated in general, because due to the structure of the state transition, the eigenvalues will always be the solution of:

$$\lambda^{n-1}(\lambda - a_{10}) = 0 \, , \tag{7.22}$$

where n is the state dimension.

c) Modeling Error. We have assumed that the plant noise components, w_k, $k = 1, \dots, M_1$ from (7.13) are zero mean and Gaussian distributed. It is important to the implementation of the ROMKF that we have an estimate of the variance $\sigma^2_{w_k}$ for each w_k. As discussed in [7.22], the following "rule-of-thumb" is successful for the determination of $\sigma^2_{w_k}$. First, we define $\sigma^2_{w_0} = \sigma^2_{w}$, the variance of $\boldsymbol{w}(i,j)$ from (7.3). Note that the estimation of $\sigma^2_{w_0}$ will be discussed in the next section. We assume that the state model supports extend M_1 rows into the past as described by (7.12). Then,

$$\sigma_{w_k}^2 = \frac{M_1 - k}{M_1}\sigma_{w_0}^2 \qquad k = 1, \dots, M_1 \ . \tag{7.23}$$

This rule appears to provide a fairly good estimation of the error term and is discussed in more detail in [7.22].

d) Extending the State. The reason approximations like the ROMKF and the RUKF [7.9] work well is that the Kalman gains for the state of (7.11) are zero outside a neighborhood of the model supports [7.23]. We have described the ROMKF by defining the state vector (7.12) of minimum size, i.e., with the minimum number of pixels. However, in reviewing the Kalman gains from the Chandrasekhar Kalman filter [7.23], it appears that we may improve the restorations by extending the state support beyond this minimum region. We have experimented with extending the minimum states for several cases. As detailed in [7.22], it appears we can obtain some improvement by a modest extension of the state immediately to the left of the minimum state support.

7.2.3 Comparison of the ROMKF with Kalman Filter Implementations

In order to put the ROMKF in perspective with other Kalman filters used for image restoration, we have compared the ROMKF with the RUKF [7.8, 9] and the Chandrasekhar Kalman filter (CKF) [7.16]. The RUKF is designed using the full 1D state-space from (7.11) to represent the image models defined by (7.1) and (7.3) with reduced error covariance updates. In other words, it is a suboptimal filter for the optimal state. The Chandrasekhar implementation is a Kalman filter employing the state vector of (7.11) without the boundary pixels, with the Kalman gain vector computed from an efficient set of recursive equations. The ROMKF implementation utilizes a true Kalman filter (Appendix 7.A) on the reduced order state of (7.12), i.e. an optimal filter for a suboptimal state. Experiments comparing the performance of these filters, detailed in [7.22], indicate comparable visual results as well as comparable mean-square errors.

7.2.4 Concluding Comment

In this section, we have introduced the ROMKF and indicated that it is suitable for image restoration applications. We have also discussed various aspects of the filter for practical implementation. We have concluded that the approximation made to reduce the state is appropriate. In addition, the ROMKF restoration results are comparable to those obtained with the RUKF and the Chandrasekhar Kalman filters. Due to the reduced state and simplicity, it will be advantageous to use the ROMKF in the maximum likelihood estimation of model parameters, which is discussed in the next section. It will also be useful for adaptive filtering as described in Sect. 7.4.

7.3 Parameter Identification

As we have mentioned before, successful restoration of noisy blurred images relies primarily upon knowledge of the system models (7.1, 3), i.e., the blur PSF, image model, and noise statistics. However, generally the only information available prior to restoration is the observed degraded image. Therefore, it is logical to assume that, for practical situations, these items must be determined from the available data. In Sect. 7.3.1, we review literature regarding parameter identification techniques for images. In Sect. 7.3.2, we introduce a maximum likelihood technique used in conjunction with the ROMKF for parameter identification. We also discuss issues related to the implementation of this technique. In Sect. 7.3.3, we present experimental results for validation of these techniques. We conclude with a brief summary in Sect. 7.3.4.

7.3.1 Literature Review

Control engineers have long been concerned with system identification and parameter estimation problems [7.24]. It is, however, an area in image restoration with a relatively short history.

Recent work in PSF identification was reported by *Tekalp* et al. in [7.25, 26]. In these, the original image was modeled as a 2D AR process as in (7.3) with the overall input-output model defined as in (7.6). For the noiseless case, it is an ARMA process with the AR parameters corresponding to the image model and the MA parameters corresponding to the PSF. ARMA identification methods identify the stable input-output transfer function, i.e., the minimum phase transfer function. This can be a problem since blur PSFs are often nonminimum phase. One approach to this problem was presented by *Tekalp* [7.25] in which the PSF is factored into four quarter-plane convolution factors which are stable in their own directions of recursion. The factors are identified using a recursive estimation algorithm then convolved to form the PSF. However, for practical implementation, this algorithm was restricted to the estimation of PSFs with nonnegative spectra, such as those with Gaussian distributions. In [7.27], *Tekalp* and *Kaufman* extended these results to the more general case of zero-phase PSFs by identifying the spectrally equivalent minimum phase (SEMP) PSF, and then adjusting the phase. A problem is that the phase adjustment is often very difficult to implement in practice for 2D PSFs. In summary, each of these methods is limited to particular PSFs. In addition, because they are spectral techniques, they are further limited to the identification of spatially invariant PSFs. Another parameter identification scheme was given by *Biemond* et al. [7.28], who determined the ARMA parameters, particularly for the implementation of the parallel Kalman filter of [7.4].

Concurrent with our effort, *Lagendijk* et al. [7.29, 30] have employed the Expectation-Maximization (EM) algorithm [7.31] to iteratively determine maximum likelihood estimates of model parameters. This algorithm is similar to the maximum likelihood technique presented next, in that both optimize the likelihood function and both result in computationally efficient algorithms which simultaneously identify and restore degraded images. The EM algorithm is described in more detail in Chap. 6 of this book.

7.3.2 Identification of Model Parameters

In this section our attention is focused on estimating the blur PSF and the observation noise variance (7.1), and the image model and the driving noise variance (7.3) from the degraded image. We will present the maximum likelihood parameter identification technique of [7.19] which is implemented in conjunction with a Kalman filter. It requires repetitive optimal Kalman restorations of the degraded image in the search for the parameters which maximize the likelihood function. This would not be practical without a fast efficient Kalman filtering algorithm such as the ROMKF. This algorithm is a spatial domain technique, making the identification of spatial varying parameters feasible. We also present a parameterization of the PSF which models a wide range of PSFs.

Although we have applauded the Kalman filter for its ability to incorporate spatially varying image characteristics, in this section we will assume image stationarity for verification of the estimator. We will discuss the identification of spatially varying model parameters in the next section.

a) The Maximum Likelihood Estimator. The following outline of the maximum likelihood method for parameter identification in the context of a recursive estimator is based upon [7.19] and [7.32]. First, we define θ as the vector of unknown model parameters:

$$\theta = \left[\left\{a_{kl}\right\}_{k,l\in R_{\oplus+}}; \left\{d_{mn}\right\}_{m,n\in R_1}; \left\{\sigma_v^2, \sigma_w^2\right\}\right] . \tag{7.24}$$

We wish to determine, given our modeling assumptions and the constraints on these models (Sect. 7.1), the θ which "most likely" resulted in our observations. In other words, we want to maximize the likelihood of the observations $\boldsymbol{y}$. Mathematically this is described by

$$\max_{\theta} p\{\boldsymbol{y}|\theta\} , \tag{7.25}$$

where $\boldsymbol{y}$ is the vector containing the observed image pixels and $p\{\boldsymbol{y}|\theta\}$ is the probability density of the observations given the model parameters θ. We will derive this expression in the context of a recursive filter by first defining

$$\boldsymbol{z}(i,j) = [y(1,1), y(2,1), \ldots, y(i-1,j), y(i,j)] . \tag{7.26}$$

The sequential ordering of the 2D data is in raster scan format as described previously. Using Bayes rule for conditional densities, we obtain

$$p\{\boldsymbol{y}|\theta\} = \prod_{i,j\in I_1} p\{y(i,j)|\boldsymbol{z}(i-1,j),\theta\} , \tag{7.27}$$

where I_1 is the support of the image. Based on our modeling assumptions (7.1), each distribution

$$p\{y(i,j)|\boldsymbol{z}(i-1,j),\theta\} \tag{7.28}$$

is Gaussian distributed with conditional mean

$$\begin{aligned}\mathcal{E}\{y(i,j)|\boldsymbol{z}(i-1,j),\theta\} &= \mathcal{E}\{D\boldsymbol{x}(i,j)+v(i,j)|\boldsymbol{z}(i-1,j),\theta\} \\ &= D\hat{\boldsymbol{x}}_b(i,j) = D\,A\,\hat{\boldsymbol{x}}_a(i-1,j)\,,\end{aligned} \tag{7.29}$$

and conditional covariance

$$\begin{aligned}\mathcal{R}(i,j) &= \mathcal{E}\{\left[y(i,j)-D\hat{\boldsymbol{x}}_b(i,j)\right]\left[r(i,j)-D\hat{\boldsymbol{x}}_b(i,j)\right]^{\mathrm{T}}|\boldsymbol{z}(i-1,j),\theta\} \\ &= D\boldsymbol{P}_b(i,j)D^{\mathrm{T}}+Q_v\,,\end{aligned} \tag{7.30}$$

where

$$\boldsymbol{P}_b(i,j) = \mathcal{E}\{\left[\boldsymbol{x}(i,j)-\hat{\boldsymbol{x}}_b(i,j)\right]\left[\boldsymbol{x}(i,j)-\hat{\boldsymbol{x}}_b(i,j)\right]^{\mathrm{T}}\} \tag{7.31}$$

is the predicted error covariance and $\hat{\boldsymbol{x}}_b$ is the predicted state estimate as defined by the Kalman filter (Appendix 7.A).

Then, (7.27) becomes:

$$\begin{aligned}p\{\boldsymbol{y}|\theta\} = &\prod_{i,j\in I_1}\frac{1}{\sqrt{2\pi|\mathcal{R}(i,j)|}} \\ &\times\exp\left\{-\frac{1}{2}\sum_{i,j\in I_1}\left[y(i,j)-D\hat{\boldsymbol{x}}_b(i,j)\right]\mathcal{R}^{-1}(i,j)\left[y(i,j)\right.\right. \\ &\left.\left.-D\hat{\boldsymbol{x}}_b(i,j)\right]^{\mathrm{T}}\right\}.\end{aligned} \tag{7.32}$$

where $|\mathcal{R}(i,j)|$ denotes the determinant of $\mathcal{R}(i,j)$. For simplification we can consider the minimization of the negative of the log-likelihood function, instead of the maximization of (7.27) or (7.32). Taking the negative logarithm of (7.32) we obtain

$$\begin{aligned}L(\theta) &= -\log p(\boldsymbol{y}|\theta) \\ &= \frac{1}{2}\sum_{i,j\in I_1}\left(\log|\mathcal{R}(i,j)|+\frac{[r(i,j)-D\hat{\boldsymbol{x}}_b(i,j)]^2}{\mathcal{R}(i,j)}\right) \\ &\quad+\frac{N}{2}\log(2\pi)\end{aligned} \tag{7.33}$$

noting that $\mathcal{R}(i,j)$ (7.30) is scalar due to the scalar observations (7.1). Eliminating the term independent of θ, we can state problem (7.27) equivalently as

$$\min_{\theta} J(\theta) \tag{7.34}$$

where

$$J(\theta) = \sum_{i,j\in I_1}\left(\log|\mathcal{R}(i,j)|+\frac{[y(i,j)-D\hat{\boldsymbol{x}}_b(i,j)]^2}{\mathcal{R}(i,j)}\right). \tag{7.35}$$

As we discussed earlier, the steady-state Kalman filter is generally used for restoration. For this, the Kalman gain is computed with the steady-state error covariance and $\mathcal{R}(i,j)$ is constant for all (i,j). We can denote this constant as $\mathcal{R}_{ss}$ and simplify (7.35). First, the distribution (7.32) becomes

$$p\{\boldsymbol{y}|\theta\} = \left(\frac{1}{\sqrt{2\pi|\mathcal{R}_{ss}|}}\right)^N \exp\left\{-\frac{1}{2}\sum_{i,j\in I_1}\left[y(i,j) - D\hat{\boldsymbol{x}}_b(i,j)\right]\mathcal{R}_{ss}^{-1}\left[\boldsymbol{y}(i,j) - D\hat{\boldsymbol{x}}_b(i,j)\right]^{\mathrm{T}}\right\}, \tag{7.36}$$

where N is the number of pixels in the image I_1. The log-likelihood equivalent function is then:

$$J(\theta) = N\log\mathcal{R}_{ss} + \frac{1}{\mathcal{R}_{ss}}\sum_{i,j\in I_1}\left[y(i,j) - D\hat{\boldsymbol{x}}_b(i,j)\right]^2 . \tag{7.37}$$

b) Discussion. As we can see from (7.32–35), the likelihood function is computed with intermediate results of the Kalman filter. The problem is to minimize this function $J(\theta)$ with respect to θ, (7.34). This cannot be accomplished analytically due to the nonlinear relationship between θ and the Kalman gain (7.A5). The use of the steady state Kalman filter implies that the Kalman gain vector is computed with the steady-state error covariance. Therefore, practical implementation requires optimization by numerical techniques.

In the numerical search for $\hat{\theta}_{\min}$ which solves (7.34), θ is varied and $J(\theta)$ computed for each θ. As a direct consequence, for each computation of $J(\theta)$, the image must be restored using the Kalman filter based on the current θ. Due to the large amount of computation involved in repetitive evaluations of $J(\theta)$, we employ the ROMKF for the restoration.

A problem common to maximum likelihood algorithms is the existence of local optima and curved ridges which make optimization difficult. Åström, [7.19] discusses this problem, suggesting the use of optimization methods based on the evaluation of the gradient and the Hessian of the likelihood function. However, due to the presence of local optima, the optimal solution $\hat{\theta}_{min}$ is initial condition dependent. In our experiments a generalized reduced gradient (GRG) [7.33] procedure is used for the optimization of (7.34).

To deal with the problem of local optima we can search for $\hat{\theta}_{min}$ from several initial conditions, or try to reduce the number of local optima. In the experiments supporting this method, we attempt to do both. We have assumed that the number of local optima is related to the dimension of θ. Therefore, by reducing the dimension of θ we may reduce the number of local optima. This is discussed later. Also, in the implementation of this method, we initialize the search from several starting points.

This algorithm is very similar in function to the EM algorithm [7.30] which alternately filters the image and estimates the parameters, converging upon parameters which minimize an index similar to $J(\theta)$. This EM algorithm uses a constrained least-squares filter for the E-step and the solution to a set of linear equations for the M-step. This is in contrast to our approach which uses the recursive ROMKF and a gradient based algorithm to determined parameter estimates.

c) Noise Variance Determination. We have not included the estimation of the noise variances by maximization of the likelihood function because the likelihood function $p(y|\theta)$ is fairly insensitive to changes in σ_v^2 or σ_w^2. These can be determined instead by the following. The estimate of σ_v^2 can be determined from a region of the observed image which would be expected to have uniform intensity, such as an area of background. This can be quantified as:

$$\hat{\sigma}_v^2 = \frac{1}{N} \sum_{i,j \in W} [y(i,j) - \bar{y}]^2 \tag{7.38}$$

where W is a region of flat intensity, and $\bar{y}$ is the sample mean of this region.

To estimate the variance of the image modeling error, $\boldsymbol{w}$, we can use the input-output model of (7.6). By taking expectations and noting the prior assumptions, we obtain

$$\hat{\sigma}_w^2 = \frac{1}{N} \frac{\sum [y(i,j) - \sum_{k,l \in R_{\oplus +}} a_{kl} y(i-k, j-l)]^2 + (\sum_{k,l \in R_{\oplus +}} a_{kl}^2 + 1)\sigma_v^2}{\sum_{m,n \in R_1} d_{mn}^2} . \tag{7.39}$$

For images with a high SNR, i.e., negligible observation noise, we can simplify this estimate to

$$\hat{\sigma}_w^2 = \frac{1}{N} \frac{\sum [y(i,j) - \sum_{k,l \in R_{\oplus +}} a_{kl} y(i-k, j-l)]^2}{\sum_{m,n \in R_1} d_{mn}^2} . \tag{7.40}$$

Let us redefine the parameter vector θ as

$$\theta = \left[\{a_{kl}\}_{k,l \in R_{\oplus +}} ; \{d_{mn}\}_{m,n \in R_1} \right] . \tag{7.41}$$

The estimate of σ_w^2 is only dependent on θ and the observed image. It is computed prior to the evaluation of $J(\theta)$ and is incorporated into the minimization of $J(\theta)$ (7.34). We assume that the observation noise variance is constant throughout the image and should be estimated using (7.38) prior to the identification of the remaining parameters.

d) PSF Parameterization. The parameterization of the PSF serves two purposes. First, the number of parameters required to represent the PSF can be drastically reduced. In laboratory settings, image restoration experiments are performed on relatively low resolution images (128 × 128, 256 × 256). Practical problems deal with images with much higher resolution such as 1024 × 1024 or better. For these images it would not be uncommon to be dealing also with PSFs which span hundreds of pixels. The identification of these parameters using (7.34) would be practically impossible due to the large dimension. Second, minimum phase estimates can be avoided for those PSFs for which symmetric modeling is appropriate. If PSF symmetry is enforced, we will not have the problem of minimum phase estimates of the PSF.

Parameterizations that we recommend are based on position relative to the center of the PSF. For example,

$$d_{mn} = \gamma^{-1} \varrho^{m^2+n^2} \tag{7.42}$$

where γ is the normalization factor used to satisfy (7.2). For a 3×3 PSF, this would be

$$D = \begin{bmatrix} \varrho^2 & \varrho & \varrho^2 \\ \varrho & 1 & \varrho \\ \varrho^2 & \varrho & \varrho^2 \end{bmatrix} \tag{7.43}$$

with $\gamma = 1 + 4\varrho + 4\varrho^2$ and d_{00} is the center pixel. Often, defocussing blur is modeled with a Gaussian distribution. This also fits the model of (7.42) by letting $\varrho = 1/\exp\{2\sigma^2\}$ where the parameter ϱ can be directly related to the variance, σ^2, of the distribution. We can also make variations on this theme such as

$$d_{mn} = \gamma^{-1} \varrho^{\sqrt{m^2+n^2}} . \tag{7.44}$$

The disadvantage of blur PSF parameterizations such as these is that the extent of the blur PSF should be known. The advantage is that symmetry is enforced and the minimum phase problems of [7.27, 28, 34] are not encountered. Another advantage is that the bounds on ϱ, $0 \le \varrho \le 1$, represent a wide range of practical blurs. At one extreme when $\varrho = 0$, the PSF represents the case of no blurring, a single pulse in the center. At the other extreme, $\varrho = 1$, the PSF is uniformly distributed. Most blurring functions of practical interest fall between these two bounds.

In some cases it may not be appropriate to model the PSF as symmetric, so we may use a parameterization such as:

$$d_{mn} = \gamma^{-1} \varrho^{|m+n|/2} \tag{7.45}$$

where d_{00} is no longer in the center. For example, $D = [1\ \varrho^{1/2}\ \varrho\ \varrho^{3/2}]$. For this PSF, we may or may not identify the minimum phase PSF due to local optima at the minimum phase and nonminimum phase roots of the polynomial. The likelihood function will have local optima at the values of ϱ corresponding to the minimum and nonminimum phase roots of the polynomial. Although we are not restricted to minimum phase estimates as in [7.27], we are not prevented from identifying them either. We suggest that for cases in which symmetry is not enforced, the restoration be performed with parameters corresponding to the local optima, i.e., both minimum phase and nonminimum phase roots. The correct parameter/restoration should be chosen by a visual criterion or by a comparison of the mean-square errors. Symmetric modeling of the PSF eliminates the possibility of minimum phase estimates.

However, for nonsymmetric PSFs, the parameterization reduces the solution space to facilitate the choice of the correct PSF.

In addition to the parameterization of the PSF, we might also consider the reduction of the number of image model parameters. However, it has been shown by *Tekalp* [7.25] that the restoration is more sensitive to the innovation which is dependent on the blur PSF than the prediction which is dependent on the image model. We observed that increasing the model support greater than the $1 \times 1 \times 1$ region does not improve the quality of the restoration with regard to the mean-square error.

7.3.3 Experimental Results

In this section we present results verifying this approach for parameter identification. For these experiments we have used a 64×64 random field generated by a zero-mean Gaussian process (7.3). The parameters used to generate the random field are displayed in Table 7.1.

In Table 7.2 we show the result of the identification of the random field image model parameters with no blur at various signal-to-noise levels. The identified values are very close to the true parameter values, also displayed in Table 7.2. As would be expected, the estimates deteriorate as the noise level increases.

In Table 7.3 we show the identification of model parameters for a 3×3 blur PSFs for the random field image. The PSF is parameterized as in (7.42). Also,

Table 7.1. The Random Field

a_{11}	a_{01}	a_{-11}	a_{10}	σ_w^2
−0.4165	0.6173	0.1445	0.6472	200.0

Table 7.2. Identification of Image Model Parameters, Synthetic Data

SNR	a_{11}	a_{01}	a_{-11}	a_{10}	σ_w^2
40 dB	−0.4169	0.6198	0.1505	0.6465	204.3
30 dB	−0.4231	0.6267	0.1478	0.6481	210.7
20 dB	−0.3826	0.6025	0.1603	0.6183	276.4
10 dB	−0.2172	0.5031	0.2172	0.4940	500.0

Table 7.3. Identification of Model Parameters, 3×3 PSF, for Synthetic Data

SNR	ρ	$\hat{\rho}$	$\hat{a}_{11}$	$\hat{a}_{01}$	$\hat{a}_{-11}$	$\hat{a}_{10}$	$\hat{\sigma}_w^2$	η_{dB}	η_{dB}^*
40	0.0	0.0165	0.0842	0.3041	0.3345	0.2772	330.0	−9.1	0.0
20	0.0	0.0402	−0.2119	0.3848	0.2631	0.5639	480.0	0.22	0.69
40	0.5	0.5326	0.1130	0.3335	0.3094	0.2440	565.0	2.1	2.1
20	0.5	0.3927	−0.2074	0.5072	0.1990	0.3191	1045.0	0.30	0.40
40	1.0	0.9899	0.0715	0.2887	0.3206	0.3191	534.0	3.4	3.9
20	1.0	0.5431	−0.0728	0.3345	0.2946	0.4441	1211.0	1.1	1.4

since the PSFs are symmetric, we report only d_{11}, d_{01}, d_{00}. The mean-square errors measured in decibels, denoted η_{dB}, are also reported. In the tables η^*_{dB} indicates the performance obtained with the true model parameters,

$$\eta_{\mathrm{dB}} = 10 \log_{10} \frac{\sum(r(i,j) - \hat{s}(i,j))^2}{\sum(s(i,j) - \hat{s}(i,j))^2} . \tag{7.46}$$

In general, the identified parameters are closer to the true value for higher SNRs. There is some tolerance in the estimate of the PSF parameter at low SNRs. This is expected because for low SNRs, the restoration process is a compromise between noise smoothing and edge sharpening, whereas it is primarily edge sharpening for high SNR images. Also, the restoration is more sensitive to the PSF model than the image model, which is the cause for the discrepencies in the estimates of image model parameters.

7.3.4 Summary

The maximum likelihood identification technique was derived in the context of a recursive estimator. For implementation, the reduced order model Kalman filter was utilized to reduce the computation involved in repetitive evaluations of the likelihood function. One of the problems with this identification method is the existence of local optima. Another is the inability to distinguish between model parameters corresponding to minimum and nonminimum phase roots of the input-output transfer function. One solution is the symmetric parameterization of the PSF. Parameterization also serves to reduce the number of unknown model parameters. Experimental results, presented here, confirm the utility of this method for parameter identification.

7.4 Adaptive Image Restoration

Although we introduced spatially variant image and observation models in Sect. 7.1 (7.1, 3), we have assumed them to be spatial invariant in the previous two sections. This section will be devoted to removing this assumption and to the identification of spatially variant models for image restoration using the maximum likelihood technique of Sect. 7.3 and the ROMKF of Sect. 7.2.

The use of a spatially invariant image model implies that the image is homogeneous. We know this is not true for most images by a visual inspection, noting changes in textures, edges, and smooth regions. A spatially invariant blur PSF model assumes that the entire image suffers from the same degradation. This is not true for the case of objects in an image which are blurred due to the motion of individual objects, or depth of field defocussing in which some objects are in focus and others are not.

Often with spatially invariant models, transitions across edges or sharp intensity changes cause ringing in the restored image. Therefore, spatially varying models should result in better restoration due to more accurate modeling and a reduction of ringing artifacts. The Kalman filter (Appendix 7.A), including the ROMKF, is ideally suited for incorporating spatially variant models.

In Sect. 7.4.1 we discuss some of the literature devoted to adaptive restoration. In Sects. 7.4.2 and 7.4.3 we describe our approaches to adaptive restoration and present experimental results. We conclude with Sect. 7.4.5.

7.4.1 Literature Review

Very little of the vast image restoration literature is devoted to spatially variant model assumptions. There are many reasons, most likely limitations in computing power and lack of means for parameter identification. Also, some techniques, such as Fourier domain techniques or [7.14, 18] can only incorporate varying parameters in a limited sense due to the structure of the filter. *Sawchuk* [7.35] and *Robbins* and *Huang* [7.36] developed inverse filters for space variant blurs which can be made space invariant by coordinate transformations. These approaches are very limited, due to few applicable PSFs and the limitations of the inverse filter.

In general, we can divide adaptive restoration techniques into two groups; continuously adaptive or region adaptive. The continuously adaptive techniques imply that the model parameters are changed at each pixel. *Tekalp* [7.25] describes a continuously adaptive RUKF in which only the blur parameters are changed throughout the image. This approach is computationally intensive. *Wellstead* and *Pinto* in [7.37] introduced self-tuning algorithms, with recursive identifiers in conjunction with ARMA filters. A shortcoming of this approach was its use of a 1D line memory. *Wagner* [7.34] improved this by allowing a 2D memory, but this memory extends into the 2D past in a reverse raster sequence and is essentially still a 1D memory.

Region adaptive techniques assume local stationarity. The image is divided into regions in which the models are assumed stationary. Several researchers [7.38–44] have applied this technique with varying criteria for segmentation. The multiple model technique, a special case of region adaptive techniques, can rapidly adapt the image and blur PSF models. This technique uses some decision logic to choose from a finite set of image and blur PSF models at each pixel in the image. The most recent research in this area is by *Tekalp* in [7.25, 42–44]. In [7.25, 43], the blur PSF is fixed and the maximum *a priori* (MAP) decision logic chooses between five image models (four edge orientations and a smooth model). These models are extended to include two PSF models in [7.42, 44]. However this technique is extremely limited because the model selection is from a finite set and these models must be determined prior to restoration. It can be further extended to include more PSF models. However, this would increase the complexity of the decision, while still providing only a limited choice of blur PSF models.

Of the adaptive techniques presented by other researchers in the literature, only [7.42, 44] considered spatially variant blur PSF models. The others limited themselves to image model adaptation. In this section, we assume that both the image and blur PSF model are nonstationary and use the maximum likelihood identification technique to identify the model parameters. We will discuss region adaptive and continuously adaptive techniques.

7.4.2 Adaptive Approaches

The Kalman filter of Appendix 7.A describes a filter with models (matrices $A(i,j)$ and $D(i,j)$) which vary with spatial location. In Sect. 7.3, we described a parameter identification scheme based on stationary model assumptions. We can combine the two by dividing the image into regions in which the models can be assumed stationary. We then use the image data in the region and (7.34) to estimate $d(m,n;i,j)$, $m,n \in R_1$ and $a(k,l;i,j)$, $k,l \in R_{\oplus +}$. It is important that these regions contain sufficient data for identification, yet be small enough for the stationarity assumption to hold.

Ideally, for images with spatial activity (edges, textures), the regions should be small. However, there is a tradeoff between this ideal and ensuring that the window contain enough data for identification. Once the image is segmented into regions, either disjoint or overlapping, the image and PSF model parameters are identified for each window by minimizing $J(\theta)$ in (7.37) using the image data within the window. The identified parameters for each window specify the filter i.e., Kalman gain, PSF model, and image (prediction) model, for each window. Once the parameters are identified for each data window, the entire image can be restored in a raster scan fashion. At each pixel, the filter appropriate to the window in which the pixel belongs is used. For the cases in which overlapping windows or regions are used, a final assignment must be made associating each pixel with one region.

There are several ways in which an image can be segmented. The simplest is partitioning the image into disjoint rectangular windows. The parameters are identified in each of the windows, and these parameters are used to restore the pixels in the window. We call this the *hopping* window technique. We call it hopping because the windows do not overlap. Alternatively, we can overlap the rectangular windows. This is called the *sliding* window technique. This would result in a more gradual transition between the parameters, but would be computationally more intensive. For this, an appropriate window size and overlap region are chosen, and then parameters are identified in each window as the window slides over the image. We would expect the parameters from one window to the next to be similar and, therefore, would use the preceding window parameters as initial conditions for the parameter identification of the next window. A weaving ordering of the windows (shown in Fig. 7.7) is used for continuity of parameters. This ordering is top to bottom, left to right for odd rows of windows and right to left for even rows. Within each window, the likelihood function is computed using a raster scan ordering.

The case in which the image slides only one pixel at a time is continuously adaptive. The parameter identification is based on the image data in a window around each pixel and the resulting parameters are used to filter only the pixel. Since the parameters should not change much from pixel to pixel, it may not be

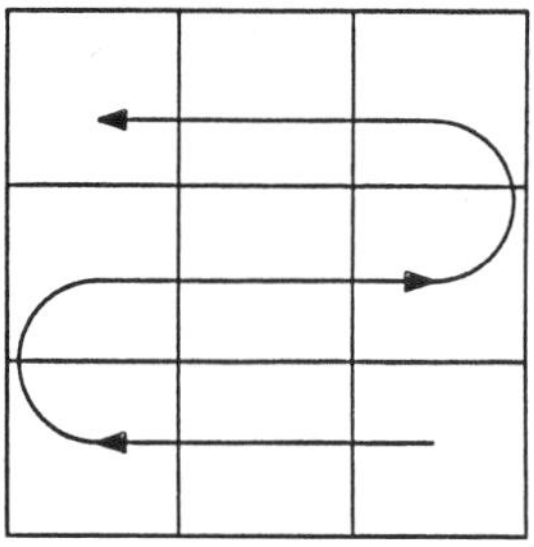

Fig. 7.7. Weaving ordering of windows

necessary to update the error covariance, or only to iterate the error covariance equations (7.A6, A7) one or two times, before computing the Kalman gain.

It would not be practical to solve the optimization problem of (7.34) at each pixel due to the computation involved. As an alternate approach, we can update model parameter estimates at each pixel using the following ideas. In the first data window, the parameters are identified by minimizing (7.37) and obtaining $\hat{\theta}_1$, and making one recursion of the Kalman filter based on these parameters. Then, sliding the window one pixel, the gradient of the likelihood function (7.37) is computed with respect to each of the components of θ. The parameter vector is then updated as follows:

$$\hat{\theta}_{k+1} = \hat{\theta}_k + \alpha \nabla J \ , \tag{7.47}$$

where ∇J indicates the gradient of J and α is an appropriate weight. One possibility for choosing α is to

$$\min_{\alpha} J(\hat{\theta}_k + \alpha \nabla J) \ . \tag{7.48}$$

After the parameter update, the pixel is filtered with the Kalman filter based on the new parameters and the window is moved to the next pixel and the process continues.

This method can be modified to further decrease the computation by updating the parameter vector less often. One possibility is to compute only a component of the gradient at each pixel, using the previously defined model parameters for filter definition. The parameter vector is updated once the gradient computation is complete. This assumes model stationarity for several pixels. Other variations might include the use of a conjugate gradient method or the use of the maximum likelihood technique for the first window of each scan line. We present these ideas as possibilities for the future. The use of parallel computer architectures for implementing these algorithms will further decrease the computation time.

Each time the parameters change, the associated error covariance and gain matrix also change. However, since the parameters are not expected to change much from window to window, the new steady-state Kalman gain can be computed with just a few iterations of the Riccati equation (7.60). The Riccati equation (7.60) will converge to steady-state for any initial nonnegative symmetric error covariance.

That is, the error covariance will satisfy the steady-state Riccati equation (7.61) after just a few iterations. The steady-state Kalman gain for the new window will be

$$K = P_{ss}D^{\mathrm{T}}\left[DP_{ss}D^{\mathrm{T}} + Q_v\right]^{-1} . \tag{7.49}$$

7.4.3 Experimental Results

We have performed several experiments to illustrate the value of adaptive filtering. The purpose of the following two experiments is to illustrate the improvement obtained by changing the model parameters in an image.

In Table 7.4 we show the necessity of adapting the model parameters for the case in which the blur PSF is not stationary. Only the left half of the camera man image is blurred with a uniform 1×5 PSF ($\varrho = 1$) with BSNR of 40 dB, shown in Fig. 7.8. The image model parameters are determined from original image data using a least squares parameter identification (LSPI). (This can not be done in a practical situation because the PSF would not be known and the original image would not be available.) The improvements for various window choices for the restored images are reported in Table 7.4. The restorations are displayed in Fig. 7.9.

Table 7.4. Adaptive-PSF Model

# windows	window size ($i \times j$)	ϱ	η_{dB}
1	122×127	0 (no blur)	0.0
		0.5	−12.9
		1 (uniform blur)	−22.9
2	122×63	1/0	−16.7
2	61×127	1/0	8.7
4	61×63	1/0	9.0
16	30×31	1/0	9.4

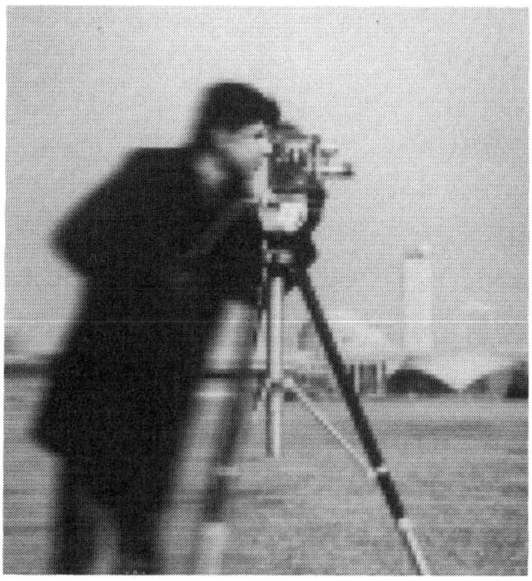

Fig. 7.8. Cameraman, half-blurred with BSNR 40 dB

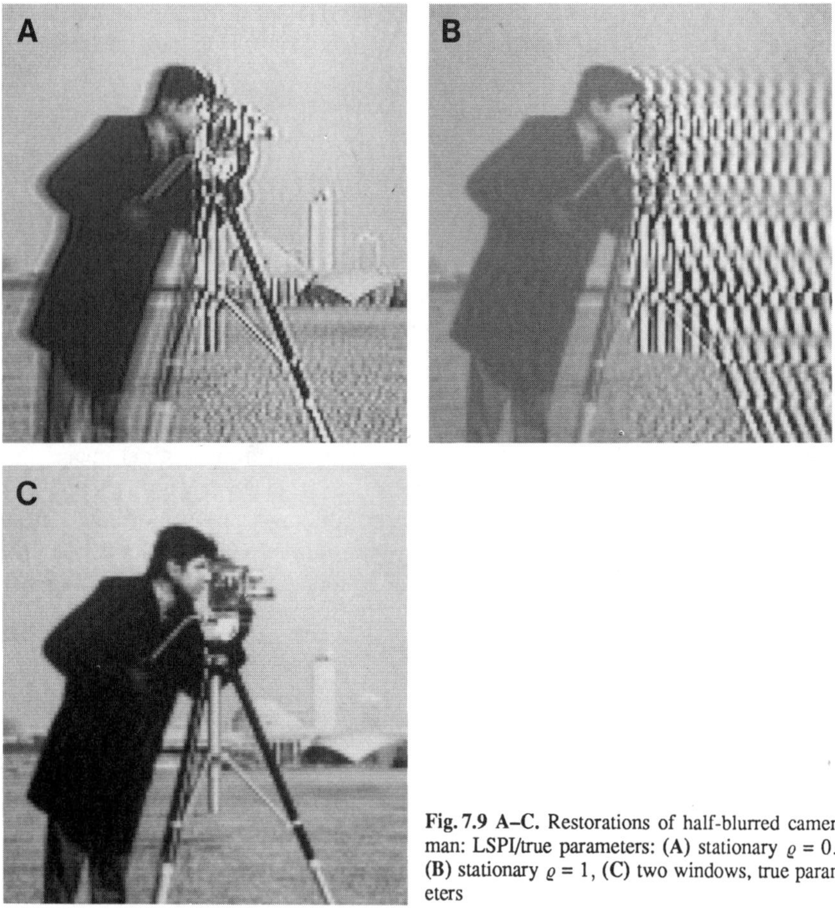

Fig. 7.9 A–C. Restorations of half-blurred cameraman: LSPI/true parameters: **(A)** stationary $\varrho = 0.5$, **(B)** stationary $\varrho = 1$, **(C)** two windows, true parameters

Here, we notice significant improvement by adapting the parameters. Stationary restoration with PSF parameter $\varrho = 1$ yields an improvement of -23 dB, and with PSF parameter $\varrho = 0$, (no blur) there is no improvement. This is in contrast to 9.4 dB improvement obtained when the PSF parameter is correctly varied for the restoration. The stationary assumption results in at least half the image restored using an incorrect PSF. For this test case, if stationary models are used, it is better not to restore the image.

Next, we show the result of using the maximum likelihood identification to determine model parameters for the half-blurred image of Fig. 7.8. The left half of the camera man image is blurred with a 1×5 uniform PSF ($\varrho = 1$), while the right half remains unblurred. In Table 7.5 we compare the parameters for one window, two windows, and four windows. The resulting images are displayed in Fig. 7.10. With stationary model assumptions, the identified parameter is zero, for no blur, resulting in no improvement. Segmentation of the image into two window and

Table 7.5. Adaptive-PSF Model, ML Identification

# windows	$\hat{\rho}$	a_{11}	a_{01}	a_{-11}	a_{10}	η_{dB}
1	0	−0.5502	0.6693	0.08904	0.7841	0.00
2	1	−0.4230	0.6807	0.1565	0.5658	8.93
	0	−0.2620	0.6820	0.0139	0.5460	
4	0.9581	0.1575	0.2299	0.1470	0.4456	8.59
	0.9774	−0.1857	0.5022	0.2472	0.4163	
	0	−0.3303	0.4964	0.1973	0.6616	
	0	−0.2436	0.7503	−0.0528	0.5261	

four square windows resulted in improvements of 8.93 and 8.59 dB respectively. The performance decreased with the four windows because the parameter estimates were not as good.

These results show that the restoration is very sensitive to inaccuracies in the blur parameter and that the stationary modeling of a nonstationary PSF results in poor restorations. However, as discussed in [7.22], stationary modeling of the nonstationary image has less severe consequences. In an image such as the geometric image, shown in Fig. 7.11, in which there are clear textures and edges, the restoration is more sensitive to the image model.

A problem that arises with rectangular windowing is that the image data may not necessarily be stationary within these windows. A better approach, although more complex, is segmenting the image into regions of similar texture. For example, an image could be segmented into flat regions and edge regions of different orientation. The resulting approach is similar to the multiple model approach of [7.25], but the parameters are identified using the maximum likelihood technique, rather than chosen from a predetermined set. Also, the segmentation must be known prior to the identification/filtering process.

We performed experiments with this type of region segmentation for the geometric image of Fig. 7.11. This image was chosen because the image could easily be segmented manually. The image was segmented into ten regions which are described in Table 7.6.

Table 7.6. 10 Regions for the Geometric Image

1	all white (flat area)
2	all black (flat area)
3	edge black-to-white 45°
4	edge white-to-black 45°
5	edge black-to-white 135°
6	edge white-to-black 135°
7	edge black-to-white 0°
8	edge white-to-black 0°
9	edge black-to-white 90°
10	edge white-to-black 90°

Fig. 7.10 A–C. Restorations of half-blurred cameraman: ML identified parameters: (**A**) One window stationary, (**B**) two windows (61 × 127), (**C**) four windows (61 × 63)

Table 7.7. Adaptive Filtering of Geometric Image, True/LSPI Parameters

description	number of windows	η_{dB}
1 × 5 PSF, 40 dB BSNR	1	7.87
	4	8.20
	10	10.69

We then compared restorations of the geometric image with spatially invariant image model assumptions, spatially variant with rectangular windows, and spatially variant with the 10 regions. The image model parameters were identified using the LSPI from the original undistorted image data, and the true blur PSF parameters were used. The improvements are reported in Table 7.7. The improvement gained with the 10 region adaptive models compared with the stationary models is signif-

Fig. 7.11. Geometric image

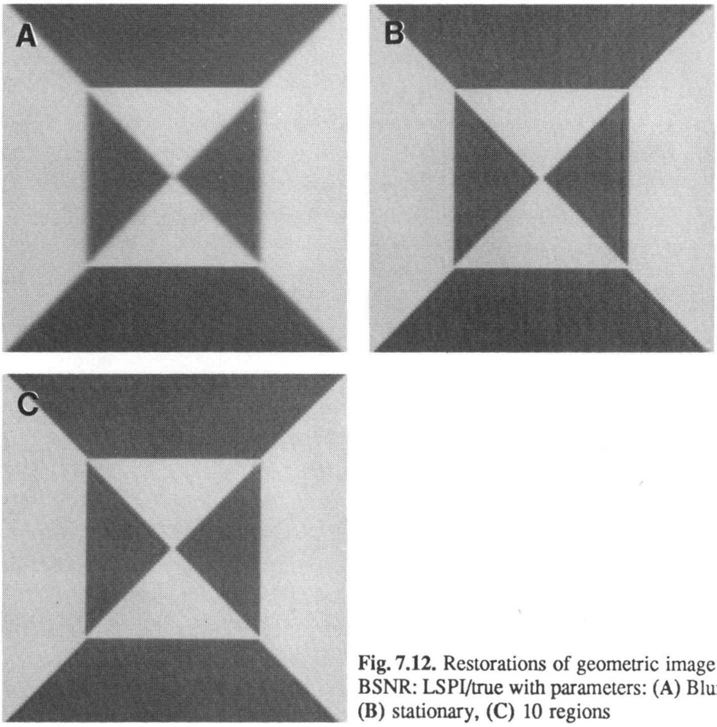

Fig. 7.12. Restorations of geometric image 1 × 5 PSF, 40 dB BSNR: LSPI/true with parameters: **(A)** Blurred 40 dB BSNR, **(B)** stationary, **(C)** 10 regions

icant; namely, 3 dB for the 1 × 5 PSF [eq. (7.44); $\varrho = 0.5$], 40 dB BSNR image. The restored images are displayed in Fig. 7.12.

7.4.4 Summary

For the geometric image, the segmentation of the image into regions of similar texture has been shown to provide better results than simple rectangular divisions. However, the actual segmentation procedure deserves discussion. Segmentation can be done by computer, using algorithms described in [7.45, 46] such as boundary detection, clustering, or thresholding. However, in addition to adding to the computational burden, they may not provide a good segmentation if edges are blurred. The segmentation can also be done interactively with the user, in which the user can decide which portion of an image should be restored and partition the image into regions. A more detailed discussion on segmentation can be found in [7.45, 46], and is beyond the scope of this chapter. For our applications, the geometric image was segmented by manually assigning the regions. However, for most images, segmentation is not so easy. The purpose of experiments here is to show that an increase in improvement results with such a segmentation.

The results shown in this section indicate that by varying the image and PSF models, improved restorations can be obtained. It is particularly important for spatially variant PSFs that the models change accordingly. This is in contrast to the image model for which restorations are fairly insensitive. An important consideration for adaptive filtering is that the regions must contain sufficient data for the identification of model parameters. As the PSF size increases, the amount of image data used for identification must also increase.

7.5 Conclusion

In this chapter, we have presented a low order state-space model for images. Its use with the Kalman filter results in the Reduced Order Model Kalman Filter. This filter was shown to be stable and to provide comparable restoration results with established Kalman filter methods. The development of the ROMKF was inspired by the desire to reduce the computation required to filter an image and to use the Kalman filter more effectively by incorporating spatially varying models.

The low level of computation was significant in making the maximum likelihood parameter identification, described in Sect. 7.3, practical. Although the image must be filtered each time the likelihood function is computed, generally very few iterations of the error covariance equations are required to compute the steady-state Kalman gain.

One of the problems with this identification technique is the existence of local optima. In some cases these suboptima correspond to minimum phase and non minimum phase parameterizations of the PSF. One technique which will avoid minimum phase PSF identification is to assume PSF symmetry, whenever possible. In other cases, we suggest restoring the image with the identified parameters corresponding to the local optima and then making a choice by visual inspection of the restoration or by comparison of mean square errors.

The reduced computation of the ROMKF makes it attractive for adaptive restoration, i.e., the incorporation of spatially varying image and blur models. We discussed several ways in which an image can be divided into regions. The most effective appears to be the segmentation according to local activity, as was done for the geometric image case. However, if such a segmentation is not possible, dividing the image into rectangular window and restoring each window based on separately identified models, results in restorations superior to stationary model assumptions.

The approach to adaptive restoration and parameter identification described in this chapter is discussed in more detail in [7.22] where these methods are also extended to color and real world images.

7.A Appendix: The Kalman Filter I

In this appendix, we acquaint the reader with the Kalman filter. The derivation can be found in [7.47] or other control systems textbooks. These equations have been extended to 2D, with one direction of recursion.

Let $\boldsymbol{x}(i,j)$ denote the state at spatial location (i,j). The dynamic model for the state is represented as a difference equation

$$\boldsymbol{x}(i+1,j) = \boldsymbol{A}\boldsymbol{x}(i,j) + \boldsymbol{B}\boldsymbol{w}(i,j) + \boldsymbol{E}\boldsymbol{u}(i,j) \tag{7.A 1}$$

and the system output model is

$$y(i,j) = \boldsymbol{D}\boldsymbol{x}(i,j) + \boldsymbol{v}(i,j)\ . \tag{7.A 2}$$

The matrix $\boldsymbol{A}$ denotes the state transition; $\boldsymbol{B}$, $\boldsymbol{E}$, and $\boldsymbol{D}$ are system matrices; $\boldsymbol{w}(i,j)$ and $\boldsymbol{v}(i,j)$ are zero-mean random Gaussian processes representing the driving (or plant) noise and the observation noise, respectively; and $\boldsymbol{u}(i,j)$ represents deterministic input.

The Kalman filter can be divided into two steps: prediction and update. In the following, the subscript b indicates prediction and a indicates update. The state prediction and update are

$$\hat{\boldsymbol{x}}_b(i,j) = \boldsymbol{A}\hat{\boldsymbol{x}}_a(i-1,j) + \boldsymbol{E}\boldsymbol{u}(i,j)\ , \tag{7.A 3}$$

$$\hat{\boldsymbol{x}}_a(i,j) = \hat{\boldsymbol{x}}_b(i,j) + \boldsymbol{K}(i,j)[\boldsymbol{y}(i,j) - \boldsymbol{D}\hat{\boldsymbol{x}}_b(i,j)]\ , \tag{7.A 4}$$

where $\boldsymbol{K}(i,j)$ is the Kalman gain matrix. It is computed by:

$$\boldsymbol{K}(i,j) = \boldsymbol{P}_b(i,j)\boldsymbol{D}^{\mathrm{T}}[\boldsymbol{D}\boldsymbol{P}_b(i,j)\boldsymbol{D}^{\mathrm{T}} + \boldsymbol{Q}_v]^{-1} \tag{7.A 5}$$

$$\boldsymbol{P}_b(i,j) = \boldsymbol{C}\boldsymbol{P}_a(i-1,j)\boldsymbol{C}^{\mathrm{T}} + \boldsymbol{D}\boldsymbol{Q}_w\boldsymbol{D}^{\mathrm{T}} \tag{7.A 6}$$

$$\boldsymbol{P}_a(i,j) = [\boldsymbol{I} - \boldsymbol{K}(i,j)\boldsymbol{D}]\,\boldsymbol{P}_b(i,j) \tag{7.A 7}$$

where

$$\boldsymbol{Q}_v = \mathrm{cov}(\boldsymbol{v}) \tag{7.A 8}$$

$$\boldsymbol{Q}_w = \mathrm{cov}(\boldsymbol{w}) \tag{7.A 9}$$

and $\boldsymbol{P}_b(i,j)$ and $\boldsymbol{P}_a(i,j)$ are the predicted and updated error covariance matrices respectively:

$$\boldsymbol{P}_b(i,j) = \mathcal{E}\left\{[\boldsymbol{x}(i,j) - \hat{\boldsymbol{x}}_b(i,j)][\boldsymbol{x}(i,j) - \hat{\boldsymbol{x}}_b(i,j)]^{\mathrm{T}}\right\} \qquad (7.\mathrm{A}\ 10)$$

$$\boldsymbol{P}_a(i,j) = \mathcal{E}\left\{[\boldsymbol{x}(i,j) - \hat{\boldsymbol{x}}_a(i,j)][\boldsymbol{x}(i,j) - \hat{\boldsymbol{x}}_a(i,j)]^{\mathrm{T}}\right\} . \qquad (7.\mathrm{A}\ 11)$$

Equations (7.A 6) and (7.A 7) can be combined into

$$\begin{aligned}\boldsymbol{P}_b(i,j) = \boldsymbol{A}\big[&\boldsymbol{P}_b(i-1,j) - \boldsymbol{P}_b(i-1,j)\boldsymbol{D}^{\mathrm{T}} \\ &\times[\boldsymbol{D}\boldsymbol{P}_b(i-1,j)\boldsymbol{D}^{\mathrm{T}} + \boldsymbol{Q}_v]^{-1}\boldsymbol{D}\boldsymbol{P}_b(i-1,j)\big]\,\boldsymbol{A}^{\mathrm{T}} \\ &+ \boldsymbol{D}\mathrm{Q}_w\boldsymbol{D}^{\mathrm{T}}\end{aligned} \qquad (7.\mathrm{A}\ 12)$$

which is also known as the Riccati equation. The steady-state Riccati equation is

$$\boldsymbol{P}_{ss} = \boldsymbol{A}\left[\boldsymbol{P}_{ss} - \boldsymbol{P}_{ss}\boldsymbol{D}^{\mathrm{T}}\left(\boldsymbol{D}\boldsymbol{P}_{ss}\boldsymbol{D}^{\mathrm{T}} + \boldsymbol{Q}_v\right)^{-1}\boldsymbol{D}\boldsymbol{P}_{ss}\right]\boldsymbol{A}^{\mathrm{T}} + \boldsymbol{D}\boldsymbol{Q}_w\boldsymbol{D}^{\mathrm{T}} . \qquad (7.\mathrm{A}\ 13)$$

Acknowledgements. The research discussed in this chapter was supported in part by grants from Eastman Kodak Company, NSF grant MIP-8703021, and NATO travel grant 0124/87.

References

7.1 B. R. Hunt: "Digital Image Processing". Proc. of the IEEE **63**, 693–708 (1975)

7.2 A. K. Jain: "Advances in Mathematical Models for Image Processing". Proc. of the IEEE **69**, 502–528 (1981)

7.3 D. L. Angwin, H. Kaufman: "Image Restoration Using Reduced Order Models". Signal Processing **16**, 21–28 (1989)

7.4 J. Biemond, J. Rieske, J. Gerbrands: "A Fast Kalman Filter for Images Degraded by Both Blur and Noise". IEEE Trans. ASSP-**31**, 1248–1256 (1983)

7.5 T. Katayama: "Restoration of Images Degraded by Motion Blur and Noise". IEEE Trans. AC-**27**, 1024–1033 (1982)

7.6 T. Katayama, M. Kosaka: "Recursive Filtering Algorithm for a Two-Dimensional System". IEEE Trans. AC-**24**, 130–132 (1979)

7.7 M. S. Murphy, L. M. Silverman: "Image Model Representation and Line by Line Recursive Restoration". IEEE Trans. AC-**23**, 809–816 (1978)

7.8 J. W. Woods, V. K. Ingle: "Kalman Filtering in Two-Dimensions – Further Results". IEEE Trans. ASSP-**29**, 188–197 (1981)

7.9 J. W. Woods, C. W. Radewan: "Kalman Filtering in Two-Dimensions". IEEE Trans. IT-**23**, 473–482 (1977)

7.10 A. Habibi: "Two-Dimensional Bayesian Estimate of Images". Proc. of the IEEE **60**, 878–883 (1972)

7.11 N. E. Nahi: "Role of Recursive Estimation in Statistical Image Enhancement". Proc. of the IEEE **60**, 872–877 (1972)

7.12 A. O. Aboutalib, L. M. Silverman: "Restoration of Motion Degraded Images". IEEE Trans. CAS-**22**, 278–286 (1975)

7.13 A. O. Aboutalib, M. S. Murphy, L. M. Silverman: "Digital Restoration of Images Degraded by General Motion Blurs". IEEE Trans. AC-**22**, 294–302 (1977)

7.14 B. R. Suresh, B. A. Shenoi: "New Results in Two-Dimensional Kalman Filtering with Applications to Image Restoration". IEEE Trans. CAS-**28**, 307–319 (1981)

7.15 R. P. Roesser: "A Discrete State-Space Model for Linear Image Processing". IEEE Trans. AC-**20**, 1–10 (1975)
7.16 A-. K. Mahalanabis, K. Xue: "An Efficient Two-Dimensional Chandrasekhar Filter for Restoration of Images Degraded by Spatial Blur and Noise". IEEE Trans. ASSP-**35**, 1603–1610 (1987)
7.17 M. Morf, G. S. Sidhu, T. Kailath: "Some New Algorithms for Recursive Estimation in Constant, Linear, Discrete-Time Systems". IEEE Trans. AC-**19**, 315–323 (1974)
7.18 Z. Wu: "Multidimensional State-Space Model Kalman Filtering with Application to Image Restoration". IEEE Trans. ASSP-**33**, 1576–1592 (1985)
7.19 K. J. Åström: "Maximum Likelihood and Prediction Error Methods". Automatica **16**, 551–574 (1980)
7.20 B. D. O. Anderson, J. B. Moore: *Optimal Filtering* (Prentice Hall, Englewood Cliffs, NJ 1979)
7.21 J. W. Woods, J. Biemond, A. M. Tekalp: "Boundary Value Problems in Image Restoration". Proc. 1975 Int. Conf. ASSP, 692–695, Tampa, FL (1985)
7.22 D. L. Angwin: "Adaptive Image Restoration Using Reduced Order Model Based Kalman Filter". Ph.D. thesis, Rensselaer Polytechnic Institute, Troy, NY (1989)
7.23 S. Koch, H. Kaufman, D. L. Angwin: "Recursive Kalman Type Filter Selection for Adaptive Image Restoration". Proc. of the IASTED Int. Conf. on Contr. and Signal Process., Honolulu, Hawaii (1989)
7.24 L. Ljung: *System Identification* (Prentice Hall, Englewood Cliffs, NJ 1987)
7.25 A. M. Tekalp: "Identification and Restoration of Noisy and Blurred Images". Ph.D. thesis, Rensselaer Polytechnic Institute, Troy, NY (1984)
7.26 A. M. Tekalp, H. Kaufman, J. W. Woods: Identification of Image and Blur Parameters for the Restoration of Noncausal Blurs, IEEE Trans. ASSP-**34**, 963–972 (1986)
7.27 A. M. Tekalp, H. Kaufman: "On Statistical Identification of a Class of Linear Space-Invariant Image Blurs Using Nonminimum-Phase ARMA Models". IEEE Trans. ASSP-**36**, 1360–1363 (1988)
7.28 J. Biemond, F. G. van der Putten, J. W. Woods: "A Parallel Identification Procedure for Images with Noncausal Symmetric Blurs". IEEE Trans. CAS-**35**, 385–393 (1988)
7.29 R. L. Lagendijk, D. L. Angwin, H. Kaufman, J. Biemond: "Recursive and Iterative Methods for Image Identification and Restoration". Proc. of the Fourth European Signal Processing Conference (EUSIPCO), ed. by J. G. Lacoume, Grenoble, France (1988)
7.30 R. L. Lagendijk, J. Biemond, D. E. Boekee: "Simultaneous Image Identification and Restoration Using the EM-Algorithm". Proc. SPIE Conference on Visual Communication and Image Processing, Cambridge, MA (1988)
7.31 A. P. Dempster, N. M. Laird, D. B. Rubin: "Maximum Likelihood From Incomplete Data". J. R. Stat. Soc. B **39**, 1–38 (1977)
7.32 A. P. Sage: *Optimum Systems Control* (Prentice Hall, Englewood Cliffs, NJ 1968)
7.33 D. G. Luenberger: *Linear and Nonlinear Programming*, 2nd ed. (Addison-Wesley, Reading, MA 1984)
7.34 G. R. Wagner: Self-Tuning Algorithms for Two-Dimensional Signal Processing. Ph.D. thesis, University of Manchester Institute of Technology, Manchester, England (1987)
7.35 A. A. Sawchuk: "Space-Variant Image Motion Degradation and Restoration". Proc. of the IEEE **60**, 854–861 (1972)
7.36 G. M. Robbins, T. S. Huang: "Inverse Filtering for Linear Shift-Variant Imaging Systems". Proc. of the IEEE **60**, 862–872 (1972)
7.37 P. E. Wellstead, J. R. Caldas Pinto: "Self-Tuning Filters and Predictors for Two-Dimensional Systems, Part 1: Algorithms". Int. J. Control **42**, 457–478 (1985)
7.38 F.-C. Jeng, J. W. Woods: "Inhomogeneous Gaussian Image Models for Estimation and Restoration". IEEE Trans. on ASSP-**36**, 1305–1312 (1988)
7.39 A. K. Mahalanabis, K. Xue: "A Window Adaptive Chandrasekhar Filtering Algorithm for Image Enhancement". Proc. 28th Conf. on Decision and Control, Los Angeles, CA (1987)
7.40 S. A. Rajala, R. P. DeFigueiredo: "Adaptive Nonlinear Image Restoration by a Modified Kalman Filtering Approach". IEEE Trans. on ASSP-**29**, 1033–1042 (1981)
7.41 W.-J. Song, W. A. Pearlman: "Edge-Preserving Noise Filtering Based on Adaptive Windowing". IEEE Trans. CAS-**35**, 1048–1055 (1988)
7.42 A. T. Erdem, A. M. Tekalp: "Decision-Directed Adaptive Image Restoration Using Multiple Image and Blur Models". Proc. Int. Conf. on Control, Jerusalem, Israel (1989)
7.43 A. M. Tekalp, H. Kaufman, J. W. Woods: "Edge-Adaptive Kalman Filtering for Image Restoration with Ringing Suppression". IEEE Trans. on ASSP-**37**, 892–899 (1989)

7.44 A. M. Tekalp, H. Kaufman, J. W. Woods: "Model-Based Segmentation and Space-Variant Restoration of Blurred Images by Decision-Directed Filtering". Signal Process. **15**, 259–269 (1988)
7.45 R. C. Gonzalez, P. Wintz: *Digial Image Processing* (Addison-Wesley, Reading, MA 1977)
7.46 A. K. Jain: *Fundamentals of Digital Image Processing* (Prentice Hall, Englewood Cliffs, NJ 1989)
7.47 A. Gelb (ed.): *Applied Optimal Estimation* (M.I.T. Press, Cambridge, MA 1972)

8. Restoration of Scanned Photographic Images

A. M. Tekalp and G. Pavlović

With 15 Figures

This chapter has two main themes: Firstly, we discuss the importance of incorporating the nonlinear sensor characteristics into the blur identification and image restoration procedures for the restoration of scanned photographic images. We propose to transform the noisy and blurred image into "the exposure domain" using the inverse of the nonlinear sensor characteristics. We further show that due to this transformation the observation noise manifests itself as multiplicative noise in the exposure domain. Secondly, we derive a linear minimum mean square error (LMMSE) deconvolution filter for the linear convolutional model in the presence of a particular type of multiplicative noise, in the exposure domain. We provide an example of a blurred image which can be restored in the exposure domain using the proposed procedure, but not in the optical density domain.

8.1 Motivation

Recorded images may be blurred due to imaging system aberrations (such as coma, astigmatism), atmospheric turbulence (an important factor in satellite imaging), out-of-focus imaging systems, and relative motion between the image and object planes. These degradations may mask important information in one of a kind documents that are in the form of photographic images. Hence, it becomes necessary to deblur photographic images to extract information from such irreplacable documents.

In the image restoration literature, it is customary to model a blurred image as the linear convolution of an "original" image with the point spread function (PSF) of the blur. The observation noise is usually assumed as additive, white Gaussian noise that is independent of the signal. However, in practice, image sensors usually have nonlinear characteristics that can be modeled as pointwise (memoryless) nonlinearity. One such example is the photographic film. Due to the well-known nonlinear relationship between the incoming light intensity and the silver density deposited on the film, given by the "$d - \log e$" curve of the film, the widely assumed linear relationship between the blurred image and the "original" image does not hold when the recording medium is photographic film. This problem is of great interest in many real-life applications, since the photographic film continues to be one of the most widely used image recording media.

The modeling of sensor nonlinearities was first addressed by *Andrews* and *Hunt* [8.1, p. 117]. They introduced a point nonlinearity $D\{.\}$ into the observation model,

Springer Series in Information Sciences, Vol. 23
A. K. Katsaggelos (ed.): Digital Image Restoration

$$b_d(x,y) = D\{h(x,y) * *s(x,y)\} + v(x,y) \ , \qquad (8.1)$$

where $b_d(x,y)$ is the image recorded on photographic film, $s(x,y)$ is the original scene, $v(x,y)$ represents the observation noise, and $h(x,y)$ denotes the PSF of the blur.

There have been some attempts in the literature to incorporate the sensor nonlinearity into image restoration algorithms. *Andrews* and *Hunt* [8.1, p. 123] propose expanding the observation model (8.1) into a Taylor series about the mean value of the observed image. Based on this expansion they derive an approximate filter for image restoration. However, they recommend that, in practice, one should process the image as though the nonlinearity was not present, since they do not obtain a significant improvement using this approach over directly processing the observed image in the density domain. *Cannon* [8.2, p. 46] confirms this recommendation based on a "low contrast assumption".

Andrews and *Hunt* [8.1, p. 193] and *Trussell* [8.3] also proposed to incorporate the nonlinear response of the photographic film through a maximum a posteriori probability (MAP) restoration formulation. However, this approach results in an iterative solution algorithm which suffers from a large computational requirement. *Cannon* et al. [8.4] also suggest that there is, in general, no significant improvement in incorporating the nonlinearity into the restoration procedure. *Angwin* and *Kaufman* [8.5] performed a comparison of image restoration using Kalman filtering in the density versus intensity (exposure) domains as an experimental study. They found that at high signal-to-noise ratios better restoration results can be obtained in the intensity domain. However, they did not consider an analytic model of the film nonlinearity and its consequences on the restoration algorithm.

In this chapter, we propose a new method to incorporate the nonlinear sensor characteristics into image restoration. We propose to transform the image into a domain where a linear convolutional relationship between the original and degraded images can be established. In the case of photographic film, this domain is known as "the exposure domain." We then show that as a consequence of this transformation, the observation noise in the exposure domain becomes multiplicative. Hence, we derive a linear minimum mean square error deconvolution filter, in the exposure domain, in the presence of multiplicative noise. We also discuss how to estimate the blur PSF, and other filter parameters from the blurred image itself.

Image formation models with multiplicative and signal-dependent noise have been proposed in the literature [8.6, 7] based on the physics of the particular image recording process. Examples include the film-grain noise in photographic imaging and photoelectron shot noise in photoelectrically emissive imaging. A number of algorithms [8.8–10] have been presented for noise suppression in the case of such noise sources. In this chapter, we study image restoration (deconvolution) in the presence of multiplicative noise. However, in our case the multiplicative noise arises in an attempt to undo the imaging sensor nonlinearity as will be discussed in detail in the following. We elaborate, by using a Taylor series expansion for the noise process, on the relationship between deconvolution in the presence of multiplicative noise and deconvolution in the presence of additive signal-dependent noise.

The outline of the chapter is as follows: In Sect. 8.2, we discuss issues related to modeling scanned blurred photographic images, such as parametric modeling of the film nonlinearity, the effect of scanner characteristics and assumptions about the noise. In Sect. 8.3, we present the theory of the restoration of scanned blurred and noisy photographic images. We first discuss the domain where the deconvolution should be implemented. To this effect, we propose to transform the image into the exposure domain where a linear convolutional relationship between the degraded and original images can be established. We also discuss the sensitivity of the restoration results on the parameters of the nonlinearity used in this transformation. We derive a linear minimum mean square error restoration filter in the exposure domain, in the presence of multiplicative noise in Sect. 8.3.2. In Sect. 8.4, we present practical issues involved in the restoration of scanned photographic images, such as identification of the blur and estimation of other filter parameters from the degraded image. We also discuss what types of blurs can be restored using the method proposed in this chapter. Finally, in Sect. 8.5, we demonstrate, by restoring some real photographically blurred images, that the proposed method results in huge improvement in resolution when compared to other existing filters neglecting the nonlinearity. In fact, we present an example of a blurred image which cannot be successfully restored in the optical density domain using conventional image restoration methods, but can be reasonably well restored in the exposure domain using our new procedure.

8.2 Modeling Scanned Blurred Photographic Images

Image restoration may be defined as applying the inverse of a mathematical model that describes the degradation in order to estimate the "original" image. The success of image restoration in a given application depends on how good the assumed mathematical model fits the real cause of the image degradation. Hence, in image restoration, it is of utmost importance to develop realistic models for the image degradations. The degradations that we are concerned with in this chapter can be broadly classified as:

(i) spatial degradations (the blur), and
(ii) random pointwise degradations (the noise).

A realistic model of the blurred and noisy scanned photographic images should include the blurring process during image formation, characteristics of the photographic film, the noise sources, and the characteristics of the image scanner. We discuss modeling the blur during image formation in Sect. 8.2.1. The information that is recorded on the photographic film is in the terms of optical density. The optical density is related to the incoming light exposure through the $d - \log e$ curve of the film, that is specified by the manufacturer. We discuss the effect of the $d - \log e$ curve on image restoration in Sect. 8.2.2. In image deblurring, one of the main limitations is the presence of observation noise in recorded blurred images.

Images recorded on photographic film are invariably contaminated by film grain noise. The severity of the effect of the film grain noise depends on the speed of the film and the amount of light present in the scene. There is also quantization noise present due to the digitization process. We discuss modeling the observation noise in Sect. 8.2.3. We also discuss the effect of scanner characteristics in modeling scanned photographic images in Sect. 8.2.3.

8.2.1 Linear Space-Invariant Blur Modeling

A blurred image can be represented by the following superposition integral in the light exposure domain [8.1]:

$$b(x, y) = \int_{-\infty}^{\infty} \int_{-\infty}^{\infty} h_1(x, y; \xi, \eta)\ s(\xi, \eta)\ d\xi d\eta\ , \tag{8.2}$$

where $s(\xi, \eta)$ denotes the object (scene) intensity distribution, $b(x, y)$ is for the light intensity (exposure) incident on the photographic film, and $h_1(x, y; \xi, \eta)$ denotes the point spread function (PSF) of the blur in the continuous coordinates.

The PSF of the blur, $h_1(x, y; \xi, \eta)$ is defined as the image of a point object of unit brightness, $\delta(x - \xi, y - \eta)$, located at (ξ, η) in the object plane. The concept of the PSF is illustrated for the case of out-of-focus blur in Fig. 8.1. In its most general form, the PSF $h_1(x, y; \xi, \eta)$ changes as the position (ξ, η) of the point object in the object plane changes. If we assume that every spatial position in the image is blurred in the same way, then we say that the blur is spatially invariant. In this case, we have

$$h_1(x, y; \xi, \eta) \doteq h(x - \xi, y - \eta) \tag{8.3}$$

where $h(x, y)$ denotes the image of a point object $\delta(x, y)$ located at the origin of the object plane. In this chapter, we consider only space-invariant blurs.

In many cases, such as out-of-focus blur and linear motion blur, $h(x, y)$ is of finite spatial extent. In many others, such as atmospheric turbulence blur, it can be

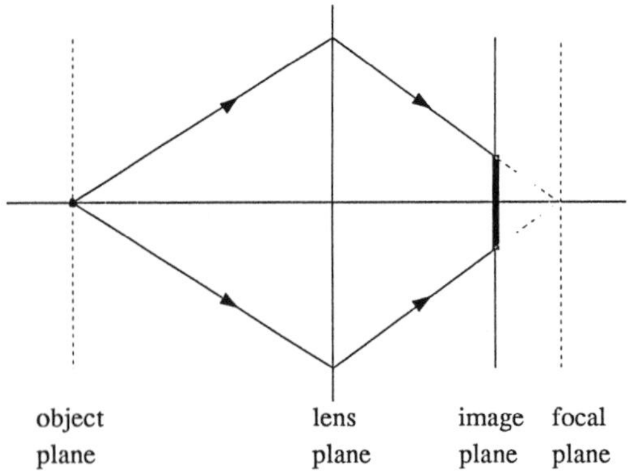

Fig. 8.1. The physical modeling of the out-of-focus image generation

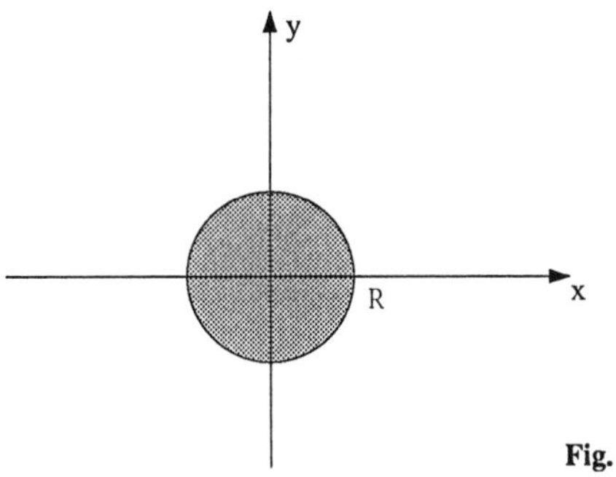

Fig. 8.2. The support of the PSF for the out-of-focus blur

assumed to be negligible outside a finite region in space, called the support of the PSF. The support of the PSF need not be causal [1], and in general, most real-life blurs are modeled with noncausal PSFs. The support of the PSF for the case of an out-of-focus blur is depicted in Fig. 8.2.

The model (8.2) for the blurred image then simplifies to the following convolution integral:

$$\begin{aligned} b(x, y) &= \int_{(\xi,\eta)\in\mathcal{B}} h(\xi, \eta)\, s(x - \xi, y - \eta)\, d\xi d\eta \\ &= h(x, y) * *s(x, y)\ , \end{aligned} \tag{8.4}$$

where $\mathcal{B}$ denotes the support of the PSF and $**$ stands for 2D convolution. Hence, according to (8.4), the exposure incident on the photographic film $b(x, y)$ is modeled as the output of a linear system, with space-limited impulse response $h(x, y)$, whose input is the object (scene) intensity distribution $s(x, y)$.

8.2.2 Effect of Photographic Film Characteristics

In recording images on photographic film, the resulting image signal is in terms of the optical density where there exists a logarithmic relation between the optical density and the incident exposure (light intensity). This relation is usually provided by the manufacturer as a $d - \log e$ curve. A typical $d - \log e$ curve of a photographic film is shown in Fig. 8.3.

Using the model proposed by *Andrews* and *Hunt* [8.1, p. 117] to represent sensor nonlinearities, we can express the blurred image $b_d(x, y)$ recorded on the photographic film as

$$b_d(x, y) = D\{h(x, y) * *s_e(x, y)\} \tag{8.5}$$

where $D\{.\}$ represents a pointwise (memoryless) nonlinearity which, in the case of photographic film, is the $d - \log e$ curve of the film. The subscript d is used to indicate the density domain explicitly. Note that, considering the physical model

[1] with respect to a particular direction of scanning

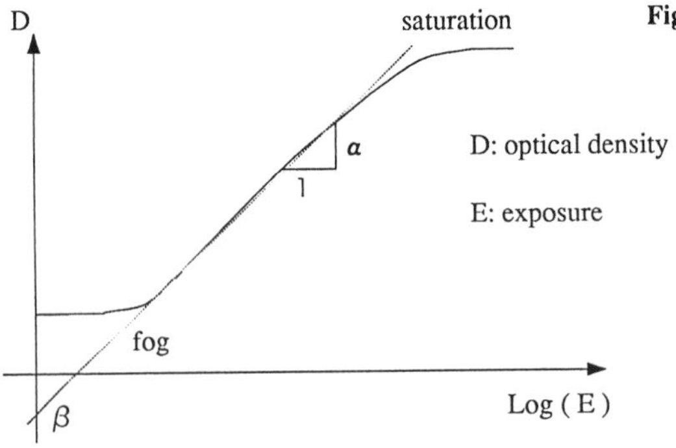

Fig. 8.3. Typical $D - \log E$ curve of a film

of the blur generation, the blurring takes place in the exposure (light intensity) domain, and the image is recorded in the optical density domain. The nonlinear function $D\{.\}$ denotes the mathematical mapping between these domains.

Assuming that incident exposure $b(x, y)$ entirely falls into the linear region of the $d - \log e$ curve, the $d - \log e$ curve can be parameterized as

$$D(E) = \alpha \log(E) + \beta \ , \tag{8.6}$$

where D and E stand for optical density and exposure, respectively, α denotes the slope of the linear region and β is the D-offset of the extrapolated linear region with respect to the origin as shown in Fig. 8.3. Hence, (8.6) is a parametric model of the memoryless sensor nonlinearity with parameters α and β. In cases where the incident exposure may partly fall into the nonlinear regions (near the toe and the shoulder) of the $d - \log e$ curve, we suggest to implement a look-up table (LUT) that represents the $d - \log e$ curve, instead of the model (8.6). However, if part of the incident exposure falls into the flat portion of either the toe or the shoulder of the $d - \log e$ curve, the respective image information may be lost permanently.

Assuming that the incident exposure remains in the linear region of the $d - \log e$ curve, and substituting (8.6) into (8.5), we get

$$b_d(x, y) = \alpha \ \log\{h(x, y) * * s_e(x, y)\} + \beta \ , \tag{8.7}$$

where the subscript e is used to explicitly indicate the exposure domain. Then, (8.7) gives the relation between the recorded image $b_d(x, y)$ in the optical density domain and the object (scene) $s_e(x, y)$ in the exposure domain, in the absence of any observation noise.

8.2.3 Scanner Characteristics and Noise

The image that is recorded on the negative is then sampled and digitized. Suppose that the image is sampled on a uniform square grid with spacing Δ in the horizontal and vertical directions, such that

$$b_d(m,n) \doteq \frac{1}{2\pi r_S^2} \int_{x^2+y^2 \le r_S^2} b_d(x+m\Delta, y+n\Delta)\, dx\, dy \ , \tag{8.8}$$

where $b_d(m,n)$ denotes the optical density at the sampling grid (m,n). In the expression (8.8), it is assumed that the sampling aperture has circular support with radius r_S and the scanning beam profile is uniform.

Then, we can approximate (8.7) by

$$b_d(m,n) = \alpha \log\{h(m,n) * * s_e(m,n)\} + \beta \ , \tag{8.9}$$

where

$$h(m,n) \doteq \frac{1}{2\pi r_S^2} \int_{x^2+y^2 \le r_S^2} h(x+m\Delta, y+n\Delta)\, dx\, dy \ . \tag{8.10}$$

Since, we assumed that $h(x,y)$ is space-limited, the Fourier transform of $h(m,n)$ is, in general, an aliased version of the Fourier transform of $h(x,y)$. This effect may be neglected if the sampling interval Δ is small enough.

There are two sources of noise in the case of scanned photographic images. They are:

(i) film grain noise, and

(ii) quantization noise. Images recorded on photographic film are generally affected by film-grain noise, $v_f(m,n)$. The film grain noise originates from the randomness in silver deposition which can be modeled by a Poisson distribution. This distribution can be approximated by a Gaussian distribution in the limit. The film grain noise is also known to be image/signal dependent. A more detailed treatment of film grain noise can be found in *Huang* [8.7]. Digital images are also affected by quantization noise, $v_q(m,n)$. The quantization noise can be modeled by a zero-mean, white Gaussian random field that is independent of the image signal.

Then, a general model for the noise present in scanned photographic images can be expressed as

$$v_d(m,n) = v_f(m,n) + v_q(m,n) \ . \tag{8.11}$$

We note that $v_d(m,n)$ is additive in the optical density domain. For practical purposes, in this chapter, we model the effect of the combined noise, $v_d(m,n)$, to some degree of accuracy, by a white Gaussian random field, independent of the image signal in the optical density domain, with zero-mean and unknown variance $\sigma_{v_d}^2$. In fact, it was suggested in [8.8] that not much improvement can be obtained by modeling the noise as signal-dependent in the image estimation problems.

Hence, the degradation model in the optical density domain including the effect of the noise can be written as

$$r_d(m,n) = \alpha \log\{h(m,n) * * s_e(m,n)\} + \beta + v_d(m,n) \ , \tag{8.12}$$

where $r_d(m,n)$ represents the observed noisy version of the blurred image. We observe from (8.12) that the relationship between the scanned photographic image

$r_d(m,n)$ and the samples of the original object (scene) $s_e(m,n)$ is nonlinear due to the presence of the logarithm.

In practice, scanners also introduce nonlinear distortions. The output of the scanner is an integer code value between 0 and $2^B - 1$, where B is the number of bits per pixel. The relationship between the output code value and the optical density, for a particular scanner, is generally known as the scanner calibration table. In the following, we assume that the calibration table of the scanner is known, and the image code values have been converted into the corresponding optical density values $r_d(m,n)$ appropriately.

8.3 Restoration of Photographic Images: Theory

In the following, we propose a new approach in order to incorporate the model (8.6) of the sensor nonlinearity into the restoration procedure. Unlike other researchers [8.1–4], we show that it is possible to obtain significantly better restorations by including the nonlinear film characteristics into the restoration procedure. Moreover, the computational load of the proposed method is almost the same as the computational load of filtering without including the nonlinearity.

8.3.1 The Domain for Deconvolution

In the observation equation (8.12) there exists a nonlinear relationship between the observed pixel values $r_d(m,n)$ and the original pixel values $s_e(m,n)$. As a first step in processing, we would like to transform the observed image in order to have a linear convolutional relationship between the transformed observations and the original image.

To this effect, we transform the observed blurred and noisy image into the exposure domain using the inverse of the model (8.6), which is

$$E(D) = 10^{(D-\beta)/\alpha} . \tag{8.13}$$

Applying (8.13) to the observation model (8.12), we obtain

$$r_e(m,n) = v_e(m,n)[h(m,n) ** s_e(m,n)] , \tag{8.14}$$

where $v_e(m,n) = 10^{v_d(m,n)/\alpha}$, and $r_e(m,n)$ denotes the observations in the exposure domain. Therefore, we observe that the additive observation noise in the density domain manifests itself as multiplicative noise in the exposure domain.

In transforming the image into the exposure domain our main goal has been establishing a linear convolutional relationship between $s_e(m,n)$ and $r_e(m,n)$. Since the transformation (8.13) is a function of the parameters α and β which may not be readily available, we show here the effect of using incorrect parameter values on the form of the model (8.14), i.e., we analyze the sensitivity of the linear convolutional model (8.14) to the inaccuracies in the parameters of the nonlinearity.

Let

$$\alpha' = \alpha + \epsilon$$

and

$$\beta' = \beta + \delta \tag{8.15}$$

where α' and β' indicate the estimates for the parameters α and β and ϵ and δ denote the inaccuracies in the estimates, respectively.

Then (8.13) can be expressed as

$$E(D) = 10^{(D-\beta')/\alpha'} . \tag{8.16}$$

Applying (8.16) to the observation model (8.12), we have

$$r'_{\mathrm{e}}(m,n) = v'_{\mathrm{e}}(m,n)[h(m,n) * * s_{\mathrm{e}}(m,n)]^{\alpha/\alpha'} , \tag{8.17}$$

where $v'_{\mathrm{e}}(m,n) = 10^{(v_{\mathrm{d}}(m,n)+\delta)/\alpha'}$, and $r'_{\mathrm{e}}(m,n)$ denotes the observations in the exposure domain using uncertain parameters.

Hence, we observe from (8.17) that we need to have $\alpha' = \alpha$ in order to establish a linear convolution expression in the exposure domain. This requires that the film type must be known prior to filtering which is usually the case if a negative is available for scanning. The sensitivity of the restoration results to the parameters α and β is discussed experimentally in Sect. 8.5. In the following, we assume that the true values of α and β are available.

8.3.2 Deconvolution with Multiplicative Noise

In this section, we derive the linear minimum mean square error filter (the Wiener filter) for deconvolution in the exposure domain in the presence of multiplicative observation noise based on (8.14).

It is well-known that the 2D Wiener filter has the frequency domain transfer function [8.11, p. 355]

$$\mathcal{W}(\omega_1,\omega_2) = \frac{S_{s_{\mathrm{e}}r_{\mathrm{e}}}(\omega_1,\omega_2)}{S_{r_{\mathrm{e}}r_{\mathrm{e}}}(\omega_1,\omega_2)} , \tag{8.18}$$

where $S_{s_{\mathrm{e}}r_{\mathrm{e}}}(\omega_1,\omega_2)$ is the cross power spectral density of the original image $s_{\mathrm{e}}(m,n)$ and the observed image $r_{\mathrm{e}}(m,n)$, $S_{r_{\mathrm{e}}r_{\mathrm{e}}}(\omega_1,\omega_2)$ is the power spectral density of the observed image $r_{\mathrm{e}}(m,n)$. The specific form of the expressions for $S_{s_{\mathrm{e}}r_{\mathrm{e}}}(\omega_1,\omega_2)$ and $S_{r_{\mathrm{e}}r_{\mathrm{e}}}(\omega_1,\omega_2)$ depends on the particular observation model that is being used. The derivation of the Wiener filter for our problem requires the evaluation of $S_{s_{\mathrm{e}}r_{\mathrm{e}}}(\omega_1,\omega_2)$ and $S_{r_{\mathrm{e}}r_{\mathrm{e}}}(\omega_1,\omega_2)$ from the observation model (8.14).

Hence, we first evaluate the cross-correlation function

$$\begin{aligned} R_{s_{\mathrm{e}}r_{\mathrm{e}}}(i,j) &= \mathcal{E}\{s_{\mathrm{e}}(m,n)r_{\mathrm{e}}(m-i,n-j)\} \\ &= \sum_{kl} h(k,l)\mathcal{E}\{v_{\mathrm{e}}(m-i,n-j)s_{\mathrm{e}}(m,n)s_{\mathrm{e}}(m-i-k,n-j-l)\} . \end{aligned}$$

If we assume that the observation noise $v_e(m,n)$ and the image signal $s_e(m,n)$ are independent and $v_e(m,n)$ is wide-sense stationary, then we have

$$\begin{aligned} R_{s_e r_e}(i,j) &= \sum_{kl} h(k,l)\mathcal{E}\{s_e(m,n)s_e(m-i-k,n-j-l)\} \\ &\quad \mathcal{E}\{v_e(m-i,n-j)\} \\ &= \mathcal{E}\{v_e(i,j)\}\sum_{kl} h(k,l)R_{s_e s_e}(i+k,j+l)\ , \end{aligned} \tag{8.19}$$

where $R_{s_e r_e}(i,j)$ is the autocorrelation of the original image.

Next, we evaluate the autocorrelation of the degraded image

$$\begin{aligned} R_{r_e r}(i,j) &= \mathcal{E}\{r_e(m,n)r_e(m-i,n-j)\} \\ &= \sum_{kl}\sum_{op} h_{kl}h_{op}\mathcal{E}\{v_e(m,n)v_e(m-i,n-j) \\ &\quad s_e(m-k,n-l)s_e(m-i-o,n-j-p)\}\ . \end{aligned}$$

Under the assumption that the signal and noise are independent, we get

$$R_{r_e r_e}(i,j) = R_{v_e v_e}(i,j)\sum_{k,l}\sum_{op} h_{kl}h_{op}R_{s_e s_e}(i+o-k,j+p-l)\ , \tag{8.20}$$

where $R_{v_e v_e}(i,j)$ is the autocorrelation of the noise process in the exposure domain.

We can express the frequency response of the Wiener filter in the presence of multiplicative noise with arbitrary distribution, by taking the Fourier transforms of (8.19) and (8.20), and substituting into (8.18), as

$$\mathcal{W}_M(\omega_1,\omega_2) = \frac{\mathcal{E}\{v_e(m,n)\}H^*(\omega_1,\omega_2)S_{s_e s_e}(\omega_1,\omega_2)}{\{|H(\omega_1,\omega_2)|^2 S_{s_e s_e}(\omega_1,\omega_2)\} **S_{v_e v_e}(\omega_1,\omega_2)}\ . \tag{8.21}$$

We note that we assumed that the signal and the noise are independent in order to arrive at (8.19) and (8.20). Otherwise, one would have to deal with third order and fourth order cross correlations of the signal and noise processes.

We then compute the mean of the noise process $\mathcal{E}\{v_e(m,n)\}$ and its power spectral density $S_{v_e v_e}(\omega_1,\omega_2)$ in order to obtain the Wiener filter frequency response for the particular multiplicative noise $v_e(m,n)$. Given that the observation noise in the optical density domain, $v_d(m,n)$, is white, Gaussian with zero mean and variance $\sigma^2_{v_d}$,

$$\begin{aligned} \mathcal{E}\{v_e(m,n)\} &= \mathcal{E}\left\{e^{v_d(m,n)\ln 10/\alpha}\right\} \\ &= \frac{1}{\sqrt{2\pi}\sigma_{v_d}}\int_{-\infty}^{\infty} e^{v_d(m,n)\ln 10/\alpha}\, e^{-v_d(m,n)^2/2\sigma^2_{v_d}}\, dv_d \\ &= \frac{1}{\sqrt{2\pi}\sigma_{v_d}} e^{\sigma^2_{v_d}\ln^2 10/2\alpha^2}\int_{-\infty}^{\infty}\exp\left\{-\frac{\left[v_d(m,n)-(\sigma^2_{v_d}\ln 10/\alpha)\right]^2}{2\sigma^2_{v_d}}\right\} dv_d \\ &= e^{\sigma^2_{v_d}\ln^2 10/2\alpha^2} \end{aligned} \tag{8.22}$$

Since $v_d(m,n)$ and $v_d(k,l)$ are jointly Gaussian, we can write

$$
\begin{aligned}
R_{v_e v_e}(i,j) &= \mathcal{E}\{v_e(m,n)v_e(m-i,n-j)\} \\
&= \begin{cases} \mathcal{E}\left\{v_e^2(m,n)\right\} & \text{for } i=0 \text{ and } j=0 \\ \mathcal{E}\{v_e(m,n)\}^2 & \text{otherwise} . \end{cases}
\end{aligned} \tag{8.23}
$$

Then,

$$
\begin{aligned}
\mathcal{E}\left\{v_e^2(m,n)\right\} &= \mathcal{E}\left\{e^{2v_d(m,n)\ln 10/\alpha}\right\} \\
&= \frac{1}{\sqrt{2\pi}\sigma_{v_d}} \int_{-\infty}^{\infty} e^{2v_d(m,n)\ln 10/\alpha} e^{-v_d(m,n)^2/2\sigma_{v_d}^2} dv_d \\
&= \frac{1}{\sqrt{2\pi}\sigma_{v_d}} e^{2\sigma_{v_d}^2 \ln^2 10/\alpha^2} \int_{-\infty}^{\infty} \exp\left\{-\frac{\left[v_d(m,n)-(2\sigma_{v_d}^2 \ln 10/\alpha^2)\right]^2}{2\sigma_{v_d}^2}\right\} dv_d \\
&= e^{2\sigma_{v_d}^2 \ln^2 10/\alpha^2} .
\end{aligned} \tag{8.24}
$$

If we let $\gamma = \exp(\sigma_{v_d}^2 \ln^2 10/\alpha^2)$, we can express

$$
R_{v_e v_e}(i,j) = (\gamma^2 - \gamma)\delta(i,j) + \gamma , \tag{8.25}
$$

where $\delta(i,j)$ is the 2D Kronecker delta function. Hence, the corresponding power spectral density is

$$
\begin{aligned}
S_{v_e v_e}(\omega_1,\omega_2) &= \mathcal{F}\{R_{v_e v_e}(i,j)\} \\
&= (\gamma^2 - \gamma) + \gamma\delta(\omega_1,\omega_2) .
\end{aligned} \tag{8.26}
$$

Given (8.21–26), the frequency response of the Wiener filter in the presence of the particular multiplicative noise $v_e(m,n)$ can be expressed as

$$
\begin{aligned}
&\mathcal{W}_M(\omega_1,\omega_2) \\
&= \left(\frac{1}{\sqrt{\gamma}}\right) \frac{H^*(\omega_1,\omega_2)S_{s_e s_e}(\omega_1,\omega_2)}{|H(\omega_1,\omega_2)|^2 S_{s_e s_e}(\omega_1,\omega_2) + (\gamma-1)\{\overline{|H(\omega_1,\omega_2)|^2 S_{s_e s_e}(\omega_1,\omega_2)}\}} ,
\end{aligned} \tag{8.27}
$$

where $\overline{X(.,.)}$ denotes averaging over all values of the independent variables.

We can make the following observations about the filter $\mathcal{W}_M(\omega_1,\omega_2)$:

(i) The filter frequency response (8.21) becomes identically zero if the mean of the multiplicative noise process is zero. However, by (8.22), $\mathcal{E}\{v_e(m,n)\}$ is always greater than or equal to one, and the equality occurs only if there is no observation noise in the density domain.

(ii) If the mean of the multiplicative noise is not equal to 1, then the mean of the observations is different from the mean of the signal by (8.14). Hence, the restoration filter, in general, has a DC-gain to compensate for this effect.

(iii) Recall that, the Wiener filter in the case of additive, white Gaussian noise (with zero mean and variance σ_v^2) which is uncorrelated with the signal is given by

$$\mathcal{W}_A(\omega_1,\omega_2) = \frac{H^*(\omega_1,\omega_2)S_{ss}(\omega_1,\omega_2)}{|H(\omega_1,\omega_2)|^2 S_{ss}(\omega_1,\omega_2) + \sigma_v^2} \ . \tag{8.28}$$

We observe that the optimal linear filter, $\mathcal{W}_{\mathcal{M}}$, in the case of the particular type of multiplicative noise $v_e(m,n) = 10^{v_d(m,n)/\alpha}$, where $v_d(m,n)$ is zero-mean, Gaussian and uncorrelated with the signal, differs from the filter $\mathcal{W}_A$ by a DC gain $1/\sqrt{\gamma}$ and in the noise power factor, $(\gamma - 1)\{\overline{|H(\omega_1,\omega_2)|^2 S_{s_e s_e}(\omega_1,\omega_2)}\}$. However, for multiplicative noise with other statistics, it is possible to obtain filter structures, from (8.18), that are considerably different from $\mathcal{W}_A$.

(iv) Although the filter $\mathcal{W}_{\mathcal{M}}$ is linear in the exposure domain, the effect of the overall restoration procedure is nonlinear in the observed image.

8.3.3 Suboptimal Restoration in the Exposure Domain

In Sect. 8.3.2, we derived the optimal linear filter in the exposure domain for the restoration of blurred photographic images given the multiplicative nature of the observation noise. Our goal in this subsection is to derive suboptimal filters in the exposure domain based on different assumptions and approximations on the effect of the observation noise. We expect that this subsection serves the reader to reach an understanding of how the restoration results vary with different approximations on the observation noise, or in other words how sensitive the restoration results are to certain approximations on the nature of observation noise. The reader may choose to skip this subsection without any loss of continuity.

We consider two approximations on the observation noise:

(i) approximation by additive, signal-dependent noise,

(ii) approximation by additive, signal-independent noise. In the second case, we clearly obtain the well-known Wiener filter expression (8.28) in the exposure domain. Hence, we will not elaborate on this assumption.

In order to derive the Wiener filter under the first approximation, we first show that it is possible to express the multiplicative observation noise in terms of additive but signal-dependent noise using a Taylor series expansion of the observation noise process $v_e(m,n)$. It is well-known that the Taylor series expansion for e^{ax} around $x = 0$ is given by

$$e^{ax} = \sum_{n=0}^{\infty} \frac{(ax)^n}{n!} \ .$$

Hence,

$$\begin{aligned} v_e(m,n) &= 10^{v_d(m,n)/\alpha} \\ &= e^{\ln 10 \, v_d(m,n)/\alpha} \\ &= \sum_{n=0}^{\infty} \frac{(\ln 10 \ v_d(m,n))^n}{\alpha^n n!} \ . \end{aligned} \tag{8.29}$$

Substituting (8.28) into (8.14), we have

$$r_e(m,n) = \sum_{kl} h(k,l)s_e(m-k,n-l)\left\{1 + \frac{\ln 10}{\alpha}v_d(m,n) + \frac{(\ln 10)^2}{\alpha^2 2!}v_d^2(m,n) + \cdots\right\} . \tag{8.30}$$

Then, we obtain an approximate observation model

$$r_e(m,n) = \sum_{kl} h(m,n)s_e(m-k,n-l) + v_e'(m,n) , \tag{8.31}$$

where

$$v_e'(m,n) = v_d(m,n)\frac{\ln 10}{\alpha}\sum_{kl} h(m,n)s_e(m-k,n-l)$$

by neglecting higher order terms (orders 2 and higher) in (8.30). Note that, in this approach, the observation noise $v_e'(m,n)$ appears as additive but signal dependent noise in the exposure domain.

Thus, the Wiener filter for deconvolution in the presence of additive, white, Gaussian, signal-dependent noise can be obtained from the approximate observation model (8.31). Under the assumption that the signal and the noise are independent in the optical density domain, and that the noise $v_d(m,n)$ is a zero mean random process, we can write

$$\begin{aligned} R_{s_e r_e}(i,j) &= \sum_{kl} h(k,l)\mathcal{E}\{s_e(m,n)s_e(m-i-k,n-j-l)\} \\ &+ \frac{\ln 10}{\alpha}\sum_{kl} h(k,l)\mathcal{E}\{s_e(m,n)s_e(m-i-k,n-j-l)v_d(m-i,n-j)\} \\ &= \sum_{kl} h(k,l)R_{s_e s_e}(i+k,j+l) , \end{aligned} \tag{8.32}$$

and

$$\begin{aligned} R_{r_e r_e}(i,j) &= \sum_{kl}\sum_{op} h(k,l)h(o,p)\mathcal{E}\left\{ s_e(m-k,n-l)s_e(m-i-o,n-j-p)\right. \\ &\quad\times\left.\left(1+\frac{\ln 10}{\alpha}v_d(m,n)\right)\left(1+\frac{\ln 10}{\alpha}v_d(m-i,n-j)\right)\right\} \\ &= \sum_{kl}\sum_{op} h(k,l)h(o,p)R_{s_e s_e}(i+o-k,j+p-l) \\ &\quad\times\left(1+\left(\frac{\ln 10}{\alpha}\right)^2 R_{v_d v_d}(i,j)\right) . \end{aligned} \tag{8.33}$$

The corresponding power spectral densities can be expressed as

$$S_{r_e s_e}(\omega_1,\omega_2) = H^*(\omega_1,\omega_2)S_{s_e s_e}(\omega_1,\omega_2) \tag{8.34}$$

and

$$S_{r_e r_e}(\omega_1, \omega_2) = |H(\omega_1, \omega_2)|^2 S_{s_e s_e}(\omega_1, \omega_2) + \left(\frac{\ln 10}{\alpha}\right)^2 \left[|H(\omega_1, \omega_2)|^2 S_{s_e s_e}(\omega_1, \omega_2)\right] ** S_{v_d v_d}(\omega_1, \omega_2) , \tag{8.35}$$

which results in the following frequency response for the Wiener filter

$$\begin{aligned} \mathcal{W}_B(\omega_1, \omega_2) &= \frac{H^*(\omega_1, \omega_2) S_{s_e s_e}(\omega_1, \omega_2)}{|H(\omega_1, \omega_2)|^2 S_{s_e s_e}(\omega_1, \omega_2) + (\ln 10/\alpha)^2 \{|H(\omega_1, \omega_2)|^2 S_{s_e s_e}(\omega_1, \omega_2)\} ** \sigma_{v_d}^2 \delta(\omega_1, \omega_2)} \\ &\frac{H^*(\omega_1, \omega_2) S_{s_e s_e}(\omega_1, \omega_2)}{|H(\omega_1, \omega_2)|^2 S_{s_e s_e}(\omega_1, \omega_2) + (\sigma_{v_d} \ln 10/\alpha)^2 \{\overline{|H(\omega_1, \omega_2)|^2 S_{s_e s_e}(\omega_1, \omega_2)}\}} . \end{aligned} \tag{8.36}$$

We note that the filter (8.36) differs from the optimal filter (8.27) in the DC gain and the noise power factor.

8.4 Restoration of Photographic Images: Practice

In practice, it is not possible to restore every blurred image, although a wide range of blurred images can be restored. There are several factors that make the restoration of photographically blurred images a very difficult task, in general.

The first step towards the restoration of a degraded image is to identify the kind of degradation that the image has suffered. If there is no available information whatsoever about the source of the blur and the noise, then this may be a very difficult problem. We discuss the problem of blur identification in Sect. 8.4.1. The estimation of the noise variance and other filter parameters are discussed in Sect. 8.4.2. We discuss some practical limitations in the restoration of photographically blurred images in Sect. 8.4.3.

8.4.1 Blur Identification

Our goal in this section is not to provide an in-depth overview of existing blur identification methods, but it is to outline the method that we used to obtain the results that are shown in Sect. 8.5, and also to list other options for blur identification.

As mentioned earlier, the most common sources of blur are out-of-focus imaging systems and relative motion between the object and film planes. Fortunately, it is possible to develop parametric models for the PSF representing these blurs from an understanding of the physical model of the blur generation. Hence, under the assumption that the image is degraded by either the uniform motion blur or the out-of-focus blur, the blur identification problem reduces to first selecting the appropriate parametric form for the PSF, and then identifying the parameters characterizing it. Of course, if we cannot satisfactorily match any of the parametric PSFs to the given blurred and noisy image, we classify the case as unsuccessful. We discuss the factors leading to unsuccessful cases in Sect. 8.4.3. In the following, we first discuss the parametric PSFs for the out-of-focus and relative motion blurs.

a) Out-of-focus blur. The PSF of an out-of-focus blur can be reasonably well-approximated by a uniform function having a circular support in the continuous spatial domain. It can be expressed as

$$h(x, y) = \begin{cases} 1/2\pi R^2, & \text{if } x^2 + y^2 \leq R^2 \\ 0, & \text{otherwise} \end{cases} \tag{8.37}$$

where R is the radius of the support. In other words, the image of a point object under an out-of-focus imaging system can be approximated by a uniform disc. This is illustrated in Figs. 8.1,2. In this case, there is only one parameter that characterizes the PSF, the radius R. In practice, the profile of the PSF may deviate slightly from the assumed uniform model. However, our results indicate that we can obtain successful restorations using the uniform PSF.

The Fourier transform, $H(u, v)$, of the PSF, $h(x, y)$ given by (8.37), can be expressed as

$$H(u, v) = 2\pi R \frac{J_1(R\sqrt{u^2 + v^2})}{\sqrt{u^2 + v^2}} \tag{8.38}$$

where $J_1(.)$ stands for the Bessel function of the first kind of order 1. Note that $H(u, v)$ is a circularly symmetric function. Hence, the information about the zero crossings of $H(u, v)$ is contained in a 1D plot of $H(u, 0)$. The magnitude of $H(u, 0)$, where u is sampled with 256 values between 0 and π, is depicted in Fig. 8.4.

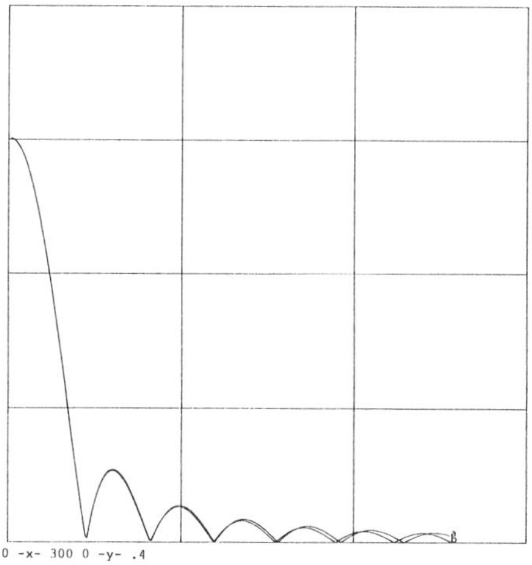

Fig. 8.4. (**a**) The line corresponding to $w_2 = 0$ from the 2D Fourier magnitude of the discrete circular PSF; (**b**) the same line from the 2D Fourier magnitude of the continuous uniform circular PSFt

The PSF $h(m,n)$ that models the blur in the discrete coordinates can be evaluated from (8.37) through (8.10). Note that (8.10) implies that the coefficients of the discrete PSF correspond to the area under the continuous PSF in the respective sampling grids. Because of the approximation errors and the aliasing effects, the Fourier transform $\tilde{H}(u,v)$ of the discrete PSF, $h(m,n)$, deviates from $H(u,v)$ slightly. The samples of the magnitude of $\tilde{H}(u,0)$, obtained by a 512×512 DFT, are also shown in Fig. 8.4. Note that this plot contains the desired information about the zero crossings.

b) Uniform Linear Motion Blur. The PSF of a one-dimensional uniform linear motion blur can be represented by a box-car function, if we assume that the motion is with constant velocity and there is no angle between the object and image planes. The PSF can be expressed as

$$h(x,y) = \begin{cases} 1/A, & \text{if } -A/2 \leq x \leq A/2 \text{ and } y = 0 \\ 0, & \text{otherwise} \end{cases} \tag{8.39}$$

where A is the extent of the blur. Physically, the extent of the blur depends on the relative velocity between the object and image planes and the duration during which the shutter remains open. In other words, a point object is smeared in the image plane due to relative motion. Again in this case there is only one parameter, the extent of the blur A, that characterizes the PSF.

The Fourier transform of the box-car function is given by

$$H(u,v) = \frac{\sin(\pi \frac{A}{2} u)}{\pi \frac{A}{2} u} . \tag{8.40}$$

Hence, the information about the zero crossings of $H(u,v)$ is contained in a 1D plot of $H(u,0)$.

We can approximate the PSF $h(m,n)$ that models the blur in discrete coordinates by

$$h(m,n) = \begin{cases} 1/N_1, & \text{if } -N_1/2 \leq m \leq N_1/2 \text{ and } n = 0 \\ 0, & \text{otherwise} \end{cases} \tag{8.41}$$

where N_1 and A are related through the sampling distance Δ.

The Fourier transform $\tilde{H}(u,v)$ of $h(m,n)$ can be expressed as

$$\tilde{H}(u,v) = \frac{\sin\left[u\left(N_1 + \frac{1}{2}\right)\right]}{\sin\left(\frac{u}{2}\right)} . \tag{8.42}$$

Hence, $\tilde{H}(u,v)$ exhibits aliasing effects around high frequencies. However a 1D plot of $\tilde{H}(u,0)$ contains the desired information about the zero crossings.

As we have seen above, both the out-of-focus blur and the uniform motion blur can be well-characterized by PSFs which contain only one parameter. In our experiments, we identify the parameter of the PSF in the frequency domain, after transforming the image into the exposure domain, using a method proposed by *Gennery* [8.12]. A related cepstral domain method for blur identification was developed by *Cannon* [8.13].

We can justify the use of the methods [8.12, 13] in the exposure domain, in the presence of multiplicative observation noise, as follows: The power spectrum $S_{r_e r_e}(w_1, w_2)$ of the observed image in the intensity domain, as derived in Sect. 8.3.2, can be given by

$$S_{r_e r_e}(w_1, w_2) = |H(\omega_1, \omega_2)|^2 S_{s_e s_e}(\omega_1, \omega_2)\} * * S_{v_e v_e}(\omega_1, \omega_2) \,. \tag{8.43}$$

Note that the multiplicative observation noise in (8.14) appears as a convolutional factor in the spectral domain equation (8.43). Under the modeling assumptions, we showed in Sect. 8.3.2 that (8.43) can be further simplified as

$$S_{r_e r_e}(w_1, w_2) = |H(\omega_1, \omega_2)|^2 S_{s_e s_e}(\omega_1, \omega_2) + (\gamma - 1)\{\overline{|H(\omega_1, \omega_2)|^2 S_{s_e s_e}(\omega_1, \omega_2)}\} \tag{8.44}$$

where $\gamma = \exp(\sigma_{v_d}^2 \ln^2 10/\alpha^2)$ and $\overline{X(.,.)}$ denotes averaging over all values of the independent variables. We observe from (8.44) that the multiplicative observation noise introduces a constant bias term to the power spectral density of the observed degraded image. This is the same effect that we observe in the case of additive white observation noise. Note that both of the techniques [8.12] and [8.13] are, in fact, deterministic techniques in the sense that they do not take the presence of observation noise into account explicitly.

In order to identify the parameter of the PSF in the spectral domain, we make the following assumptions [8.12, 13]:

(i) The "original" image signal spectrum does not have zero-crossings.
(ii) The effect of the observation noise does not mask the desired information.

From (8.44), we see that the effect of the observation noise, in the spectral domain, manifests itself as an additive constant term, which we refer as "intensity domain noise level" in the following.

Hence, the zero crossings in the spectrum of the observed blurred and noisy image, if any, can be attributed to the zero crossings in the Fourier magnitude of the blur PSF. As mentioned above, both the out-of-focus blur and uniform linear motion blur possess characteristic zeros in their Fourier magnitudes. In fact, it is sufficient to detect just the first zero-crossing frequency in both cases. As a matter of fact, it is often easy to detect the first zero crossing, and more difficult to detect the zero crossings at higher frequencies, since the signal to noise ratio is lower at high frequencies. The parameter of the PSF can be found from the frequency of the first zero crossing in these cases as follows.

In the case of the out-of-focus blur, the radius of the circle can be found from

$$R = \frac{3.83(NFFT)}{2\pi K} \tag{8.45}$$

where 3.83 corresponds to the first zero crossing of the normalized Bessel function of the first kind of order 1, $NFFT$ is the size of the fast Fourier transform, and K

is the frequency where the first zero crossing in the spectrum of the blurred image is detected.

In the case of the uniform linear motion blur, the extent of the blur can be found from

$$A = \frac{(NFFT)}{K} \tag{8.46}$$

where K is the frequency of the first zero crossing as above. If no zero crossings can be detected the method is unsuccessful.

In our experiments, we found that, in general, it is not possible to identify the parameter of the PSF for blurred photographic images using these techniques in the optical density or code value domains. However, we observed that these techniques work reasonably well to identify real blurred images, in the *exposure domain*, with 20 dB or higher signal-to-noise ratio which is the case when we used Kodak VR-G 200 film and 8 bit quantization. Hence, the incorporation of the film $d - \log e$ curve, plays an important role in blur identification as well as in the restoration.

The cepstral domain method is a straightforward extension of the spectral method. *Cannon* [8.13] reports that it is possible to distinguish between the uniform linear motion blur and the out-of-focus blur by inspecting the cepstral domain information.

If it is not possible to detect any zero crossings in power spectral density of the degraded image, then we suggest using a spatial domain blur identification technique. For example, the atmospheric turbulence blur is usually modeled by a PSF in the form of a truncated Gaussian function. Hence, its Fourier-magnitude function does not have any zero crossings if the effect of the truncation is not significant. Spatial domain blur identification using ARMA modeling of the blurred and noisy images was first proposed by *Tekalp* et al. [8.14, 15]. Maximum likelihood formulation in the presence of noise and the EM algorithm implementations were later studied [8.16], see also Chap. 6.

8.4.2 Estimation of Other Filter Parameters and Procedure

In this section we first consider the estimation of the other filter parameters, which are the variance of the observation noise in the optical density domain and the power spectral density of the original image in the exposure domain. We then summarize the procedure for the restoration of photographic blurred images.

a) Estimation of the Noise Variance. We estimate the variance of the observation noise in the optical density domain, since the noise is additive in that domain. As is usually the case, we choose a segment of the image where the image is more or less uniform. We estimate the variance of this segment as the variance of the observation noise.

b) Estimation of the Power Spectrum of the Image. There are two approaches to estimate the power spectrum of the original image:

(i) Estimate the power spectrum of the image from a similar prototype,

(ii) Approximate the power spectrum of the original image with that of the noisy and blurred image. We have chosen the second approach to obtain the results shown in Sect. 8.5. In order to estimate the power spectrum of the observed image, there are again two approaches:

(i) nonparametric estimation, such as using the Welch's method,

(ii) parametric approach by first fitting an AR model to the observed image, and then using the parameters of this model to compute the power spectrum of the output of this model. In our experiments, we observed that the power spectrum estimate obtained by fitting a 1×1 nonsymmetric half plane (NSHP) AR model to the observed image is acceptable in order to obtain good restoration results. However, for certain images the nonparametric spectrum estimate yielded better restorations.

Finally, we summarize the proposed procedure for the restoration of noisy and blurred scanned photographic images as follows:

Procedure for Monochrome Images

1) Assuming that each pixel of the image is stored as a byte, i.e., as a code value that ranges between 0 and 255, we first convert the image from the code value domain to the corresponding optical density values using the calibration table of the scanner/digitizer.

2) We transform this density domain image into the exposure domain by using the $d - \log e$ curve of the film. The parameters α and β can be obtained by fitting a straight line to the $d - \log e$ curve, as shown in Fig. 8.3.

3) We restore the image in the exposure domain using the filter (8.27). In order to compute the filter frequency response, we use the estimates of the PSF of the blur, the parameter $\sigma^2_{v_\mathrm{d}}$, and the spectrum of the original image $S_{s_e s_e}(\omega_1, \omega_2)$ which are obtained as described above.

4) We display processed images in the optical density or exposure domains after proper scaling. We usually use linear min-max scaling, i.e., we scale the restored image linearly between the minimum and maximum values in the image.

Procedure for Color Images

In order to process color images, we either (i) process the red, green and blue channels independently in the exposure domain; or (ii) after step (2) we transform the image into the Y-I-Q domain [8.11, p. 423], and process the Y-component only in the "Y-exposure" domain. We then transform back to the red, green and blue exposure components after step 3.

8.4.3 Limitations in Restoring Photographically Blurred Images

The most important step in the restoration of photographic blurred images is the blur identification. In general, if we can accurately identify the blur, then we can restore it. We have stated in Sect. 8.4.1 that it is relatively easy to identify linear space invariant (LSI) out-of-focus and LSI uniform motion blurs. If the image is blurred due to one of these factors, and we have the negative (film) available for scanning, then we expect to be successful.

However, there are several limitations that lead to unsuccessful cases. Some of the limitations in restoring photographically blurred images are:

(i) The PSF of the blur, in general, varies spatially within an image. This is one of the most important limitations, since it necessiates blur identification at every pixel using the pixels within a neighborhood of that pixel under the assumption that blur PSF varies slowly in spatial coordinates. Sometimes it is even difficult to justify this assumption. There is also a trade off between having a big enough window for blur identification, and the validity of assumption that the PSF is stationary within the window.

(ii) There is observation noise. The presence of observation noise imposes a fundamental limitation on how much we can restore the resolution of the image before the filtered noise starts dominating the restored image. Also, the film grain noise is usually signal-dependent, which causes theoretical difficulties.

(iii) There are ringing artifacts in the restored image. The ringing artifacts are visually objectionable. Moreover, they sometimes mask important image information. It is possible to suppress ringing artifacts to a certain extent, however we need adaptive filtering algorithms which are computationally demanding.

(iv) The extent of the PSF of the blur should be, in general, at least an order of magnitude smaller than the size of the segment that we would like to restore. This poses a limitation in the processing of spatially variant blurs.

(v) One needs high resolution and high quality (hence, expensive) scanners to digitize blurred images in order to obtain good restoration results.

(vi) If a negative (film) is not available, one needs to take into account the printing conditions and the response of the photographic paper.

8.5 Results

We processed three scanned photographic images two of which are blurred due to an out-of-focus camera, the third image is blurred due to uniform linear motion of the object. These images are taken using a 35 mm Kodak VR-G 200 film. One of the out-of-focus images is a moderately blurred image of a car (shown in Fig. 8.5), whereas the other out-of-focus image is more severely blurred (shown in Fig. 8.6). These images were taken from two different distances with the same settings of the camera. We placed white frames on these images to indicate the area of interest. As can be seen, we are interested in reading the license plate of the car. It is

Fig. 8.5. The "license plate" image which is moderately blurred due to an out-of-focus camera, with the area of interest indicated by the frame

Fig. 8.6. The "license plate" image which is severely blurred due to an out-of-focus camera, with the area of interest indicated by the frame

possible to read the license plate of the car from the first blurred image, but the dealer's name is not readable. In the second image, the plate area appears almost at uniform brightness, and it is not possible to read any information at all. The image that is blurred due to uniform linear motion blur is shown in Fig. 8.7. This is a highly blurred image of a moving train. Again the white frame indicates the

Fig. 8.7. The "train" image which is blurred due to uniform horizontal motion of the train

area of interest. In the following, we process only the area of interest indicated on these images.

The images are scanned by using a microdensitometer (courtesy of Eastman Kodak Company). The scanner characteristics and the $d - \log e$ curve of the film are also provided by the Eastman Kodak Company. Note that the $d - \log e$ curve of the film is measured from the same roll of VR-G 200 photographic film.

The PSF of the out-of-focus blur is modeled by a uniform circle. For both images, the diameter of the circle, that indicates the severity of the blur, has been estimated by using the spectral method, explained in Sect. 8.4.1, in the exposure domain. We show in Fig. 8.8 b a plot of $log\{S_{r_e r_e}(w_1, 0)\}$ that is obtained from the exposure domain image in the case of moderately blurred license plate image. This plot clearly indicates a zero crossing that corresponds to $2\hat{R} = 14$, where $\hat{R}$ is the estimate of the radius. However, the same plot obtained from the density domain image, shown in Fig. 8.8 b, does not indicate any zero crossings. Thus, we see that the incorporation of the $d - \log e$ curve into the identification algorithm enables us to identify the blur in this case, which could not otherwise be identified in the density domain. Fig. 8.8 a shows the logarithm of the Fourier magnitude of a uniform function having a circular support with diameter 14 pixels. Figure 8.9 a–c shows the same set of results in a simulation experiment. In the simulation, we blurred a sharp image using a circular PSF with diameter 14 pixels in the exposure domain. Then, we converted the image back into density domain and added 17 dB observation noise in the density domain. Figure 8.9 b shows the result of blur identification in the exposure domain, whereas Fig. 8.9 c shows the result in the density domain. The results are very much similar to the results obtained on the real blurred image and indicates the necessity of incorporating the $d - \log e$ curve into blur identification.

We show in Fig. 8.10 b a plot of $log\{S_{r_e r_e}(w_1, 0)\}$ that is obtained from the exposure domain image in the case of severely blurred license plate. Figure 8.10 c

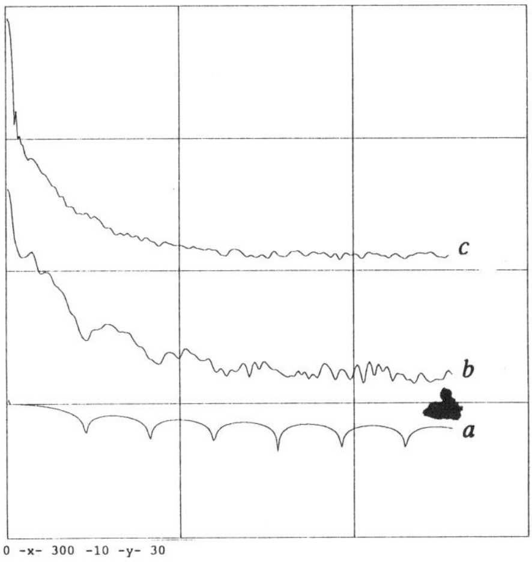

Fig. 8.8. Blur identification results on license plate image with moderate out-of-focus blur. (*a*) The logarithm of the Fourier magnitude of the discrete circular PSF with diameter 14 pixels; (*b*) the logarithm of the power spectrum of the observed image in the exposure domain; (*c*) the logarithm of the power spectrum of the observed image in the density domain

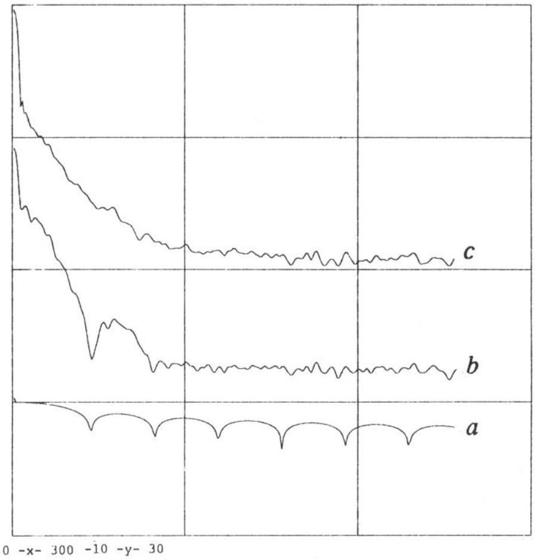

Fig. 8.9. Blur identification results on a simulated out-of-focus blur with D = 14 and 17 dB signal-to-noise ratio (*a*) the logarithm of the Fourier magnitude of the discrete circular PSF with diameter 14 pixels; (*b*) the logarithm of the power spectrum of the observed image in the exposure domain; (*c*) the logarithm of the power spectrum of the observed image in the density domain

shows the same plot obtained from the density domain image. Again note that the density domain plot does not show any indication of a zero-crossing. Hence, by inspection of this plot alone, we would have declared the case as unsuccessful. However, inspection of Fig. 8.10 b suggests that a zero crossing which corresponds to either $2\hat{R} = 19$ or $2\hat{R} = 23$ is present. We found by trial and error that $2\hat{R} =$

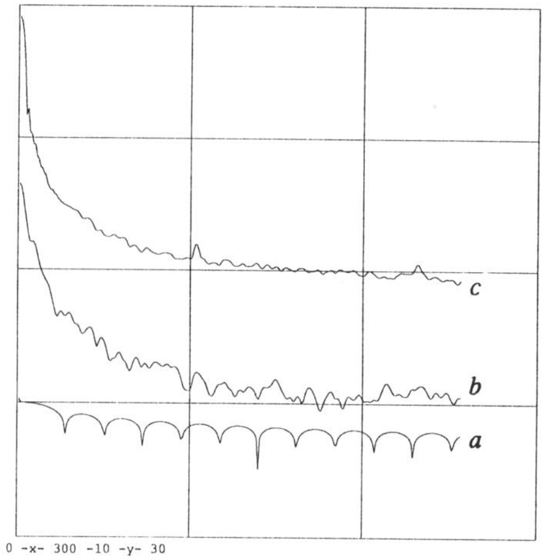

Fig. 8.10. Blur identification results on license plate image with severe out-of-focus blur: (*a*) the logarithm of the Fourier magnitude of the discrete circular PSF with diameter 23 pixels; (*b*) the logarithm of the power spectrum of the observed image in the exposure domain; (*c*) the logarithm of the power spectrum of the observed image in the density domain

Fig. 8.11. Moderately blurred photographic image: (**A**) displayed in density domain; (**B**) displayed in exposure domain; (**C**) restored image using the proposed filter displayed in exposure domain; (**D**) restored image using the conventional Wiener filter displayed in density domain

23 yields a better restoration. Figure 8.10 a shows the logarithm of the Fourier-magnitude of a uniform function having a circular support with diameter 23 pixels. We estimated the signal-to-noise ratio in both license plate images as 20 dB.

Application of our procedure to restore these images resulted in huge improvement in resolution. In the first case, the blurred image within the area of interest is shown in Figs. 8.11 A, B in the density and exposure domains, respectively. The

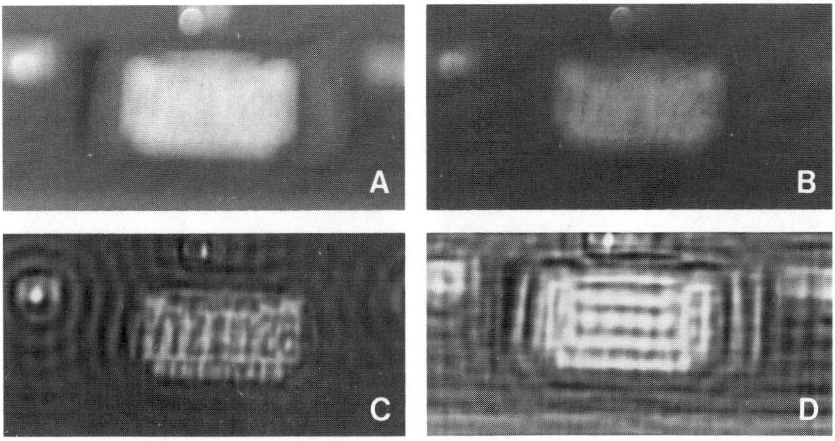

Fig. 8.12. Severely blurred photographic image: (A) displayed in density domain; (B) displayed in exposure domain; (C) restored image using the proposed filter displayed in exposure domain; (D) restored image using the conventional Wiener filter displayed in density domain

image that is restored by our new filter, (8.27), is shown in the exposure domain in Fig. 8.11 C. It is possible to read the dealer's name clearly from the restored image in the first case. We prefer to view the restored images in the exposure domain, because transforming the result back into the density domain sometimes amplifies the ringing artifacts. The result of restoration by the conventional Wiener filter in the density domain is shown in Fig. 8.11 D. The improvement obtained by using our procedure over using the conventional Wiener filter in the density domain is noteworthy.

In the second case, the blurred image within the area of interest is shown in Fig. 8.12 A, B in the density and exposure domains, respectively. The restored image using our procedure is shown in the exposure domain in Fig. 8.12 C, while Fig. 8.12 D shows the image that is restored by the conventional Wiener filter in the density domain. It is possible to read the license plate of the car after restoring the image using our filter, but the dealer's name is still unreadable. There is no visible improvement in the case of the conventional Wiener filter. Hence, this is a case where one cannot resolve the letters without using the $d - \log e$ curve of the film in the restoration process. It is not possible to give a numerical measure of the improvement in either case, since a perfectly registered "original" image is not available. We have also carried out the restoration in the exposure and density domains with a simulation example as outlined above. The results are very similar to the case of the real blur and verify the necessity of the use of the $d - \log e$ curve in restoring photographic blurred images.

In the case of the Train image degraded by the uniform linear motion blur, the blur identification results are shown in Fig. 8.13. Again, Fig. 8.13 b, c show the power spectrum of the degraded image in the exposure domain and the density domain, respectively. In this example, it is possible to successfully identify the

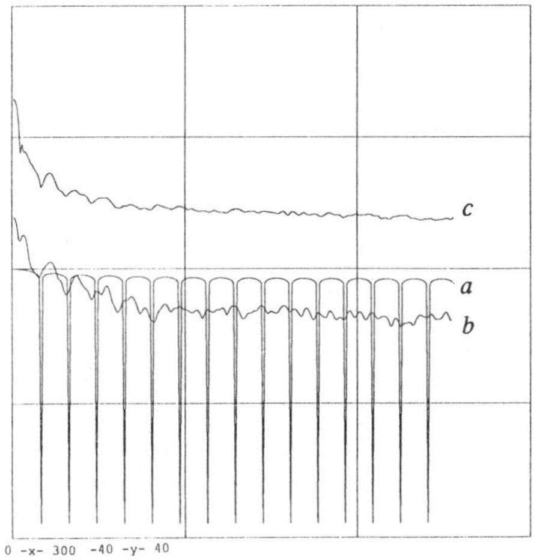

Fig. 8.13. Blur identification results on train image with uniform horizontal motion blur: (*a*) the logarithm of the Fourier magnitude of the discrete box-car PSF with extent 32 pixels; (*b*) the logarithm of the power spectrum of the observed image in the exposure domain; (*c*) the logarithm of the power spectrum of the observed image in the density domain

first zero crossing in both the exposure and density domains. We obtain $\hat{A} = 32$ in either domain. Figure 8.13 a shows the logarithm of the Fourier magnitude of the box-car PSF of extent 32 pixels. The blurred image within the area of interest is shown in Fig. 8.14 A, B in the density and exposure domains, respectively. The restored image using our procedure is shown in the exposure domain in Fig. 8.14 D, while Fig. 8.14 C shows the image that is restored by the conventional Wiener filter in the density domain. Although, the density domain restoration does improve the resolution for this image, the exposure domain restoration is still much better.

We conclude from these experiments that the best results are always obtained when the image is restored in the exposure domain. However, an improved image can sometimes be obtained even if the image is restored in the density domain. Our analysis indicates that if the histogram of the degraded image in the exposure domain is confined to a narrow exposure range close to zero, then the restoration obtained in the density domain may also be acceptable. This can be justified using the approximation $\log(1 + x) \approx x$, which holds for $|x| \ll 1$, where x denotes the exposure. In order to demonstrate that this is indeed the case, we show the histograms of the blurred "License plate" and "Train" images in the exposure domain in Fig. 8.15. In these figures, the x-axis is scaled from 0.0 to 1000.0, which correspond to 0.0 and 2.4 in the exposure scale, respectively, and the y-axis indicates the normalized frequencies of occurence of the respective x values. Figure 8.15 a, b show the histograms of the "License plate" images shown in Figs. 8.11 B and 8.12 B, respectively. In these images the exposure values are in the range 0.0095 to 2.13, and the approximation $\log(1 + x) \approx x$ is not valid. In the "Train" image, the exposure values are in the range 0.002 to 0.15, as can be seen from the

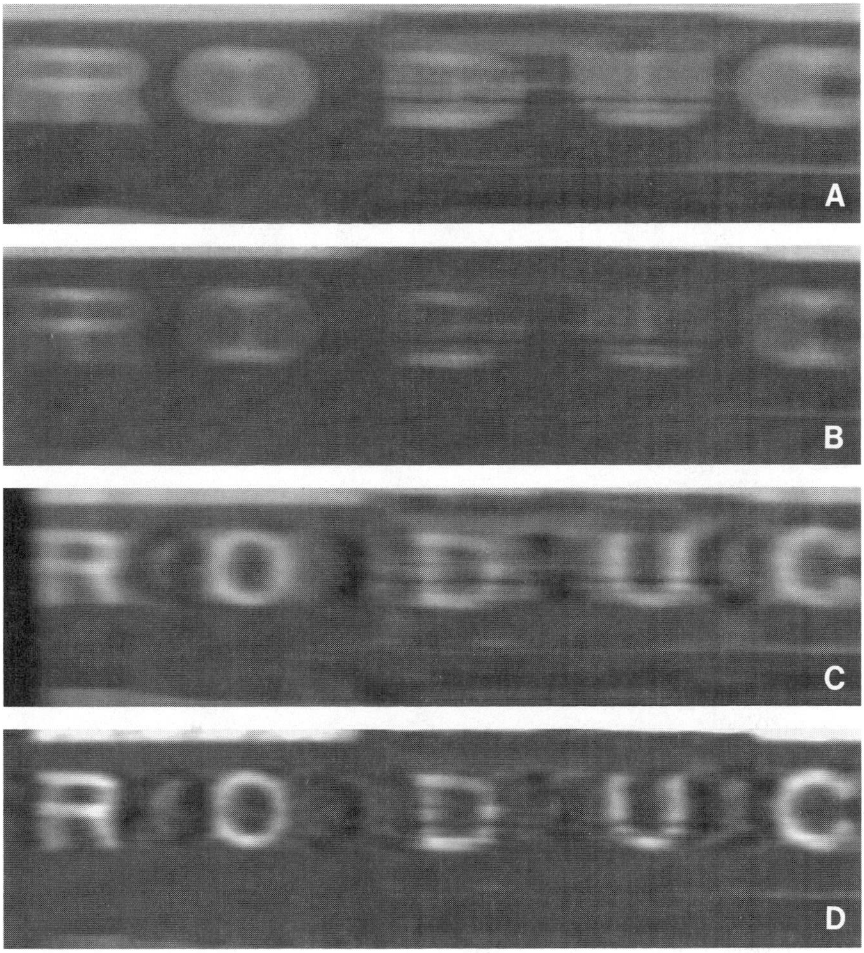

Fig. 8.14. (**A**) Blurred photographic image displayed in density domain; (**B**) blurred photographic image displayed in exposure domain; (**C**) restored image using the conventional Wiener filter displayed in density domain; (**D**) restored image using the proposed filter displayed in exposure domain

histogram which is depicted in Fig. 8.15 c. Hence, the approximation $\log(1+x) \approx x$ can be justified in this case.

Finally, in order to investigate the sensitivity of the results to the actual values of the parameters of the nonlinearity, we perturb the values of α and β, and use these values in the restoration procedure. We found that acceptable restoration results can be obtained within a $\pm 10\%$ range around the true parameter values.

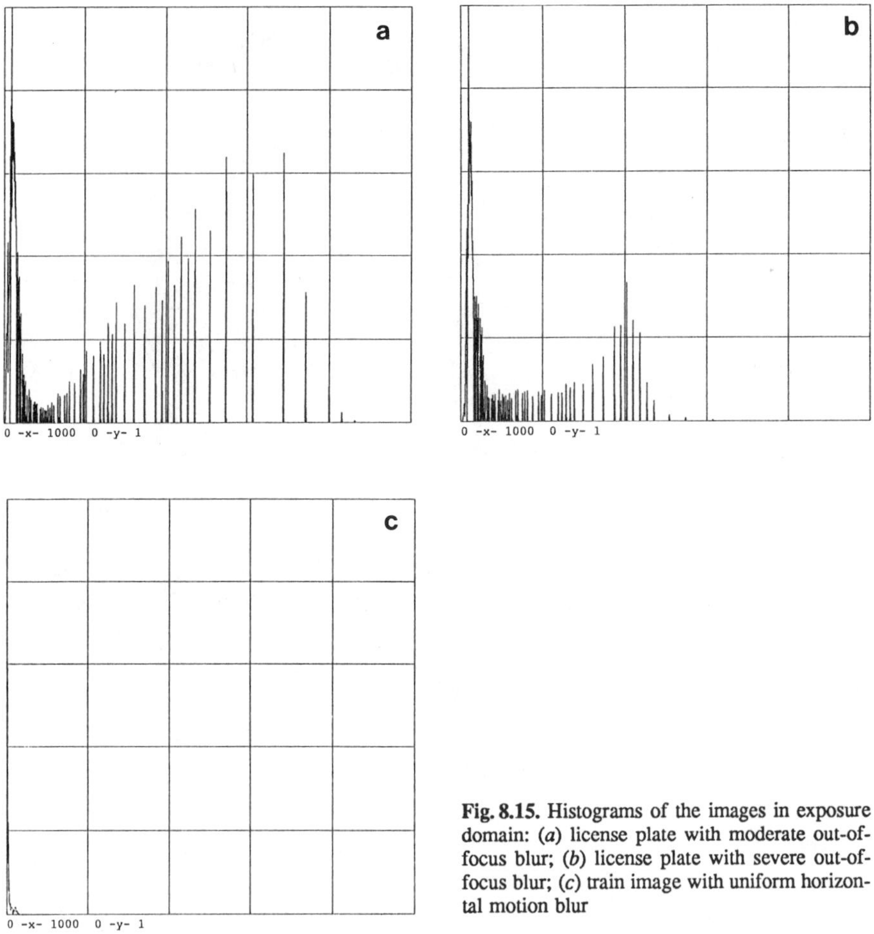

Fig. 8.15. Histograms of the images in exposure domain: (*a*) license plate with moderate out-of-focus blur; (*b*) license plate with severe out-of-focus blur; (*c*) train image with uniform horizontal motion blur

8.6 Conclusion

This chapter has offered two main contributions:

(i) We discuss the importance of incorporating the nonlinear sensor characteristics into the blur identification and image restoration procedures for the restoration of scanned photographic images. We provide a sensitivity analysis to show that a linear convolution relationship between the original and the observed images exists if and only if one uses the correct nonlinear sensor characteristics in the transformation. We also show that due to this transformation the observation noise manifests itself as multiplicative noise in the exposure domain.

(ii) We derive a linear minimum mean square error (LMMSE) deconvolution filter for the linear convolutional model in the presence of a particular type of multiplicative noise. The reader can use the same steps in order to derive the LMMSE deconvolution filter in the presence of multiplicative noise with other probability distributions.

We would like to comment that deconvolution in multiplicative noise differs from signal/image estimation in multiplicative noise. A common approach for signal estimation in multiplicative noise is to transform the multiplicative noise into additive noise using a homomorphic transformation [8.17]. This cannot be followed in the deconvolution problem since the homomorphic transformation, although results in additive noise, destroys the linear convolutional relationship. In fact, in this chapter, our motivation in dealing with the multiplicative noise has been obtaining a linear convolutional relationship between the original and degraded images.

The future research directions are the restoration of photographic images where the blur is space-variant, and the reduction of ringing artifacts in photographic blurred images. We are currently working on these problems.

Acknowledgements. This article is based upon research performed under grant number 88-IJ-CX-0038 from the National Institute of Justice and NSF grants MIP-8809291 and CDA-8820693. We extend our thanks to Eastman Kodak Company, and in particular to Dr. Ibrahim Sezan who helped us with scanning the photographic images used in this chapter and provided us with the data regarding the scanner calibration and the $d - \log e$ curve of the particular film.

References

8.1 H.C. Andrews, B.R. Hunt: *Digital Image Restoration*, (Prentice Hall, Englewood Cliffs, NJ 1977)

8.2 T.M. Cannon: "Digital Image Deblurring by Nonlinear Homomorphic Filtering," Ph.D. Thesis, University of Utah, Salt Lake City, Utah (1974)

8.3 H.J. Trussell, B.R. Hunt: "Improved Methods of Maximum A Posteriori Image Restoration," IEEE Trans. C-**27**, 57–62 (1979)

8.4 T.M. Cannon, H.J. Trussell, B.R. Hunt: "Comparison of Image Restoration Methods," Appl. Opt. **17**, 3384–3390 (1978)

8.5 D.L. Angwin, H. Kaufman: "Effects of Modeling Domains on Recursive Color Image Restoration," Proc. IEEE Int. Conf. Acoust., Speech and Sign. Proc., Dallas, Texas (1987)

8.6 A.W. Lohmann: "Image Formation and Multiplicative Noise," J. Opt. Soc. Am. **55**, 1030–1031 (1965)

8.7 T.S. Huang: "Some Notes on Film-Grain Noise," NASA Summer Study on Atmospheric Degradations, Woods Hole, Mass. (1968)

8.8 J.F. Walkup, R.C. Choens: "Image Processing in Signal-Dependent Noise," Opt. Eng. **13**, 258-266 (1974)

8.9 D. Kuan, A.A. Sawchuk, T.C. Strand, P. Chavel: "Adaptive Noise Smoothing Filter for Images with Signal-Dependent Noise," IEEE Trans. PAMI-**7**, 165-177 (1985)

8.10 C.R. Moloney, M.E. Jernigan: "Nonlinear Adaptive Restoration of Images with Multiplicative Noise," in Proc. IEEE Int. Conf. Acoust., Speech and Sign., Glasgow, Scotland (1989) pp. 1433–1436

8.11 J.S. Lim: *Two-Dimensional Signal and Image Processing*, (Prentice Hall, Englewood Cliffs, NJ 1990)

8.12 D.B. Gennery: "Determination of Optical Transfer Function by Inspection of Frequency Domain Plot," J. Opt. Soc. Am. **63**, 1571–1577 (1973)

8.13 M. Cannon: "Blind Deconvolution of Spatially Invariant Image Blurs with Phase," IEEE Trans. ASSP-**24**, 58–63 (1976)

8.14 A.M. Tekalp, H. Kaufman, J.W. Woods: "Identification of Image and Blur Parameters for the Restoration of Noncausal Blurs," IEEE Trans. ASSP-**34**, 963–972 (1986)

8.15 A.M. Tekalp, H. Kaufman: "On Statistical Identification of a Class of Linear Space-Invariant Blurs Using Nonminimum Phase ARMA Models," IEEE Trans. ASSP-**36**, 1360–1363 (1988)

8.16 R.L. Lagendijk, J. Biemond, D.E. Boekee: "Simultaneous Image Identification and Restoration Using the EM Algorithm," Proc. SPIE Int. Conf. Visual Comm. Imag. Proc., Cambridge, Mass. (1988) pp. 2–9

Additional References

Chapter 1

S.J. Reeves, R.M. Mersereau: "Optimal Estimation of the Regularization Parameter and Stabilizing Functional for Regularized Image Restoration", Opt. Eng. **29**, 446–454 (1990)

M. Zervakis, A.N. Venetsanopoulos: "M-estimators in Robust Nonlinear Image Restoration", Opt. Eng. **29**, 455–470 (1990)

S.N. Efstratiadis, A.K. Katsaggelos: "Adaptive Iterative Image Restoration with Reduced Computational Load", Opt. Eng. **29**, 1458–1468 (1990)

N.B. Karayiannis, A.N. Venetsanopoulos: " Regularization Theory in Image Restoration – The Stabilizing Functional Approach", IEEE Trans. ASSP-**38**, 1155–1179 (1990)

A.K. Katsaggelos, J. Biemond, R.W. Schafer, R.M. Mersereau: "A Regularized Iterative Image Restoration Algorithm", IEEE Trans. SP-**39** (4), 914–929 (1991)

P.L. Combettes, H.J. Trussel: "The Use of Noise Properties in Set-Theoretic Estimation", IEEE Trans. SP-**39**, 1630–1641 (1991)

M.G. Kang, K.T. Lay, A.K. Katsaggelos: "Phase Estimation Using the Bispectrum and its Application to Image Restoration", Opt. Eng. **30**, 976–985 (1991)

Chapter 3

M. Sezan, H. Stark, S. Yeh: "Projection Method Formulations of Hopfield-type Associative Memory Neural Networks", Appl. Opt. **29**, 2616–2622 (1990)

S. Yeh, H. Stark: "Learning in Neural Nets Using Projection Methods", Optical Computing and Processing **1**, 47–60 (1991)

Chapter 4

F.C. Cheng, J.W. Woods: "Compound Gauss-Markov Random Fields for Image Estimation", IEEE Trans. SP-**39**, 683–697 (1991)

S. Rastogi, J.W. Woods: "Image Restoration by Parallel Simulated Annealing Using Compound Gauss-Markov Models", Proc. Int. Conf. Acoust., Speech, Signal Processing, Toronto, Canada, May 1991, pp. 2961–2964

F.C. Jeng, J.W. Woods, S. Ratogi: "Compound Gauss-Markov Random Fields for Parallel Image Processing", in *Markov Random Fields: Theory and Application*, edited by R. Chellappa, A. Jain (Academic, New York; to appear)

S. Lakshmana, H. Derin: "Simultaneous Parameter Estimation and Segmentation of Gibbs Random Fields Using Simulated Annealing", IEEE Trans. Pattern Anal. Machine Intell. **11**, 799–813 (1989)

Chapter 5

A. Rangarajan: "Representation and Recovery of Discontinuities in Some Early Vision Problems", Ph.D. Dissertation, University of Southern California, Los Angeles, CA, Jan. 1991, pp. 2697–2700

A. Rangarajan, R. Chellepa: "A Unified View of Continuation Methods for Image Estimation", Proc. Conf. on Information Sciences and Systems, The Johns Hopkins University, Baltimore, MD, March 1991

Chapter 6

R.L. Lagendijk, J. Biemond, D.E. Boekee: "Identification and Restoration of Noisy Blurred Images Using the Expectation Maximization Algorithm", IEEE Trans. ASSP-**38**, 1180–1191 (1990)

A.K. Katsaggelos, K.T. Lay: "Identification and Restoration of Images Using the Expectation Maximization Algorithm", IEEE Trans. SP-**39**, 729–733 (1991)

Chapter 7

S. Koch, H. Kaufman: "Boundary Value Selection Problem for Image Restoration Using the Reduced Order Model Kalman Filter", Proc. Int. Conf. Acoust., Speech, Signal Processing, Toronto, Canada, May 1991, pp. 2941–2943

Chapter 8

M.E. Zervakis, A.N. Venetsanopoulos: "Generalized Transformation in Nonlinear Image Restorations", Proc. Douziene Colloque Gretsi, Nice, France, June 1989, pp. 727–730

Subject Index